"This carefully researched and reported ac FBI adds, new, what Einstein might call 'dii tory but maybe even to our own present-da it was in the moral vacuum of the McCarthy ... vvai and too many ill-conceived adventures overseas, come to maturity in this current precarious hour. Sometimes what worries the FBI can also serve as a clue to what, somewhere back in our national soul, lingering and toxic, has been eating away at us. In redeeming from the forces favoring general amnesia this essential set of connections, Fred Jerome has given us back a piece of our history, and hopefully of our conscience as well."

— Thomas Pynchon

"Fred Jerome's investigative gem detailing the other life of Albert Einstein, the one most of us have never even heard about—Einstein the social activist and the target of Hoover-McCarthy Gestapoism—could not have arrived at a more timely moment. The comparisons between then and now are scary: deportations and threats of deportations (aimed even at Einstein), preparations for the detention of thousands, lawless lawmen on a rampage, given a green light by their leaders.

"To defy racist right-wingers, to join in protest marches demanding anti-lynching laws, in those days were dangerous activities; and friendship with Paul Robeson, aiding leftists and radicals and, worse, actual communists, were deemed treasonous. Yet despite the hysterical times, readers of this breakthrough book will draw hope from discovering the strength and courage that complimented Einstein's genius.

It is about time!"

—Paul Delaney, former *New York Times* reporter and editor and founding member of the National Association of Black Journalists

"In troubled times like these, it is heartening to be reminded that Albert Einstein was not only a man determined to speak truth to power, but unafraid to take action in support of these truths, even in the face of such a formidable opponent as the FBI. For almost two decades, Fred Jerome has devoted much of his research and writing talents to the task of revealing the oft-forgotten—or purposely hidden— political role of the great scientist. Now, in this new edition of his first book on Einstein, Jerome has added an *Update* summing up and adding much new information on this topic. I have learned much from his work, and I'm sure other readers will too. May Einstein's—and Jerome's—example inspire us to action in the face of our current crises!"

—John Stachel, founding Editor of *The Collected Papers of Albert Einstein*, author of *Einstein from 'B' to 'Z'*.

"Jerome has unearthed a side of Einstein that has been lost in most biographies."

—*Independent Weekly*

The Einstein File

Fred Jerome

The Einstein File

The FBI's Secret War Against
the World's Most Famous Scientist

Baraka
Books

Montréal

"Do you think it's right to rake up the past?"

"I don't feel that I know what you mean by raking it up.
How can we get at it unless we dig a little?
The present has such a rough way of treading it down."

—Henry James, *The Aspern Papers*

POPE: This man [Galileo] is the greatest physicist of our time.
He is the light of Italy, and not just any muddlehead.

INQUISITOR: Would we have had
to arrest him otherwise?

—Bertolt Brecht, *Galileo*

ISBN 978-1-77186-130-4 pbk; 978-1-77186-144-1 epub; 978-1-77186-145-8 pdf; 978-1-77186-146-5 mobi/pocket

Book Design and Cover by Folio infographie
Editing and proofreading: Bronwyn Averett and Robin Philpot

Legal Deposit, 2nd quarter 2018

Bibliothèque et Archives nationales du Québec
Library and Archives Canada

Published by Baraka Books of Montreal
6977, rue Lacroix
Montréal, Québec H4E 2V4
Telephone: 514 808-8504
info@barakabooks.com

Printed and bound in Quebec

Trade Distribution & Returns
Canada and the United States
Independent Publishers Group
1-800-888-4741 (IPG1);
orders@ipgbook.com

Contents

Einstein and McCarthyism – Old and New

"Trenches of ideas are more powerful than weapons."

José Marti

The re-release of Fred Jerome's *The Einstein File: J. Edgar Hoover's Secret War Against the World's Most Famous Scientist* could not have come at a more crucial moment. Today the United States is in the grip of what many consider to be a "new McCarthyism," and—like the McCarthyism of the 50s where Fred Jerome reminds us that "at the center of McCarthyism stood not McCarthy, but Hoover and his FBI"—the Federal Bureau of Investigation (FBI) is once again a major player in today's sequel of mass ideological intimidation and control.

With the publication of *The Einstein File* in 2002, which detailed the curious targeting of Albert Einstein by J. Edgar Hoover and his Federal Bureau of Investigation, many people were surprised but not shocked that the FBI labeled Einstein a national security threat and monitored the world's most famous scientist. And certainly, it was not beyond the pale of acceptable speculation for a book to be published that questioned the motivation and even legality of these actions by the FBI, especially under the leadership of its mercurial director J. Edgar Hoover.

But the U.S. is a very different place today than it was just a few years ago. In 2002, civil and human rights activists were resisting efforts by the U.S. government to expand the power of the national security apparatus in response to the traumatic attacks on the U.S. on 9/11. The Patriot Act, the establishment of the Department of Homeland Security, the war against the press, and mass racial profiling, as well as the mandatory registration and questioning of Muslims, were some of the issues that inspired vigorous opposition to the national security state.

However, in the era of Russia-gate, today the FBI and the intelligence community are defended as paragons of integrity whose motivations are beyond reproach. It seems as if people have forgotten about the excesses of COINTELPRO targeting the Black Liberation Movement and the anti-war movement; the illegal surveillance and infiltration of environmental groups; the nation-wide military assaults on members of the Black Panther Party and the American Indian Movement; and the FBI's current designation of some elements of the Black Lives Matter movement as potential "Black identity extremists."

This mass cultural amnesia has enabled the open collaboration between the state and the multinational media conglomerates to limit the public's access to information in the name of national security with almost no public opposition.

Therefore, the re-release of *The Einstein File* is vitally important. It serves as a reminder that there is abusive power beyond the reach of democratic control and that many of the individuals who populate those structures have agendas and vendettas that, unchecked, have had devastating consequences for individuals and even nations.

Corporate-state targeting of dissent is constructed on the idea that the public must be protected from subversive ideas promulgated by dangerous foreign governments. This ideological position is the product of a dubious campaign orchestrated by the main intelligence agencies of the U.S. state, with the FBI playing a lead role. The acceptance of this narrative has created a political environment in which Orwellian corporate-state collusion to limit alternative information and analysis is quickly becoming normalized.

Facebook's announcement that it will institute a process of "counter speech," Twitter's messages to individuals alerting that they have been re-tweeting information from foreign sources, and Google's manipulation of its search functions to disappear, de-rank, and marginalize alternative —i.e. radical—sources of news, information, and analysis barely generates a yawn from the public.

The Einstein File is an important corrective to the naive belief that the interests of the state and the interests of the people are the same.

Being reminded of the existence of the state's repressive power and the extent that it will go to attempt to intimidate and silence opposition gives a new urgency to the story of FBI counter-intelligence actions that were directed at Albert Einstein. If Einstein—a political refugee from fascist Germany, an advocate of peace, and a renowned scientist who passionately believed in the possibility of collective humanity to rise above war, social injustice, and racism—could be identified as a national security not only that any of us can become targets of state repression but that the values that this country pretends to be committed to are, and have always been, a lie.

The story that comes to life in *The Einstein File* is not just about the obsessive focus on Einstein by J. Edgar Hoover. It is also the story of a particular kind of mindset that continues to dominate thinking behind U.S. counter-intelligence operations.

Why did Hoover fixate on Einstein? In order to answer that question, Jerome excavates the rotting underbelly of racism, anti-Semitism, irrational anti-communism, and pro-fascist sentiments that were not ideological anomalies just confined to Hoover. During the period when Hoover first emerged on the political scene in 1919 and up until the year Einstein passed away in 1955, the anti-communist paranoia, vicious racism, and anti-Semitism characterized the thinking and world views of U.S. decision-makers from both parties and a good segment of the ruling elite.

During the lead-up to World War II, U.S. and Western hypocrisy were on full display as fascism and racism dominated Europe and the Roosevelt administration in the U.S. refused to support an anti-lynching law to protect African-Americans. That hypocrisy was apparent to Einstein who held beliefs quite different from the leaders of his new nation.

From Einstein's early teens when he renounced his German citizenship to avoid the draft to his career as a young scientist, he believed that human beings could and should resist the manipulations of their leaders to engage in war. With the outbreak of World War I, Einstein was part of a group that issued a "Manifesto to Europeans" calling for an end to war and for European cooperation.

Einstein's commitment to peace was challenged by the events that would overtake Europe with the rise of fascism—a fascism that received significant support from all of the capitalist "democracies." As German Jews desperately contacted Einstein for help emigrating from Nazi-controlled Germany, the U.S. was collaborating with German authorities who provided their U.S. counterparts with information on Jews suspected of being communists. Cordell Hull, the U.S. Secretary of State under liberal president Franklin Delano Roosevelt, refused to issue any statements of concern regarding German Jews, but he did issue condemnations of what he characterized as exaggerated accounts of terror and atrocities against Jews in Germany!

Based on information supplied by the Germans, they were automatically barred from emigrating to the U.S. As a consequence, many of those Jews who sought refuge in the U.S. ended up in German concentration camps never to be seen again.

Einstein clearly understood that prevailing anti-Semitism in U.S. culture and the fact that Hull and others in the Roosevelt administration saw Germany as a deterrent to the Soviet Union explained why officials of his adopted country turned their collective backs on the Jews of Europe.

Jerome weaves together a fascinating tale that will allow readers to draw their own conclusions on both the personal motivations of J. Edgar Hoover and the political meanings and implications for us today when powerful individuals wield institutional power beyond the reach of the people.

There are many factors that might explain Hoover's obsession with Einstein and why Einstein seemed to represent everything he loathed: Einstein's commitment to peace, his support for W.E.B. Dubois during the McCarthy repression of the 50s as well as Paul Robeson's American Crusade to End Lynching, or the fact that Marian Anderson, the world famous black opera singer, was a personal friend of Einstein who always stayed at his home whenever she was in Princeton. Certainly Einstein's Jewishness grated on Hoover, a notorious anti-Semite who only vacationed in spaces closed to Jews. And, of course, Einstein's radical positions in support of socialism were anathema to the anti-Communist crusader.

The Einstein File provides an insight into the mind of J. Edgar Hoover and denaturalizes *the patriotic smokescreen that continues to serve as an ideological shield for state repression today.* Liberal pragmatism and collaboration with right-wing forces during the 1930s mirrors the opportunism of the Bush and Obama administrations' collaboration with right-wing autocratic regimes in Saudi Arabia, the Gulf states, and Israel to pursue its objectives in the Middle-East.

For those of us who are members of oppressed peoples, naivety in the face of the awesome power of this state is a luxury that we cannot afford. Holding on to the myth of the FBI as a noble force can even be deadly.

In their hysterical opposition to President Trump, liberals have championed the FBI as a noble institution that is above politics. *The Einstein File* represents a timely reminder that without democratic accountability, fierce oversight, and the determination to fight for democratic and human rights, freedom and self-determination are only slogans.

Ajamu Baraka
February 2018

Squelching Scientists Then and Now

The Einstein File documents the shocking story of the deliberate effort by the FBI to undermine the reputation and influence of one of the greatest scientists in history. Now, more than half a century later, the manipulation of scientists and their work in areas such as climate change, energy, pharmaceuticals, toxic pollutants, and many others, makes this history involving Einstein all the more relevant and frightening. That's because human beings have become so numerous, our technology so powerful, and our consumptive demand so great, while our economy has exploded into a global force, that we are overwhelming the capacity of the biosphere to sustain us.

This is the Anthropocene Epoch, when our species has become the major factor altering the physical, chemical, and biological properties of the planet on a geological scale. There has never been another single species as capable of transforming the Earth as we are, and this change has happened with explosive speed. But we don't know enough to anticipate and avoid the deleterious consequences of all we do, so we end up undermining the very support systems of all life: air, water, soil, photosynthesis, and biodiversity.

A cursory examination of popular media quickly reveals our obsession with politics, economics, celebrity, and sports, while we ignore the reality that the most powerful force shaping our lives and the world today is science, when applied by industry, medicine and the military. For more than forty years, leading scientists of the world have been warning us that humanity—driven by economic forces that have formed deadly partnerships with powerful political interests—is headed along a very dangerous path.

My entire career in popularizing science on television and radio has been predicated on my belief that when the public is armed with the best facts—in my case, that means scientific facts—they will be able to make better, more informed decisions. We are living in a time when that belief seems quaint and totally unrealistic. This is a time of "fake news," where the perpetrators of this kind of misinformation accuse legitimate and credible media outlets of the very same crime.

Today, through the Internet, any ordinary person has access to more information than ever before in history, but rather than accessing the best evidence to form knowledgeable opinions, many find it easier to search for a website or "authoritative source" that confirms their beliefs. In other words, they don't have to change their minds if they can validate their views, regardless of whether the source or information has real credibility.

Social media is touted as the democratizing outlet providing platforms for everyone. But without the ability to assess the value and credibility of the information, bias, vested interest, greed, racism, sexism—you name it—can all make their case with equal ease. Today we are learning how the popular channels of information access and exchange, like Google, Twitter, and Facebook, are contaminated by corporations and foreign governments with their own selfish agendas.

Humanity is confronted by the existential crisis of our time: climate change. Despite the overwhelming scientific evidence supporting the contention that human use of fossil fuels is creating the problem, religions and industries have successfully created doubt or disbelief, even in the face of evidence. The criminal hacking of thousands of emails between climatologists failed to reveal bias or distortion of data among them, yet labeling them as a "scandal" ("Climategate") and creating apparent exposés by using short snippets out of context have made skepticism and denial of human-induced climate change widespread.

Scientists are not omniscient and, when they get carried away by an idea or invention, can become self-interested promoters just like a business or corporation. Then it becomes important for other scientists to raise questions or concerns. The great strength of science is in *description* of the world and universe around us, because we have so much yet to learn. But our ignorance remains vast, and so scientists often lack the ability to come up with problem-free *prescriptions* for how we can apply our observations or inventions.

But scientists do have knowledge that is often hidden from public view by arcane jargon or secrecy, so they are needed in all discussions about social and environmental issues. The attempt by the Bush-Cheney government in the United States, and then by Stephen Harper in Canada, to squelch scientists' discussions about climate attests to the power of industry and right-wing billionaires to steamroll opposition.

We must be ever vigilant to the suppression of information and ideas coming from the scientific community, from young scientists, who are most vulnerable to threats of grant loss, to the most famous and revered. Fred Jerome's *The Einstein File* reminds us this.

David Suzuki
February 2018

Preface

What I like most about Einstein is that he was a troublemaker. An agitator. A questioner of authority.

Without fully understanding his scientific theories, I, like most people, understand they were critically important, that they totally transformed our view of the universe and prepared the ground for all the great technological steps of the twentieth century—from space exploration to computers, and including, for better or worse, nuclear power. But for me, the most admirable part is that Einstein refused to be fit into a mold. He didn't wear socks. He talked to children as if they were real people. And in politics, too—when the Red scare of the 1950s silenced a generation, Einstein remained outspoken. Dangerous. And doubly dangerous because of his universal public appeal.

Unable to destroy him or to intimidate him from speaking out against injustice while he was alive, the authorities found another way of muffling his voice: After his death, they turned him into a saint.

I first came across the Einstein file quite by accident—something like stumbling on an old map with an X marked on it while rummaging around an attic. I was researching a projected book (still projected) on the most prominent science stories of the twentieth century and reading through clips on Einstein published after his death in 1955. (Einstein himself is arguably the most widely covered, continuing science story in history.) And there on page seventeen of the business section of the *New York Times* of September 9, 1983, next to the weather map, a small headline declared:

FBI FILED REPORTS

ON EINSTEIN AS A SPY

AND KIDNAP PLOTTER

Richard Alan Schwartz, a Florida English professor and author of *The Cold War Reference Guide,* had obtained the FBI's dossier on Einstein after three years of FOIA requests—and after the FBI blacked out and withheld some 25 percent of the file. He told the *Times*: "It would make wonderful absurdist drama. I'm really tempted to write one." The bad news is that Rick Schwartz never wrote that drama. The good news is that he shared the Einstein file with others, and when I visited him in Miami a few years ago, he was happy to make it available to me. The FBI has since made it readily accessible to the public, and in February of 2000, even put it on their Web page.

Additional good news is that after more than two years of my own FOIA requests, and with indispensable help from the Public Citizen Litigation Group in Washington, I was able to obtain those sections of the file previously "redacted" out—more than three hundred pages and blacked-out paragraphs that had been withheld for seventeen years. The Bureau's declassifiers still blacked out a few items, mainly names and code numbers of FBI agents and confidential informants—some of whom I've identified through other means.

Initially, I had thought the FBI's Einstein file would make a good magazine piece—simply because most people had no idea it even existed. But reading it through, page after alarming page, revealed a bigger story which I have attempted to recount in this book: the little-known campaign by J. Edgar Hoover's FBI (in cooperation with other federal agencies) to destroy Einstein's good name, including the effort to link Einstein to Soviet espionage—an effort that some of Hoover's followers continue to pursue today.

What also emerges from the FBI's dossier, through its obvious anti-Einstein bias, is a political dimension of Einstein's life, largely unknown to the public: his intense commitment to social justice, his anti-racism, and his response to McCarthyism. If the government's secret campaign to undermine the world's greatest scientist is headline news to most readers, Einstein's politics are the story behind the headline, the *why* of that campaign.

Finally, the fact that so few people have any inkling of Einstein's political dimension reflects another, more intriguing component of this story: the attempted rewriting of history to erase Einstein's radical politics from his public image—portraying him as the kindly professor, forgivably absent-minded since his brain roams a higher plane than the rest of us, so engrossed in great thoughts that he has no time for merely mortal concerns.

I think it was when I realized how much had not been told to us about the life of this "Man of the Century"—I felt as though I'd been robbed—that I decided to put a book together. As a science writer, I had known for years that Einstein was always a good story. Any issue of *Time* with his picture on the cover was the year's top seller, according to Henry Grunwald, the magazine's former editor in chief.[1] But I was astounded to discover the extent of Einstein's political commitment and humanitarian outreach—why hadn't I known? A valuable shipment of history had vanished, and no one had even reported it missing. Why didn't the whole world know?

This is not another biography of Einstein—some two hundred have already been written. Indeed, Einstein has been biographied, bibliographied and chronologied, dramatized and televised, vetted and now (of course) Interneted more than any other scientist in the history of the world. There's an *Einstein Dictionary*, and even an *Einstein for Beginners* cartoon book. Recent years have brought a spate of articles, TV programs (including a two-hour *Nova* special), and at least three books on Einstein's love letters, relationships with his sons, wives, and "others." Even Einstein's brain has been sized, analyzed, and publicized across the world.

The one area of Einstein's life that's been neglected by biographers,[2] letter collectors, and video producers—the one area virtually ignored by the mainstream media when they headlined Einstein's selection as *Time's* "Person of the Century"—is his politics.*

While Einstein was, to be sure, a questioner of authority, his politics were more than just maverick. Forged by his firsthand view of the rise of Nazism in Germany, his outlook was above all anti-fascist, including his public opposition to McCarthyism in the United States. He was a pacifist, an internationalist, a socialist, and an outspoken anti-racist, but he was not simply a passive commentator on world events. The FBI file provides a window onto the nature of Einstein's politics, the depth of his public involvement, the generosity of his prestigious endorsement of organizations he supported. It was that activism, and not Einstein's numerous political articles and speeches, that Hoover's Bureau considered dangerous. Einstein, the FBI file alleges, was "affiliated or his name extensively associated with literally hundreds of pro-Communist groups."[3]

Einstein, of course, saw it differently:

---

* *Time* magazine's "Person of the Century" issue includes a rare exception: Its article subtitled "Relativity's Rebel" by veteran science writer Fred Golden paints a fairly comprehensive political portrait—with one significant omission: As if the executives at *Time* decided to go so far but no farther, their article makes no mention of Einstein's socialist convictions. (*Time.* December 31, 1999.)

If a man has such esteem... it is his obligation and duty to use this power to do good for his fellow men. For this reason, I have used every opportunity to help the underdog, but, of course, only [when] the person is within his rights.[4]

But the absence of Einstein's politics from his popular image became curiouser the more I researched the events cited in the FBI's dossier. ("Curiouser and curiouser," said Alice as she explored Wonderland.) Almost all of Einstein's outspoken political stands were major news stories at the time. His public call for witnesses to defy Senator McCarthy and other congressional "inquisitors" (his term) made not one but two front-page stories during 1953 in the *New York Times* and media around the world. Indeed, while he was alive, in virtually all his public activities, even sticking out his tongue at a reporter, Einstein equaled news. Yet, since his death in 1955, while Einstein himself has become an icon, the once-major news of his anti-establishment politics has become a non-story.

"It's the process of canonization," says Freeman Dyson." When you put someone on a pedestal, you don't call attention to his feet of clay."[5] Einstein would no doubt have objected to that description of his politics—to him, they were far from feet of clay—but Dyson has provided an essential insight: The iconization of Einstein has reduced him from astute social critic to genial, absentminded professor with his head in the clouds. No waves on this cruise, nothing that might even slightly sway the boat.

So history is sanitized. With Einstein, as with Casals, Copland, Dreiser, Neruda, O'Casey, Picasso, and many more, we are taught the acceptable half-lives of our heroes. Only what is supposed to be admirable about their lives is served up to each generation—biographical pap, pureed, boneless, nothing to chew on. We may admire and eulogize Einstein as a genius, but as a role mode! for young people, a genius who is *also* anti-racist, anti-war, and pro-socialist is simply not permitted—and thus easily omitted from all approved versions of history.

I came to write this book not without a point of view. Born as what is now known as a "Red diaper baby," I grew up in a family with its own extensive FBI file. During the very years that the FBI was putting together the Einstein file, my father, one of the Communist Party officials convicted under the Smith Act, was serving three years in the federal penitentiary at Lewisburg, Pennsylvania. I remember FBI agents in their telltale identical gray-flannel suits and fedora hats following my family, my teenage friends and me in and out of the New York City subways; even following me when I went on some of my earliest dates. (Talk about a conversation starter!)

Nonetheless, I have tried to approach *The Einstein File* as a reporter, describing the Cold War atmosphere in this country and Hoover's conviction that he needed to take extreme measures to save the nation from communism.

I cannot say I have always been objective. If objectivity means non-partisanship, standing above the fray, I don't believe it is either possible or (if it were possible) desirable.[6] As the old story goes, "objective" is the man who, on a visit to his grandmother's house, finds her being attacked by a bear and stands to one side shouting, "C'mon, Grandma! C'mon, Bear!" Accuracy, of course, including a fair presentation of the opposing views (understanding *why* the bear attacked Grandma—perhaps it was hungry), is essential in reporting, and I have meticulously checked facts and documented allegations, interviewed numerous former FBI officials (only some of whom agreed to let their names be mentioned), and digested a plethora of government documents besides the Einstein file.

More than a few readers may find it hard to understand how Einstein could have been attracted to the left and to the defense of Communists. It wasn't really so unusual, especially for anti-fascists, including many Jewish refugees, who knew that communists were Hitler's first victims and—except during the 1939-1941 Stalin-Hitler nonaggression pact—were among the most militant fighters against the Nazis and Nazi imitators in virtually every country. For many African-Americans and other equal-rights advocates, the strongest and sometimes the only voices raised against racism came from communists, who organized Southern share-croppers, exposed the rape frame-ups of the Scottsboro defendants, Willie McGee, and many others, launched the first integrated trade unions, and led anti-Jim Crow protests decades before the civil rights movement of the 1960s. The CP also provided many of the organizers for the movement, marches, and battles to build industrial unions and win reforms such as unemployment insurance.

"Yes, they were starry-eyed," one former communist recently wrote, "over the emergence of the world's first nation to proclaim itself social-ist and place people above profits, and yes, they were lamentably slow to accept the reality that Stalinism had butchered the socialist dream." But "American Communists, despite their sins... advocated something more human than corporate capitalism...and fought hard and effectively for social justice...".[7]

My first inclination was to say nothing here about "America's New War" and "Homeland Defense," launched in the wake of the horrific terror-ist attack that has come to be known as 9-11. The book was in its final copy-editing stage, with publication just a few months away. But after living with Einstein for a number of years, it's impossible to remain silent.

One can never be sure, of course, what Einstein would have said or done, but it's fairly safe to say that he would have shared the world's horror at the terrorist attack and the killing of several thousand innocent people on September 11. It is also quite likely that abhorrence of that awful act would not have made him indifferent to other offenses, that he would have been alarmed and angered by Washington's increasing reliance on military attacks abroad and repression at home—the unapologetic bombing of civilians; the roundup, admittedly with no evidence, of thousands of Arabs or people who look Middle Eastern; the USA Patriot Act permitting unlimited detention of non-citizens; and the edict authorizing secret military trials (with death-sentence power) for aliens "suspected" of helping terrorists.

(Quite a few Americans, while uneasy about military involvement, may be unconcerned about the new repression because the restrictions on liberty don't affect them, but apply only to aliens. Despite history, there are always some, it seems, who feel relieved because they are not immigrants, not blacks, not homeless, not gays, not Jews, not yet.)

To Einstein, the most alarming aspect of "America's Homeland Defense" would quite likely be the anti-immigrant and anti-Arab racism that, already present before September 11, has become rampant. We can imagine his sense of sorrow, anger, and déjà-vu, had he watched Virginia's Senator John Warner on the Larry King show, November 7, 2001, instructing viewers: "You must think of yourself as an agent, not to spy on your neighbor, but to judiciously report anything that looks suspicious."

And what would Einstein have said, what could possibly have expressed his profound sadness about the *Wall Street Journal's* front-page report on November 21—just two weeks later—that nearly half a million Americans had called the FBI to turn in their neighbors, mostly Arab or Arab-looking:

THE TATTLERS
A NATION OF TIPSTERS ANSWERS FBI'S CALL…
IT'S NEIGHBOR VS. NEIGHBOR,
AS AGENTS ARE SWAMPED BY 435,000 CITIZEN LEADS.
EVEN THE PRIEST IS SNOOPING

Wrapping repression in the flag and calling it patriotism is a tactic Einstein knew only too well. Indeed, Attorney General Ashcroft's plan to designate forty-six groups as "terrorist" or "pro-terrorist" sounds eerily imitative of the "subversive organization" lists of the fifties. In 1949, as McCarthyism and suppression of civil liberties were rapidly subverting America's freedom, Einstein, in a little-known statement, declared: "The flag is a symbol of the fact that man is still a herd animal."[8]

In conversations over the past few years, I've found that the FBI's Einstein file sounds an alarm. That Hoover and his Bureau would go after Einstein—resorting to an array of techniques, from tapping phones and opening mail to secretly breaking into private residences—seems to bring home to many people just how far and wide McCarthy-Hooverism, and the fear it generated, reached.

Whether Einstein's endorsement of groups that shared his concerns about social justice threatened America's security, as Hoover believed it did, is a judgment the reader and history must make. But if his FBI file helps to revive public interest in Einstein's political principles, it would be a delicious twist to Hoover's secret anti-Einstein crusade.

Introduction

Sam Papich, the FBI's former liaison officer with the CIA, spoke quite openly when I called him on December 4, 1999, to ask what he knew about the FBI's Einstein file:

FJ: [after introductions] This is for a book on the FBI's file on Einstein.
SP: On who?
FJ: Einstein. Albert Einstein.
SP: I'll be darned.
FJ: You're surprised to hear that such a file existed?
SP: Well, I am...To be very honest with you, I don't know of any investigation that the FBI conducted of Einstein.
FJ: You were the liaison with the CIA?
SP: Yes...beginning in fifty-three, and then on for about fifteen years.
FJ: Well, this file covered up until about fifty-five. Einstein died in fifty-five. Is there any reason you can think of that Hoover would have wanted to develop such a file?
SP: None whatsoever. What information do you have that there was any investigation?
FJ: What I have is the file itself, which is—
SP: What you need to keep in mind is that people really get confused when it comes to these files...It's possible—I'm just speculating, mind you—that someone maybe wrote a letter accusing Einstein of associating with known communists or something and it was checked out and it was filed...a miscellaneous junk file...or there could have been a file on Einstein strictly on his scientific pursuits...but to be very honest, I didn't know of any such...You know, in those days, we were pretty much of a big family and if you were investigating some celebrity or some well-known individual, it would get around within the office. I never heard of a rumor or any kind of indication that we looked at Einstein. What did you get from Freedom of Information? Or did you?

FJ: I have the FBI's file that is eighteen hundred pages long.
SP: Eighteen hundred?
FJ: Right.
SP: I'll be damned.

J. Edgar Hoover had every reason to keep his investigation of Albert Einstein tightly under wraps. That top FBI officials such as Papich hadn't even heard about Hoover's Einstein file shows just how secret it was.[*]

Yet for nearly a quarter-century, from Einstein's arrival in the United States in 1933 until his death in 1955, Hoover's FBI, in cooperation with seven other federal agencies, conducted an investigation into Einstein's political ideas and activities, collecting more than eighteen hundred pages of "derogatory information" in a campaign to undermine his credibility and influence.[1] (The file contains virtually nothing about Einstein's science.) The FBI's most intensive anti-Einstein effort came between 1950 and 1955, at the height of this country's Red-scare hysteria.

Hoover may well have intended to make his case against Einstein public…eventually. This was not one of the FBI chief's "personal" secret files used primarily as leverage to "influence" (some have used the word "blackmail") their subjects.[2] At the right time, going public with the Einstein file could have brought Hoover a publicity bonanza—but only when all his ducks were lined up, or, in this case, when his witnesses checked out and his evidence proved that Einstein was a danger to America. Until then, he bent over backward to avoid a leak. Agents were instructed to use the utmost "discretion," and no one was permitted to interview Einstein, his family, or his friends for fear that someone would blow the whistle. The file itself has numerous references to this preoccupation with secrecy. One example warns agents to be especially cautious because of "Einstein's prominence throughout the world."[3]

No one ever accused Hoover of being publicity-shy, but if it got out prematurely that he was investigating the world's most admired scientist and America's most famous refugee from Nazi Germany, he knew that he and his FBI—and quite possibly the entire United States government—would face a storm of international outrage and derision.

---

[*] "Einstein? Albert Einstein? Why would we ever have a file on *him?*" The incredulous question came during a phone conversation on October 23, 1997 with Donald K. Moore, who had been the FBI's deputy director for counterintelligence beginning in 1956, only a year after Einstein's death. Charming, affable, and quite open to questions, Moore changed his story somewhat when I interviewed him in his house on November 6, 1997. What he had meant to say, he now said, was that he simply didn't know any specifics about the Einstein file. "I might probably have heard about it, but just didn't know any details."

An FBI file on Einstein simply doesn't compute with his public image. When *Time* anointed Einstein as "Person of the Century," the magazine's promotional description celebrated that image:

> One person clearly stands out as both the greatest mind and paramount icon of our age: the kindly, absentminded professor whose wild halo of hair, piercing eyes, engaging humanity and extraordinary brilliance made his face a symbol and his name a synonym for genius, Albert Einstein.[4]

But a kindly, absentminded icon-genius could hardly have threatened America's national security. It's no longer news that Hoover had files on a wide array of celebrity "subversives," from Ernest Hemingway to John Lennon.* The FBI kept files on some *ten million* Americans.** But Einstein? The FBI's Einstein is a total disconnect from the public's image. Instead of *Time's* "kindly...engaging humanity," the Bureau's dossier declares:

> Professor Einstein is either the Chairman of, member, sponsor, endorser, patron or otherwise affiliated with 10 organizations which have been cited by the Attorney General, 13...cited by the House Committee on Un-American Activities and 10...cited by the California House Committee on Un-American Activities, all as being Communistic groups. (FBI's Einstein file, Section 1)

> In 1946, a professional associate of Dr. Einstein's, whose reliability is unknown, stated that in his opinion Dr. Einstein had been led to back those who favored the turning over of the atomic bomb to Russia. (Section 9)

> ...it seems unlikely that a man of his background could...become a loyal American citizen. (Section 1)

J. Edgar Hoover's hostility to dissenters and political activists is no longer news. The news is that through its hostility, the Bureau's dossier begins to describe a dimension of Einstein's life almost completely omitted from his popular image:

"My life is divided between equations and politics," Einstein said on several occasions. To be sure, the equations came first for him, with politics in second place. But he spent a lot of time and energy on second place, publishing at least 195 essays and articles on political topics. More than

---

* Groucho Marx, Frank Sinatra, and Mickey Mantle are the latest names to surface in Hoover's Hall of Fame files. A sampling of others includes Leonard Bernstein, Pearl Buck, Aaron Copland, W. E. B. Du Bois, Robert Frost, John Garfield, Graham Greene, Dashiell Hammett, Lillian Hellman, Langston Hughes, A.J. Liebling, Norman Mailer, H.L. Mencken, Arthur Miller, Dorothy Parker, Paul Robeson, Frank Silvera, John Steinbeck, James Thurber, Gore Vidal, Mark van Doren, and Thomas Wolfe.

** You can read a variety of figures on how many millions of security files Hoover actually kept. David Wise, author of numerous works on the FBI and U.S. security operations, says 9.6 million. (FBI's Greatest Hits.)

150 of his interviews, letters, and speeches on politics were quoted in the
New York Times alone.[5]

He was an ardent democrat, believing in the equality of all men (to a
lesser extent, women)* and the right and duty of each person to question
authority and resist tyranny. His political outlook might best be summarized in the principles of the French revolution: *liberté, egalité, fraternité*—
dangerous words to would-be thought controllers everywhere, including
those who dominated this country's politics during the McCarthyism of
the 1950s.

---

* Einstein's male chauvinism and his shabby treatment of his first wife, Mileva, as well
as others, has been described in extensive detail in recent articles and books. While his
attitude and several affairs may not stand out as unusual for his time—indeed, White
House watchers today might find his social life humdrum—there is no doubt about
(and no justification for) Einstein's sexism.

PART 1

Discovering America

1

"What's This, an Inquisition?"

As they left their country home in Caputh, Germany, in the autumn of 1932 to return to their Berlin apartment and prepare for their coming visit to the United States, Einstein turned to his wife, Einstein, Elsa, and said, "Before you leave this time, take a good look at the villa."

"Why?" Elsa asked.

"You will never see it again."[1]

As the year drew to a close, so did Germany's thirteen-year attempt at a liberal democracy, the Weimar Republic. With one out of three workers unemployed and inflation out of control, millions of angry, hungry Germans turned to Hitler's new nationalism for simple, soothing answers, and a convenient scapegoat for all their problems: "the international Jewish-Bolshevik conspiracy."[2]

Winning 230 of the 608 seats, the Nazis had become the largest group in the German Reichstag (although they never won a majority and their vote actually declined by two million before Hitler came to power and did away with elections). The pro-Nazi press grew increasingly shrill in its attacks against Jews, with Einstein prominent among the targets. These press accounts, as we shall see, came to play a significant role in Einstein's FBI file.

In 1931, a Leipzig publishing house produced a book of essays entitled *100 Authors Against Einstein;* the following year, a top German Army general reportedly sent a warning to Einstein that his life "is not safe here anymore."[3] Violent, often armed street battles between uniformed Nazi gangs and leftists erupted daily, and the exodus of German intellectuals began. Among those moving to Russia were author Arthur Koestler and the architect Hannes Meyer. The artist George Grosz and his wife, after receiving numerous death threats, sold their large house and moved to the United States. Marlene Dietrich, who had become famous while visiting

Hollywood, came home to Berlin in 1932, surveyed the political scene, and returned to America—this time for good. What's remarkable is not that so many German artists and writers fled the country in 1932, but that so many held out hope and stayed until after the Nazis seized power in 1933. The latter included Kurt Weill, his wife Lotte Lenya, Bertolt Brecht...and Einstein.[4]

Without question, the world's most celebrated scientist was becoming increasingly apprehensive about the rise of Nazism and assaults against the Jews in Germany. "Einstein...for all his serenity, was anxious," reported Norman Bentwich, an attorney friend, after visiting the scientist in Berlin and observing "grim signs of a rising anti-Semitic flood...many Jewish shops had been sacked..." But despite Einstein's anxiety and his premonition about their house in Caputh,* he and Elsa planned to stay in the United States for only a few months, fully expecting to be back in Berlin by the spring.[5]

For the third year in a row, Einstein planned to spend the winter as a guest faculty member at the California Institute of Technology in Pasadena. On their way home, he and Elsa had scheduled a brief visit to Princeton, where he had accepted an appointment at the soon-to-open Institute for Advanced Study. Under his arrangement with the Institute, Einstein would continue living in Berlin but spend half of each year in Princeton.

As they packed for their trip to America that first week in December 1932, they undoubtedly looked forward to a vacation from the tension that was daily life in Germany. On previous trips, Einstein had visited the United States and other countries as an unofficial representative of the Weimar Republic, which handled his travel and visa arrangements. But by December 1932, the government was in a shambles, teetering on the brink of collapse. For the first time, the Einsteins had to make their own visa arrangements. The details were simple enough; they had no trouble with the forms. Or so it seemed.

---

* Einstein's summer house was originally promised as a gift of "appreciation" from Berlin's city government on the scientist's fiftieth birthday in 1929. But in a series of improbable and ostensibly accidental blunders, the Municipal Council repeatedly "discovered" that the house or land they had approved was actually not theirs to give. After changing the proposed gift several times (each offer was a little less attractive than the previous one), this comedy of "errors" finally exasperated the Einsteins. At their own expense, they bought the land and built the house in Caputh, using almost all their savings. Three years later, the Einsteins left Germany, never to return, and their house in Caputh was seized by the Nazis. Philipp Frank argues that the fiasco was planned by Berlin city officials. (Frank, p. 221-223.) For the most detailed description of this story, see Grüning, Ein Haus für Albert Einstein.

Albert and Elsa Einstein on their way from Germany to Pasadena, CA in 1931.

On the morning of December 5, Einstein received an unexpected call from the U.S. Consulate General in Berlin, requesting that he and Elsa come by to answer a few questions related to their visa application. He was busy, Einstein said, and asked if they couldn't simply send him the visa, but the consular authorities insisted. Assuming it was just the routine mechanism of bureaucracy, he and Elsa agreed to stop in during the afternoon[6]. It would be anything but routine.

Even as a half-time resident, Einstein's presence in America was a prospect that set off a Red-alert in the Woman Patriot Corporation. When it was launched fourteen years earlier (April 1918) in Washington, during the heady last months of World War I, the organization's weekly newspaper, *The Woman Patriot,* proclaimed across the top of its front page: FOR THE HOME AND NATIONAL DEFENSE, AGAINST WOMAN SUFFRAGE, FEMINISM AND SOCIALISM.

Almost all its officers and board members used their husbands' names—such as Mrs. James Wolcott Wadsworth, Jr. *(See* endnote 11.) While this was in keeping with their antifeminism, it also left no doubt that these were ladies of substance—the wives and widows, daughters and dowagers of some of the most prominent families in Eastern politics and business. Several Woman Patriot leaders also held office in the National Association Opposed to Woman Suffrage, but the new group linked antifeminism to a more comprehensive agenda. Headlines in their paper's first issue included:

MAKE THIS YOUR WAR...VICTORY OR ENSLAVEMENT FOR AMERICA

ANTI-SUFFRAGISTS TO WAGE

UNCEASING WAR AGAINST

FEMINISM AND SOCIALISM

WOMEN SUFFRAGE VS. PROHIBITION

The editorial statement proudly declared the group "stands for a strong and safe suffrage,...[and] the exemption of women from unnatural responsibilities, voting duty, jury duty and political turmoil." After the Nineteenth Amendment was ratified (despite the Woman Patriot's best efforts), the group turned to other targets, crusading against the proposed Constitutional amendment outlawing child labor—an amendment they denounced as "a communist plot."

But by 1932, the Woman Patriot Corporation had fallen on lean times.

They had moved twice to smaller offices in Washington and their weekly newspaper was now a monthly, reduced from tabloid to newsletter size. In fact, the group had never recovered from the devastation of seeing women enter voting booths. With that battle lost, most of the better-known names and much of the organization's funding gradually dropped off.

Nonetheless, the remaining Patriots valiantly upheld the flag, focusing their fire on protecting America from dangerous ideas. In 1928, their president, Mrs. Randolph Frothingham, made headlines when she helped the Daughters of the American Revolution compile a "blacklist of speakers" they sought to bar from public appearances. Mrs. Frothingham's public-enemy nominees to the DAR's blacklist included William Allen White, Roscoe Pound and Felix Frankfurter (both at Harvard Law School), college presidents Neilson of Smith and Woolley of Mt. Holyoke, Clarence Darrow, Norman Hapgood, David Starr Jordan, and Rabbi Stephen S. Wise.[7]

By 1932, she and her fellow Patriots had decided to concentrate their remaining forces on guarding America's gates against "undesirable aliens"—communists, pacifists, feminists, and other un-American types seeking to enter the United States. Along with playwright George Bernard Shaw and the grandson of Karl Marx, Einstein had earned a top spot on the Woman Patriot keep-out list.

In August, when the Institute-in-formation at Princeton announced that Einstein's half-time residency would begin the following year, Mrs. Frothingham set to work. Within three months, she submitted a memo to the State Department arguing that Einstein should be barred from the U.S. under the Alien Exclusion and Deportation Law. As revised in June 1920, that law forbid "aliens" from entering the United States (or if they had managed to enter, from staying) if they were anarchists or wrote, spoke, or even thought like anarchists. It was designed specifically to "correct" the "gaps" found in the law after the "Palmer raids" of January 1920. (The vast majority of immigrants arrested in those raids had to be released when someone discovered that they had committed no criminal acts. Six months later, the rewritten law decreed that aliens could be denied entry, deported, or even jailed, simply for possession of literature or expression of anarchist opinions, even if they had committed no overt actions.[8])

But the Woman Patriot group did not limit its anti-Einstein allegations to anarchism. Mrs. Frothingham accused the scientist of virtually every politically subversive sin, including treason and inciting troops to shoot their officers. Asserting that Einstein should be barred from the United States because he was the "leader of the new 'militant pacifism,'" the document states:

> Who is the acknowledged world leader, who, by direct affiliation with Communist and anarcho-communist organizations and groups, and by his own utmost personal efforts, is doing most to "shatter" the "military machinery" [as] the "preliminary condition of any people's revolution"?
>
> ALBERT EINSTEIN is that leader. Not even Stalin himself is affiliated with so many anarcho-communist international groups to promote this "preliminary condition" of world revolution and ultimate anarchy, as ALBERT EINSTEIN.
>
> ALBERT EINSTEIN...advocates "acts of rebellion" against the basic principle of all organized government...he advocates "conflict with public authority;" admits that his "attitude is revolutionary;" that his purpose is "illegal" and that he intends to organize and lead...a "militant opposition" and to "combat" the basic principle of our Constitution...he teaches and leads and organizes a movement for unlawful "individual resistance" and "acts of rebellion" against officers of the United States in time of war, which is almost impossible without the assaulting or killing of such officers as a necessary

consequence of such "acts of rebellion," and which…"revolutionary" "combat," "conflict" or "rebellion" (as Albert Einstein himself names his objectives) must promote treason, desertion or other "crimes against the existence of the Government;" he believes in or advocates a system of organized sabotage against all preparations of the United States to defend itself…[9] [Underlining and capitalization in original.]

The Woman Patriot "brief" is anything but. The charges against Einstein continue in the same vein and tone for sixteen legal-sized, single-spaced pages. It is doubtful that such a massive arsenal of allegations could be collected—or even concocted—by one person working alone in just three months. But among the unofficial network of small but busy far-right groups—with names such as Daughters of 1812, National Security League, National Patriotic Council—who may well have helped out with the anti-Einstein research, none saw fit to claim responsibility.[10] No source is given for any of the quotations or, in fact, for anything cited in the document. While Mrs. Frothingham promises (page 4) to submit "documentary evidence on these points" as soon as it "is completed," such evidence apparently never materialized.

Having promised future proof, Mrs. Frothingham does not hesitate to offer more speculation, scientific as well as political. As the reader might guess, she is not a fan of Einstein's physics:

> [His] frequently revised theory of "relativity" is of no more practical importance than the answer to the old academic riddle, "How many angels can stand on the point of a needle…?"

Of all Einstein's sins, however, the most sinful to the Woman Patriots was his "negation of organized religion." Spurred by spiritual as well as patriotic zeal, their memo declares:

> This alien, more extensively and more potently than any other revolutionist on earth, promotes confusion and disorder, doubt and disbelief and…has promoted lawless confusion to shatter the Church as well as the State—and to leave…the laws of nature and the principles of science in confusion and disorder…

Finally, if further proof were needed of Einstein's unsavory character, Mrs. Frothingham informs us that he "apparently cannot talk English."*

---

* Before moving to the United States, Einstein's interviews were usually conducted in German with an interpreter present, although he gave at least one speech in English, an anti-Nazi address in London's Albert Hall on October 3, 1933. Living in America, he was soon able to give virtually all his public speeches and interviews in English, despite a thick German accent. It's a safe bet that Mrs. Frothingham understood only too well Einstein's public statements criticizing militarism and economic inequality.

The document is an appropriate opener to the FBI's Einstein file. Sent to Hoover by the State Department, it comprises the file's first sixteen pages.

If Mrs. Frothingham were a character created by Charles Dickens, we would chuckle at the novelist's talent for coming up with apt names. Far from being a laughing matter, however, the family name was a source of pride for generations of Frothinghams, dating back to the Mayflower Pilgrims. Indeed, virtually all the ladies of the right who founded the Woman Patriot Corporation in 1918 carried prestigious pedigrees.[11] But none was more prestigious than the Frothinghams of Massachusetts. Mrs. Louis A. Frothingham was not only a founding Woman Patriot, but also vice-president of the National Association Opposed to Woman Suffrage. Her husband, a Mayflower descendant and leading New England banker, was elected to four terms as U.S. Congressman from Massachusetts.[12] Had he not died suddenly in 1928 while sailing on his yacht *Winsome*, Louis Frothingham might have remained a member of Congress for many more years. Of the six country clubs he belonged to, four in Boston and two in Washington, not one admitted Jews or people of color.

It seems fitting, then, that in 1932, it should fall to another Frothingham to lead the Woman Patriots into battle against Albert Einstein— Mrs. Randolph Frothingham, cousin by marriage to the late Congressman of Mayflower descent.

When he heard about the Woman Patriot diatribe (Mrs. Frothingham had sent copies to the press[13]), Einstein's first reaction was to laugh. He dashed off a tongue-in-cheek essay that was printed on the front page of the *New York Times* (December 4, 1932):

> Never yet have I experienced from the fair sex such energetic rejection of all advances, or if I have, never from so many at once.
>
> But are they not perfectly right, these watchful citizenesses? Why should one open one's doors to a person who devours hard-boiled capitalists with as much appetite and gusto as the ogre Minotaur in Crete once devoured luscious Greek maidens—a person who is also so vulgar as to oppose every sort of war, except the inevitable one with his own wife? Therefore, give heed to your clever and patriotic women folk and remember that the capital of mighty Rome was once saved by the cackling of its faithful geese.[14]

Einstein had every reason to feel confident his little satire would be the end of the episode. Every country had its crackpots, and this group of elite superpatriots clearly did not represent the America he and Elsa had come to know in the past two years. Certainly no one in his right mind could take that memo seriously. But he had not figured on the U.S. Department of State. When the anti-Einstein "brief" arrived in late November, State Department officials could easily have treated it as one of the many pieces of crank mail they frequently received. They didn't.

Maybe it was the lingering influence of the Woman Patriot family names. (Besides Mrs. Frothingham, the group's vice-president in 1932 was Mrs. John Fremont Hill, whose late husband had been Republican governor of Maine for eight years.) More likely, it was the conservative bias that characterized that outgoing Republican Administration—not least, the State Department. In any case, within a week (which included the Thanksgiving holiday), officials forwarded the Woman Patriots' document to the U.S. Consulate in Berlin—in time to arrive before the Einsteins' scheduled departure for America.

While there is no evidence of State Department collusion in the Woman Patriot's crusade, the Department's behavior in this case appears unusually cooperative. On December 1, 1932, Assistant Secretary of State Wilbur J. Carr notified Mrs. Frothingham that the Department had acted "in order that consular officers may examine [Einstein] in reference to those [Woman Patriot] charges *in addition to* the examination which they would ordinarily make as to his admissibility."[15] [Emphasis added.]

If the Einsteins had had any hint that their scheduled interview at the U.S. Consulate was connected to the "watchful citizenesses" who had authored the critique, he and Elsa might never have arrived there on the afternoon of December 5.

Since U.S. Consul General George Messersmith was out of town, Assistant Consul Raymond Geist conducted Einstein's interview.[16] From Geist's very first question, the discussion was as comfortable as fingernails scratching a blackboard.

"What is your political creed?"

Surprised, Einstein thought it over and then burst out laughing. "Well, I don't know. I can't answer that question."

"Are you a member of any organization?"

Einstein ran his hand through his hair, turned to Elsa for help, and declared, "Oh yes, I am a War Resister."*

"Who are they?"

"Well, they are my friends."

---

* Einstein was a member and later honorary chairman of the War Resisters League, an international pacifist organization.

After several more routine questions, such as the purpose of Einstein's trip to the United States ("to do some scientific work"), Geist finally pulled the trigger:

"What party do you belong to or sympathize with? For instance, are you a Communist or an anarchist?"

This was a piece of America he had not seen before. It was almost German. According to an Associated Press report:

> Professor Einstein's patience broke. His usual genial face stem and his normally melodious voice strident, he cried:
>
> "What's this, an inquisition? Is this an attempt at chicanery? I don't propose to answer such silly questions.
>
> "I didn't ask to go to America. Your countrymen invited me; yes, begged me. If I am to enter your country as a suspect, I don't want to go at all. If you don't want to give me a visa, please say so. Then I'll know where I stand."

As he reached for his hat and coat, Einstein asked, "Are you doing this to please yourselves or are you acting upon orders from above?" Without waiting for an answer, he and Elsa walked out.

We can only imagine their shock and anger as they talked during the cab ride back to their apartment, but by the time they arrived, they had a plan. First, Einstein phoned the consulate. If he did not receive a visa by the next afternoon (twenty-four hours), he told them, he would cancel his trip. Next, Elsa called the *New York Times* and the Associated Press correspondents in Berlin and gave them a blow-by-blow account of the consulate confrontation. Elsa also told the AP reporter she had six trunks packed and ready. "If they're not sent to Bremen by tomorrow noon, it will be too late for the sailing. That will be the end of our going to America." The Einsteins' sophisticated use of the media in this skirmish belies—as early as 1932—the kindly, bumbling, absentminded-professor image so universally accepted today. The political implications were unmistakable when Elsa told the *Times* her husband had stated, "Wouldn't it be funny if they won't let me in? The whole world would be laughing at America."

Someone in Washington must have had the same thought. A late-night press release from the State Department announced that Consul General George Messersmith had suddenly returned from his trip, reviewed Einstein's case, and "will issue a visa tomorrow."* On December 10, the Einsteins, with their six trunks, sailed from Bremen for California.

---

* Messersmith didn't actually return to Berlin for several days, according to The Woman Patriot, December 1932. It seems plausible that fabricating a story about his reviewing the case was the best Washington could or would do to save face. Of course, they might have simply apologized to Einstein.

Despite that quick reversal, concern about the government's goof was widespread. In New York, a group of prominent women met at the home of Mrs. Gerard Swope, wife of the president of General Electric, and adopted resolutions "in the name of the intelligent American people," rebuking the State Department for paying any attention at all to the "absurd document of a so-called patriotic society," and asking for the recall of Consul Messersmith because of "his ignorance" and for "humiliating America and making it a laughingstock second only to the Scopes trial in Tennessee."

Mrs. Einstein told the *Times* reporter that she and her husband had received many cables from "Americans of all classes…deeply disturbed over the case."[17]

For the Woman Patriot Corporation, it was the last hurrah. Their flame gave one final splutter in January 1933; attempting to block Einstein from disembarking when his ship arrived in California, Mrs. James Cunningham Gray, on behalf of the Woman Patriot Corporation, made a formal request to cancel his visa under the Alien Exclusion Act. Mrs. Gray, according to a *New York Times* report (January 9, 1933), said her organization "sought only 'equal enforcement of the law for all alien Reds.'" She also cited Professor Thomas Jefferson See, who had publicly attacked Einstein's theory of relativity as "a crazy vagary, a disgrace to our age." It was the group's last publicly reported activity. They never published another copy of *The Woman Patriot* after the Einstein issue (December 1932).[18]

On January 12, 1933, the Einsteins arrived in California. On January 30, Hitler seized power in Berlin. In May, the house in Caputh was raided and ransacked by Nazi SS men ostensibly searching for a hidden cache of weapons intended for a planned uprising against the Third Reich. When they found no weapons, they confiscated the property anyway, claiming it was "obviously" about to be sold to finance anti-Nazi activities. A year later, Einstein, with his wife Elsa, daughter-in-law Margot, and their friend and assistant Helen Dukas, moved to Princeton. He never returned to Germany.

It would seem simple to dismiss Mrs. Frothingham and her cohorts as a Neanderthal right-wing fringe group. Einstein certainly viewed the Woman Patriots as more cracked than the Liberty Bell; so did Mrs. Swope and her influential circle. Yet the U.S. State Department, pursuing the group's anti-Einstein charges, almost stopped his trip to America. In the coming years, the State Department would reveal its conservatism—

among its more publicized actions, blocking Jewish refugees from Nazism from entering America.* But it wasn't just the State Department where officials shared—sometimes secretly, often openly—many of the views espoused by those self-appointed sentinels. As the Einstein file reveals, similar seeds were sprouting and flowering in—at least—Hoover's FBI, the War Department (now Defense), and the INS.

Eight years later, well into the New Deal administration of Franklin Roosevelt, the Woman Patriots' memo was to be decisive in a key decision affecting Einstein's life and America's national security. In this second act of the drama, a new player—J. Edgar Hoover—enters from stage right.

---

* Under the Republicans in December 1932 (Roosevelt did not take office until March 1933), the State Department was a bastion of America-first attitudes—anti-immigrant and anti-Semitic. But under Roosevelt, "State" remained at least as bigoted. In January 1934, Secretary of State Cordell Hull (supported by the President) intervened to block passage of a Senate resolution expressing "surprise and pain" at the Nazis' treatment of Jews. During most of World War II, the State Department's chief official in charge of refugee policy was Breckenridge Long, a virulent anti-Semite who praised Hitler's Mein Kampf as "eloquent in opposition to Jewry" and referred to Jews as "exponents of Communism and Chaos."(Wyman, Paper Walls; Offner, American Appeasement; Zinn, p. 111; Wistrich, p. 119; and Morse, p. 133.) But "Long was only one of many State Department opponents of humanitarian action on behalf of Jews…" (Simon Wiesenthal Center Online, 1997.)

2

Flashback

Growing up in Kaiser Wilhelm's expanding, militaristic German Empire in the 1880s and 1890s must have been a little bit like living through sixteen years of basic training. But even as a child, Einstein was marching (or more likely dancing) to a different drummer. Perhaps he was born that way. Perhaps growing up in a family whose business was making and selling electric dynamos—at a time when Western Europe was rushing to switch from gaslight to electricity—stimulated him to value innovation and creativity. (It also introduced him to electromagnetism, which was to be so central to his future theories.) Whatever the combination of causes, it was clear very early in his life that Einstein was not much for regimentation.

The violin perhaps best illustrates the point: His mother Pauline, an excellent pianist, hired a succession of violin teachers for her son, starting when he was six. But young Albert rejected all the technical practice and étude drills—too boring and tedious. It was not until, at thirteen, after he had discovered and "fallen in love with" Mozart's sonatas that he decided to commit himself to mastering the violin.

> My wish to reproduce them to some degree in their artistic content and their unique gracefulness forced me to improve my technique; this I acquired with those sonatas without practicing systematically. I believe altogether that love is a better teacher than a sense of duty—at least for me.[1]

This was obviously not a good Prussian *soldat*. In 1895, at the age of sixteen, Einstein renounced his German citizenship and moved to Switzerland, leaving behind family, friends...and the Kaiser's military draft. He attended the liberal *cantonal* [high school] at Aarau and lived with the Winteler family. Jost ("Papa"), Rosa ("Marna"), and their seven children remained his lifelong friends.[2] (Einstein's sister Maja married the Wintelers' son Paul.) "Papa" Winteler's tierce opposition to German chauvinism undoubtedly bolstered Einstein's internationalist outlook.

Einstein moved to Zurich in 1896 to study at the Polytechnic Institute and thrived in the freewheeling, free-thinking, university community. Turn-of-the-century Zurich was a haven for socialist and anarchist student groups and exiled revolutionaries from throughout Europe. Einstein, never fond of classroom studies, often (in his own words) "played hookey," choosing instead to do a part of his learning at the Odeon Café, a popular gathering place for radical Russian refugees such as Alexandra Kollontai, Leon Trotsky, and later, Lenin (quite likely already contemplating their uprising against the Czar). While there is no evidence that he met any of the more celebrated exiles, Einstein's circle encompassed the newly organized, anti-militarist Swiss Society for Ethical Culture. He also spent time with a group of Serbians, including Mileva Marie (soon to become his first wife), her girlfriends, and later, their husbands, some of whom were political radicals. But perhaps the most radical of Einstein's Zurich colleagues was Friedrich Adler,[3] a junior lecturer in physics and an ardent socialist whose father, Victor, was the head of the Austrian Social Democratic Party. To Einstein, Friedrich was "the purest, most fervent idealistic character" he'd ever met.*

Choosing to stay in the relatively unrepressed intellectual atmosphere of Switzerland rather than return to an increasingly militaristic Germany, Einstein—after graduating from the Polytechnic Institute—adopted Swiss citizenship.

It took the world's greatest scientist two years before he finally landed work, and then only with help from an old friend who had influential contacts. In 1902, he took a job as a clerk in the Swiss Patent Office in Bern, where he remained for seven years. Einstein wrote to Mileva, who was staying with her family in Hungary, that the "annoying business of starving" was over and they could finally afford to set up house together. In 1903, they were married, and their first son, Hans Albert, was born a year later. A second son, Eduard, was born in 1910, by which time Einstein had become a professor at the University of Zurich.**

In Switzerland, Einstein also developed some of his most important work in theoretical physics, challenging the prevalent view (of Heinrich Hertz and others) of the electrodynamics of moving bodies and the

---

* In 1916, Friedrich Adler assassinated the prime minister of Austria. Einstein submitted a statement on his behalf that may have helped convince the postwar (World War I) Austrian officials to grant Friedrich amnesty.

** The Einsteins also had a daughter, Lieserl, born before they were married, and apparently put up for adoption. Despite recent literary speculation, her fate remains unknown.

"I often think in music. I live my daydreams in music." Einstein plays the violin
to celebrate his 50th birthday in Berlin, March 14, 1929.

concept of "the Ether," a substance then believed to occupy all space. In 1905—often called Einstein's *annus mirabilis* (miracle year)—he produced four major theories,* including the Special Theory of Relativity with a supplement (also in 1905) containing what has become the world's most quoted formula: $E = mc^2$. In January of that "miracle year," Europe had reverberated with explosive news of a different kind—the near-revolution in Russia: CZAR'S SUBJECTS ARM FOR REVOLT, declared the *New York Times* headline, followed by DOWAGER CZARINA FLEES AND RUMORS OF OUTBREAKS IN FINLAND AND ELSEWHERE. The *Times* report began: "St. Petersburg's streets were the theatre today of scenes unparalleled in the history of the world." While a direct cause-and-effect connection between society's political eruptions and Einstein's revolutionary physics is unlikely—Einstein himself denied any such link—one historian argues: "At least on a preconscious level, Einstein's own thought seems to have been influenced by [that political] instability."[4]

---

* Einstein's other major 1905 papers were on Brownian motion, light quanta, and the photoelectric effect (for which he later won the Nobel Prize).

During his years in Bern, Einstein earned his doctorate, which enabled him to become a professor—first in Zurich in 1909, then in Prague in 1911, and in Zurich again in 1912, this time at his alma mater, the Polytechnic Institute. Einstein was now recognized as one of the top theoretical physicists in the world, and at the age of thirty-two, he was the youngest participant in the first Solvay Conference of the world's leading physicists, held in Brussels near the end of 1911.

As Europe's universities competed for top scientific and academic brain-power, Einstein was definitely in demand. The German establishment, in tierce competition with England and France for international influence (and colonies), viewed scientific and technological research and development as critical to their economic (and military) success. Through their most famous scientist, Max Planck, who visited Einstein in Zurich in 1913 ("Planck looked me over as if I were a prize hen"[5]), the Germans made him a promising bid. Though he had given up his German citizenship and dodged their draft, the government offered Einstein a full professorship (with no teaching responsibilities) and a large amount of money if he would return to develop his theories in Berlin.

It was an offer he found too good to refuse, and Einstein moved back to Germany—with no way of knowing World War I was about to erupt. Moving from Zurich to Berlin in 1914 was like canceling a camping trip to take a cabin on the *Titanic*. Four months after his arrival in April, German troops invaded Belgium. Personal upheavals on the Einstein home front paralleled the world crisis. His marriage to Mileva, on the rocks for years, was all but over. Shortly after their arrival in Berlin, Mileva left with their two sons to return to Zurich when she discovered he was having an affair with his cousin Elsa, soon to become his second wife.

The four war years in Berlin were a baptism of fire for Einstein's anti-militarist and internationalist ideas. Nearly all German scientists—including his friend Max Planck—quickly became superpatriots, many with war-industry jobs. Einstein and a few other academics were a small anti-war island in the sea of Prussian nationalism. As the war began, ninety-three German intellectuals, including Planck, issued a "Manifesto to the Civilized World," attempting to justify Germany's expansionism and attack on Belgium. In a foretaste of Nazi manifestos a generation later, the document argued that Germany had to defend its *Kultur* against the "shameful spectacle...of Russian hordes...allied with Mongols and Negroes...unleashed against the white race."

In response, Einstein and only three others issued a "Manifesto to Europeans," calling for an end to the war and for European cooperation. The counter-proclamation, banned in Germany, was not published until

1917 in Switzerland. It denounced those Germans "—primarily scientists and artists—[who] have so far...failed to speak out for peace":

> Nationalist passions cannot excuse this attitude which is unworthy of what the world has heretofore called culture. It would be a grave misfortune were this spirit to gain general currency among the intellectuals. It would ... not only threaten culture as such, it would endanger the very existence of the nations for the protection of which this barbarous war was unleashed.

Anti-war activism in Germany (as in France, England, and the United States) could be bad for your health. Pacifists were often assaulted, jailed, or forced to flee the country. (Georg Nicolai, author of the "Manifesto to Europeans," served time in prison and then fled to Denmark.) But Einstein was a special case. Because he was such a valuable asset to Germany, the government permitted him freedom to make anti-war statements. As long as he continued to use the office provided for him on the outskirts of Berlin, Einstein was allowed to work on his research and even to travel, despite his public dissent from the war fervor, but he was excluded from most of the events and activities of Berlin's academic elite. Even when, in 1916, he announced his General Theory of Relativity and changed the course of physics, his refusal to support the war meant he "remained one of [the] political outsiders in Germany." [6]

Einstein's opposition to the war was not limited to declarations. His participation in the outlawed New Fatherland League—which circulated appeals and petitions against the war, advocated peace with no annexations, and called for "a United States of Europe"—launched his political activism. Moreover, that activism, as so often happens, helped to radicalize his political outlook:

> At the beginning, Einstein seems to have attributed wars solely to human folly or wickedness. But through his interaction with pacifist circles, he came to realize the force of economic and social factors.[7]

The "war to end all wars" and "to make the world safe for democracy" did neither, but it did topple the German Kaiser, the second autocrat to fall in two years. A year before the war ended, the world witnessed what John Reed called "ten days that shook the world"—the Bolshevik revolution in Russia (as well as uprisings and almost-revolutions in several other countries, including Germany).

The "Czar of all the Russias" was dead. The Russian Empire was dead. Even the once-invincible Kaiser and the vaunted military machine Einstein had fled as a teenager were dead. Authority, it seemed, no matter how powerful and permanent it proclaimed itself, could be dethroned. It was a grand time for change...and for political mavericks.

If Einstein thought his life would change after the war, he never could
have guessed how dramatically or quickly. In November 1919, when
British scientists measured a deflection of starlight around the sun, thus
confirming the General Theory of Relativity, a war-weary world, hungry
for heroes, suddenly discovered Albert Einstein. Headlines in the *London
Times* of November 7 announced:

> REVOLUTION IN SCIENCE, NEW THEORY
> OF THE UNIVERSE. NEWTONIAN
> IDEAS OVERTHROWN.

Three days later, the *New York Times* joined in:

> LIGHTS ALL ASKEW IN THE HEAVENS,
> EINSTEIN THEORY TRIUMPHS

In the next few years, Einstein won the Nobel Prize (1921),* received
invitations to write and speak to audiences in scores of countries, and was
honored and celebrated throughout the world. One trip took the Einsteins
to China, Japan, Palestine, and Spain, where they were cheered by hundreds of thousands of people.

But in Germany, Einstein attracted a different kind of public attention.
From its start, the ghosts of anti-Semitism and nationalism haunted the
post-war Weimar Republic's attempt at liberal democracy. In early 1920,
a new organization, calling itself the Working Party of German Scientists
for the Preservation of Pure Scholarship, launched an attack on Einstein,
labeling the Theory of Relativity "Jewish perversion," and a group of
students that one newspaper called "an anti-Semitic mob" disrupted
Einstein's lecture at the University of Berlin.[8] He began to receive death
threats. One right-wing student publicly promised to "cut the throat of
that Jew," and the press publicized his statement. Such threats had to be
taken seriously. On June 24, 1922, Einstein's friend Walther Rathenau, the
Jewish foreign minister of the fledgling German Republic, was shot and
killed by a fascist on a Berlin street.

Reports that the Einsteins were thinking of leaving the country
prompted German government and scientific officials to take immediate
steps to suppress the attacks on him, if only for reasons of self-interest:

---

* Einstein had been nominated for the Nobel Prize in ten of the previous twelve years,
yet it wasn't until he had become a world-renowned celebrity that the Nobel Committee
agreed to award him their prize. Irving Wallace, author of *The Prize*, uncovered the
intriguing story of international politics and anti-Semitism behind this delayed action.
(See Chapter 15, p. 209, fn.)

The attacks on Professor Einstein and the agitation against the well-known scientist are making a very bad impression [in Great Britain]. At the present moment in particular, Professor Einstein is a cultural factor of the first rank... known in the broadest circles. We should not drive out of Germany a man with whom we could make real cultural propaganda.[9]

The campaign against Einstein in Germany suddenly stopped...or went underground. More than a decade before Hitler seized power, the French Post-war Army of Occupation in Düsseldorf arrested thirty members of "a German variety of armed Ku Klux Klan," secretly organized inside the defeated German Army. The group was modeled after the American KKK and was reported to have sixteen thousand men in an underground network throughout Germany. One target of the group's propaganda was Albert Einstein.[10]

Meanwhile in Washington, the war's aftermath had also provided the launching pad for the career of J. Edgar Hoover and the new government agency he would head: the Federal Bureau of Investigation. A postwar recession had resulted in labor unrest and strikes—thirty-six hundred strikes in 1919 alone, involving some four million workers. Attorney General Palmer assigned his young special assistant J. Edgar Hoover to plan and supervise a series of raids to arrest radicals, anarchists, immigrants, and militant union members in cities across the country.

On the night of January 2, 1920, ten thousand people in twenty-three states were arrested in the now-notorious "Palmer raids"—under Hoover's direct supervision. To lay the groundwork for those raids, Hoover had prepared a report on the newly formed Communist Party, which, he concluded, "would destroy the peace of the country and thrust it into a condition of anarchy and lawlessness and immorality that passes imagination." One of Hoover's proudest "achievements" during those years was the arrest and deportation of the Jewish anarchist leader Emma Goldman and her lover Alexander Berkman in December of 1919.

When the Palmer raids brought an unexpected public backlash, and Congress launched an investigation into possible violations of human rights, Hoover publicly minimized his role in the raids and kept a low profile as he maneuvered his way to appointment as director of the new FBI. At the same time, he quietly began to develop his extensive files on suspected "Reds" and others he didn't like.

In the immediate wake of World War I, "world peace" seemed like a dream about to come true, and pacifists found widespread support throughout Europe. In a world worn out by bloodshed," Einstein for once marched with the crowd rather than against it." He continued to work with pacifist groups such as the War Resisters International and agreed to serve on the prestigious International Committee for Intellectual Cooperation, an arm of the League of Nations.* On the committee, his main interest was in transforming education, especially at the elementary-school level, from a source of national chauvinism within each country into a teacher of international cooperation.[11]

But as the League of Nations proved ineffective against resurgent nationalism and a worldwide military buildup—unable or unwilling, for example, to stop Japan's blatant invasion of Manchuria—Einstein increasingly reached out directly to the public, advocating grassroots action as the way to ensure world peace. An international celebrity and much-invited speaker, Einstein carried the pacifist message to audiences in every continent. Although the official reason for those invitations was scientific, he often found audiences eager to hear his political views and had no problem with discussing relativity at a university lecture in the morning and, on that same evening, urging young people to refuse military service.

In the winters of 1930, 1931, and 1932, when, with Elsa, he visited the United States as a guest faculty member at Caltech, Einstein found in America an audience eager to hear his political views. In a New York speech on December 14, 1930, he presented his "two-percent" solution to war: "If only two percent of those assigned to military service" would refuse to fight, "governments would be powerless. They would not dare send such a large number of people to jail." Six weeks later, in an interview with American author and socialist, Upton Sinclair, for the magazine *New Leader*, Einstein said the Depression could be solved by a reorganization of the economy.[12] Even at Caltech, his activity was not limited to scientific topics: One Einstein talk early in 1932 called for an international economic boycott of Japan to counter that country's invasion of Manchuria; another was an appeal for a more equitable economic system. Pointing to the worldwide Depression, he declared:

> At a time when we are rich in consumable goods and means of production as in no previous generation before us, a great part of humanity suffers severe want; production and consumption falter to an increasing degree, and confidence in public institutions has sunk as never before...It is not in intelligence that we lack for overcoming evil, but in unselfish, responsible devotion [to] the common weal.[13]

Einstein's pacifist and socialist leanings seemed to mesh with the dominant American mood, desperate for radical economic reform—a mood that was about to sweep Roosevelt into the White House.

---

* Committee members included Marie Curie, Hendrik Lorentz, Gilbert Murray, and Paul Painlevé.

Although a few fervent patriots considered Einstein's speeches and friendship with people like Upton Sinclair as dangerous, Einstein's public appearances throughout America attracted a bevy of fans that would have been the envy of most Hollywood stars. One widely publicized event took place on January 30, 1931. That evening, the premiere of Charlie Chaplin's movie *City Lights* in the lavish, new Los Angeles Theater on Broadway "went down in legend as the greatest Hollywood had ever seen." From early afternoon, crowds poured into downtown, hoping to catch a glimpse of glamour. So many fans turned out that they blocked all traffic, and their crush broke several department-store windows. Squads of LA police were assigned to control the crowds, and according to press reports, at one point they threatened to use tear gas to prevent a riot. The glittering event attracted virtually every luminary and power broker in Hollywood: the Vidors, De Milles, Zanucks, Schencks, Barrymores, Warners, Gloria Swanson, Marion Davies, and, of course, columnist Hedda Hopper. Her firsthand account reported that Chaplin's personal guests of honor, Professor and Mrs. Albert Einstein, received a standing ovation when they entered the star-studded auditorium.[14]

(More than twenty years later, at the height of the Red scare, another Hopper "item" on Einstein's friendship with Chaplin became an item in each man's FBI file.[*])

Einstein's status as an international celebrity had always been a puzzle to him. Not that he didn't enjoy the attention. He never shied away from an interview and seemed to relish bantering with the press. Reporters delighted in his quick wit and pithy expressions. But Einstein could see no logical reason that his every move should attract such public applause. At first, he thought it was a passing fad that would soon die down and give way to another star. But each year, his popularity continued to grow. After the standing ovation from Hollywood's elite at the *City Lights* premiere, Einstein asked his new friend Chaplin if he could explain what lay behind such celebrity status. The movie genius turned to Einstein and said: "People cheer me because they all understand me, and they cheer you because nobody understands you."

---

[*] TO: Director, FBI FROM: SAC, Los Angeles Date: 5/11/54
SUBJECT: ALBERT EINSTEIN, IS-R [for Internal Security—Russia]
"Hedda Hopper's Hollywood" in the January 11, 1939 issue of the Los Angeles "Times" states that EINSTEIN and CHARLIE CHAPLIN were "great friends," their friendship having started "way back in 1931" when they met aboard a boat coming to California; that CHAPLIN later entertained EINSTEIN and took him to the opening of the film entitled, "City Lights." (Einstein file, Section 10.)

Understood or not, Einstein continued to draw crowds. When his cross-country train stopped in Chicago on March 3, 1931, the large group of fans who came to the station to see him were not disappointed. In an anti-war speech from the train's rear platform, Einstein called on "brave and courageous war resisters" to refuse to serve in the military:

> I am convinced that the only way is the denial of military service... It is an illegal fight, but a fight for the real right of the people...when [governments] demand criminal actions from their citizens.[15]

It would not be the last time Einstein advocated civil disobedience as an effective tactic against oppressive government rule.

Despite his superstar popularity—or maybe because of it—Einstein did not especially take to America during those visits in the early 1930s. Even during an earlier trip to the United States in 1921:*

> There is no doubt that he hated [the] excessive recognition, well aware that in spite of what he had done, he was in some ways like the men on Everest who metaphorically stood upon the shoulders of their predecessors. He was never in any doubt about his own worth; he had no reason to be. But he hated the hubbub created around him... "I feel like a prima donna," said Einstein as he turned to the [New York] reporters and prepared for the worst.... "He does not like to be what you call a showcase," [Elsa] explained.[16]

Besides the unrelenting celebrity treatment he received, Einstein's less-than-positive image of America may have come from the racial prejudice he found so rampant...and so repugnant. During his United States visit in the winter of 1931, he wrote an article criticizing racism for the NAACP magazine *The Crisis,* and earlier that year, he had joined Theodore Dreiser's committee in defense of the nine African-American "Scottsboro Boys" falsely accused of rape and sentenced to death. (See Chapter 6.)

After his 1930-31 United States visit, Einstein said he was glad to return "to old Europe" despite "its pains and hardships." And a year later, after another bout of nonstop lionizing, he called America "a boring and barren society."[17] But all of that did not prevent him and Elsa from returning at the start of 1933. The "pains and hardships" in Europe had grown harder and more painful. And as for America, besides welcoming the warm temperatures in California, the Einsteins were especially eager to witness the social reforms promised by Roosevelt's election. The change of climate from Germany, both meteorological and political, would be refreshing, even for just a few months.

---

* The Einsteins first visited the United States with Zionist leader Chaim Weizmann on a fund-raising trip in 1921 for a Hebrew University in Jerusalem.

3

Refugee

The earth literally shook on the day in 1933 when Einstein told a press conference in Pasadena he would not be returning to Germany.

As long as I have any choice in the matter, I shall live only in a country where civil liberty, tolerance and equality of all citizens before the law prevail... These conditions do not exist in Germany at the present time.

Evelyn Seeley reported in the *New York World Telegram* of March 11, 1933, that as he walked away from the interview at Caltech, "Dr. Einstein felt the ground shaking under his feet. Los Angeles was being visited by the worst earthquake in its history." The LA quake was over in seconds, by today's standards hardly worth a press notice. But the sharpest trembler that area had yet seen was an apt symbol of the upheaval in Einstein's life.

What had been planned as a one-semester visit to Pasadena—his third winter as a guest faculty member at Caltech-became a permanent exile when, after Hitler seized power on January 30, the Nazis confiscated all Einstein's belongings and pro-Nazi newspapers put a price on his head equivalent to $50,000. On hearing the news, Einstein quipped, "I didn't know I was worth so much." [1] But when he and Elsa visited Belgium in the summer of 1933, round-the-clock police guards were assigned to protect him from a threatened Nazi assassination. America was a safer haven: the Woman Patriot group seemed only a passing annoyance. And when the Institute for Advanced Study in Princeton offered him a lifetime appointment, that settled it.

After renting an apartment in Princeton for a year, they bought the house at 112 Mercer Street, where Einstein spent the last twenty years of his life. Elsa had become deeply depressed after the death of her daughter Use from tuberculosis in Paris a year earlier. She had no new job to occupy her, and "[Ilse's] death broke Elsa's spirit, aging her beyond recognition," according to her friend Antonina Vallentin. "It was like a wound that refused to heal."[2] Within months of their move, Elsa developed a serious kidney and circulatory illness, and after suffering for more than a year, died in December 1936.

Following Elsa's death, Einstein's Mercer Street "family"—his step-daughter Margot and housekeeper-secretary Helen Dukas (and his sister Maja, who arrived from Italy in 1939)—became totally devoted to supporting his work. His search for a Unified Field Theory (linking the fundamental forces of nature—gravity and electromagnetism—to one underlying force) had so far been without success, but that didn't faze him. When it came to seeking answers to scientific questions, no one was more stubborn.* His main frustration was in the world of politics.

During his early years as a U.S. resident, Einstein more often than not disagreed with Roosevelt's policies toward events in Europe. The topics varied, but the basic issue was always the same: How seriously would FDR resist Nazism? Einstein's activity on behalf of Jewish refugees during the 1930s put him at frequent loggerheads with the Administration. As noted earlier, the immigration policy of Roosevelt's State Department seemed designed, at least partly, to keep Jews out of the country.[3] Secretary of State Cordell Hull, who viewed Berlin as a deterrent to Moscow, resisted demands to denounce Nazi anti-Semitism. When a visiting delegation from the American Jewish Congress and B'nai Brith appealed to him to speak out in 1933, Hull told them the cables he had received from the U.S. Embassy in Berlin "would not appear to bear out the gravity of the situation." But the Secretary of State was not totally silent. He criticized what he called "exaggerated accounts of terror and atrocities" in reports about "the alleged mistreatment of Jews" in Germany.

At least one State Department official reflected a more explicitly political bias in explaining why Jewish refugees from Germany should not be admitted to the United States:

> It may be added with regard to a possible increase in immigration from Germany in view of recent reported troubles in that country that it has been alleged that undesirable classes including Communists will wish to come to this country...[4]

To enter the United States of America in the 1930s, a refugee had to present a birth certificate (in duplicate), a military-service record, a job guarantee or an affidavit of support from a relative or friend who prom-

---

* "I am not more gifted than anybody else. I am just more curious than the average person and I will not give up on a problem until I have found the proper solution." (Bucky, p. 29.)

Albert Einstein chats with New York City
Mayor Fiorello H. La Guardia in February, 1936.

ised to be financially responsible for the new resident, and one more item:
a police certificate of good character for the previous five years.[5] These
requirements were, of course, prohibitive for most* (While fleeing from
the Nazis, you simply stop by the local Gestapo headquarters on your way
out of the country and pick up a good-character voucher.)

With fear suffocating most of Europe, desperate pleas for help from
Jewish refugees deluged Einstein's house in Princeton. At times, his
desk seemed buried by these appeals. While referring many to friends

---

* The U.S. immigration law (1924) allotted each country a limited number of annual
immigrants. But requirements imposed on would-be immigrants were so restrictive—
such as the need to obtain a good-character certificate—that even these limited quotas
could not be filled. One of the more disgraceful statistics in American history shows that
between 1933 and 1943 over 400,000 quota slots for immigrants from Nazi-ruled countries went unfilled (Morse, pp. 61-62). It wasn't until 1944, with the war nearly over, that
Roosevelt finally acted, appointing a War Refugee Board, directed by Treasury Secretary
Henry Morgenthau. With the help of Rabbi Wise, Morgenthau had prepared a report for
Roosevelt on "The Acquiescence of this Government in the Murder of the Jews."

who could help, to businessmen and others who might offer jobs or take financial responsibility for refugees, Einstein himself wrote numerous affidavits of support for Jewish artists, teachers, and scientists attempting to enter the United States. One of those Einstein helped escape was the legendary photographer Philippe Halsman. In 1947, after Halsman took his most famous portrait-photo of Einstein, the photographer asked why he never wore socks. Einstein replied: "When I was young, I found out that the big toe always ends up by making a hole in the sock. So I stopped wearing socks." To Halsman, this was "symbolic of Einstein's independence of thought."[6]

But Einstein's sponsorship didn't always help. The State Department denied admission to any refugee who had a record with the Gestapo. If the Nazis claimed you had "communist sympathies," that was all the United States authorities needed—you were barred. (Until the United States entered the war in December 1941, Washington and Berlin maintained diplomatic relations, and the exchange of police records was common practice through the international police agency Interpol, in which the Germans played a leading role.) Not only that, but Einstein's recommendation for a refugee with such a "record" might be cited as more "derogatory data" in the FBI's Einstein file. Here's one of several examples in the file's newly released pages (Section 9)[7]:

> New York Confidential Informant [code number blacked out] advised that…
> the German playwright Georg Kaiser…was listed…October 19, 1941 [among]
> a group of "German intellectuals…with [police] records of active Communist
> sympathies"….Bufiles [Bureau files] contain derogatory data concerning sev-
> eral of Kaiser's sponsors in addition to Albert Einstein.

Besides seeking to help individual refugees, Einstein, with his friends Rabbi Steven Wise, Otto Nathan, and others, lobbied—with little success—to convince the Administration to open its doors to more refugees. In 1939, a bill they supported, which would have bypassed the quota system to allow twenty thousand refugee children from Central Europe to enter the United States, was opposed by the State Department and killed by Congress. Einstein, Wise, and Nathan even appealed to Eleanor Roosevelt to intervene with her husband to help reverse "a policy…which makes it all but impossible to give refuge in America to many worthy persons who are victims of fascist cruelty in Europe." The First Lady promised to show their letter to FDR, but no change occurred.[8]

It was Einstein's vigorous support for the anti-fascist forces in the Spanish Civil War that most sharply conflicted with the Roosevelt Administration—specifically its foreign policy of neutrality. This policy included an embargo against sending arms or troops to either side in the

1936-1939 civil war in Spain. If the United States was accused of being
"neutral in favor of Franco," it may have been because the principal supplier of fuel for Franco's forces was the American oil company Texaco.[9]
So while Hitler and Mussolini supplied Franco with heavy weapons, the
German and Italian planes in Franco's air force flew on mostly American
oil,˙ bombing Spanish villages. Defying Roosevelt's "neutrality" embargo,
some 2,800 Americans made their way to Spain to fight the fascists. Many
traveled to Paris as "tourists" and then, aided by French anti-fascists,
moved south through France and across the Pyrenees to Spain, where they
joined an army of thirty-five thousand volunteers from fifty-two countries
fighting to defend the democratically elected Spanish government against
Franco's army. The Abraham Lincoln Brigade—the U.S. contingent—
included young volunteers from all regions of the country and all walks
of life. It was the first racially integrated military unit in the history of
the United States.[10] Einstein's anti-fascism made him an early and ardent
supporter of "the Lincolns."

While the international anti-fascist military operation in Spain was
openly organized by the communists (Comintern), at the height of its
popularity in the mid-1930s, its cause and its slogan—"Make Madrid the
Tomb of Fascism"—enlisted a broad political spectrum. Einstein joined
a world wide array of writers, artists, and political activists, including, in
America, Ernest Hemingway, Langston Hughes, Helen Keller, Gene Kelly,
Gypsy Rose Lee, Dorothy Parker, A. Phillip Randolph, and Paul Robeson,
as well as literally thousands of British and American scientists,˙˙ many
of whom were themselves refugees from Hitlerism. Defending Spanish
democracy became the international rallying cry of protest meetings and
fund-raisers, not to mention books, essays, poems, songs, and paintings,
many of which remain popular today.

Despite the array of celebrities supporting the Spanish anti-fascists,
Einstein was singled out for special attack by Franco's many American

---

* Similarly, American "neutrality" did not interfere as U.S. oil companies did a boom-
ing business with Italy during its aggression against Ethiopia. Standard Oil and others
continued to profit from their German sales as late as 1941, until the United States for-
mally declared war on Germany.
** Among the thousands of scientists supporting the anti-fascist fight in Spain:
Nobel Prize-winning chemist Harold Urey, geneticist L. C. Dunn, zoologist Selig
Hecht, engineer Walter Rautenstrauch, astronomer Harlow Shapley, physicists Arthur
Compton and J. Robert Oppenheimer, pathologist John Peters, mathematician Dirk
Struik, and leading figures in American anthropology, Franz Boas and Ruth Benedict,
and physiology, Walter Cannon and A.J. Carlson. In England, the long list of anti-fas-
cist scientists was headed by the noted crystallographer and political activist J. D.
Bernal.

friends, including, as we shall see, the hierarchy of the Roman Catholic Church. HUAC, the congressional investigating committee, cited Einstein's "subversive" affiliation with anti-Franco groups such as the Abraham Lincoln Brigade. The FBI's Einstein dossier (Summary Report, Section 8) first repeats HUAC's charge that "the so-called Abraham Lincoln Brigade in behalf of Loyalist Spain ... is a subversive and Communist organization," and then cites an article in the February 5, 1937 *New York Times* [in the midst of the Spanish Civil War]:

> ...a message from EINSTEIN to "a prominent Spanish personality" declared that he felt ashamed that the Democratic nations had failed to support the Loyalist Government of Spain...EINSTEIN remarked, "At this moment, I... assure you how intimately united I feel with the Loyal Forces and with their heroic struggle in this great crisis of your country."

But in 1938, it was Roosevelt's foreign policy, not the FBI or HUAC, that Einstein saw as the main obstacle to defeating fascism in Spain. In the spring, he joined a group of Princeton University professors in an unsuccessful appeal to Washington to lift the U.S. embargo on weapons to the Spanish (anti-fascist) government.

Nonetheless, Einstein warmed toward America as the FDR Administration warmed toward those fighting the Nazis. Beginning in 1939, just months before Hitler began his blitzkrieg across Europe, Roosevelt took steps to tilt U.S. foreign policy toward the Allies. After Hitler's invasion of Poland in September, Roosevelt pushed through amendments to the Neutrality Acts to allow the United States to supply arms and planes to England and France. The FDR Administration had clearly decided it was now in the national interest to add American money, machinery, and manpower to the anti fascist alliance.[11] While still officially neutral, America was now increasingly "neutral against Germany."

Imagine the doctor in 1655 London who first recognizes that the mysterious, screamingly painful death of several gland-swollen patients was caused by the Plague, the killer epidemic known to have decimated entire populations. Imagine what desperate, frightened thoughts race through his mind at the sudden realization that tens of thousands of unsuspecting people face a gruesome death from this menace against which there is no known protection.* You now have some sense of what Leo Szilard must have felt when he first realized in 1939 that the Nazis had begun work on an atomic bomb. In April, the Nazis had taken over Czechoslovakia, and, Szilard had learned, they had banned the export of uranium ore from the

---

* Before subsiding in 1656, the Plague killed more than 100,000 Londoners.

Czech mines. It was the clearest sign yet that they planned to stockpile the strategic metal for use in preparing an atomic bomb.

Szilard, the brilliant physicist from Hungary who played a pivotal role in first building and later battling nuclear weapons, concluded that to stop Hitler's potential atomic monopoly, his best chance was to enlist the help of his old friend and colleague, Albert Einstein. Besides sharing much of the same worldview, beginning in 1926 in Berlin (where Szilard had come to study after fleeing the repressive and anti-Semitic Horthy regime in Hungary), the two had collaborated to invent and patent a new pump for use in refrigeration.* This time, Szilard proposed that they work together on a more important project.

It was Saturday morning, July 15, 1939, and Szilard and fellow Hungarian-Jewish refugee physicist Eugene Wigner, had driven from New York City to Peconic, Long Island, to interrupt Einstein's sailing vacation. The drive out to Long Island took them directly past a sight that must have been awesome even to the two world-traveled scientists. In a city still wracked by the Depression and unemployment lines, from the middle of a marsh incongruously called Flushing Meadow, rose the mammoth, globe-shaped "Perisphere" and other sleek, futuristic structures of the New York World's Fair. Highlighted by General Motors' "Futurama" exhibit, the Fair promised "The World of Tomorrow," when everyone would have comfortable homes with TVs, washing machines, and ice-making refrigerators, and take two-month vacations in new cars (made by GM) on a vast network of superhighways. For all that Szilard loved inventions and the benefits of technology, at that moment the glitzy exhibition must have seemed an ironic backdrop to the catastrophic drama he sensed was about to unfold.

It is often a little incident that most vividly portrays the full meaning of a disaster. In the case of Nazi-occupied Czechoslovakia, that morning's *New York Times* had such a story at the top of Page 3. It's easy to imagine Szilard reading the item aloud as Wigner drove:

PRAGUE JAILS FIRST COUPLE IN 'MIXED MARRIAGE' CASE

PRAGUE, July 14-A German doctor of Jewish ancestry and his non-Jewish German wife, residents of Czecho-Slovakia since 1936, were brought today before a Prague German court on a "race-shame" charge. The doctor was

---

* Never used in refrigerators, their pump was later adapted for the circulation of coolants in the controversial fast-breeder nuclear reactor—"an irony that would not have been lost on either Einstein or Szilard." (Bernard Feld, Einstein and Nuclear Weapons, Holton and Elkana, p. 391.) Also: "The Einstein-Szilard Refrigerator" by Gene Dannen, Scientific American, January 1997.

sentenced to two and one-half years of penal servitude and his wife to two years.

The prosecution alleged that the doctor, after living four years out of wedlock with this woman, had married her after the publication of the Nuremberg Laws, leaving Germany in order to do so....

Here they were arrested by the German secret police five days after the occupation. Since the end of April, both have been held in prison.

Dressed in an undershirt and rumpled, rolled-up pants, Einstein welcomed them to his summer cabin, and the three physicists sat on the screened-in porch, sipping tea on a balmy July afternoon, trying to figure out how to save humanity. When Szilard explained why he was convinced that the Nazis were beginning an atom-bomb project—German scientists' participation in recent scientific breakthroughs* and new evidence that Germany had begun stockpiling uranium—Einstein was alarmed. He nodded agreement when Szilard declared that if Hitler got the bomb first, he would hold the world hostage. "He was very quick to see the implications," Szilard later wrote, "and perfectly willing to assume responsibility for sounding the alarm."[12]

Einstein had been a pacifist, even if only semiconsciously at first, for most of his life—at least since he left Germany at sixteen to avoid serving in the Kaiser's army. But beginning in 1933, as the Nazi military machine spread death and dread first through Germany and then across Europe, Einstein was forced to rethink his pacifism. His belief that injustice and oppression could be defeated without guns was trampled beneath the goose steps of Nazi storm troopers and pulverized by the fascists' terror-bombing of civilians in towns like Guernica during the Spanish Civil War.

Only months after Hitler took power in Germany in 1933, Einstein first advocated the use of military force. "What I will tell you will greatly surprise you," he wrote to a Belgian pacifist who had asked his support for two imprisoned conscientious objectors. Because Nazi Germany was "obviously pushing toward war with all available means," Einstein warned, countries such as Belgium and France had no choice but to

---

* The international array of scientists whose discoveries had recently made the atomic bomb not just a theoretical but a practical possibility included: Otto Hahn in Berlin and Lise Meitner in Stockholm (nuclear fission); Enrico Fermi (a refugee from Mussolini's fascism) and Szilard in New York; and Frederic Joliot Curie in Paris (nuclear chain reaction). Meitner, an Austrian Jew who had worked with Hahn for years, was forced to flee to Sweden after the Nazi Anschluss (takeover of Austria) in March 1938. While in Sweden, she suggested the explanation for their earlier experimental results. (Hahn was awarded the 1944 Nobel Prize. For a critical review of the Nobel Committee's non-recognition of Meitner, see Ruth Sime's biography.)

build their military defense. "Imagine Belgium occupied by present-day Germany! Things would be far worse than in 1914, and they were bad enough then." [13]

Einstein's shift drew angry letters and articles from pacifists around the world, who felt that he had abandoned the cause. In fact, it was not such a total about-face. Four years earlier, describing his own pacifism, Einstein told a magazine editor: "My attitude is not the result of an intellectual theory, but is caused by a deep antipathy to every kind of cruelty and hatred..."[14] Now cruelty and hatred had become the government of Germany, and as fascism expanded in the 1930s, Einstein expressed alarm at Japan's invasion of Manchuria, Italy's invasion of Ethiopia and Albania, and especially at the Hitler-Mussolini support for Franco's assault in Spain. Though it infuriated many pacifists, Einstein increasingly advocated force as the only alternative. As Doty summarized it, "Peace was not above survival or saving... civilization from fascism."[15]

By 1939 when Einstein and Szilard met on Long Island, Hitler's regime had gone from book-burning to the anti-Semitic Nuremberg Laws to *Kritallnacht*. On November 10, 1938, any hopes that the Nazi nightmare might die peacefully Jay shattered with the glass of Jewish homes, shops, and synagogues on the streets of cities throughout Germany and Austria. Incited by SS men in civilian clothes, mobs rampaged throughout the two countries assaulting, raping, and killing Jews, and destroying their property, leaving streets so littered with broken glass that the assault became known as the "night of broken *glass*"—*Kristallnacht*. More than one hundred Jews were killed.

With the rest of the world, Einstein got the news the next morning:

> ...a wave of destruction, looting and incendiarism unparalleled in Germany since the Thirty Years' War...police confined themselves to regulating traffic and making wholesale arrests of Jews "for their own protection."[16]

Thirty thousand Jews were rounded up during *Kristallnacht* and sent to Dachau, Oranienburg-Sachsenhausen, and Buchenwald concentration camps, where they joined Communists, Socialists, labor "agitators," and Catholic oppositionists the Nazis had arrested earlier.*

---

* The Nazis' earliest concentration camps, such as Dachau, built during Hitler's first year in power (1933), were for members of the left-wing resistance. During 1936—two years before Kristallnacht—the Nazis arrested 11,687 Germans for "illegal socialist activity." Gestapo reports revealed more than 300,000 Germans either in "preventive detention" for political reasons or in prison or awaiting trial for "political misdemeanors." Nazi documents show that between 1933-1945, "about three million Germans were held in a concentration camp or prison for political reasons," for periods ranging from a few weeks to the entire sixteen years." (Hoffman, History of German Resistance, 1933-1945, p. 16.)

After *Kristallnacht* and Franco's military victory in Spain, Einstein became even more insistent on the need for armed force to stop the fascists. "Europe today resembles a town in which the thieves and murderers are thoroughly organized," he wrote early in 1939, "while law-abiding citizens are unable to decide whether they should create a police force." Later, he spelled it out more directly:

> With the rise of Fascism, I recognized that one could not maintain such a [pacifist] point of view except at the risk of allowing the whole world to fall into the hands of the most terrible enemies of mankind. Organized power can be opposed only by organized power. Much as I regret this, there is no other way.[17]

It's not surprising, then, that Einstein quickly agreed with Szilard and Wigner that they needed to take immediate steps to prevent Germany from becoming the first nation to build an atomic bomb. After considering several plans, the group decided the tactic with the most impact would be a letter from Einstein to President Roosevelt, urging him to consider a crash program to develop a nuclear bomb before the Germans built theirs.[18] On August 2, Einstein sent his now-famous letter—drafted in collaboration with Szilard—to Roosevelt. It began:

> *Sir,*
> *Some recent work by E. Fermi and L. Szilard...leads me to expect that the element uranium may be turned into a new and important source of energy in the immediate future. Certain aspects of the situation seem to call for watchfulness and, if necessary, quick action on the part of the Administration....*

The letter then went on to inform the president that it "appears almost certain" that scientists in America could, in the immediate future, set up "nuclear chain reactions in a large mass of uranium" to produce enormous amounts of power and "large quantities of radium-like elements." Einstein also told the president that it was possible, though not certain, that this new phenomenon would lead to the construction of "extremely powerful" bombs:

> *A single bomb of this type, carried by boat or exploded in a port, might well destroy the whole port with some of the surrounding territory...*

The letter urged the president to establish ongoing contact between the Administration and physicists experimenting with chain reaction in America. Einstein suggested that a liaison between the White House and the scientists could, among other things, address the problem of obtaining a supply of uranium ore and arrange for additional funding to speed up the pace of the experiments. Einstein's final paragraph brought the president a pointed piece of news:

I understand that Germany has actually stopped the sale of uranium from the Czechoslovakian mines which she has taken over....[19]

It wasn't quite so simple. Initially, the Administration allocated only a token $6,000 to the uranium project. It took a second Einstein-Szilard letter to FDR, urging the President to move more quickly. It also took a shift in U.S. policy from neutrality to alliance with Britain, France, and the Soviet Union against Germany and Japan, before the Manhattan Project was launched. But it was launched (nearly three years after the Einstein-Szilard letter to Roosevelt), and while Hitler's effort fizzled, U.S., British, and Canadian scientists went on to build the world's first atomic bomb.

It might well have happened without them, but in that tense summer of 1939, Einstein, Szilard, and their colleagues were convinced the letter to Roosevelt could be decisive. The President's increasingly anti-Nazi actions had persuaded them that regardless of past differences, America was the world's best hope to stop a worldwide fascist takeover. Moreover, America had the strength, resources and, potentially, the will to beat Hitler to the bomb.

For Einstein, this was a sea change in attitude from the days when he viewed this country as "a boring and barren society"—a new high in his up-and-down affair with America. He planned eagerly for its consummation, and decided that he would become an American citizen.

He might eventually have become a U.S. citizen anyway. But his decision to do so in 1940, along with his stepdaughter Margot and Helen Dukas, seemed like a political vote of confidence in the country. To be sure, Einstein's fondness for America was something less than a passionate commitment sworn on the altar of eternal love. He remained angry over Roosevelt's molasses-like movement toward supporting Britain. In August, while RAF planes were battling Nazi bombers daily over London, Einstein wrote to Harold Urey: "America's attitude towards the present war, particularly toward England, is…disastrous, [offering] halfhearted and insufficient measures instead of unconditional solidarity."[20] But, slowly, Roosevelt *was* joining the anti-fascist war. And at home, just eleven days after taking office, Roosevelt's new attorney general, Robert Jackson (best remembered today as a judge in the Nazi war-crimes trials at Nuremburg and, later on, the U.S. Supreme Court) dropped all charges against the eleven Lincoln Brigade members the FBI had arrested. It was a clear rebuke to Hoover…and a hopeful signal to anti-fascists like Einstein.

Signals from FDR or not, when it came to hope for beating fascism, there were few choices in the summer of 1940. Western Europe, except for England, had fallen to Hitler and Mussolini, and as for the Soviets,

Einstein, like many other liberals and leftists, was angered by Stalin's treaty with Hitler (and the Red Army's subsequent invasion of Finland).

In a nationwide radio broadcast on June 22, 1940, even as Nazi troops were goose-stepping through Paris, Einstein gave what was probably his most pro-American statement.* The broadcast, sponsored by the U.S. Immigration and Naturalization Service, was part of an NBC network series, *I Am an American,* in which notable immigrants were interviewed. Einstein declared unequivocally that pacifism was not enough to stop the fascists, and essentially called on the American people to lead the resistance:

> I do not think words alone will solve humanity's present problems. The sound of bombs drowns out men's voices. In times of peace, I have great faith in the communication of ideas among thinking men, but today, with brute force dominating so many millions of lives, I fear that the appeal to man's intellect is fast becoming virtually meaningless …
>
> Making allowances for human imperfections, I do feel that, in America, the development of the individual and his creative powers is possible, and that, to me, is the most valuable asset in life….
>
> In some countries, men have neither political rights nor the opportunity for free intellectual development. But for most Americans, such a situation would be intolerable. In this country, it has been generations since men were subject to the humiliating necessity of unquestioning obedience. Hence, it is all the more important for them to see to it that these liberties be preserved and protected.[21]

The FBI did not cite Einstein's "I am an American" speech in his dossier. Instead, even as he prepared for the broadcast, the FBI and Army Intelligence were secretly targeting him for attack.

---

* After FDR's re-election, Einstein sent him warm congratulations. But even during the war, as most of America rallied behind Roosevelt, the Einstein-U.S. romance continued to blow hot and cold. In September 1942, he wrote to Frank Kingdon: "Why did Washington help to strangulate Loyalist Spain? Why has it an official representative in fascist France? Why does it not recognize a French government in exile? Why does it maintain relations with fascist Spain? Why is there no really serious effort to assist Russia in her dire need? It is a government to a large degree controlled by financiers the mentality of whom is near to the fascist frame of mind. If Hitler were not a lunatic, he could have remained friends with the Western powers…." (Letter to Kingdon, Einstein Archives, Princeton.)

4

Banned from the Bomb

A year after Einstein and Szilard first wrote to FDR, their proposal that the United States develop a nuclear bomb before the Nazis did was only inching forward on the slow track from one government station to another. Roosevelt had set up the National Defense Research Council under the chairmanship of Vannevar Bush, an electrical engineer and former president of the Carnegie Institution, to be responsible for developing the bomb project. But Bush, a New England conservative, was not convinced that anyone could make such a bomb and was in no hurry to move the project along.[1] Despite Bush's caution, the NDRC began sparingly to fund nuclear research (at MIT and Columbia) and to begin planning what would become the Manhattan Project.

To help pull the project through the swamp of Washington's bureaucracy, Roosevelt established a top-level Advisory Committee and submitted the names of thirty-one scientists to Army Intelligence (G-2) for clearance. Since this was a weapons-development project, G-2 was responsible for checking the political loyalty of nominees.[2] But G-2 sought help from the FBI with background checks on some of the scientists. In June—as Einstein was preparing his radio address—G-2's chief, General Sherman Miles, wrote to Hoover,* asking the FBI "to check the names of certain scientists who are under consideration as advisors in matters pertaining to the War Department" and requesting "a summary" of the

---

* The letter was addressed to "Lieut. Colonel J. Edgar Hoover" (Hoover's commission in the Army Reserves). A possible explanation for the military form of address is that "for months the FBI director had been in a turf battle with General Miles over which of their agencies had what intelligence authority." (Gentry, p. 266.) Miles may have felt that since this was a military project, Hoover would be more likely to cooperate if he "pulled rank."

FBI's file on Albert Einstein.) In 1940, Hoover didn't yet have much of a file on Einstein—it was barely a year since Roosevelt had authorized an FBI investigation of "subversive activities."* What he did have was a copy of the eight-year-old, sixteen-page "brief" from the Woman Patriot Corporation urging that Einstein be barred from America.[4] When General Miles' letter arrived, Hoover pulled together all the items he could collect from FBI offices around the country. The bulk of the file, fully 80 percent, was the Woman Patriots' anti-Einstein attack. The second part was Hoover's cover letter summarizing items he'd collected from various Bureau offices:

> Information has been received that a "World Congress Against War" was held in Amsterdam, the Netherlands, in August, 1932, under the chairmanship of "a distinguished French Communist," Henri Barbusse. It is reported that this meeting was called at the instance [sic] of the Communist International and that Dr. Albert Einstein was a member of the International Organizing Committee....

In fact, Einstein had refused to attend the 1932 congress, calling it "entirely under Russian-Communist domination." Supporting the meeting's pacifist and anti-fascist goals, Einstein did send a message denouncing Japan's invasion of Manchuria and "the unrestrained lust for profits..." He charged that Japan's intention was "to weaken Russia with a military assault and hinder its economic growth." But he refused an invitation to join the post-conference Anti-War Committee because of Russian influence. ("I am anxious to avoid partisan ties."[5])

The false allegation that he helped organize and lead the conference was repeated throughout the FBI's Einstein file and, over the years, in numerous communications between Hoover and other government agencies. As with other false charges, once in the file—whether or not the FBI knew it was false—the allegation was there to stay.

---

* Hitler's army invaded Poland on September 1, 1939, and two days later, France and England declared war on Germany. That same week, President Roosevelt announced that the FBI would have primary authority to investigate espionage, sabotage, violations of neutrality regulations, as well as "subversive activities."

Roosevelt was determined that with its expanded power, the FBI would keep close tabs on his opponents at home—including isolationists in Congress, Nazi sympathizers like the Liberty League and Father Coughlin's Christian Front—and track clown, if recent reports were true, the growing number of Nazi spies operating inside the United States. Besides, Roosevelt had never liked or trusted the communists, and was delighted that Hoover would keep an eye on them-especially now that Stalin had signed a nonaggression pact with Hitler. (FDR was also considering running for an unprecedented third term and was not above using the FBI for a little intelligence work against potential opponents.) To the FBI chief, the new power was an opportunity to build both the Bureau and his own prestige by hunting not so much Nazis as his favorite quarry: communists.

Hoover's letter to G-2 then lists other presumably dangerous groups and activities where "it has been reported" (sometimes "by a confidential source") that Einstein was associated:

> ...in February, 1933, Dr. Albert Einstein was chosen as Honorary Chair man of the "War Resisters League," reportedly a pacifist organization alleged to be the American affiliate of the War Resisters International, whose headquarters were at Middlesex, England.
>   ...reported to be a member of the German-American League for Culture.
>   ...endorsed the national convention of the "American League Against War and Fascism" held in Pittsburgh, Pennsylvania in November, 1937....
>   ...in December, 1937, was a member of the Advisory Committee of the North American Committee to aid Spanish Democracy....
>   ...was a member of the National Committee of the "Friends of the Abraham Lincoln Brigade," whose alleged aim it was to obtain the safe return to this country of American members of the so-called "Abraham Lincoln Brigade," fighting in the Spanish Revolution. [sic]
>   On Feb. 5, 1939, an article appeared in the New York Times newspaper stating that the Spanish Embassy, Washington, DC, made public on February 4, 1939, a statement made by Dr. Albert Einstein to "a prominent Spanish personality," whose identity was not revealed, declaring that he felt ashamed that the democratic nations had failed to support the Loyalist Government of Spain.

Finally, the packet of Einstein "information" Hoover sent to G-2 included a brief "Biographical Sketch" rife with factual errors and notable for its extremely hostile tone and a political bias echoing the pro-Nazi press in Germany. Indeed, the "sketch" is so inflammatory that G-2 chief General Miles appended a handwritten note to his copy, warning that there could be a public backlash if it ever leaked out. (Miles' exact words were: "There is some possibility of flameback."[6])

The unsigned document was highly unusual for the FBI, whose agents were trained to note meticulously the authorship of every report (though agents' names are blacked out of the files released by the FBI "for security reasons"). From its content and style, it's evident that the eight-paragraph "Biographical Sketch" had been recently prepared by someone outside the Bureau, someone not very knowledgeable about Einstein and not particular about accuracy. After getting Einstein's name and birth date right, the document states that Einstein "has one child by his first wife" (they had a daughter and two sons); is "located at Princeton University" (he was at the Institute for Advanced Study); and was "ousted from Germany as a Communist" (he was not ousted—Hitler seized power while Einstein and his wife were in the United States, visiting Caltech). But these misstatements appear to be merely honest ignorance compared to the document's overall import. Calling Einstein "an extreme radical," the author declares that "a great deal of material on him can be found in the files of the State Department." Virtually the only Einstein material then in the State Department files was the eight-year-old anti-Einstein diatribe from Mrs. Frothingham's Woman Patriot Corporation.

The FBI's "Biographical Sketch" further alleges that Einstein...

has been sponsoring the principal Communist causes in the United States, has contributed to Communist magazines, and has been an honorary member of the USSR Soviet Academy [of Science] since 1927. The Soviet's enthusiastic birthday greeting to Dr. Einstein appears in the Communist party newspaper, the "Daily Worker" of March 18, 1939.

No examples are cited of either Communist "causes" or "magazines," nor does the document mention the many other internationally prominent scientists who were honorary members of the Soviet Academy or any of the hundreds of other greetings Einstein received on his sixtieth birthday. But the core of the "Sketch" is its version of the Einsteins' life in Germany in the 1920s:

...in Berlin, even in the political free and easy period of 1923 to 1929, the Einstein home was known as a Communist center and clearing house. Mrs. and Miss Einstein were always prominent at all extreme radical meetings and demonstrations. When the German police tried to bridge some of the extreme Communist activities, the Einstein villa at Wannsee was found to be the hiding place of Moscow envoys, etc. The Berlin conservative press at the time featured this, but the authorities were hesitant to take any action, as the more radical press immediately accused these reporters as being Anti-Semites.

As a result, the document warns:

In view of his radical background, this office would not recommend the employment of Dr. Einstein on matters of a secret nature, without a very careful investigation, as it seems unlikely that a man of his background could, in such a short time, become a loyal American citizen.

On October 1, 1940, Einstein, stepdaughter Margot, and Helen Dukas became U.S. citizens in the Federal District Court in Trenton, New Jersey. Newspapers across the country featured the story, often with a wire-service photo of the three, hands raised, taking the oath of allegiance. Significantly perhaps, Einstein never gave up his Swiss citizenship, but there's no doubt he was enthusiastic about his new status as an American. The *New York Times* reported Einstein was so delighted that he said he "would even renounce" his cherished sailboat if such action were required as "a part of my citizenship."

Citizen Einstein: Albert Einstein became a citizen of the United States on October 1, 1940, accompanied by his stepdaughter Margot (right) and Helen Dukas.

One can't help but wonder if Einstein would have been quite so effusive if he had known that on July 26, General George V. Strong of G-2 had denied his security clearance,[7] barring him from the Manhattan Project that he and Szilard had proposed just a year earlier.

Einstein was never informed of the ban. But it had to be clear to him within several months that he was off the atomic invitation list. When, just a month into Einstein's American citizenship, two FBI agents had come by to ask him about Leo Szilard, he'd had no reason to doubt that his own clearance would soon follow. The agents asked Einstein about Szilard's history and raised several politically pointed questions about his loyalty. Without hesitation, Einstein gave his friend Leo his strongest possible endorsement:

> Professor EINSTEIN…stated that SZILARD is a very idealistic man who is not at all politically minded. He stated that he had never been connected with any organizations, societies, or political groups abroad [and is] absolutely honest, reliable and trustworthy…as anti-Nazi as he himself is and an outspoken democrat…[who could be trusted] without any fear whatever that Szilard might disclose confidential information to a foreign government.[8]

That FBI agents should seek Einstein's recommendation on someone else's loyalty at the same time that Hoover and G-2 were denying his clearance is further evidence that the FBI chief had kept his anti-Einstein project a top secret even within the Bureau.

Whether Einstein's recommendation helped or not, Szilard was cleared by G-2 and played a key role in building the atomic bomb. Einstein surely had a sense of what Szilard was doing. Even before the Manhattan Project was launched, Leo would visit him once every week or ten days to discuss "his work on the uranium experiment." Though he didn't know the details, Einstein was surely aware that a huge government project was underway—"virtually all nuclear physicists [in the United States], as well as countless scientists from other disciplines, had vanished, their addresses unknown."[9] It was an easy guess that the project's goal was an atomic bomb—after all, he had proposed it in the first place.

Based on General Groves's denial of clearance, presumably reinforced by G-2 and/or FBI agents, Vannevar Bush decided not to discuss the bomb project with Einstein: "I wish very much I could place the whole thing before him and take him fully into confidence, but this is utterly impossible in view of the attitude of people here in Washington who have studied his whole history."[10]

Ironically, Einstein, the once and future pacifist, could not have been more eager to contribute to the work of the anti-Nazi war. He finally had his chance in May 1943, when the Navy hired him as a consultant on submarine warfare and high explosives. Unlike the Army's G-2, the Office of Naval Intelligence had cleared Einstein for war work. On July 10, 1940, just sixteen days before their Army counterparts said no, ONI reported: "Chief of Naval Operation does not abject to [Einstein's] employment."

Einstein (paid $25 a day) couldn't have been more devoted to his new work. "He felt very bad about being neglected," according to the head of the Navy research team who formally enlisted Einstein. "He had not been approached by anyone to do any war work." Einstein boasted to friends that he had managed to get into the Navy without the required haircut, and told his close friend Gustav Bucky that he loved working for the Navy: "So long as the war lasts, I do not want to work on anything else." From June 18, 1943 to October 15, 1944, Einstein sent Navy Lieutenant Stephen Brunnauer regular, detailed reports—some handwritten, others typed, including his handdrawn diagrams—on problems relating to high explosives. Brunnauer later reported that Einstein's solutions had been confirmed in weapons' tests to be completely accurate.[11]

After publicity photos appeared of the famous scientist as a "Navy man," Vannevar Bush asked Einstein to serve as a consultant to the Office of Scientific Research and Development. It was quite a change for the man who less than two years earlier, had found it "utterly impossible" to confide in Einstein. Perhaps the Navy's decision to hire Einstein had made it "safe" for Bush to approach him, too—Bush denied this, insisting he hadn't known about the Navy's action[12]—or maybe it was the change in political climate that followed the Russian victory over the Nazis at Stalingrad. The first major defeat for Nazi troops, widely seen as turning the tide of the war, warmed many American hearts, minds, and politicians—at least temporarily—toward the Russians.*

If his letter to Roosevelt weren't proof enough, Einstein's enthusiastic work for the Navy leaves no doubt that he endorsed the war effort and, as Balibar writes, "supported the national effort to develop nuclear energy and bombs."[13] Yet,—perhaps because he resented having been barred from the Manhattan Project—when Bush finally asked him to serve as a consultant, Einstein turned down the offer.

WHY EINSTEIN?

Why did the FBI and G-2 single out the world's most famous scientist to exclude from what was then the world's most important scientific effort?

The evidence is scanty. The witnesses are dead. The key document, the letter from G-2's General George Veazey Strong denying Einstein's security clearance, has vanished. We know about the letter because it is cited in the FBI's Einstein file (Section 2, p. 175) and a note from Vannevar Bush on December 2, 1941, which stated:

> ...nearly a year and a half ago, the name of Professor Albert Einstein, of the Institute for Advanced Study at Princeton, was submitted to the Army and Navy for clearance....The Navy gave its assent; but in a letter dated July 26, 1940, General Strong stated that the Army could not clear.[14]

But the actual letter from General Strong is missing. Responding to an FOIA request in 1983, the Military Archives Division of the General Services

---

* After a grueling and gruesome battle lasting nearly five months, Nazi field marshal Friedrich von Paulus surrendered his remaining troops to the Russians on February 2, 1943. The previous November, while the battle raged, a Congress of American Soviet Friendship, held in New York's Madison Square Garden, received messages of greeting and support from, among others, President Roosevelt and General Eisenhower; Mayor LaGuardia declared November 8, 1942, "Stalingrad Day," and a "Special Issue" of Life magazine on March 29, 1943, with a heroic-looking portrait of Stalin on the cover, was devoted to the Soviet Union.

Administration stated: "We have been unable to locate the letter...."[15] (Nor did it turn up in the National Archives, despite an exhaustive search.) Curiously, of all the documents in Einstein's FBI and G-2 files—some of them outrageous, a few ludicrous, almost all controversial—this one letter blocking Einstein's clearance is the only document to have vanished. (It is pure coincidence, of course, that if that letter had appeared on the front page of a newspaper anywhere in the world, it would have been a disaster for America's international prestige—and for General Strong's career.)

Without the letter and without witnesses, an investigative reporter would begin by checking out the most likely reasons that the government might have barred Einstein from work on the bomb. Hoover (and no doubt General Strong, who was his political ally) believed Einstein's left-of-center views made him a danger to America, not to be trusted with military secrets.* But many Manhattan Project scientists received security clearance despite detailed FBI and G-2 dossiers on their radical, socialist, or even communist activities. Here, for example, is a memo from G-2's General Miles on Nobel Prize-winning chemist Harold Urey, then at Columbia University:

> Subject: Loyalty of Certain Individuals.
> A check of the records of Federal Bureau of Investigation reveals the following summary of information:
> H. G. Urey—Columbia University/Chairman of meeting on February 12, 1939, of the Lincoln Birthday Committee for Democracy and Cultural Freedom, made statement re "In Defense of Bill of Rights" and was speaker at four annual conferences of the American Committee for Protection of Foreign [Born]" (very left-wing) [comment in original]; member of the American Committee for Democracy and Cultural Freedom 1939....

All the organizations cited in General Miles' Urey memo were considered by the FBI to be communist-front groups. Indeed, the American Committee for Protection of Foreign Born (Miles' memo left off the last word) also appears on every list of Einstein's "subversive" connections. Moreover, Urey's FBI file shows numerous other left-leaning activities, including thirteen "Communist-front organizations." Among these are Friends of the Abraham Lincoln Brigade and three other anti-Franco groups "in support of Spanish democracy," as well at the National Council of American Soviet Friendship.[17] Yet, the Army gave Urey thumbs-up.

Urey was far from the most left-wing of the scientists Hoover and G-2 cleared for atom-bomb work. In the best-known case, Robert

---

* Roosevelt did not share this insecurity about Einstein: In April, just three months before G-2 denied Einstein clearance, the President invited him to attend—and suggest other participants—an enlarged meeting of the Advisory Committee on Uranium.

Oppenheimer was selected to head the Manhattan Project although his Red-front associations—known to the FBI and G-2 (his FBI file runs well over seven thousand pages)—were far Redder than Einstein's. His wife Kitty's first husband had been killed fighting in Spain with the Lincoln Brigade, and his brother Frank, who also worked on the Manhattan Project, was known to have been a Communist Party member. After the war, it was no surprise when Oppenheimer told *Time* magazine he'd had "lots of Communist friends."[18] While Oppenheimer is the most publicized, numerous others, such as Szilard and Phil Morrison, also worked on the bomb although they were known to lean at least as left as, and often farther left, than Einstein.

But once the decision was made to build an atomic bomb, the FDR Administration recruited the talent required to do it—wherever that talent came from. Faced with either an American bomb made by (some) Red and pink scientists or no bomb, the choice was clear. (Later, once the bomb had been produced, tested, and presented to the government, the scientists who made it were as disposable as red wrapping paper on a Christmas gift.) Einstein's maverick politics, then, would not have been enough reason to ban him from the bomb. In our hunt for the why, "too Red" is crossed off the checklist of possibilities.

"Too Jewish" is also crossed off. There's no doubt that anti-Semitism was a part of Hoover's and his Bureau's outlook. Anti-Semitic incidents in the FBI were frequent and ignored, according to former agent Jack Levine. One supervisor told his training class there was nothing subversive about the American Nazi Party, because "all they are against is Jews."[19] While Einstein was aiding Jewish refugees from Nazism, Hoover reportedly spent his Christmas vacations before World War II at a Miami Beach hotel that displayed a sign: "No Dogs, No Jews." While the Miami hotel changed its anti-Semitic policy after the war (and the large influx of Jewish residents to the area), Hoover continued to vacation every year at another resort that barred Jews, the Hotel del Charro in La Jolla, California.* Nonetheless, so many of the Manhattan Project's scientists

---

* Owned by Hoover's friend Texas oilman Clint Murchison, the hotel even refused to admit attorney Roy Cohn in 1953 when he arrived with his boss Joe McCarthy, who hadn't heard about the Gentiles-only policy. While barring Jews (and blacks), Murchison's Hotel del Charro welcomed a broad spectrum of moneyed America as its guests, including movie stars (Clark Gable and Elizabeth Taylor), politicians (Texas Governor John Connelly, HEW Secretary Oveta Culp Hobby, and Vice-President Nixon), and organized crime figures (Johnny Drew and Carlos Marcello, from Chicago and New Jersey): Theoharis (The Boss), p. 296. One insider has described Murchison as a good friend of the Mob. (Bonanno, p. 85.)

were Jews (and immigrants) that if Hoover's anti-Semitism had set the standard for participation, it would have crippled the atomic-bomb effort, if not killed it altogether.

Is it possible that Einstein was rejected for the Manhattan Project because he simply wasn't needed, had nothing to contribute technologically to building an atomic bomb? No less a figure than Hans Bethe, Nobel Prize-winning physicist and one of the leading scientists in the Manhattan Project, writes that Einstein was not asked to participate because: "We needed experts in nuclear physics and explosives. Einstein, though he was the greatest physicist of the century, had never worked in these fields."[20]

Yet there is at least some evidence that Einstein could have contributed. As discussed earlier, for more than a year beginning in 1943, Einstein worked for the U.S. Navy, successfully solving problems in the very field—high explosives—in which Bethe says, "We needed experts." And in at least one instance, Einstein's expertise seemed to be just what was needed during the early stage of planning for the bomb. In December 1941, Vannevar Bush wanted Einstein's input on a specific problem related to isotope separation. Conscious of G-2's security ban, Bush tried a convoluted approach to Einstein without telling him what the information was needed for. It was a clumsy and patronizing attempt to deceive one of the smartest men in history, which fooled no one.[21] But it demonstrates that at least at that early stage, Einstein's expertise *was* in demand.

How much technical expertise Einstein could have contributed is questionable, and history certainly demonstrates that he wasn't essential to building the bomb. But no one, least of all Bethe, argues that Einstein's lack of essential expertise was a reason for denying his security clearance.

If it wasn't simply anti-communism and anti-Semitism, what drove Hoover to go after Einstein as early as 1940? To find the answer requires taking a brief time-out from Einstein to explore what the FBI chief was up to, and with whom. When it came to picking a side for or against the Nazis, the head of the FBI hesitated. In the language of the lawman whose favorite outdoor sport was gambling on the ponies, Hoover hedged his bets.[22] Until the United States actually declared war on Japan and Germany in December 1941, the FBI chief's ties and friendships with the pro-Nazi camp continued to be close...and sometimes secret.

During the last years of official U.S. neutrality, American public opinion was mixed. Reports of *Kristallnacht* and other Nazi atrocities alarmed many, especially as fascist armies rolled over most of Europe. But polls showed the majority of Americans still favored keeping the country out of any overseas war. Support for this isolationism came from both left, the U.S. Communist Party (during the Hitler-Stalin pact, until Germany invaded the Soviet Union in 1941), and right, the Hearst papers, and other conservative media, as well as major corporations trading heavily with Germany and Japan.*

Until President Roosevelt announced his candidacy in the 1940 election, many observers doubted he would run for a third term.** The political right wing hummed with anticipation, smelling victory if they could avoid facing FDR's charisma. The strong isolationist bloc in Congress planned an all-out drive for Senator Burton Wheeler of Montana as its presidential candidate. "If I had my way, the first thing [America] would do would be to start minding our own business," Wheeler told a *New York Times* interviewer. In Berlin, the Third Reich also smelled an opportunity: The Nazis made secret campaign contributions to thirteen congressmen and seven U.S. senators—including Wheeler. It was on this right-wing long shot that Hoover placed his political hedge bet. According to one insider's report, Wheeler's isolationists secretly met with Hoover and promised him the job of attorney general—a job Hoover had long yearned for—in their would-be administration.[23]

If Roosevelt suspected a Hoover-Wheeler alliance, it explains one otherwise puzzling event: When FDR asked Hoover in 1940 to conduct a secret investigation of his political opponents, the President put Senator Wheeler on a separate list. In a highly unorthodox step, Roosevelt secretly enlisted Britain's top anti-Nazi agent in the United States, William Stephenson, better known today as *A Man Called Intrepid*, to check out Wheeler (who ran against FDR in the Democratic Party's primaries). The President's choice of Stephenson turned out to be unfortunate for

---

* A new organization called America First, with Sears Roebuck Chairman Robert Wood at its head, support from media mogul William Randolph Hearst, and Charles Lindbergh as its most celebrated spokesman, conducted a well-financed national campaign to "keep America out of Europe's wars." FDR's popularity remained high, but America First tapped into a deep vein of mind-our-own-business sentiment. In New York City, the group packed Madison Square Garden's 20,000 seats for a mass meeting. After the Japanese attack on Pearl Harbor on December 7, 1941, America First was dissolved as an organization, although not necessarily as a state of mind. Eerily echoing the German postwar claim that "We didn't know about the [concentration] camps," one of America First's founding members, Bob Stuart (later CEO of the Quaker Oats Company and U.S. Ambassador to Norway under President Reagan), writes: "Some of the events going on in Europe, such as Kristallnacht, really didn't get the coverage that we now know they deserved. So our awareness level wasn't very high."(Jennings, p. 208.)
** By tradition, no president before FDR had served for more than two terms. In 1951, six years after Roosevelt's death, Congress approved the 22nd Amendment limiting a president to two terms.

Wheeler...and for Hoover. Nicknamed "Little Bill" because of his short stature, Stephenson's cloak-and-dagger operation was anything but small.* Behind a façade called the British Passport Control Office, in New York's Rockefeller Center, he set up what one expert has described as "the most successful covert action operation in history."[24]

Stephenson's staff not only found evidence of the German government's secret campaign contributions to Wheeler (and other isolationists in Congress), but within a matter of months, the "Intrepid" team uncovered proof that more than one million copies of pro-Nazi propaganda had been sent out from Wheeler's office through the U.S. mail, illegally using his congressional free-postage franking privilege.** When the news "leaked" out to the press, it was a body blow to Wheeler's career, and the end, at least for a few years, of Hoover's maneuvers to become attorney general.[25]

Einstein, of course, was ardently anti-isolationist, arguing publicly and privately for America to join the anti-Nazi struggle. In 1940—the year Einstein was denied security clearance—Hoover's links to the isolationists would have made Einstein a top target.

One of Hoover's favorite sources of information was a book published in 1934, *The Red Network* by Elizabeth Dilling, a rabid anti-Semite who was later tried for being a Nazi agent. If the Aryan Nation were searching for a public-relations director, Elizabeth Dilling, if she could be reincarnated, would be an ideal choice. Richard Gid Powers, far from an anti-FBI historian, describes her as "a bizarre figure who made herself the center of a tiny, but noisy, group of wildly irresponsible, anti-Semitic countersub-

---

* In the shadow world of espionage, as a rule, the less publicity, the better the spy—for obvious reasons. James Bond was so well known that if he'd been a real agent, he couldn't have uncovered his own bed. To "Intrepid," operating in virtually total secrecy, no scheme was too bold or too devious if it helped expose the Nazi danger. His no-holds-barred network included experts who secretly opened diplomatic mail and broke into embassies to steal code books, a group of several hundred prostitutes who seduced Nazi diplomats and pro-German U.S. politicians, and more than 2,000 men and women working to place anti-Nazi stories (sometimes true) in the press. At first, Stephenson cooperated with the FBI, feeding Hoover information on Nazi agents and collaborators in the United States, including corporations secretly doing business with Berlin—more than 100,000 confidential reports on the Nazis' North American network. But when the FBI failed to act on these reports, Stephenson began to question the chief's loyalties and shut down the information pipeline to Hoover. (Gentry, p. 266.) Stephenson felt Hoover "spent more time spying on the British than on Nazi agents." (Loftus/Aarons, p. 74.)

** Wheeler finally admitted he "sold" a million of his franked envelopes to the America First organization. While Wheeler's office was the center of the operation, he wasn't alone. A total of 1,173,000 copies of pro-Nazi propaganda were mailed out through the offices of 24 members of Congress. (Stevenson, p. 293.)

versives on the lunatic right during the 1930's." More succinctly, Powers calls her "a crackpot."[26]

The question is not whether Dilling was a crackpot. The question is how much Hoover and his Bureau relied on this crackpot for "derogatory information." Dilling's *Red Network* "was one of J. Edgar Hoover's most useful aids to compiling his files," according to Natalie Robbins, who reviewed the FBI files on 148 American writers. In her book *Alien Ink,* she reports the files on writers such as Josephine Herbst, Fannie Hurst, Malcolm Cowley, Granville Hicks, and Edmund Wilson are "liberally peppered" with Dilling's dubious allegations. "In many files, the language of Dilling's book is used word for w ord."[27] Like the Nazis, Dilling saved a prominent spot for Einstein on her enemies list—perhaps because she was such a rabid anti-Semite. When it comes to Jew-baiting, her booklet *The Plot Against Christianity* makes *Mein Kampf* seem like a Boy Scout manual.

Dilling's *Red Network* lists the names of hundreds of "subversives," along with thumbnail descriptions, but she identifies six individuals as particularly dangerous Reds, devoting two or three pages to each of them. Among these are Gandhi, Jane Addams, and Einstein. She allots half of her Einstein space to citing antirelativist "authorities" such as Thomas Jefferson See and Arthur Lynch, who denounced Einstein's theories. She also quotes extensively from the Woman Patriot tirade. And as proof positive of his Redness, she reports that Einstein "called the grotesque art of Communist Diego Rivera 'a gift to the world.'" Like the isolationists, Dilling could have nudged Hoover even farther into the anti-Einstein camp.

Hoover's sympathy for the far right was not limited to American fascists. He also maintained cordial ties with Nazis in Germany. Recently released FBI files reveal that Hoover sent Hitler's Gestapo chief Heinrich Himmler a personal invitation to attend the 1937 World Police Conference in Montreal, and the following year, welcomed one of Himmler's top aides to the United States. The Gestapo chief was on the FBI's mailing list until April 1939—just months before the Nazis invaded Poland. But even after Himmler was removed from the Bureau's list, Hoover kept up his own pen-pal correspondence with several Nazi police officials. In June 1939, with Nazi SS and police conducting savage attacks on Jews, Gypsies, and homosexuals throughout Germany, Hoover personally autographed a photo of himself and sent it, in response to a request, to the chief counsel for KRIPO, the Nazi criminal police agency. He continued communication with Nazi police groups and officials until December 4, 1941, just three days before Pearl Harbor.[28]

Once the United States officially entered the war, Hoover suddenly (if temporarily) became an ardent anti-fascist. But in the spring and summer of 1940, when he sent the Bureau's dossier on Einstein to Army Intelligence, the FBI chief was apparently keeping close company with this country's native Nazis, as well as friendly ties with officials in Berlin.

The discovery of Hoover's far-right leanings and possible pro-Nazi linkages suggests a motive for the FBI chief to target Einstein in 1940. The Nazis' reason for singling Einstein out was obvious: Like all racist regimes, the Third Reich fed its followers a carefully constructed mythology about the "inferior race," drummed out in mind-numbing repetition of stereotypes—ugly, lazy, evil, conspiring against the system, and, above all, not as smart as those in power. The very existence of a world-renowned Jewish genius subverted the entire mythology.

Was Einstein's name really on a Hitler hit list? Just months after the Nazis took power in 1933, as we've noted, the pro-Nazis press announced a price on his head. More evidence comes from an unlikely source—the FBI's Einstein file. As part of an unrelated investigation, agents interviewed an Interior Department official, Thomas W. Hunter:

> Mr. Hunter stated that he personally had seen a list of names described to him as Hitler's "black list"...of Jewish refugees wanted by the Nazis "dead or alive." He recalled...this list...included Albert Einstein, the famous scientist.[29]

That the Nazis were out for Einstein's head is hardly news, but if they also had a hand in Hoover's investigation, it might help to explain why Einstein became a special FBI target. It's worth taking a second look at the FBI/G-2, unsigned "Biographical Sketch" of Einstein that provided the rationale ("...it seems unlikely that a man of his background could... become a loyal American citizen.") for denying his security clearance.

The "Sketch" reeks with circumstantial evidence of a pro-Nazi author, echoing unfounded Nazi reports that the Einsteins' home was "a Communist center and clearing house." Einstein was—quite publicly—affiliated with several anti-fascist, left-of-center organizations in pre-Hitler Germany, but the FBI/G-2 document parrots stories in the "conservative" (pro-Nazi) German press claiming the Einsteins were "always prominent at all extreme radical meetings and demonstrations" and calling their summer house in Caputh "the hiding place of Moscow envoys." (No envoys, hidden or open, from Moscow or anywhere else, were ever identified.) In addition, the document describes 1923-1929 Germany—a time of escalating street-violence by Nazi gangs—as a "political free and easy period."

If the "Biographical Sketch" of Einstein was not twisted by a pro-Nazi author, the document nonetheless reflects a mindset, a world-view prevalent in the FBI and G-2 at the time:

...the Bureau's fervent anti-communist ideology...prompted the writer of the biography [sketch], even as late as 1940 to accept the accounts of the conservative press and to deny the reality of the Nazi campaign against the Jews, dismissing charges of anti-Semitism as rhetoric from the radical press.[30]

How likely is it that one or more of Hitler's helpers did have a hand in creating the FBI/G-2 anti-Einstein "Sketch"? There is no doubt about it, according to historian Klaus Hentschel of the University of Goettingen, who sees the document as a painting finger:

[It] was either picked up from the German radical right-wing press (e.g. *Volkischer Beobachter),* in which incompetent propagandists...published their polemical articles, or suggested by informants originating from these nationalistic circles.

Hentschel also found evidence of continued FBI reliance on pro-Nazi sources a decade later, during the McCarthy era.[31]

For Einstein, this would not be the last time the Nazi connection played a role in Hoover's campaign against him.

Aside from any Nazi influence on the FBI, the U.S. Army had its own reasons for banning Einstein from the bomb: control of the Manhattan Project. While the Army clearly had the ultimate legal and physical control, the bomb could be built only if scientists remained convinced it was for an essential cause—in this case, beating Hitler. From the outset, the Manhattan Project was a shaky partnership between the two camps. General Leslie Graves and the other top military officials worried about how to ensure military command of the operation and viewed some of the scientists as prima donnas.[32]

The Army and General Graves had to have known that Einstein's prestige and universal popularity could sway other scientists—and even more important, public opinion—if a policy controversy were to arise inside the Manhattan Project. Einstein was probably the only scientist who might have threatened the military's complete control of the bomb project. No one, not Urey, not Bethe, not even Oppenheimer, could elicit anywhere near the immediate public sympathy and support.

As it became clear by the end of 1944 that the Nazis would not succeed in building an atomic bomb and Washington began to lay plans for using the bomb against Japan instead of Germany, scores of Manhattan Project scientists protested, and several considered quitting. Only one, Joseph Rotblat (who won the Nobel Peace Prize in 1996), actually left; despite their qualms, none of the others followed Rotblat's walkout.[33] But had Einstein been in those walking shoes, he might well have had more impact on colleagues and, without doubt, have influenced public opinion to oppose using the bomb, at least against civilian populations. In barring him from the Manhattan Project, the Army, consciously or simply following military "instinct," was maintaining control of its turf. The unforeseen effect was to block Einstein from leading any protest against the bomb—until after it had been dropped on Hiroshima and Nagasaki.

Einstein shared the world's elation at the defeat of Hitler, but peace was a long way from paradise. He was not about to repeat the mistake he had made after the First World War. In 1918, after four years of war had cost the lives of more young men than any conflict in history, the victorious Allies proclaimed the world "safe for democracy." Einstein's words were never more wrong than when, at the age of thirty-nine, he wrote from Berlin to his mother in Switzerland: "The great event has happened!...Militarism and bureaucracy have been thoroughly abolished here."[34]

This time, he knew better: Only four months after the war's end, he told a Nobel anniversary dinner in New York:

> The peoples of the world were promised freedom from fear; but...fear among nations has increased enormously since the end of the war. The world was promised freedom from want; but vast areas of the world face starvation, while elsewhere people live in abundance. The nations of the world were promised liberty and justice; but even now we are witnessing the sad spectacle of armies...firing on peoples who demand political independence and social equality...

He concluded: "The war is won, but the peace is not."[35]

PART II

Postwar Fallout

5
Emergency Committee

On July 25, 1945, President Harry S. Truman wrote in his diary:

> This weapon is to be used against Japan between now and August 10. I have told the Sec. of War, Mr. Stimson, to use it so that the military objectives and soldiers and sailors are the target and not women and children...we as leaders of the free world for the common welfare cannot drop this terrible bomb on the old Capital or the new...The target will be a purely military one and we will issue a warning statement....

Less than two weeks later, on August 6, a U.S. Air Force bomber—with no warning—dropped an atomic bomb on Hiroshima, killing nearly 100,000 civilians of all ages. Another 100,000 would perish from radiation poisoning.[1] On August 9, a second bomb fell on the city of Nagasaki and its civilian population, with similar numbers of casualties.

A historical novelist might spin an intriguing conspiracy plot from the total disconnect between the President's diary and the bombing. But if it disturbed Truman, there is no record of it.[*] When the Federal Council of Churches cabled him expressing the distress of "many Christians" over the bombing's "indiscriminate destructive effects" and its "extremely dangerous precedent for the future of mankind," Truman's response gave no sign of the concern for Japanese civilians he had professed two weeks earlier:

---

[*] By the time he met with Oppenheimer in 1946, the President seemed unperturbed by the bombing. Never known for agility with words, Truman reportedly answered Oppenheimer's outpouring of conscience—"I feel like I have blood on my hands"—with: "Don't worry, it will all come out in the wash." (Davis, p. 258.) Another version of the conversation, in Merle Miller's biography of Truman, has the President offering a handkerchief to Oppenheimer with the comment: "Well, here, would you like to wipe off your hands?" Later, Truman referred to the former head of the Manhattan Project as "that crybaby scientist." (Herken, p. 401.)

The only language they seem to understand is the one we have been using to bombard them. When you… deal with a beast, you have to treat him as a beast.[2]

It was the kind of statement that fueled charges—primarily from people of color—that racism was behind the nuclear attack. Roy Wilkins, editor of the NAACP's magazine *The Crisis,* accused Washington of treating the Japanese as subhuman, adding that the U.S. devastation of Hiroshima and Nagasaki raised the question, "Who is barbarian and who is civilized?"[3]

Einstein blamed the atomic bombing of Japan on Truman's anti-Soviet foreign policy. He had enthusiastically supported Roosevelt's wartime alliance with Moscow against Nazism,[4] and he told an interviewer from the *Sunday Express* of London that if FDR had lived through the war, Hiroshima never would have been bombed. The interview was immediately added to Einstein's FBI file:

ROOSEVELT WOULD HAVE BANNED
A-BOMB USE, EINSTEIN BELIEVES

Professor Albert Einstein…said today that he was sure President Roosevelt would have forbidden the atom bombing of Hiroshima had he been alive, and it probably was carried out to end the Pacific war before Russia could participate….[5]

Questions about the motives behind the atomic bombing of Japan have persisted, but Einstein was not alone in his view. "There are several tantalizing hints that President Roosevelt was troubled about the basic question of using the weapon against Japan in a way that his successor never was," according to McGeorge Bundy, National Security Adviser to Presidents Kennedy and Johnson. Historians have also come up with considerable evidence that Truman's Secretary of State James F. Byrnes saw the bombing "as a way to end the war before the Red Army entered Manchuria."[6]

Einstein's *London Express* interview also provided what was then a rare public glimpse of how some nuclear scientists had tried to stop the atomic bombing:

"A great majority of scientists were opposed to the sudden employment of the atom bomb," he said … Einstein explained that scientists favored a demonstration of the bomb "to prove to the enemy its existence and its massive destructive powers" before it was used as an instrument of war.

Whether or not Roosevelt would have ordered the A-bombing of Japan, conscience-plagued scientists in the Manhattan Project believed he was their best chance to block the use of the bomb they had built. When it became clear in mid 1944 that the Germans would not succeed in developing the bomb, the scientists were plunged into debate over the ethics of continuing what had originally been an anti-Nazi cause. For the many European (mostly Jewish) scientists, the bomb was intended to stop Hitler.

Though barred from the Manhattan Project, Einstein learned about the argument when his longtime colleague Otto Stern, one of the Project's worried scientists, visited him in Princeton to discuss the bomb's awesome potential and his fears about its future. In December, Einstein wrote to Niels Bohr, urging that they approach leading scientists from key countries—including Russia—who could influence their governments "to bring about an internationalization of military power." It was "the one possibility, however slight," Einstein argued, to prevent a future where "secret [nuclear] war preparations...will lead inevitably to destruction..." Bohr shared Einstein's fears, but had been warned by Churchill and Roosevelt that if any word, or even a hint, about the atomic-bomb project got out, especially to scientists in other countries, it would be a dangerous breach of security. Bohr, when contacted by Einstein, rushed to Princeton, and after a long discussion, persuaded Einstein that wartime security required them to remain silent.*

Meanwhile, several Manhattan Project scientists headed by Leo Szilard sought to convince Roosevelt not to use the bomb against Japan, and in March 1945, Szilard enlisted Einstein's help. Less than six years after the two scientists had first proposed that Roosevelt launch the bomb project, Einstein wrote to FDR again, urging the President to meet with Szilard immediately, adding, "I have much confidence in [Szilard's] judgment."[7] A day after Roosevelt's death on April 12, 1945, Einstein's letter was found on his desk, unopened.

With Hitler's defeat in sight but not quite in hand, FDR's death left Truman in the commander's seat, and the scientists got nowhere at all with him. In June, a group of the Manhattan Project scientists at the University of Chicago's Metallurgical Laboratory, led by Szilard and Nobelist James Franck, sent a report to Secretary of War Henry Stimson, warning that using the bomb against Japan would compromise America's moral leadership. As Einstein later told the *London Express,* the Franck Report recommended that the United States conduct a demonstration of the bomb in an uninhabited area to convince the Japanese to surrender

---

* Bohr, who was working on the bomb at Los Alamos in 1944 (after he and his son made a dramatic escape in a small boat from Nazi-occupied Denmark), had tried but failed to convince Churchill and Roosevelt to invite the Soviets to join in planning for cooperative postwar control of nuclear energy. Churchill and Roosevelt told the world-famous Danish physicist his proposal would threaten U.S. and British security. They also ordered him monitored to "make sure he is responsible for no leakage of information, especially to the Russians." Churchill went farther, claiming that Bohr was "very near the edge of mortal crimes." (Sherwin, p. 110, and Clark, pp. 697-701.)

without nuclear devastation. More than 150 Manhattan Project scientists signed a petition, circulated by Szilard, containing essentially the same message.[8]

The scientists' campaign had no effect on White House policy, but it did provide experience, contacts, and heightened awareness for the committees to come.

Unlike the wild celebrations in Times Square, Red Square, and Piccadilly Circus when the Nazis had surrendered in May, the public's reaction to the Allied victory over Japan was tempered by uncertainty and awe at the massive destructive power of the bomb. Most Americans, to be sure, rejoiced at the end of the war, and supported the bombing. A month after Hiroshima, a nationwide Gallup poll showed 69 percent thought it was "a good thing," with only 17 percent in opposition. For the U.S. troops assigned to the war in the Pacific, and their families and friends, anything that shortened that fighting was cause for cheering. One former Navy man recalls: "Our ship was headed to Japan when we heard about Hiroshima— we all started whooping it up and tossing our gear overboard."[9]

Harry Truman was on board the Navy's USS *Augusta* (sailing home from the Potsdam Conference with Churchill and Stalin) when news of the Hiroshima bombing reached him. "This is the greatest thing in history," the President told a group of sailors dining at his table. The Navy men cheered.[10]

More than 98 percent of the U.S. press editorials welcomed the news from Hiroshima and Nagasaki. The nation's keynote editorial in the *New York Times* blamed the Japanese, who, "by their own cruelty and treachery... had invited the worst we could do to them." As throughout the war, racist terms and caricatures of a slant-eyed, bucktoothed enemy appeared frequently in editorials and cartoons on Hiroshima. The *Philadelphia Inquirer* denounced "the whining, whimpering, complaining Japs," and *Newsweek* headlined, "The Jap Must Choose Between Surrender and Annihilation." Nor would the left-wing media be outdone when it came to editorial applause for the bombing. The *New Republic* welcomed the news; the *Nation* hailed the bomb's "spectacular success," adding that two billion dollars "was never better spent"; and the left-leaning *PM* called for dropping "a few" atom bombs on Tokyo to "clear the bases for democracy after the war." The Communist Party's *Daily Worker* cheered: "We are lucky to have found The Thing [the atom bomb] and that we are able to speed the war against the Japanese before the enemy can develop countermeasures."

But the national celebration was far from unanimous, and even the majority's positive assessment was laced with worry. A *Fortune* opinion poll showed only 47 percent felt the bomb had decreased the chances of another World War, and the Social Service Research Council reported that 64 percent of people they surveyed felt there was "a real danger" that nuclear bombs would some day be used against the United States.[11] "[It's] as if we had put our hands upon the levers of a power too strange, too terrible, too unpredictable …for any rejoicing over the immediate consequences," the *New York Herald Tribune* declared on the morning after the bombing. And the banner headline in the *Des Moines Register* was anything but euphoric:

DESTROY 60 PCT. OF CITY!

On CBS radio, Edward R. Murrow reported an unprecedented national "sense of uncertainty and fear…a realization that survival is not assured." And even the usually promilitary *Life* magazine reflected the national nervousness: "The people of the world, although thrilled by the prospect of peace, were shaken by the new weapon."[12]

Besides nervousness, a careful listener could hear growing numbers of American voices raised in criticism: In September, several leaders of the Catholic Church denounced the bombing as "the most powerful blow ever delivered against Christian civilization and the moral law." Father James M. Gillis, editor of the *Catholic World,* wrote: "The action taken by the U.S. Government was in defiance of every sentiment and every conviction upon which our civilization is based." A blue-ribbon commission of theologians set up by the Federal Council of Churches declared that "the indiscriminate slaughter of noncombatants" was "ghastly," and "[the] surprise bombings of Hiroshima and Nagasaki are morally indefensible" and "unnecessary for winning the war," adding:

> As the power that first used the atomic bomb under these circumstances, we have sinned grievously against the laws of God and against the people of Japan.[13]

A handful of journalists refused to join the media cheering section. *New York Post* columnist Marquis Childs, on August 10, called the atomic bombing of Japan "a supreme tragedy…" And the *Christian Science Monitor's* Richard L. Strout questioned: "How can the U.S. in the future appeal to the conscience of mankind not to use this new weapon?"[14]

More condemnation came from the African-American community. With many black troops assigned to the Pacific war, the African-American media's initial reaction to Hiroshima was mostly positive. But within weeks, perhaps reacting to such racially charged statements as

Truman's "treat him as a beast" pronouncement, skepticism and anger became their dominant theme. Besides Roy Wilkins' editorial in the NAACP's *Crisis*, the *Washington Afro-American* declared that Hiroshima "revived the feeling in some quarters that maybe the Allies are fighting a racial war after all." Noting that "the 7,000 black workers at [the Manhattan Project's research center in] Oak Ridge lived in segregated, inferior housing and performed menial jobs only, with no school provided for their children [unlike for the white workers]," the paper asserted the United States had spared the Germans, who, "after all, represent the white race," and "saved our most devastating weapon for the hated yellow men of the Pacific." By mid September, the *Chicago Defender* had carried articles by poet Langston Hughes, NAACP Chairman Walter White, and W. E. B. Du Bois, siding more with the Japanese victims than with the U.S. government.[15]

While polls showed a majority continuing to express approval of the bomb and its use against Japan, newspapers in several U.S. cities reported an increasing flow of letters criticizing the killing of noncombatant civilians in Japan, calling it inhuman, and protesting "our disregard of moral values."[16] Truman insisted that Hiroshima was a target with military importance, and that atomic-bombing the two Japanese cities actually saved tens of thousands of lives on both sides. If, as Einstein and others charged, he had acted in order to thwart Russian's entry into the Pacific war, such international power politics were, then as now, rarely included in official explanations of military action:

> When Japan surrendered a few days after the bomb was ordered dropped on August 6, 1945, the military estimated that at least a quarter of a million of the invasion forces against Japan and a quarter of a million of Japanese had been spared complete destruction and that twice that many on each side would, otherwise, have been maimed for life…
>
> I think the sacrifice of Hiroshima and Nagasaki was urgent and necessary for the prospective welfare of both Japan and the Allies.[17]

But the anti-nuclear activists responded by reprinting a report of the U.S. Strategic Bombing Survey that stated: "Hiroshima and Nagasaki were chosen as targets because of their concentration of activities and population." The USSBS also estimated that Japan would have surrendered within months even without the U.S. nuclear attack.

And a week after the bombing of Nagasaki, conservative editor David Lawrence, one of the few dissenting journalists, wrote:

> Military necessity will be our constant cry in answer to criticism, but it will never erase from our minds the simple truth that we of all civilized nations, though hesitating to use poison gas, did not hesitate to employ the most

destructive weapon of all times indiscriminately against men, women and children.[18]

In the fliers and pamphlets of the growing anti-nuclear movement, the official U.S. Air Force photograph of the atomic bomb explosion over Hiroshima became a symbol of devastation. James Faber, the National Press Photographers Association's historian, called it "a picture that represents the instantaneous death of almost 80,000 people."[19]

Blaming Truman for the devastation of Hiroshima and Nagasaki did not relieve the sense of responsibility that gripped many (though not all) of the Manhattan Project scientists. By the traditional standard of appointments and awards (including Nobel prizes), these were men of brilliance. Trained in the careful observation and analysis of unexpected events, they had devoted several years of their energy and enthusiasm to building a weapon they believed would save democracy from Hitler's terror. Now they recoiled in shock.

"The time will come when mankind will curse the name of Los Alamos and Hiroshima," Philip Morrison declared after flying over the devastation caused by the bomb he'd helped to make. ("One bomber and one bomb had...turned a city of three hundred thousand into a burning pyre.") Szilard called the bombing of Hiroshima and Nagasaki "one of the biggest blunders in history" and "a flagrant violation of our own moral standards." The most dramatic conscience-cry was Oppenheimer's somber *mea culpa* from the Bhagavad Gita,* "I am become death."[20] Even Edward Teller, the Hungarian-born physicist, later one of the most ardent advocates of nuclear weapons, declared in 1945: "I have no hope of clearing my conscience. The things we are working on are so terrible that no amount of protesting or fiddling with politics will save our souls...."[21]

But many concerned scientists (not Teller) did turn to politics. Driven by guilt, or by what they saw as the real threat of global annihilation (or both), organizations of alarmed, anti-nuclear scientists sprouted across America. Only a few months after the Hiroshima bombing, a group of Manhattan Project members formed the Federation of Atomic Scientists (later broadened to the Federation of American Scientists), aimed at seeking international control of nuclear weapons. Within a year, FAS had helped form two more organizations: the National Committee on Atomic Information, which represented some fifty unions, churches, and civic organizations; and the Association of Scientists for Atomic Education,

---

* Originally composed in Sanskrit, the Bhagavad Gita is a central text of the Hindu religion.

which sent scientists to speak to meetings across America and distributed a colorful, cartoon-filled "Handbook" on the hazards of nuclear weapons. Yet another group, the Atomic Scientists of Chicago, launched the *Bulletin of Atomic Scientists*, with Einstein as an unofficial "godfather." The first issue called on the American people [to] work "unceasingly for the establishment of international control of atomic weapons as a first step towards permanent peace."[22]

The problem, the scientists soon discovered, was that all that publishing, mailing, and traveling to meetings, cost money. Financial planning was not the forte of these scientists-become-activists, so the FAS leadership retained professional fund-raiser Harold Orum. To Orum, the solution to their money problems was obvious and living in Princeton. Even supporters of a cause like nuclear disarmament are more likely to contribute money when solicited by a star, and what brighter star for that purpose than Albert Einstein?

In May 1946, Orum and Szilard recruited Einstein to head the new, Nobel-studded Emergency Committee of Atomic Scientists (ECAS),* designed primarily to raise funds for other anti-nuclear groups. Except for Einstein, all the ECAS members had worked on building the bomb, and the Committee answered both an urgent national need and a call from their collective conscience. The new group planned "to arouse the American people to an understanding of the unprecedented crisis in national and international affairs," but its "Information" page also declared that the scientists felt "a deep sense of responsibility" for "the part they had borne" in developing nuclear weapons.[23] The ECAS immediately sent out an appeal, signed by Einstein, seeking to raise $200,000 "to inform the American people that a new type of thinking is essential if mankind is to survive and move to higher levels." In early June, Einstein repeated the fund-raising pitch in movie newsreels and, later that month, told the *New York Times* the ECAS wanted to bring about "a great chain reaction of awareness and communication" to block nuclear w eapons.[24]

More than eleven thousand people responded to Einstein's appeals during the first year, contributing $400,000 to ECAS. The group mailed and broadcast their warnings of potential nuclear catastrophe to more than a quarter of a million Americans and thousands more around the world. On the policy front, the ECAS lobbied Congress to help stop passage of the

---

* ECAS members included Vice-Chairman Harold Urey, Harrison Brown, and Thorfin Hogness (all from the University of Chicago), Hans Bethe (Cornell), Selig Hecht (Columbia), Philip Morse (Brookhaven National Laboratory), Linus Pauling (Caltech), Frederick Seitz (Carnegie Institute of Technology), Victor Weisskopf (MIT), and Szilard, who was, according to Fölsing (p. 724), "the driving force behind this enterprise."

May-Johnson bill that would have handed authority over all atomic energy research to a new and completely secret agency dominated by the military.

Americans' support for nuclear weapons, uncertain to begin with, declined considerably during the two years following Hiroshima. By October 1947, a Gallup poll showed that public support for the bomb had fallen from its 1945 level of 69 percent to 55 percent, and anti-nuclear sentiment had more than doubled, from 17 percent to 38 percent. The bomb had released—into both the air and the public's consciousness—atomic radiation, a mysterious force with a much-publicized potential for medicine and cheap energy, but also the frightening and invisible potential for mass murder. "Strange," Einstein later wrote, "that science which, in the old days seemed harmless, should have evolved into a nightmare that causes everyone to tremble."[25]

One thin volume published a year after the war, more than any other single argument, cut to the conscience of America. John Hersey's *Hiroshima* first appeared as a long article in the August 31, 1946, *New Yorker*—the issue sold out-and quickly became a best-seller. Millions more heard it broadcast on ABC radio.[26] It was, and still is, haunting:

> ...their faces were wholly burned, their eye sockets were hollow, the fluid from their melted eyes had run down their cheeks....
>
> Not many people walked in the streets, but a great many sat and lay on the pavement, vomited, waited for death, and died....
>
> The apparently uninjured people who had died so mysteriously in the first few hours or days had succumbed in[the bomb's] first stage. It killed ninety-five percent of the people within half a mile of the center, and many thousands who were farther away.

Einstein bought a thousand copies of Hersey's book and distributed them to friends.

But in the relative prosperity of postwar America, the country's bleeding conscience clotted quickly. Hersey's images of Hiroshima horror faded, and like sinners who feel better on Monday morning after a hell-and-brimstone sermon on Sunday, millions of Americans turned to settling the suburban frontier. The baby boom was more immediate than the bomb. As the antinuclear scientists seemed to grow farther apart from most of the public, Einstein lamented that too many people had "dismissed this warning from their consciousness."

Fear may have been as much a factor as apathy in the public's mood as new Cold War tensions undercut support for weapons reduction. Even among the former Manhattan Project scientists who had joined FAS, a 1947 poll asking, "Should the United States proceed with the production of atomic bombs?" showed an astonishing 242 to 174 in favor. Within the next three years, the sharp drop in FAS membership, according to one historian, "suggests the degree to which activism was undercut by Cold War compulsions."[27]

In another sign of the changing times, Einstein made a futile effort in 1947 to meet with Secretary of State George C. Marshall, hoping to convince him that only a world government with military power could prevent a catastrophic nuclear war. Marshall assigned Einstein's letter to Lewis Strauss, then a member of the new Atomic Energy Commission (and the man who later led the effort to discredit J. Robert Oppenheimer), and Strauss sent his thirty-seven-year-old aide, investment banker William T. Golden, to interview Einstein in Princeton. Golden reported that Einstein told him, "It pains me to see the development of a spirit of militarism in the United States," and that he compared Americans to the German people at the time of the Kaiser. Einstein also warned: "Americans are beginning to feel that the only way to avoid war is through a Pax Americana, a benevolent world domination by the United States," and argued that "history shows this to be impossible and the certain precursor of war and grief." Golden clearly disagreed,* concluding that Einstein "seemed naïve in the field of international politics and mass human relations."[28]

American foreign policy had clearly shifted with the arrival of the Cold War, and Einstein's hopes for peace through sharing were now clearly out of favor with the new foreign-policy experts. One historian, commenting on Golden's report, has pointed out that, "Nowhere in the report is there any analysis of Einstein's ideas, nor does Golden refute his observations. Instead, one is left to conclude that Einstein's ideas are naïve because they run counter to State Department policy."[29]

Atomic weapons had shattered "the outmoded concept of narrow nationalism." That was Einstein's message as ECAS chairman. But as the Cold War emerged, nationalism became more strident on both sides. In January 1948, the committee mailed out thousands of copies of Einstein's article "Atomic War or Peace," calling for world government and criticizing both Washington and Moscow for blocking the idea.[30] And, three months later, accepting the "One World Award" at a ceremony in Carnegie Hall, Einstein warned: "The proposed militarization of the nation not only immediately threatens us with war, it will also slowly but surely undermine the democratic spirit and the dignity of the individual in our land."

---

* Golden recently gave the New York Times (May 1, 2001) a totally different version of that interview: "Einstein said it was essential that a world army be created, under the leadership of the U.S. Unless this was done, there would be an atomic war in the next 10 years." Golden's original memo leaves no doubt that Einstein, far from calling for an American-led world army, specifically denounced the trend toward U.S. militarism.

But 1948 would be the Committee's last year of any real activity. Disagreements over several issues, including how much to support the United Nations' Atomic Energy Committee (Einstein felt the UN had been "ineffectual"), diluted the group's public statements and private resolve. But above all, the growing Cold War undermined the ECAS, with some members arguing the group should work more closely with the U.S. State Department, and, as we've seen, a majority of FAS scientists favoring more U.S. nuclear weapons.[31]

Understandably edgy about guarding the nation's nuclear monopoly, the FBI saw the Emergency Committee as a national-security catastrophe about to happen. The Bureau began monitoring the Emergency Committee as soon as it was formed in 1946—barely a year after the atomic bombing of Japan. Acknowledging that the ECAS was dedicated to "educating the public as to the peril from the atomic bomb [and advocating] international control and the elimination of war," the Bureau's internal memos made it clear that Hoover's agents considered the group—most of whom had just emerged from top-secret research on the bomb—a bunch of bleeding-heart scientists, and "educating the public" sounded to FBI ears like revealing nuclear se crets.[32]

But it was the Emergency Committee's chairman, Albert Einstein, who primarily triggered the FBI's Red alert. Einstein not only advocated cooperation with the Russians, but his popularity and headline potential made the ECAS particularly dangerous to Hoover and his Bureau. The FBI's dossier makes it clear that with Einstein as its head, the ECAS seemed certain to spill the nuclear beans:

> Leader and chief spokesman [for ECAS] was Professor Albert Einstein, who in the past has been used by various Communist Front organizations as a "big name" "innocent" sponsor.
> ...EINSTEIN has been led to back those who favor turning over the bomb to Russia.... [Informant's name blacked out] said that he did not believe that Dr. Einstein was actually a Communist, but that he was becoming old and was very easily led by younger men...[33]

And an entry in the FBI file on February 14, 1947 cites an article on the ECAS in that day's Washington *Times Herald*:

> SCIENTISTS SEEK FUNDS TO REVEAL ATOM SECRETS
> A campaign to raise $1,000,000 to finance efforts to divulge information concerning atomic energy which the American Government was trying to keep secret...was launched by a group of scientists...headed by ALBERT EINSTEIN...the Emergency Committee of Atomic Scientists.

Even more threatening, an internal FBI memo tells Hoover:

Einstein...has been carrying on correspondence with scientists in more than 60 foreign countries concerning international atomic energy control and related matters. Through this committee, attempts are made to keep foreign scientists informed on developments in the United States in the field of pure science.[34]

But what caused the Bureau's most severe anxiety is that *for two years,* its agents incorrectly believed Einstein had worked on the atomic bomb and had "complete information" on American nuclear secrets. As early as January 1945—with World War II still intense and seven months before Hiroshima—an FBI memo stated:

...Albert Einstein was head of the School [sic] of Advanced Study at Princeton, New Jersey and was reported to have complete information relative to the DSM [Manhattan] project, which project was one of the most confidential of the United States Government.

Within the next fourteen months, the FBI's Washington and Newark offices issued additional memos repeating the m is inform ation.[35] At best, it was sloppy police work: The FBI, which only five years earlier had been instrumental in having Einstein denied security clearance and barred from the atomic-bomb project, failed to check its own records as agents kept ultra-close tabs on the same Einstein to prevent him from giving nuclear secrets he didn't know to the Russians. (Sloppiness is also reflected in two relatively minor misstatements in the entry above: It is the Institute, not the School, for Advanced Study, and Einstein was never its head.) It may not have been so much a case of institutional amnesia as simply a reflection of the haphazard, scattergun status of the FBI's Einstein records—a status soon to change dramatically.

Alarmed by their own misinformation, on March 7, 1947, FBI agents brought their security fears about Einstein to the Atomic Energy Commission. The AEC discreetly told them:

[The Manhattan Project] never had any close contact with Einstein...he did not contribute anything during the...development of the bomb...he was not a consultant....[36]

It's easy to imagine two grim-faced FBI men striding into the AEC offices—determined that the nuclear agency take action against a national-security threat named Einstein, a scientist who had acquired America's nuclear secrets while working on the bomb and now wanted such knowledge to be "shared"—and the same officials exiting a few hours later, at least somewhat less stridently.

Perhaps chagrined by their ignorance, Hoover's men reduced their surveillance of ECAS. In November 1947, the Bureau noted that the Foreign Press Association of the United Nations presented an award to Einstein as chairman of ECAS for "his valiant efforts to make the world's nations understand the need of outlawing atomic energy as a means of war." But by this time, the FBI's interest in the Emergency Committee was waning, with only infrequent reports on the group's activities.

Having overreacted to Einstein, the FBI now seemed indifferent to the Committee, even though all its other members had worked on the Manhattan Project. The final assessment from the FBI's New York office paints the group with political pastels instead of scarlet.

> [The ECAS consisted of] scientists who were interested in atomic energy... headed by Albert Einstein and some prominent American physicists. Some Communist sympathizers were associated with the organization which was not, however, under the control or influence of pro-Communist or pro-Russian elements.[37]

Despite its own "clearance," the FBI's dossier on Einstein continued for the next seven years—indeed, to this day—to list the ECAS among his "Communist front" groups. Apparently, like negative entries in a credit record, once on the list, always on the list.

Raising public consciousness was the central ECAS strategy. The idea, Einstein had told the *New York Times,* was to spark a public dialogue about nuclear weapons "in every newspaper, in schools, churches, town meetings, private conversations and neighbor to neighbor...."[38] The committee did reach hundreds of thousands of concerned citizens. But most Americans shrugged at the arrival of the nuclear age, preoccupied with new homes, cars, and families, and un-alarmed about the dangers from atomic weapons...until the Russians exploded their bomb in 1949. Then the Soviet bomb would also become a weapon for Hoover, McCarthy, and their cohorts, who used its threat to justify the anti-communism and fear that dominated the 1950s.

ECAS was, at best, only partially successful. Nonetheless, Einstein and the Committee opened a door for at least two generations of anti-nuclear protesters and cracked the mold of scientist-as-recluse, focused only on equations and test tubes, hidden and hiding from the world.[39]

At the end of 1945, just months before the Emergency Committee was formed, Einstein observed, "Today, the physicists who participated in forwarding the most formidable and dangerous weapons of all times are harassed by a feeling of responsibility, not to say guilt."[40] But Einstein insisted that he himself did not feel guilty about the bomb. In 1952, in response to a series of challenging questions from Katusu Hara, editor of the Japanese magazine *Kaizo* ("Why did you cooperate in the production of the atomic bomb although you were well aware of its tremendous destructive power?"), he argued first that he had not worked on the bomb ("My part…consisted in a single act: I signed a letter to President Roosevelt"), and second, that even after the horror of Hiroshima, building the bomb was justified because it was intended to stop the greater horror of Hitler and the Nazis. If the two arguments appear contradictory, it was a contradiction he endured. Even when he wrote to Linus Pauling, "I made one great mistake in my life— when I signed the letter to President Roosevelt recommending that atom bombs be made." Einstein added: "But there was some justification—the danger that the Germans would make them."[41]

6

American Crusade to End Lynching

During the last twenty years of his life, Einstein almost never spoke at universities. He considered the honorary-degree ceremonies to which he was frequently invited to be "ostentatious."[1] Moreover, the abdominal aneurysm that would eventually take his life caused him increasing pain and made it difficult to travel. Given the constant stream of university invitations, he found it easiest to adopt a just-say-no rule. In May 1946, he broke that rule to speak at Lincoln University in Pennsylvania. Both the year and the choice of school are significant.

About sixty miles from Princeton, Lincoln University was chartered in 1854 as, in the words of its eighth president, Horace Mann Bond, "the first institution found anywhere in the world to provide a higher education in the arts and sciences for male youth of African descent." In 1946, when Dr. Bond invited Einstein to Lincoln, the student body consisted of 265 men. "It was still a small school," Mrs. Julia Bond, Dr. Bond's widow, recalls. "But of course, everyone came to hear Einstein. We didn't have a hall big enough, so we held the ceremony outdoors in the grove."[2]

"On Friday, May 3, a very simple man came to Lincoln University," one student wrote a few days later in the school newspaper:

> His emaciated face and simplicity made him appear as a biblical character. Quietly he stood with an expression of questioning wonder upon his face as... President Horace Mann Bond conferred a degree. Then this man with the long hair and deep eyes spoke into a microphone of the disease [racism] that humanity had. In the deep accents of his native Germany, he said he could not be silent. And then he finished and the room was still. Later he lectured on the theory of relativity to the Lincoln students.
>
> That night, Albert Einstein went back to Princeton....[3]

Dr. Bond's son chuckles today when he looks at an old photo of Lincoln faculty members' children with the famous scientist: "Family lore has

Einstein telling me, 'Don't remember anything that is already written down.' And although I do not recall this exchange"—he was barely six years old at the time—"I have followed this advice ever since."[4] (Whether Einstein's advice helped or not, Julian Bond grew up to become a civil-rights activist, state assemblyman, TV talk-show host, and chairman of the NAACP.)

In accepting the invitation, Einstein clearly intended to send a message to a wider audience. But the media then—like the media since then—had different news priorities. While almost all of Einstein's public speeches and interviews were widely covered by the major media, in this case, most of the press treated the address by the world's most famous scientist at the world's oldest black university as a non-event.[5]

"There is...a somber point in the social outlook of Americans," Einstein reportedly told the Lincoln University audience:

Their sense of equality and human dignity is mainly limited to men of white skins. Even among these there are prejudices of which I as a Jew am clearly conscious; but they are unimportant in comparison with the attitude of "Whites" toward their fellow-citizens of darker complexion, particularly toward Negroes...

The more I feel an American, the more this situation pains me. I can escape the feeling of complicity in it only by speaking out.

I do not believe there is a way in which this deeply entrenched evil can be quickly healed. But until this goal is reached, there is no greater satisfaction for a just and well-meaning person than the knowledge that he has devoted his best energies to the services of the good cause.[6]

To understand the full significance of Einstein's visit to Lincoln— and of its miniscule coverage—we need to recall the racial situation in America in what might be called "the Bloody Spring of 1946."

Black GI's came home after World War II in no mood for racism. Despite their segregated, second-class status in the army, they had put their lives on the line, faced bullets and bombs, and lost arms, legs, and buddies, fighting for freedom and democracy. One notable example, the 761st Tank Battalion, known as the Black Panthers, was designated by General Patton to play a key role in the Battle of the Bulge. The all-black unit subsequently fought against German troops in Europe for 183 straight days, capturing or destroying thirty major towns, four airstrips, ammunition dumps, and hundreds of armored vehicles and tanks. The Battalion received the Presidential Unit Citation—but not until 1978, after years of letters and requests to the Defense Department. The 761st, like other black units in World War II, adopted as its unofficial insignia, "Double V"—for victory over the Nazis in Europe and over racism back home.[7]

"Segregation is a disease of white people," Einstein said
at Lincoln University in Pennsylvania where he received an honorary
degree from Lincoln President Horace Mann Bond.

But at home, the war was far from over; only the enemy had changed uniforms and now wore sheets or sheriff's badges... or both. In the first fifteen months after Hitler's defeat, a wave of lynching and other anti-black violence—mostly, but not only, in the Southern states—killed more than fifty African-Americans, with recently returned veterans the targets of some of the most bestial lynch mobs. The resurgent racist terrorism—not seen since the Ku Klux Klan rampages following the return of black soldiers from the First World War, a quarter-century earlier*—included a number of police shootings of unarmed civilians, in the North as well as in the South. One of the most widely publicized cases occurred in the small town of Columbia, Tennessee.

---

* In 1919, W. E. B. Du Bois wrote: "This is the country to which we Soldiers of Democracy return....But by the God of heaven, we are cowards and jackasses if now that the war is over, we do not marshal every ounce of our brain and brawn to fight a sterner, longer, more unbending battle against the forces of hell in our own land." (*The Crisis*, April 1, 1919.)

On the morning of February 25, 1946, a white radio repairman, William Fleming, "slapped, struck or kicked" a black woman, Mrs. Gladys Stephenson, and, according to news reports, "was promptly knocked through a plate-glass window by her son James Stephenson," a nineteen-year-old Navy veteran recently returned from the Pacific. Both Mrs. Stephenson and her son were arrested. At about 6:00 P.M., a white lynch mob paraded around the jailhouse, and at least part of it then headed toward the black section of town, known as Mink Slide. A number of black veterans organized an armed defense of their neighborhood. Two armed white men "under the influence of alcohol" (according to court testimony months later) and four city policemen who went into Mink Slide that night were wounded by gunfire from blacks, convinced that a lynching was about to occur. According to one report, "four or five" men in the white mob were killed, "but the local authorities would not admit to it."[8]

African Americans firing on white policemen was enough for the governor to rush in five hundred state troopers with submachine guns. They attacked Mink Slide, destroying virtually every black-owned business in the four square-block area, seizing whatever weapons they could find and arresting more than one hundred black men. Two of the detainees were shot and killed inside the jail by troopers during what police called "a spontaneous outburst." Of the others, twenty-five were indicted for "attempted murder." A young NAACP lawyer named Thurgood Marshall, chief defense attorney for the twenty-five, angrily declared:

> The action of the Tennessee State troopers in roping off the Negro section of Columbia, Tennessee, and firing at will and indiscriminately was closer to… German storm troopers than any recent police action in this country.[9]

Shortly after Marshall's statement appeared in the *New York Times* in March, Einstein joined the National Committee for Justice in Columbia, Tennessee, headed by Eleanor Roosevelt and including an array of celebrities such as Mary Mcleod Bethune, Colonel Roy Carlson (Carlson's Marine Raiders), Marshall Field, Oscar Hammerstein II, Helen Hayes, Sidney Hillman, Langston Hughes, Harold Ickes, Herbert Lehman, Sinclair Lewis, Joe Louis, Henry Luce, Adam Clayton Powell, Jr., A. Philip Randolph, Artie Shaw, and David O. Selznick.[10] Perhaps because of its political breadth, it is one of the few Einstein political affiliations not included on the FBI's list of "Communist front" groups.

With Marshall leading a four-man interracial defense team, twenty-four of the twenty-five defendants were acquitted. (The twenty-fifth defendant, Lloyd Kennedy, was released after serving ten months of a five-year sentence.) The legal victories came despite two acrimonious trials in segregated Tennessee courtrooms before hostile judges and all-white juries. After the second trial, Marshall himself narrowly escaped from a lynch mob (including local police) that nearly succeeded in murdering the future Supreme Court Justice.[11]

Foretelling its investigations into civil-rights abuses during the 1960s, the FBI sent an all-white team of agents to Columbia to interview witnesses, ostensibly about possible violations of civil rights. But the African-Americans they questioned reported the agents seemed mainly interested in finding out which black people had fired guns. (Only a few months later, Hoover was asked why he had sent only white agents to investigate a horrific lynching in Monroe, Georgia; he replied that Monroe had "a very ignorant type of Negro," who wouldn't have talked to black agents.*) A "top-secret" FBI memo, dated March 2, 1946, ignores the police attack on the black community in Columbia, and without indicating a cause, as if it were describing spontaneous combustion, refers to the events simply as "race riots." The memo was sent from an agent in Tennessee to Hoover's man in charge of the Mink Slide investigation, D. M. (Mickey) Ladd—a name we shall come to know well in the Einstein case. Within less than two weeks, the Bureau produced a 197-page, single-spaced report, citing only white witnesses and totally exonerating the local and state police. The black population was described as threatening, local officials as restrained, and the state police as operating completely within the line of duty.[12]

If Einstein and the other members of the committee thought their prestige would restrain the lynching, disappointment didn't keep them waiting long. The total failure of the President, the attorney general, and government officials at any level, to take action against the state and city authorities behind the Mink Slide attack begat only more terror. The lynchers could not have asked for a greener light than the FBI's report. White mobs throughout the South, often aided by police, went on a lynching rampage, primarily targeting World War II veterans.

In the heat of July and August 1946, the wave of unpunished lynching seemed to swell. In successive weeks, African-American veterans J. C. Farmer in Bailey, North Carolina, and Macio Snipes, described as "the only Negro to vote" in his district of Taylor County, Georgia, were shot down by bands of white men. As his mother stood a hundred yards away, Farmer was killed by bullets from a posse of twenty to twenty-five "dep-

---

* In fact, Hoover could not have sent black agents if he had wanted to. There was only one bona fide black agent in the entire FBI in 1946: James E. Amos, 68, the man Hoover had sent to infiltrate the Marcus Garvey movement more than twenty years earlier. Five other "agents" within the Bureau served as Hoover's chauffeurs and other personal-service staff.

uties" in eight cars. An hour earlier, while waiting for a bus, he had gotten into a scuffle with a policeman. Snipes was gunned down on the porch of his home by ten white men.[13]

The media missed or ignored a number of such murders,* but on July 27, a front-page story in the *New York Times*, which Einstein read every morning, reported one of the more gruesome cases, and lynching in America suddenly became national and international—and unavoidable—news:

GEORGIA MOB OF 20 MEN MASSACRES
2 NEGROES, WIVES; ONE WAS EX-GI

MONROE, Ga., July 26—Two young Negroes, one a war veteran who served in the Pacific, and their wives were lined up last night near a secluded road and shot dead by an unmasked band of twenty white men....

The ghastly details of the multiple lynching were told by Loy Harrison, a well-to-do white farmer who was taking the Negroes to [work on] his farm and was held at gunpoint [when his car was waylaid] by the mob.... The Negro men were taken out of the car first and led down the side road. The women were held at the automobile. Then a member of the mob said one of the Negro women had recognized him.

"Get those damned women, too," the mob leader shouted. Several of the men then...dragged the shrieking women from the automobile....

The story also reported that the victims had been shot at least sixty times, and that the bodies were "scarcely recognizable" because of the mass of bullet holes. Two days later, the *Times* reported:

MONROE, Ga., July 28—Close relatives of two of the four Negroes killed by a white mob here Thursday failed to appear at funeral services today and friends voiced the belief that they were "too frightened" to appear.

A Grand Jury heard testimony from 106 witnesses in this case, and then returned no indictments. Another lynching report, two weeks later, described the complicity of local authorities in Louisiana:

John C. Jones, 28, discharged veteran of European services, was found dead two miles from Minden in Dorcheat Bayou. His body had been horribly beaten with "some flat object—such as a wide leather belt or a thick plank," his face and body burned with a blowtorch so that his eyes were "popped" out

---

* Hoping the pressure of international opinion might spur Truman and the Congress to stop the racist terror, two organizations, the National Negro Congress in 1946 and the NAACP in 1947, submitted separate petitions to the United Nations documenting lynchings often unreported by the press. The NAACP had begun to distance itself from those on the left like Paul Robeson and the National Negro Congress. Ironically, the NAACP's petition to the UN was written by W. E. B. Du Bois, who would soon be expelled for his left leanings and willingness to work with communists.

of his head and his light complexion seared dark. His wrists were mutilated with a cleaver and he had been partially castrated.....

The report confirmed that Jones and seventeen-year-old Albert Harris had been turned over to a mob by the sheriff a few minutes after release from a local jail, where they had been confined for a week on charges of attempting to break into the house of a white woman. (She refused to press charges.) The young men were driven to the bayou, where Jones was tortured and killed. Harris, although beaten, shot in the shoulder, and left for dead, managed to escape. The article concluded:

> Jones, who had brought a German automatic from Europe, had been told by a white neighbor that he would get Jones' gun if he had to kill him to do it.[14]

It is impossible to imagine that Einstein had not been shaken by these news reports when, in early September, a telegram arrived from Paul Robeson, proposing to set up a group called the American Crusade to End Lynching and to hold a mass rally in Washington on September 23—the anniversary of Lincoln's Emancipation Proclamation. The protest, to be led by black veterans, would demand punishment for lynchers and prompt passage of a federal anti-lynching law. W. E. B. Du Bois and several other prominent citizens, white and black, were already on board as ACEL sponsors.[15] Now Robeson's telegram asked Einstein to be co-chairman.

Race had not been a central consideration when Einstein moved to Princeton thirteen years earlier. He was seeking a quiet work space, a violin-playing, pipe-smoking space, and a refuge from media attention. "Into this small university town," Einstein wrote during his early days in Princeton, "the chaotic voices of human strife barely penetrate. I am almost ashamed to be living in such peace while all the rest struggle and suffer." It turned out to be more wish than observation, but Princeton seemed—at first—"a banishment to paradise."[16]

Not that he had been oblivious to racism in America. In 1931, shortly before moving to America, as we've seen, he had joined the campaign to save "the Scottsboro Boys,"* and the NAACP had published his article in *The Crisis*, expressing admiration for the "determined effort of American Negroes."[17] Nonetheless, on arriving in Princeton, his most striking impression had to be the contrast with Berlin—the absence of SS agents and the young boys with swastika armbands roaming the

---

* The worldwide campaign to save the nine African-American teenagers from Alabama, falsely accused of rape and sentenced to death in 1931, continued for 19 years before they were all eventually freed. For Einstein, the Scottsboro case was a harbinger of campaigns to come; for the FBI, it was his first "Communist Front."

streets. Princeton must have promised an enclave, a safe haven. Even the name of the street they lived on when they first moved to Princeton—Library Place—symbolized sanctuary.

But anyone living in Princeton in the 1930s and 40s could not miss the racism. The idyllic little sanctuary turned out to be not so idyllic. On the campus, as at all the Ivy League schools, the university's quota system allowed for only a few Jewish students. Of only two Jewish faculty members, one—Einstein's good friend Otto Nathan—was fired after teaching economics for just one year, an act Einstein considered blatantly anti-Semitic.* And if you were black, whether student or faculty, the university was totally off-limits. Perhaps because it was the southernmost of the Ivy League colleges, Princeton attracted a high percentage of students from Southern states. As late as September 1942, while United States and Allied troops were battling fascism overseas, the *Princeton Herald* "explained" that admitting black students to the university, while morally justified, would simply be too offensive to the large number of Princeton's Southern students.[18]

The town itself was as racially divided as its movie theater, where whites and blacks sat in separate sections until well after World War II had defeated Hitlerism. The black population, about 20 percent of the town, moved about unobtrusively, mostly outside the white world—a segregated civilization beginning just behind Princeton's main street and continuing on down to the unpaved "avenues" next to the trolley tracks and past the garbage dump. Until 1948, all Princeton's African-American primary-school children attended the Witherspoon School, as color-coded as any school in Alabama, and on Sunday mornings, segregated prayers arose from the Witherspoon Street Presbyterian Church. Rumors of "incidents" between blacks and the all-white police force were frequent. Einstein told friends he often heard white townspeople "talking against Negroes." Robeson, who was born in Princeton, called it a "Georgia plantation town."

Nor did Princetonians restrict their bigotry to people of color. During his first months there (before the local citizenry decided they would benefit from having a famous Jew in their town), Einstein felt a definite "coldness" toward him—a Jew in what one writer called "that enclave of WASP-dom."[19]

Another example of Princeton prejudice came on April 16, 1937, when the great diva Marian Anderson gave a concert to a standing-room only

---

* One of the trustees of Princeton was none other than Breckenridge Long, one-time lobbyist for Franco and an anti-Semite, whom we met in a previous chapter as the State Department's man in charge of immigration.

Einstein with friend and economist Otto Nathan. Einstein considered Nathan's firing by Princeton to be blatantly anti-Semitic. Otto Nathan, on whom the FBI also had a file, was also Einstein's financial advisor and co-trustee of his literary estate with Helen Dukas. (Photo: Philippe Halsman, courtesy Doris Nathan)

audience at Princeton's McCarter Theatre. "Complete artistic mastery of a magnificent voice...from the first Handel aria to the last Negro spiritual," reported the daily *Princetonian,* adding, "It is hard to discuss such a performance without the excessive use of superlatives." Nonetheless, Princeton's Nassau Inn refused the African-American contralto a room.* Einstein immediately invited her to stay with him and Margot in the house on Mercer Street; she accepted, and their ensuing friendship lasted for the rest of his life. She stayed with them whenever she came to Princeton. The last time was in January 1955, two months before Einstein died. When she left, he came downstairs, with difficulty, to say good-bye. The world-renowned diva later wrote that she felt "honored," and that she knew "this was really good-bye."[20] (Two years after the Nassau Inn incident, the Daughters of the American Revolution refused to allow her

---

* The Nassau Inn ended its white-only policy after World War II, and in 1946 was the site of the founding conference of the Emergency Committee of Atomic Scientists.

to perform at their Constitution Hall in Washington. Eleanor Roosevelt promptly resigned from the D.A.R. and helped arrange an outdoor concert at the Lincoln memorial where 75,000 people came to hear Marian Anderson sing.)

After becoming a citizen, Einstein was even more outspoken on racial issues; he told friends he now felt less like a guest in America's house. Dedicating the Wall of Fame at the 1940 World's Fair, Einstein said that America "still has a heavy debt to discharge for all the troubles and disabilities it has laid on the Negro's shoulder...." During the war years, despite the global issues in the air—or perhaps because of them—he helped sponsor the NAACP's new Defense Fund and (although it's never been reported) he took part in at least one meeting of the organization's Princeton chapter. Lifelong Princeton resident Fanny Floyd recalls, as a youngster, seeing Einstein at a local NAACP meeting in 1942 or 1943.[21] He also supported the campaign to block the extradition of Sam Buckhannon, a refugee from a Georgia chain gang. (See Chapter 10.)

But it's doubtful that anyone expected the extent of the postwar racist terror that erupted in America, echoing the horror the world had just defeated. During the first year following the defeat of fascism in Germany and Japan, racist violence in the United States killed fifty-six blacks—most of them returning veterans. That is only the number of lynched African-Americans that was reported to, and reported by, the local police. (In 1941, the last year before the United States entered World War II, the number of lynchings reported was four.[22])

Busy as he was with the new Emergency Committee of Atomic Scientists, Einstein could not shrug his shoulders at Robeson's invitation—or at lynching. If his increasing abdominal pains prevented his travel to Washington for the September 23 protest, he would send a letter to President Truman, to be delivered by the protest leaders, urging an immediate anti-lynching law. Either way, his answer to Robeson was yes.

Twelve pages of the FBI's Einstein file concern the American Crusade to End Lynching—considerably more space than most of his affiliations. Perhaps this was because Hoover and his Bureau viewed the anti-lynching campaign—much as they would later view the civil-rights movement of the 1960s—as a threat to America's national security. Racism in the FBI has been extensively reported, including Hoover's vendetta against Martin Luther King and several lawsuits by African-American agents documenting bigotry throughout the Bureau. But Hoover learned his racism long before joining the FBI. It was the fourth "R" in the white-only schools he attended, along with the white-only churches in the white-only world that was his sector of one of America's most segregated Southern cities, Washington, D.C. One of Hoover's first Justice Department security files, set up in 1919, was labeled "Negro Activities."* It denounced black-owned newspapers, including A. Philip Randolph's *Messenger* and the NAACP magazine *The Crisis,* edited by Du Bois:

> ...something must be done to the editors of these publications as they are beyond doubt exciting the negro [sic] elements of this country to riot and to the committing of outrages of all sorts.[23]

The Einstein file's ACEL section begins with a report from Army Intelligence (G-2), described by the FBI as "a completely reliable source":

> ...When in Washington, the delegation planned to call on the White House and national figures to demand action by the administration. A parade was scheduled to be led by colored and white veterans who were to march to the Lincoln Memorial where a national religious ceremony would be held and persons who escaped lynch mobs were to be presented...Dr. Albert Einstein was scheduled to appear.

As with most of Einstein's political activities, the FBI's reports on the ACEL rely heavily on news stories and other published material:

> *The Philadelphia Inquirer...*dated 9/23/46...stated EINSTEIN wrote a letter to President HARRY S. TRUMAN assailing lynching. This letter was to be delivered to President TRUMAN by a group headed by PAUL ROBESON. The *People's Voice* dated 10/5/46...stated in part that EINSTEIN and PAUL ROBESON were co-chairmen of the ACEL...

> The three-point program for the ACEL included: (1) apprehension and punishment of all lynchers; (2) passage of a Federal anti-lynching law; (3) removal of [Mississippi] Senator Theodore Bilbo. Dr. Albert Einstein has been selected as co-chairman with Paul Robeson of the Crusade....

> A report in the September 14, 1946 issue of the *Baltimore Afro-American* states that a one hundred-day "Crusade to End Lynching" would begin in

---

* Hoover's early files described back-to-Africa advocate Marcus Garvey as "a notorious negro [sic] agitator" and claimed that Garvey's newspaper (Negro World) "upheld... Soviet Russian rule" and engaged in "open advocation [sic] of Bolshevism." Hoover's first black agent was assigned to infiltrate Garvey's movement in the 1920s. There is no evidence of any Hoover file on the Ku Klux Klan, which at that time was on a rampage of lynching and cross-burning. Like most racism, Hoover's was not restricted to one target group. One instance of his anti-Hispanic bigotry came after the attempted assassination of President Truman by Puerto Rican nationalists in 1950, when Hoover said "jokingly," "You never have to worry about a President being shot by a Puerto Rican or a Mexican. They don't shoot very straight. But if they come after you with a knife, beware." (*Washington Post* obituary, May 5, 1972.)

Washington, DC with a huge rally on September 23…in the afternoon, delegations will be appointed to confer with government officials [about] definite
programs to stop lynching.…

[The ACEL pamphlet states] "Lynching cannot be permitted to continue
unchecked in a nation founded upon…justice and equality…America must
rid itself of the crime of unpunished lynching.…" Signers, "morally indignant
over this lawless violence," include ALBERT EINSTEIN.[24]

Defending the FBI against accusations of political bias, Hoover frequently insisted the Bureau was nothing more or less than a fact-collection
agency. In 1953, he told the *New York Times*: "It is the ironclad practice of
the FBI never to evaluate any of the information it receives from its own
investigators or any other source."[25] Yet as early as 1946, the FBI's report
on the American Crusade to End Lynching declared:

…in view of some of the endorsers, this Crusade has all the earmarks of
another Communist attempt to instill racial agitation.
The above information is evaluated in this report as having been received
from a usually reliable source whose information was probably true.[*]

A subsequent entry in the FBI's report on the ACEL states:

Paul Robeson, who has a long record of Communist affiliations, was the moving spirit in what was known as the American Crusade to End Lynching and
organized a pilgrimage to Washington, D.C. for 9/23/46. This venture was
actively supported by the Communist press…

And in a harbinger of hundreds, if not thousands, of FBI reports to
come, one entry on the ACEL concludes by labeling the group with a tag
line that summarizes the Bureau's view of civil rights protests, generally:

RE: *Foreign Inspired Education among the American Negroes*
Internal Security-C [for Communist][26]

Similarly, a 1947 memo from the FBI's New York office identifies the
Committee to Oust [Mississippi Senator] Bilbo with the tag line: "Internal
Security-C."
The government's anti-communism policy, most extreme during (but
not at all limited to) the 1950s, relied on the argument that the commun-
ists were threatening to take over the world, and a crackdown—with the
FBI as watchdog and pointer—was necessary to stop them. The only thing

---

* "No matter how much Hoover claimed his was only a fact-finding agency [of] strictly
investigative nature…the FBI during the McCarthy era became an infiltrative organization, gathering 'intelligence'…more likely to compromise, embarrass, and ruin those
investigated than merely supply 'facts.'" (Nash, p. 106.)

that mattered in the Bureau's evaluation of a suspect organization—or of a suspect individual like Einstein—was whether or not they collaborated with "Reds" like Robeson. The suggestion that the FBI might investigate lynching itself as a subversive threat to democracy would have been considered a diversion from Hoover's (and his Bureau's) main task: catching communists.

When his illness prevented him from attending the Washington anti-lynching rally, Einstein sent a letter to be delivered to the President by Robeson and the other ACEL leaders, but in view of what occurred at the White House, it is uncertain that Einstein's letter was ever handed to Truman.

After the rally, which drew at least three thousand protesters, a multi-racial delegation, including Robeson, Rabbi Irving Miller of the American Jewish Congress, and Mrs. Harper Sibley, president of the United Council of Church Women and wife of the former president of the U.S. Chamber of Commerce, met with Truman in the Oval Office. The gentlest term that might describe their meeting is "confrontational." The following exchange emerges from a variety of newspaper accounts, the most detailed in the African-American press. Almost as soon as Robeson began reading the group's statement calling for immediate executive action to stop the lynch mobs, the President interrupted.

The timing was not yet right for an anti-lynching law, he said, and the delegation ought to appreciate the fact that America and Great Britain were "the last refuge of freedom in the world." Somewhat less than appreciative, Robeson answered that Britain was one of the world's "great enslavers of human beings." Truman insisted that the moment was not propitious for a forthright statement from the Chief Executive, according to a report in the leading black weekly, the *Chicago Defender,* which added:

> In terms which left no doubt in the minds of the delegation from the American Crusade to End Lynching, President Truman today emphatically refused to take the initiative to end mob violence and the spread of terrorism in America...[declaring] the whole question o lynching and mob violence was one to be dealt with in political terms and strategy...and patience must attend the final solution.
>
> When Mrs. Sibley made a comparison between fascism...against the Jews in Europe and fascism in America as levied against Negroes, the President showed impatience and a flare of temper.
>
> Robeson...said returning [black] veterans are showing signs of restiveness and indicated that they are determined to get the justice here they have fought for abroad. Robeson warned that this restiveness might produce an emergency situation which would require Federal intervention. The President, shaking his fist, stated this sounded like a threat.

Robeson's implied ultimatum that if the government would not provide protection black people would defend themselves, was apparently too much for Truman, who promptly ended the meeting. (Robeson later told the press that his remarks were "not a threat, merely a statement of fact about the temper of the Negro people.")[27]

The ACEL delegation left the White House without having presented its complete statement or, by all accounts, Einstein's letter. But Truman or his aides had to know about the letter. A copy had been mailed to the White House, and it had been excerpted in that morning's *New York Times*:

> The delegation will deliver to Mr. Truman a letter from Dr. Albert Einstein stating that security against lynching is "one of the most urgent tasks of our generation.
>
> Endorsing the crusade "in the conviction that the overwhelming majority of the people favor security for all against illegal violence," Dr. Einstein wrote.
>
> "There is always a way to overcome legal obstacles whenever there is an inflexible will at work in the service of so just a cause."

Although Robeson and the other organizers had hoped for a much larger turnout, the ACEL contributed to the growing movement for anti-lynching legislation. The protest rally received extensive media coverage: The *New York Times* and the *Washington Post* both headlined their stories with Robeson's implied ultimatum that the government must act to end lynching—"or Negroes will." The African-American press, on the other hand, emphasized Truman's weakness: The *Chicago Defender's* headline declared, "Truman Balks at Lynch Action," and the *Baltimore Afro-American* proclaimed: "Robeson Proves Ability to Handle Situation."[28] The anti-lynching protest and the publicity seemed to spur the NAACP to intensify its own efforts against "mob violence." Refusing to work with "Reds" like Robeson, the NAACP had boycotted the ACEL protest,* but afterward accelerated a separate, more subdued lobbying effort—including a more cordial meeting with Truman and other top Washington officials.

In spite of Truman's hostility toward Robeson, just six weeks after their Oval Office face-off, the President appointed a Committee on Civil Rights, charged with determining how "current law-enforcement measures…may be strengthened…to safeguard the civil rights of the people." Between Truman's confrontation with Robeson in September and his Executive Order 9008 on December 5, establishing the Civil Rights Committee,

---

* Ironically, a decade later, Hoover denounced the NAACP's planned 1956 March on Washington as "in line with Communist policy" and "spearheaded by Communists." (Powers, Secrecy and Power, p. 331.)

the Democrats had suffered a resounding defeat in the congressional elections. At least one historian points to a connection: "The perception of Truman's weakness on civil rights issues...led African-Americans to desert the Democratic Party en masse in...November 1946....After analyzing the electoral defeat, the President [established his] Committee on Civil Rights...."[29]

While Einstein and the ACEL had urged Truman to take immediate action to outlaw lynching, J. Edgar Hoover argued that even the appointment of a committee was too radical a move. Headed by General Motors President Charles E. Wilson, the President's Civil Rights Committee was hardly a nest of sedition,* but the FBI chief viewed the committee as "capitulation to communist pressure groups," and internal FBI memos described it as part of "a widespread smear campaign" by "selfish and conniving elements" with "ulterior and often veiled motives":

> Certain elements active in the United States are capitalizing upon every alleged** violation of civil rights...for the ultimate purpose of launching and perpetuating an organized attack against...law enforcement agencies.[30]

Within a year, the President's Committee proposed that Congress enact an anti-lynching law, as well as an end to voting discrimination, a Fair Employment Practices Commission, and desegregation of the armed forces. It was a platform that helped Truman's upset re-election victory in 1948, a platform designed by his aides to gain votes that would otherwise have gone to third-party candidate Henry Wallace.*** (Einstein and Robeson actively backed Wallace, who campaigned for immediate anti-lynching laws and refused to hold campaign meetings in any segregated Southern auditorium.)

But the sharpest spur prodding Washington to clean up the most visible symbols of America's racism was neither Truman's election-year

---

* Years later, as secretary of defense under President Eisenhower, Wilson became an embarrassing public-relations problem for the Administration when he bluntly declared: "What's good for General Motors is good for America."

** Memos between Hoover and other top FBI officials frequently referred to "alleged" civil-rights violations and "alleged" lynchings. One memo to Hoover from the head of the Bureau's San Francisco office referred to "alleged persecution of negroes [sic] in South Africa." (O'Reilly, p. 29, fn. 49.)

*** "Proper handling of the Civil Rights issue...can virtually assure the re-election [of Truman] by cutting the ground out from under Wallace...."(Memo from Oscar Ewing to Clark Clifford: Goldfield, pp.253-254.) In 1947, a campaign led by civil rights leader A. Philip Randolph urged African-Americans to refuse to serve in a segregated army. And, in March 1948, early in the presidential campaign, one Minnesota poll showed 54 percent of black voters leaning toward Wallace. (Duberman, p. 325.) A large majority of them ended up voting for Truman.

tactics nor any moral principle. Rather, it was the Cold War competition with Moscow to influence developing countries. As the three biggest nations in Asia—China, India, and Indonesia—erupted in revolutionary upheavals, America's racist laws and unpunished violence were an embarrassing obstacle to U.S. influence around the world. In case the President and other decision-makers couldn't figure it out, Truman's Civil Rights Committee made it plain, warning that America could not afford to "ignore what the world thinks of us or our record" because:

> The world's press and radio are full of [our Civil Rights record]…Those with competing philosophies…have tried to prove our democracy an endless fraud and our nation a consistent oppressor of underprivileged people…[31]

An item in the *Chicago Defender* provides an exclamation point to the Committee's concern and—in retrospect—a remarkable historical signal. On September 28, 1946, the same day the *Defender* covered the Robeson-Truman confrontation, it also carried an interview by widely acclaimed correspondent George Padmore with a foreign leader described as the head of a "little country seeking independence." In the interview, the foreign leader criticizes lynching in America as "barbarism" and evinces "great concern about the status of American Negroes and…a surprising knowledge of the American situation." Accompanying the interview is a large photo of the foreign leader—a young, handsome, brown-skinned man with intensely focused eyes. His name is Ho Chi Minh. His "little country seeking independence" is Vietnam.

Despite its ambitious name, the American Crusade to End Lynching was essentially a one-protest organization and ceased activity after its Washington demonstration. But it was a vital part of the ongoing tradition of confrontational struggle—as opposed to total reliance on legal suits and appeals—for civil rights in America. It would be another ten years before Rosa Parks and other working women of Montgomery took on that town's segregated buses, and several more years before tens of thousands of young people joined in mass anti-racist actions, but in 1946, the rumblings had begun that would erupt into the civil rights movement of the 1960s.

For Einstein and Robeson, although they had met before, the ACEL marked their mutual discovery that they shared a common wavelength. Their bond would grow into an ongoing alliance and a friendship—albeit little known for two such public figures. (See Chapter 10.)

7

The Einstein Watch

On February 2, 1943, Albert Ascher Wollenberger, a German Jewish refugee living in Cambridge, Massachusetts, was summoned to the FBI's Boston office for questioning. While he was there, FBI agents surreptitiously entered and searched his apartment at 19 Irving Street. The FBI's official explanation for the break-in was that Wollenberger was a "German alien" living in the U.S. while the nation was at war with Germany.

But Wollenberger had fled from Hitler's Germany and was widely known as an anti-Nazi. In fact, as the FBI knew, he was chairman of the Cambridge chapter of Friends of Free Germany, an anti-fascist group totally supporting the war then raging against Hitler. The tag line on the FBI's memo on June 16, 1943, describing the break-in, reveals the Bureau's real purpose: "Internal Security-C" [for communism]. The memo's final sentence declares:

> Wollenberger stated that through the assistance of his maternal aunt, Miss Helen Dukas, secretary to Professor Albert Einstein, Institute for Advanced Studies [sic], Princeton, New Jersey, he obtained a scholarship at Springfield College, Springfield, Massachusetts, where he spent two scholastic years.[1]

Until recently, available evidence provided no hint of how closely the FBI monitored Einstein. But in March 2000, thanks to the dogged efforts of the Public Citizen Litigation Group in negotiating the release of three hundred-plus previously withheld pages and paragraphs, the picture changed.[2] (Some of the newly released data have been integrated elsewhere in this story.) What is perhaps the most significant news in those pages is the extreme measures the FBI took to collect information on Einstein, his friends and contacts, during the l940s—what would later be called "dirty tricks"—monitoring phone calls, opening mail ("mail cover"), rummaging through garbage ("trash watch"), and surreptitiously entering and searching several homes and offices.

The 1940s in America comprised two quite different, although not alto-gether unconnected halves: the World War II years, 1941-1945, when the United States and England were allied with the Soviet Union in the war against fascism; and the early Cold War years of 1946-1950, when Russia (and communism) became America's main enemy. But even during the World War II years, when the United States and Soviets were wartime allies, the FBI and HUAC conducted their own mini-Cold War, investi-gating, spying, and holding hearings on people and groups—especially union activists, teachers, and writers—they perceived as exerting com-munist influence in America.

The Wollenberger case, for example, was part of a larger FBI/HUAC effort to harass and monitor a group of left-leaning German refugees who had come to America to escape Hitlerism. Just as with Wollenberger, these agencies used the war with Germany as a pretext to spy on these *anti-fascist* Germans. In his recent book *(Communazis)*, Alexander Stephan cites hundreds of government files to expose how, during the World War II years, the FBI and other agencies targeted and harassed German refugee writers such as Bertolt Brecht, Thomas and Heinrich Mann, Lion Feuchtwanger, and Erich Remarque, not because they were suspected backers of Hitler, but because they were known anti-fascists, often having communist contacts or socialist ideas. Einstein was in touch with many of these artists, shared their hatred for Nazism, and in some cases, such as Thomas Mann, shared a role in several political protests-and FBI reports.

The anti-left surveillance policy was not limited to refugee writers. Throughout the war years, the FBI continuously spied on American writ-ers and artists the Bureau viewed as "Red," or leaning in that direction. For example, one "Confidential" FBI memo to Hoover in 1943 warned that Ernest Hemingway had been "active in aiding the Loyalist cause in Spain [and] his views are 'liberal' and...he may be inclined favorably to Communist political philosophies." A year later, as American troops were landing in Normandy to fight the Nazis, a memo on "Communist influ-ence or control" in the Writers War Board (a government agency headed by Rex Stout, which had begun as a conservative, anti-communist group, but had become increasingly involved in the anti-fascist war effort) stated: "It is significant to note that the name of Langston Hughes appears with the advisory council...Hughes, you will recall, is the Negro Communist poet famous for the Communistic, atheistic poem, 'Goodbye Christ.'"[3]

Of course, with America's national slogan "All Out for the War Effort," the FBI and HUAC had to conduct their Red hunts behind the headlines. Nonetheless, while posters plastered across the country showed deter-mined Americans, sleeves rolled up, joining the Army, becoming nurses,

Einstein in 1946 teaching a class at Lincoln University.

working in defense plants, and doing everything to win the war against fascism, from rationing food to buying war bonds, HUAC continued its hearings on the menace of communism and the threat from Russia, then America's ally. The FBI never stopped compiling, albeit quietly, its lists of "Reds."

During the 1941-1945 period, Einstein's name appeared in several FBI investigations and HUAC hearings:

- In two separate hearings, he was cited as a friend of the North American Committee to Aid Spanish Democracy.
- In another hearing, a HUAC witness fingered Einstein as having "signed an open letter to the Mayor of Stalingrad in June 1943" (a few months after the Nazi defeat in that city had changed the course of the war).[4]
- On August 14, 1943, the FBI reported that Einstein signed a fundraising appeal for the Legal Defense and Education Fund for the NAACP.

But in all these and several similar cases during the war years, Einstein's name was simply dragged in with a host of others by the widespread

Hoover-HUAC net. There was no direct FBI surveillance of Einstein during World War II—that did not begin until the start of the Cold War.

If you are a baseball fan, 1946 is the year Jackie Robinson breaks the color line. If you are President Truman, 1946 is the year you set up the Central Intelligence Group to lay plans for the CIA. If you are Winston Churchill, it's the year you make your "Iron Curtain" speech in Fulton, Missouri, signaling the opening of the Cold War with Russia. And if you are the Special Agent in Command (SAC) of the Newark office of the FBI, 1946 is the year you start surveillance of Albert Einstein.

An internal FBI memo, dated March 8, 1946, and tagged "Internal Security-R [for Russia]" reports:

> The Newark Field Division obtained a number of telephone numbers and listings. These numbers include Princeton 1-606, which was a nonpublished number of Doctor Albert Einstein, 112 Mercer Street, Princeton, New Jersey.

A "Correlator's note," typewritten in 1952 by someone who may have felt the memo could lead a reader to think the FBI intended to tap Einstein's phone, adds: "The purpose in obtaining the above-mentioned telephone numbers and listings is not indicated in this reference."[6] Actually, the Bureau requested permission from the attorney general to place a tap on Einstein's phone, but the AG, perhaps worried about a possible leak, said no. A notation in ink appeared beside the request in Einstein's dossier: "Not considered advisable."[7]

Nonetheless, the Newark office—then operating locally without a coordinated anti-Einstein effort controlled by Hoover and headquarters (which began in 1950)—monitored many of Einstein's incoming and out-going calls, keeping a list of the phone numbers and, where known, the individuals on the other end.

In nearly five years of surveillance, the FBI identifies calls and letters to Einstein and his secretary Helen Dukas from several Russians and other individuals who once worked with communists and the Communist International (Comintern) during its period of influence (1920s and 1930s). A number of these had since broken with the Soviet leadership, and one (Otto Katz) was subsequently executed by the Moscow-dominated regime in Czechoslovakia. It is important to note that throughout this period of surveillance, the FBI made no allegation of any conspiracy involving Einstein.

Targets of the FBI's surveillance of Einstein and his colleagues during the postwar years of 1946-1950 also included dozens of leading scientists. The newly released Einstein-file pages provide a rare acknowledgment by the Bureau of how Hoover's agents operated, which included intercepting and opening private mail:

A mail cover placed on the residence and business address of Victor Frederick Weisskopf in October and November, 1947, revealed that he received a communication from V. Bargmann, Palmer Physics Laboratory, Princeton University, New Jersey.

Victor Weisskopf, a leading physicist in the Manhattan Project, was a member of the Emergency Committee of Atomic Scientists, which Einstein chaired. Valentin Bargmann was one of Einstein's research assistants.

Another mail intercept involved Einstein's close colleague, mathematician Kurt Gödel, who had escaped from Nazi-occupied Austria and after an adventurous trek through Siberia and Japan, arrived in Princeton and the Institute for Advanced Study in 1940:

> On February 14, 1951, the Bureau was furnished by the Censorship Group, Vienna Austria, the following intercept of a letter dated January 11, 1950 from Dr. Kurt Goedel to Marianna Goedel, Vienna.
>
> "Einstein warned the world not to try to attain peace by re-armament and intimidating the adversaries…and he was quite right…one thing is certain: Under the slogan 'Democracy' America is waging war [in Korea] for an absolutely unpopular regime…."

While the FBI often read telephone records supplied by AT&T, actual phone taps were less frequent—but not unknown:

> On November 10, 1947, Dr. [Thorfin] Hogness contacted Dr. Edward Condon in Washington D.C. from New York regarding a previous telephone conversation the day before. The conversation that took place was quite lengthy…[at one point] Hogness agreed with Condon and stated "Weil (garbled) Einstein believes the same thing…"
> Source: Technical Surveillance
> Reported by [agent's name blacked out]

The file also reports mail or phone intercepts or "trash watches" on several other Einstein colleagues, including physicists Peter Bergmann, Leopold Infeld, and Melba Phillips, and astronomer Harlow Shapley, as well as many nonscientist friends and associates.

On March 14, 1949, Einstein celebrated his seventieth birthday. On the same day, Hoover's sleuths recorded the undeniable fact that he received a telegram "sent from the telephone at University 4-5762…containing the following message: 'Congratulations and much luck,' signed Patsy, Jonny and Matthew."[8]

What is most remarkable about the dozens of searches and intercepts described in this document is their casualness. At no time did the FBI agents seek, or even think about, a warrant to enter and search a residence; nor did anyone ever seek court permission to tap a phone or open private letters. It's as if the agents woke up in the morning, brushed their teeth, and opened somebody's mail. Routine. The only indication of anything wrong, or even unusual, is that the FBI kept these reports classified—and blacked out from the version of the Einstein dossier they released—for seventeen years.

What were Hoover's agents looking for? What crime did they hope to uncover or prevent with their Einstein watch? The only logical conclusion, if logic has a role here, is the bomb. America's sudden emergence as a nuclear power placed the FBI in the high-pressured, high-stakes role of guardian of the queen's jewels: atomic secrets. When the Emergency Committee of Atomic Scientists set up its headquarters in Princeton, we know that the local FBI agents agonized over Einstein's role as ECAS chairman because they mistakenly believed he had worked on the Manhattan Project and knew its secrets. Hoover didn't tell Newark he had helped ban Einstein from the bomb project, and he may well not have known that Newark had included Einstein on its surveillance list.

So at least until the FBI learned from the Atomic Energy Committee in March of 1947 that Einstein had been kept out of the atomic-information loop, the Newark agents were most likely watching for Einstein—deliberately or otherwise—to create a national-security calamity by letting the nuclear cat out of its classified bag.

But what about after March 1947, when the Newark agents learned of Einstein's nuclear innocence from the AEC? The monitoring continued—it was two years later that the G-men intercepted the "congratulations" birthday telegram to Einstein from the three well-wishers, "Patsy, Jonny and Matthew." Why keep the Einstein watch going?

One explanation is simple inertia. With apologies to Newton's First Law of Motion: An investigation in motion tends to stay in motion. Another possible explanation is the early but unmistakable growth of the Red scare, the increase in finger-pointing and, as we shall see, the number of people, including Einstein, at whom the fingers were pointed. However, the newly released sections of the FBI's Einstein's file reveal another likely reason for the continuation of the Bureau's Einstein watch: nothing less than the sworn declaration of one of America's leading authorities on communism.

From July 19 to July 23, 1948, the Washington State Committee on UnAmerican Activities, one of the most active mini-HUACs at the state level, held hearings in Seattle. Its star witness was the former director of research for the federal HUAC, J. B. Matthews, who had since been demoted to the rank of professional witness* and whose job, he told the

---

* Throughout the Red scare, the government paid a slew of ex-communists to travel around the country from one Congressional hearing or trial to another, where they

Washington State Committee, was "researching communism." Matthews was such a loose cannon that even J. Edgar Hoover considered him irresponsible.[9]

Although the topic of the hearings was "Un-American Activities in Washington State," and its aim was to blacklist half a dozen left-wing professors at the University of Washington, Matthews could not resist speaking on a variety of themes from his repertoire of anti-communist testimony. He was especially eager to discuss Einstein, who, according to Matthews "rarely lets a month go by that he does not sound off on some political question."

As evidence of Einstein's "Red" character, Matthews approvingly cited a somewhat unusual source: "It was often averred by the Nazis that Einstein's mathematics were Communist mathematics." But the meat of Matthews' testimony was his suggestion that Einstein could be giving America's nuclear secrets to the Russians. After asserting "it was Einstein who first completely conceived the possibility of the atomic bomb," Matthews described what he called Einstein's "direct report to President Roosevelt suggesting setting aside some two billion dollars…to build an atomic bomb. That is some indication," Matthews continued, "of the importance of Professor Einstein in the whole field of nuclear fission, the atomic bomb and our topmost military secrets." Having designed the stage, Matthews presented his drama, here described in the FBI's Einstein file:

> Matthews further stated that few visiting scientists from Soviet Russia have come to the US without [conferring] with Professor Einstein. He pointed out that it would be possible for Einstein to confer…without disclosing important secrets but he was not sure any man should be entrusted with a responsibility for deciding whether or not [to] disclose such secrets….

Sworn testimony that Einstein might be giving the Russians our atomic secrets-even though the source was not completely reputable, and even though it was at a local hearing—might well have made national headlines for Canwell and his committee, except that his timing was bad. The Washington State HUAC hearing and Matthews's anti-Einstein testimony came during the same week the FBI was arresting the top twelve officials of the U.S. Communist Party, a story that filled the newspapers and radio newscasts.

Matthews's testimony, like all HUAC and mini-HUAC transcripts, was copied to the FBI, where it received the utmost respect. So, despite

---

would appear as "expert witnesses." During the 1948 hearings, Washington State HUAC chairman, former Sheriff Albert F. Canwell, brought in six paid witnesses, including journalist Howard Rushmore, who later wrote an attack on Einstein.

recent information from the AEC that Einstein had not worked on the bomb and did not possess nuclear secrets, the State HUAC report from Seattle provided Hoover's agents with an "official" reason—if they needed a reason—to maintain their Einstein watch. With its clear inference of espionage, Matthews' testimony may have been the first spy charge leveled against Einstein. It certainly was not the last.[10]

We need not wonder how Einstein would have felt had he known he was under surveillance. The fact is, he did know. And his words make it quite clear that what he felt was anger. At a dinner party in July 1948, Einstein told the Polish Ambassador to the United States:

> I suppose you must realize by now that the US is no longer a free country, that undoubtedly our conversation is being recorded. This room is wired, and my house is closely watched.

We know that Einstein made those comments, because as he spoke, the FBI was taking down his words.[11] Whether or not Einstein knew all the details of his surveillance, his comments were very close to the mark. Einstein biographer Abraham Pais believed that Einstein had no knowledge of any specific FBI investigation; still, it was "common knowledge" among physicists in Princeton that their activities were "under surveillance."[12] Indeed, the anger in Einstein's words seems not so much about his own target status as about the onrushing storm from the right.

8

Right Time

McCarthyism in America couldn't wait for McCarthy. The Wisconsin senator's anti-communist antics didn't hit the headlines until 1950, but the Red scare and the "ism" that would bear his name began almost as soon as the war ended in 1945. One of the earliest targets was Albert Einstein.

"It's about time the American people got wise to Einstein… He ought to be prosecuted." It was the floor of Congress on October 25, barely two months after the Japanese surrender. The speaker was Mississippi's John Rankin, one of the bloc of Southern Democrats continually re-elected, thanks to Dixie's white-only voting laws, and a senior Democratic congressman on HUAC. What prompted Rankin's attack was Einstein's signature on a letter urging the U.S. government to break diplomatic and commercial relations with the fascist regime in Spain.* Rankin was a fan of Spanish dictator Franco, and any enemy of Franco was an enemy of Rankin:

> This foreign-born agitator…in order to further the spread of Communism throughout the world…is using the mail to raise money to propagandize us into breaking relations with Spain, which…would mean another war probably….
> I call on the Department of Justice to put a stop to this man Einstein.[1]

But Rankin's analysis had little influence outside of a few white voters in Mississippi. In any case, for most Americans, it was too soon after the war to be defending one of Hitler's friends. Spain had been technically neutral during the war, but Franco's friendship with Hitler and Mussolini was well known, and "neutral" Spanish bases were used to refuel German

---

* Five years later, in another anti-Einstein tirade, Rankin proclaimed: "Ever since he published his book on relativity to try to convince the world that light had weight, he has capitalized upon his alleged reputation as a scientist." (*Dallas Times Herald*, February 14, 1950.)

submarines and Luftwaffe planes bombing American and Allied troops in North Africa. Pictures of the Nazi atrocities were still too fresh in the public's mind, as were the memories of American GI's embracing Russian soldiers when the two armies met at the river Elbe on their way to the end of the Nazi nightmare.

In November 1945, thousands of people crowded into New York's Madison Square Garden to hear the President, the Secretary of War, and America's top general publicly endorse the Washington-Moscow alliance. An item in the Einstein File reports:

> ...Confidential National Security Informant [informant's code-number blacked out] reported that on November 14, a rally was held in Madison Square Garden under the auspices of the National Council of American-Soviet Friendship....Messages of greetings, according to the informant, were sent by President Truman, Admiral King, General Eisenhower, Secretary of War Patterson, Eleanor Roosevelt, Professor ALBERT EINSTEIN and others.[2]

To the FBI, as soon as the Second World War ended (if not sooner), anything friendly to the Russians was anti-American. Einstein's endorsement of the friendship rally was one more piece of "derogatory information" for his dossier, reconfirming his subversive nature. If it wasn't "derogatory," Hoover wasn't interested. A revealing handwritten notation on an internal memo in Einstein's file declares: "No dissemination, as report contains no pertinent derogatory in form ation."[3] Communist ideas, links to communists, and especially sympathy for Russia, were the inches and feet on Hoover's "derogatory" yardstick, and he was convinced that sooner or later, the people who counted in Washington would again see it his way. It was sooner. The Madison Square Garden event was one of the last celebrations of the brief World War II alliance.

Indeed, the first obstacle to the new Cold War was the widespread compassion and friendship many Americans had developed for the Russians during the war just ended. (Twenty million Soviet citizens had been killed by the Nazis, yet the Red Army had beaten Hitler's troops at Stalingrad and then battered the German armies back to Berlin.) Before the end of the first winter of peace, former British Prime Minister Winston Churchill, speaking in Fulton, Missouri, with Truman at his side, said that a Soviet "Iron Curtain" had fallen across Europe, and thanked God for giving the atomic bomb to America. One speech, of course, does not a Cold War make, but Churchill's "Iron Curtain" address publicly signaled a new

---

* In February 1946, a month before Churchill's address, Stalin had given his "Two Camps" speech in which he argued that Western designs against the Soviet Union would make coexistence virtually impossible.

course and intensified the debate over relations with Moscow. The speech drew criticism from prominent liberals, including Eleanor Roosevelt and columnist Walter Lippmann. Inside the Truman Administration, the principal dissenter from America's foreign-policy U-turn was Secretary of Commerce Henry A. Wallace.

An agriculturalist and businessman, Wallace had been Roosevelt's secretary of agriculture and then vice president (from 1940-1944). The son of prominent Midwestern Republicans, he nonetheless became a leader in the liberal wing of FDR's New Deal Administration. Whether or not Roosevelt would have continued the wartime alliance with Moscow is open to debate, but it was certainly the position of a faction within his Administration. Now virtually alone in Truman's post-war Cabinet, Wallace stood for—and stood by—that policy of U.S.-Soviet cooperation.

"The United States owes Russia an undying debt of gratitude....The citizens of the Soviet Union paid a heavier price for our joint victory over fascism than any other people," he declared two weeks after Churchill's "Iron Curtain" speech, adding:

> [Just] as some [American] military men profess that the only road to peace is atomic bombs, bases [and] huge appropriations for armaments...so the Soviets may feel that the only road to peace is for them to give the capitalistic nations tit for every tat....
>
> The only way to defeat communism in the world is to do a better and smoother job of maximum production and optimum distribution....Let's out-compete Russia in the most friendly spirit possible, for we must realize that, militarily speaking, there could be no final victor in any armed conflict between our two great nations.[4]

It was six months before Truman fired Wallace. In the meantime, Wallace continued to criticize the Administration's increasingly anti-Soviet policies, particularly the U.S. proposal for "international control" of nuclear power*. The United States would share its atomic energy with

---

* Truman didn't fire Wallace right away, partly because during the spring and summer of 1946, the country was swept by one of the largest waves of strikes and labor unrest in its history. Throughout the war, most unions had adopted a no-strike policy (sup-ported by the U.S. Communist Party), focusing all efforts on a military victory. But the war had been good for the bottom lines of American corporations, and now unions were seeking a share. (Textile mill profits rose 600 percent from 1940 to 1946, while wages increased 36 percent. (Zinn, p. 120.) Three million U.S. workers went on strike in just the first half of 1946, and nearly five million by year's end. In May, with striking coal and railroad workers nearly shutting down their industries, Truman sent federal troops to seize the mines and railroads and threatened to draft railroad workers into the Army so he could order them, as soldiers, back to work. (Brecher, pp. 228-229.)

the rest of the world if Russia would promise not to build any atom bombs and allow U.S. inspectors entry to inspect Soviet technology sites to make sure they weren't cheating. Meanwhile, the United States would be able to continue manufacturing nuclear weapons. Wallace ridiculed that proposal, as "hypocritical" and something the Russians would obviously never accept, and he called for a real effort at cooperation.

The day Truman fired him, September 20, 1946, Wallace became leader of the resistance. He received some eight thousand letters and telegrams from Americans, well-known and unknown, worried about the trend toward militarism, angry about federal inaction against lynching, and some from people who simply admired a man who stood by his principles. One of the earliest messages came from Einstein: "Your courageous intervention deserves the gratitude of all of us who observe the present attitude of our government with grave concern."

Support for Wallace came also from Helen Keller, Thomas Mann, Congressman Claude Pepper, columnist Max Lerner, and Anita McCormick Blaine, heiress to the International Harvester fortune, who enclosed a check for ten thousand dollars. A conference co-sponsored by the CIO, and the NAACP, the National Farmers Union, and other liberal organizations cabled Wallace that he had "the support of millions and millions who believe in the program of Franklin Roosevelt."[5] The new year began with the formation of the Progressive Citizens of America and speculation, both public and private, about a third-party presidential campaign in 1948. But we are getting ahead of the story.

Wallace's dismissal from the Cabinet not only mobilized the left, it rallied the right. If Truman had been resisting pressures from the Republicans and the conservative wing of the Democratic Party, his firing of Wallace signaled his capitulation. The President's diary leaves little doubt:

But Truman was sinking fast in the popularity polls, dropping 30 points between January and June. At the end of June, the expiration of wartime price controls (FDR's Office of Price Administration had set and, for the most part, enforced strict controls on prices) allowed companies to raise their prices-food prices soared 13.8 percent in July. For months, with Truman's encouragement, Wallace toured the country, speaking before audiences of workers, African-Americans, liberals, and leftists, urging them to stick with the Democratic Party, despite its flaws. (Culver, pp. 415-418.)

Despite Truman's repressive measures, the strikes succeeded in wresting concessions from corporate America. Indeed, a case can be made that after tough struggles, U.S. workers, as well as industries, benefited from World War II. "The biggest gains were in corporate profits, which rose from $6.4 billion in 1940 to $10.8 billion in 1944. But enough went to workers and farmers to make them feel that the system was doing well for them." (Zinn, p. 127.)

[Wallace] is a pacifist one hundred percent. He wants to disband our armed forces, give Russia our atomic secrets and trust a bunch of adventurers in the Kremlin Politboro....The German-American Bund...was not half so dangerous. The Reds... and the "parlor pinks" seem to be banded together and are becoming a national danger[6].

More than Churchill's "Iron Curtain" speech, Truman's firing of Wallace marked the start of the Cold War for America. During the coming months, while the United States sent hundreds of millions of dollars and military advisers to help defeat pro-communist guerrillas in Greece, and successfully beat back Red electoral challenges in France and Italy, the Soviets installed pro-Moscow governments in the Eastern European countries their troops had occupied during the war. And in China, Mao's communist guerrillas, with the support of millions of peasants, defeated the American-backed nationalists and took power in 1949.

Just as disturbing to the United States and other Western governments, although less publicized, was the international upsurge of independence movements in former colonies. In Asia, revolutionary movements were ablaze—in Indochina against the French, in Indonesia against the Dutch, in Malaysia against the British, and in the Philippines, where armed rebellion broke out against U.S. troops. In Africa, too, discontent was on the rise, with exceptionally militant strikes in French West Africa, Kenya, and South Africa, where a hundred thousand gold miners stopped work until they were forced back by the army.

Yet only in the United States—unlike other anti-Soviet, Western, colonial states such as England and France—did the country's leaders feel it necessary to link the Cold War to the Red scare, which came to be called McCarthyism. In England, communists were a just a handful; in France and Italy, they were millions (the largest political party in both countries); but only America made them outlaws. Within months of Wallace's dismissal, Truman's Secretary of Labor Lewis Schwellenbach proposed a constitutional amendment to outlaw the Communist Party. While most officials were not prepared to go so far in abandoning civil liberties, Schwellenbach's statements spurred the pre-McCarthyites in Congress to pass (over Truman's veto) the Taft-Hartley Act, which barred communists from holding union offices and gave McCarthyism an effective weapon to drive communists and Red-led unions out of the organized labor movement.[*]

---

[*] Schrecker (*Many Are the Crimes*) makes a convincing case that the primary target of McCarthy-Hooverism was the left-wing influence in labor unions. Even in Hollywood, the Red scare was most welcome by the big studios because it helped them "to get rid of militant trade unionists." (Lawson, p. 13.)

But the lynchpin of pre-McCarthy McCarthyism (before 1950) was Truman's loyalty-security program decreeing that government employees would be fired if they were found to be "disloyal." Executive Order 9835, issued March 22, 1947, required every federal worker to undergo political screening, and assigned the Department of Justice to make a list of "subversive organizations." A remarkably prophetic headline in the next morning's *New York Times* reported:

> PRESIDENT ORDERS INQUIRY
> ON DISLOYAL JOBHOLDERS;
> COMMUNISTS FIRST TARGET

Suddenly, more than two million federal employees had to be screened for loyalty. Another four million working for private companies with defense contracts were soon included under the Federal Industrial Security Program. With some qualms, Truman agreed to give total screening authority to J. Edgar Hoover's FBI.[7]

At the center of McCarthyism stood not McCarthy, but Hoover and his FBI. He was there before McCarthy came to power, and he continued to wave the Red-scare flag for years after the Wisconsin senator's demise. The FBI chief provided McCarthy with key staff people, and while indignantly denying it, secretly gave him (and other congressional investigating committees) a steady supply of allegations from faceless informants. "I can say unequivocally that is an absolute lie," Hoover declared, responding to charges that he "leaked" secret files to selected members of Congress. But after his falling-out with Hoover, former Assistant FBI Director William Sullivan revealed, among other things, how much McCarthy relied on the FBI for his "information": "The FBI kept Joe McCarthy in business....We gave McCarthy all we had....[Hoover] had us preparing material for [McCarthy] regularly, [we] kept furnishing it to him while [Hoover] publicly denied that we were helping him." The FBI chief, wrote Theoharis (in 1988), "had more to do with undermining American constitutional guarantees than any political leader before or since."[8]

Hoover had never stopped keeping files on communists. "There was no question in his mind that Godless, atheistic, monolithic communism was a threat," explained a former Justice Department official: "Hoover [saw] Communists coming up out of the sewers." In 1936, he started a program to prepare for the "grave danger" from subversives in a national emergency. It involved "indexing" people and groups such as "known espionage agents, known saboteurs, leading members of the Communist Party, and the German Bund." On September 2, 1939, with Roosevelt's

authorization, Hoover ordered his agents to prepare reports on dangerous types such as "Germans, Italians and Communists." Initially, the
program was called the Custodial Detention Index, later renamed the
Security Index. In 1943, Attorney General Biddle, angered at discovering
a secret Hoover investigation of First Lady Eleanor Roosevelt, ordered the
FBI chief to do away with the Custodial Detention Index. Hoover simply
changed its name to the Security Index and told his agents to keep quiet
about its existence.[9]

In a similar move shortly before World War II ended, Hoover ordered
all FBI field offices to begin collecting evidence on "the illegal status and
activities" of U.S. communists, evidence that could be used to prepare an
indictment that would put the Party out of business. His memo added,
"The importance of this project cannot be overemphasized." For the next
two years, FBI agents compiled names, places, and allegations against CP
members around the country, while headquarters put together a "brief"
that Hoover would soon use against the Party.[10]

In March 1947, just four days after Truman announced the new loyalty-security program, Hoover launched a public attack on the CP. Testifying
before HUAC, the FBI chief declaimed direly that the Communist Party
was out to take over America. For Hoover, it was nothing new. What *was*
new was that the *Times* editors placed the story atop Page 1:

> FBI HEAD BRANDS
> COMMUNIST PARTY
> A 'FIFTH COLUMN'
> Allegiance to Russia, He Testifies, and
> Overthrow of Our Government Is Goal

The term "overthrow of our government" was not a casual choice.
Hoover wanted to make communism a crime and to start by arresting
the Party's top leadership. But at that early stage of the Red scare, it would
have been hard to sell the public on jailing people just for their ideas.
Hoover lobbied Attorney General Tom Clark to indict top party officers
under the Smith Act for "conspiracy to teach and advocate the overthrow
of the government by force and violence" and sent him the brief his agents
had been working on for two years-containing some two thousand pages
on the CP. Within fifteen months, Hoover's pressure and the Bureau's brief
brought results: In July 1948, the Department of Justice issued Smith Act
indictments and FBI agents arrested the twelve top CP officers. "That was
the one case Hoover really wanted prosecuted," a law-enforcement official said later.[11] The Smith Act prosecution, however, was not exclusively,
or even primarily, Hoover's decision. As Theoharis points out, Hoover's

J. Edgar Hoover tries to make a point about the "red menace" before HUAC
in 1947. Hoover and the FBI were at the center of McCarthyism.
They kept on brandishing the "red menace" after the demise of Senator McCarthy.

authority depended on "powerful national leaders* [who] shared the FBI
director's obsessive anti-communism and yet sought to mask their own
complicity and indifference to the law."[12]

---

* Hoover's personal connection to the power elite was George E. Allen, a financier
and lobbyist, and his closet friend outside the FBI. (Clyde Tolson, the FBI's second in
command, was Hoover's almost constant companion.) Allen served as a director of
numerous industrial and insurance companies, including Republic Steel, and was a
friend to Presidents Roosevelt, Truman, and Eisenhower. He played poker regularly
with Truman, who appointed him to the Reconstruction Finance Corporation and later
became Eisenhower's golf and bridge partner. His unique brand of modesty is revealed
by the title of his book: Presidents Who Have Known Me.

During a friendship that spanned forty years, Allen and Hoover usually had
dinner together twice a week at Harvey's restaurant, went to the racetrack together
almost every Saturday, and vacationed together—summers in Florida and winters in
California. Other friends who sometimes joined their vacation party included wealthy
Texas oilmen Clint Murchison and Sid Richardson. (For more on the Allen-Hoover
friendship, see Demaris, The Director; also Esquire, September 1974.)

Another Hoover buddy was Lyndon Johnson. For nineteen years, the FBI chief and
LBJ lived across the street from each other, "trading gifts and gossip in a relationship
approximating, as closely as either... would ever know it, genuine friendship." Once,
Hoover gave LBJ a beagle: LBJ named the dog "Edgar." (Welch, p. 93.)

Einstein protested the arrests of the CP officers, as did several liberal and left-wing groups in the United States. But on the whole, the jailing of American communists upset Europeans much more—perhaps because of their recent, firsthand experience with Nazism. Editorials in several West European newspapers drew analogies to Hitler's initial steps outlawing and jailing communists in Germany.

* * *

For all his patriotic zeal in the anti-communist cause, Hoover still found time to promote the cause of Hoover, and the 1948 elections offered a chance he couldn't pass up. It was no secret that the FBI director and Truman did not get along. In Hoover's view, the President, despite his loyalty program, was "soft" on communism. Hoover's Republican friends were planning an election campaign that accused the Democrats of covering up "Red infiltration" into government. Truman, who had his own anti-communist agenda, thought Hoover was out to grab too much power, and warned aides that the FBI could become another Gestapo.

Hoover was confident his problems with Truman would be over by Election Day. It was eight years since his last scheme to become attorney general had failed when his partner in the alleged plot, Senator Wheeler, was done in by publicity about pro-Nazi propaganda mailed from his office. This time, Hoover's script had a far more promising leading man: Republican presidential candidate and odds-on favorite to win the White House in November, Thomas Dewey.

The Hoover-Dewey deal was not complicated. In exchange for "information" on Dewey's opponents, president-elect Dewey would appoint Hoover as attorney general and Tolson as assistant attorney general, allowing them to continue their close collaboration...and companionship.* Dewey also promised to make Hoover a Supreme Court Justice when

---

* Reports that Hoover and Tolson were secretly lovers have been widely disseminated in recent years, as well as stories that Hoover was a closet cross-dresser. The most extensive treatment of these reports was Anthony Summers' 1993 bombshell book. The Secret Life of J. Edgar Hoover, but others have since added to the evidence. Bill Bonanno's recent book about his father, the Mafia boss, cites photos of Hoover "in drag." (Bound by Honor, pp. 134-135.) On the other hand, several former FBI officials, like Donald Moore, continue to deny the charges. Cartha DeLoach spends an entire chapter of his book (Hoover's FBI, pp. 61-81) attempting to refute Summers' charges. But more significant than the FBI chief's alleged secret homosexuality, the reports underscore the hypocrisy of Hoover's puritanical moral code, strictly enforced for all Bureau employees, including an absolute ban on anyone even suspected of gay sexual tendencies.

132 THE EINSTEIN FILE

the next vacancy occurred. Besides information, the FBI would provide Dewey with position papers on several topics, including communism.[13]

Anticipating his long-sought prize, Hoover spent the summer of 1948—besides arresting the CP officers—leaking allegations against Alger Hiss to a HUAC member from California named Richard Nixon, allegations that would help get Nixon headlines during the committee hearings on the Hiss case.* Most of the headlines had an anti-Truman slant, increasing the odds of a Dewey victory in November.

The election had to be one of Hoover's biggest disappointments. Every high-school student in America has seen the news photo of the re-elected President Truman, grinning broadly after his upset victory and holding up the DEWEY DEFEATS TRUMAN headline that had been printed before all the results were in. It was as close as Hoover would ever get to a promotion.

If Hoover was the quarterback of the Red scare, its front line was the House Un-American Activities Committee—HUAC.** While the Communist leaders may have been Hoover's top-priority target, HUAC's biggest headlines came from California. In March 1947, as the FBI chief prepared his "fifth-column" attack on the CP, Mississippi's Rankin announced HUAC would hold hearings in Hollywood, aimed at politically cleansing the movies. The hearings opened in October, almost a year before the Hiss case, amid a mob of flashbulbs and autograph seekers.

By now, the public has learned a good deal about Hollywood blacklisting, thanks to movies such as *The Front*, *The Way We Were*, *Guilt by Suspicion* and *Trumbo* and the nationwide debate in 1999 over awarding an Oscar to producer and one-time informer Elia Kazan. When TV documentaries periodically remind us of those hearings—top movie writers refusing to name names before the Committee and going to jail for contempt; others like Walt Disney and Ronald Reagan, with no such qualms; a delegation of stars, including Humphrey Bogart,*** Lauren Bacall, and Danny Kaye, flying to Washington to protest the Committee's attack on the First Amendment—it is clear that only Hollywood could have given

---

* For HUAC's Republican chairman, J. Parnell Thomas, the Hiss hearing was a last happy headline—a few months later, he was in a federal prison serving time for embezzlement.
** Actually named the House Committee on Un-American Activities, HUAC was an easier acronym to pronounce. Opponents often called it simply "the Un-American Committee." Established by anti-New Deal forces in Congress in 1938, it immediately denounced the Roosevelt Administration as "a tool of Stalin," and never changed its ultraconservative spots.
*** Movie tough-guy Bogart was not nearly so tough fighting for principles. Within just weeks of his Washington trip under pressure from studio executives, Bogie said the protest had been "ill advised."

HUAC such publicity. But from the start, the Red scare aimed at—and reached—well beyond Tinseltown, impacting labor unions, schools, and scientists, especially those with defense-related jobs.

Early in 1947, Hoover began sending Truman a series of reports stating that several leading scientists were communists, or sympathizers. One of the first on Hoover's list was Harlow Shapley, director of the Harvard Observatory and a Wallace supporter, who became, with Einstein and others, increasingly active in efforts to stem McCarthyism. Testifying before HUAC in December 1946, from the witness stand, Shapley called Mississippi's Rankin "fascist!" In one of Hoover's more bizarre attempts to discredit Shapley, the FBI chief labeled Shapley's efforts to bring about a federally funded National Science Foundation a "tactical scheme very similar to the general operational procedures of the Communist Party."[14] FBI surveillance of Shapley included monitoring his phone and mail contacts with Einstein.

Another name on Hoover's suspect-scientist list and the center of an early public controversy was physicist Edward U. Condon, an authority on microwave electronics and recently elected head of the American Physical Society, who had worked briefly at Los Alamos as deputy to Oppenheimer. Condon's first "subversive" activity was having been appointed director of the National Bureau of Standards by (then Secretary of Commerce) Henry Wallace. His second was issuing "An Appeal to Reason," challenging the State Department's restrictions on scientists' travel—Condon himself had been denied a passport in 1945 to attend a scientific conference in Moscow—and the exchange of scientific information:

> What is going on? Prominent scientists are denied the privilege of traveling abroad. Physicists are not allowed to discuss certain areas of their science with each other...Let us cast this isolationist, chauvinist poison from our minds before we corrode our hearts.[15]

Defying the Cold War trend, Condon invited a delegation of Russians to visit the Bureau of Standards in 1947. When the conservative *Washington Times Herald,* reportedly fed by HUAC Chairman J. Parnell Thomas, ran a series of stories linking Condon to the American-Soviet Science Society and other subversive-sounding organizations. Condon requested that Secretary of Commerce Averell Harriman run his name through a security investigation. Harriman referred the case to the AEC, and—while the FBI interviewed more than three hundred people as part of Condon's "loyalty review"—Nixon and other HUAC members denounced him as "one of the weakest links in our national security," and a Chicago paper headlined: ATOM CHIEF LINKED TO SPY RING.[16]

Again, Einstein joined the protesters—science societies, civil-liberties groups, and others, who rallied to Condon's defense—and was among a hundred and fifty scientists who sponsored a New York dinner where University of Chicago President Robert Hutchins declared: "If Ed Condon, whose Americanism sticks out all over him and all over his record, can be linked to a spy ring, anybody could be linked to a spy ring.... nobody is safe." Although the AEC finally cleared Condon, stating there was "no question whatever" about his loyalty, his case foreshadowed harder trials to come.[17]

What was happening in postwar America—the growing Red scare and Cold War militarism—was not just upsetting to Einstein, it was ominous. In May 1947, just weeks after Truman decreed his loyalty-security program, Einstein felt "compelled to voice this honest warning":

> [In] Germany, I saw how excessive nationalism can spread like a disease, bringing tragedy to millions. Now...I recognize indications of the disease... also in this country.[18]

To understand how acutely anxious Einstein felt about this nationalist "disease," consider that during the same postwar years, he was suffering from a debilitating intestinal illness that periodically laid him low with spasms of pain and vomiting. In December 1948, he underwent exploratory surgery, and doctors found the cause of his suffering was a large aortic aneurysm. Today, such an aneurysm can be surgically removed; in 1948, it was essentially a death sentence, depending only on how fast the aneurysm grew. At the same time, he was busy as chairman of the Emergency Committee of Atomic Scientists, actively writing and speaking out against racism, and continuing his scientific work in pursuit of a Unified Field Theory. For all of that, at sixty-nine, he took on another campaign.

On April 1, 1948, Einstein wrote to Shapley, then head of the National Council of the Arts, Sciences and Professions (ASP), proposing "a strong counterattack [against] the people in power in Washington, pushing systematically toward preventive war." Americans want peace, Einstein argued, and "while the country's democratic institutions are still alive, it is the duty of intellectuals to see that our people's political aspirations gain influence and become dominant while there is still time."[19]

In the next two months, Einstein, Shapley, Thomas Mann, and several others, began planning an international gathering of cultural and scientific leaders—a weekend of artistic and intellectual exchange between East and West, and especially between the United States and the Soviet Union. The "Cultural and Scientific Conference for World Peace," sponsored by ASP, was scheduled for the following spring in New York's Waldorf

Astoria hotel. Shapley was the primary organizer, but the Einstein and Mann names helped the ASP enlist 550 sponsors-educators, religious leaders, scientists, and artists, including Lillian Hellman, Langston Hughes, Dorothy Parker, George Seldes, and Louis Untermeyer.

In March 1949, scores of participants arrived in New York from around the world, the largest delegations coming from Russia and Eastern Europe. While permitting Soviet-bloc delegates to attend, the U.S. State Department denied visas to at least twenty delegates (because of their leftist affiliations) from Western countries, including British crystallographer and radical J.D. Bernal and three Canadians. Indian Prime Minister Nehru sent greetings to the conference, as did Pablo Casals, Sean O'Casey, Michael Redgrave, Diego Rivera, and George Bernard Shaw. Americans attending included artists such as Leonard Bernstein, Aaron Copland, and Norman Mailer. Einstein's surgery in December made it impossible for him to attend the event, but he continued his support. His FBI file reports that in March 1949, Einstein was a "sponsor on the program."[20]

Two days of workshop discussions (one on education included W. E. B. Du Bois and three professors fired by the University of Washington after the State HUAC hearings mentioned earlier) provided interesting and often intense debates between pro-Moscow delegates and many who believed there had to be a non-Soviet alternative to "the American Century." The conference's final resolution called for more cultural and scientific exchanges between the United States and the Soviets. But it was like swimming against the rapids.* As one observer put it: "There was a right and a wrong year to advocate cultural coexistence with Russia, and none was more wrong than 1949."[21]

Most of the U.S. media paid little attention to the conference sessions or serious interviews, focusing instead on the anti-Soviet pickets outside ("God Save America!" "Kill the Red Killers") and coming up with witty one-liners ("A let's-all-love-Russia clambake") and clever headlines (PINK COMINFORM WILL HUDDLE IN LUXURY). No coverage was more

---

* The conference may have suffered as much from its own weaknesses as from rightwing attacks against it. In particular, the virtual absence of delegates from Asia and Africa undermined the conference's goal of "World Peace." The single Asian delegate, Indian mathematician D.D. Kosambi, told the gathering: "The countries I come from suffer from hunger, [which] twists and warps and corrodes the mind and soul of human beings....Even the atomic bomb should be no more horrible than year after year, generation after generation of having your mind filled with no other thought than that of food....One of the first things I heard here was that a million bags of potatoes had been dumped into the ocean [to keep the market price competitive]. You are using a far more terrible means of warfare than the bacteriological or the atomic."

graphic than *Life* magazine's four-page photo essay on April 4, titled: RED
VISITORS CAUSE RUMPUS.

One way to measure the rising hysteria for any given year of America's
Red scare is to see who was attacking Einstein. In 1945, when the Red scare
was barely born, it was a rabidly racist congressman from Mississippi,
representing a fairly small percentage of the American population, even
a small percentage of the Mississippi population if you include people of
color. At the height of the Red-scare hysteria, 1953, the attack on Einstein
came, as we will see, from the mainstream, agenda-setting media, the
New York Times and the *Washington Post*. In 1949, it was *Life* magazine.
Owned and slanted by the conservative Henry Luce, *Life* attracted millions of readers every week not so much with its new or right-of-center
views as with its oversized pages of large, colorful, sometimes brilliant,
always lively photographs. *Life* advertised itself as "the picture magazine"
at a time when—difficult as it is to imagine—most American homes did
not have television.

Life's report on the Cultural and Scientific Conference for World
Peace called the gathering "an oddly assorted group of thinkers from
all over the world," and stated: "The foreign guests at the meeting...
mostly from Russian-dominated countries, [included] composer Dmitri
Shostakovich...." The magazine carried photos of the pickets outside the
hotel, most of them refugees from East European countries. One plac-
ard declared: "Stop Stalin, Save Slovakia"; another, held up by an angry-
looking young man in a suit and tie, read: "Shostakovich! Jump Thru The
Window!" But the highlight of *Life's* photo essay was a two-page spread,
headed DUPES AND FELLOW TRAVELERS DRESS UP COMMUNIST FRONTS,
with photos of fifty well-known Americans who, the magazine charged,
were helping international communism by sponsoring "front" organizations and events like the Waldorf Astoria conference. In the center of the
left-hand page, surrounded by photos of writers, musicians, professors,
scientists, and ministers—and just beneath the photo of Congressman
Adam Clayton Powell, Jr.—is Albert Einstein.

Media criticism was far from new to Einstein. It had begun in Berlin
during World War I for his pacifism, and increased after the war as
anti-Semitic, German nationalists foreshadowed Hitler. While the rest
of the world hailed Einstein, the conservative German press denounced
his "Jewish science." The media attacks intensified after Foreign Minister
Rathenau's assassination in 1922, until Germany's struggling Weimar government cracked down on the rightists ...for a while. Within a few years,
Hitler's gangs roamed German streets, and Einstein was a frequent target
of the pro-Nazi press.

Life Magazine ran this two-page spread at the height of the "red scare" on April 4, 1949 charging that these 50 well-known Americans were aiding international communism by "fronting" for organizations and events. Einstein was among them.

In the United States, too, most of the media attacks came from far right field. "I'll bet that Einstein fellow eats with a knife," Father Coughlin announced on his Christian Front radio program on Thanksgiving weekend, 1938, adding that the scientist "is fooling everyone with his relativity theory." Einstein almost never responded to media critics.

A rare exception occurred near the end of his life, when Einstein asked Helen Dukas to call comedian Sid Caesar to tell him how much he enjoyed Caesar's TV character "The Professor" (a German-accented, Einstein spoof on *Your Show of Shows* variety program) and to invite him to Princeton for a visit.* As for the *Life* article, if Einstein saw it, he ignored

---

* At first, Caesar thought someone one was pulling his leg. When he realized the call was actually from Einstein, he was overwhelmed: "I was so shocked I almost dropped the phone. Einstein wants to talk to me... It was like Copernicus calling up....I mean, what am I gonna say to Einstein? 'You know, I think you made a mistake in there. I don't think it is E equals MC squared: it is EM squared to the unda-eighteenth power....' You know, what am I gonna tell him? I knew I would just sit there like a little boy and listen...." Einstein died before the meeting could be set up, but Caesar later wrote: "The fact that Albert Einstein knew who I was... It was one of the most beautiful moments of my life." (Caesar's essay in Jennings & Brewster, p. 333.)

it—unless we consider his letter to the writer Max Brod two weeks *before* the magazine's publication as his response:

> There have already been published by the bucketfuls such brazen lies and utter fictions about me that I would long since have gone to my grave if I had let myself pay attention to them.[22]

But Einstein would not shrug off the rapidly spreading political attacks against others on the left. His FBI file provides a summary of the most important battles he joined in the resistance to pre-McCarthy McCarthyism:

> Newark Confidential Informant (code # blacked out) advised that on 3/46 the House Committee on Un-American Activities cited for Contempt all members of the Executive Board of the Joint Anti-Fascist Refugee Committee for [not] producing books and records...when called before the Committee... According to the informant, the JAFRC sent a telegram to every Congressman urging they vote against the [contempt citation]. The signatures...included the name of EINSTEIN and four others.... (Section 8, p.44.)

On March 16, 1948, French nuclear scientist Irene Joliot Curie arrived in the United States and was immediately "detained" on Ellis Island by U.S. authorities. A reception committee of scientists organized protests, and after four days, Mme. Curie was released.

> It is noted that Madame Irene Joliot Curie [is] the wife of Frederic Joliot Curie, head of the French Atomic Energy Commission, a French delegate to the UN Commission on Atomic Energy, and an admitted member of the CP of France....EINSTEIN was one of those who invited her to visit the US.
>
> The Joint Anti-Fascist Refugee Committee was urging telegrams...protesting Madame Curie's treatment and detention upon arrival in the US. According to the Informant, Professor EINSTEIN sent a telegram and was asking all scientists on the reception committee to do likewise. (Section 8, pp. 45-46.)

> Harlow Shapley...and nine others [including] Albert EINSTEIN [launched] the Committee of One Thousand to seek the abolition of the Un-American Activities Committee. (Section 5, p. 766.)

> EINSTEIN was among individuals named...as having petitioned the US Supreme Court for a rehearing of the prison sentences imposed on [John Howard] Lawson and [Dalton] Trumbo and eight others ("The Hollywood Ten") for contempt of Congress. (Section 8, p. 78.)

Einstein's most controversial stand was in defense of the indicted communists. Hitler's round-up of communists, in Einstein's view, had been the first step toward a concentration-camp society. So, unlike many liberals in the United States, and despite his criticisms of the Soviet Union and Stalin, Einstein protested the arrests in 1948:

Nobel Prize winner Irene Joliot-Curie chats with Einstein at his Princeton
home in 1948 after she had been detained at Ellis Island.

Among the names and organizations [in an article on January 30, 1949, in *The Worker]* which protested the trial of the twelve [stating] "the entire leadership of the Communist Party, a legal political party, has been indicted for teaching the social science of Marxism"…was Dr. Albert EINSTEIN. (Section 6, p. 958.)

On 9/10/49…the Committee to defend the rights of the twelve Communist leaders…listed as sponsors EINSTEIN and others. (Section 8, p.76.)

When, during the trial of the CP officials, Federal Judge Harold Medina cited their attorneys for contempt of court:

Albert EINSTEIN, Thomas Mann, Professor Thomas Emerson and thirteen others denounced a trend toward disciplinary action against lawyers who defend "political minorities, racial minorities and labor organizations." The statement mentioned the contempt citations by Judge Medina against…counselors for the Communist leaders. (Section 3, p. 409.)

During the same postwar years, two other causes also kept Einstein actively writing articles, statements, and letters: the campaign for World Government and formation of the United World Federalists in 1947; and the Zionist movement, before and after the establishment of Israel in 1948.

Both of these issues were complex, and they involved Einstein in debates, sometimes heated. Yet his FBI file contains no significant references to either.

While he had long supported the Zionist cause—first visiting the United States in 1921 on a fund-raising tour with Zionist leader Chaim Weizmann—Einstein often clashed with its leaders by urging cooperation with the Arabs.* He considered himself primarily a cultural rather than a political or territorial Zionist. In 1930, while Zionist policy called for a Jewish state in Palestine, he proposed a power-sharing arrangement for the nation-to-be (a Joint Council of four Jews and four Arabs, modeled after the Swiss Constitution), but both sides rejected the plan. Eight years later, Einstein said he "should much rather see a reasonable agreement with the Arabs based on living together in peace than the creation of a Jewish state"** and warned against "the inner damage Judaism will sustain...from the development of a narrow nationalism within our ranks." In a little-known letter to Weizmann, he argued:

> If we do not succeed in finding the path of honest cooperation and coming to terms with the Arabs, we will not have learned anything from our two-thousand-year-old ordeal and will deserve the fate which will beset us.[23]

Cooperation with the Arab population, in Einstein's view, was both the only "practical possibility" and "moral justification" for Zionism. A 1998 collection of Einstein's letters and statements, published by the Hebrew University of Jerusalem's Albert Einstein Archives, explains further: "He urged a solution to the Arab-Jewish conflict in Palestine based on mutual understanding and consent." Until the summer of 1947, Einstein "advocated a bi-national solution in Palestine," writes Ze'ev Rosenkranz, curator of the Archives at the Hebrew University, adding: "Following independence [in 1948], he strongly supported the State of Israel, yet remained highly critical of its political leadership."[24]

It's well known that when Weizmann, who was Israel's first president, died in 1952, the Israeli government offered Einstein the presidency, but he declined. Less widely reported is the comment Israeli Prime Minister Ben

---

* This book originally appeared in 2002. Shortly after, I researched, wrote and had published *Einstein on Israel and Zionism* (St. Martin's Press, 2009), which provides much more information on Einstein and his relationship with Israel and Zionism. See page 317 below.

** Einstein was also critical of Arab nationalism. In two long articles in the Princeton Herald in 1944 (April 14 and 28), Einstein and author Eric Kahler argue with the "one-sided" views of Philip. K. Hitti (described as "an authority on matters relating to the Moslem world"), and deplore Arab leaders who have done little or nothing to improve the impoverished living conditions of their people.

Gurion made at the time to a close associate: "Tell me what to do if he says yes! I've had to offer the post to him because it's impossible not to. But if he accepts, we are in for trouble." When he turned down the offer, Einstein told his stepdaughter Margot, "If I were to be president, sometime I would have to say to the Israeli people things they would not like to hear."[25]

One can find numerous published statements by Einstein endorsing Israel and Zionism. (In 1952, he told his good friend, Israeli statesman Abba Eban,* "My relationship to the Jewish people has become my strongest human bond...") But considering the unrestrained racism ravaging the Mid-East today, it's important to note that until the end of his life, Einstein insisted: "The most important aspect of our [Israel's] policy must be our ever-present, manifest desire to institute complete equality for the Arab citizens living in our midst....The attitude we adopt toward the Arab minority will provide the real test of our moral standards as a people."[26]

If Einstein's ideas on Israel were not completely welcomed by most Israeli leaders, his advocacy of World Government was emphatically rejected by many of the world's governments. (Not to be confused with the "globalization" that is currently the target of anti-corporate demonstrations, the campaign for World Government proposed to prevent future wars primarily through a supranational military force, open to all nations, with a monopoly on major weapons.) While it was briefly popular after World War II among a wide spectrum of American intellectuals,** the movement—and especially Einstein, its best-known advocate—was assailed from the right and the left.

To Mississippi's Rankin, it was just one more reason that Einstein "should have been deported for his communistic activities years ago."[27] Einstein easily ignored attacks from Rankin, but when four top Soviet scientists in 1947 denounced his support for World Government, including the charge that "...such ideas represent the imperialist aims of capitalist monopolists," Einstein wrote a long response.*** The Soviets feared that "Einstein's suggestion [for World Government)...would only serve as a

---

* A week before Einstein's death in 1955, Eban came to visit. He reportedly told Einstein that the new technology of television would make it possible for him to be seen and heard by some sixty million people. Einstein answered: "You see, I still might become famous, after all!" (Bucky, p. 158.)

** United World Federalist alumni included such far-from-leftists as Thomas Finletter, who later became Secretary of the Army, and Cord Meyer, whose New York Times obituary carried the headline, "Communism Fighter at the CIA."

*** Einstein clashed with the Russians again in August 1948 when the Soviet-dominated World Congress of Intellectuals, meeting in Wroclaw, Poland refused to present a statement he had sent (at their invitation) advocating World Government. (See "How Red?" fn.9. Exhibit B.)

screen for an offensive [by Western powers] against [Socialist] nations…"
Einstein acknowledged the repeated military and political attacks by
Western nations that "Russia has suffered…during the last three decades,"
but argued that to avoid nuclear destruction, both sides had no choice.
"There is no other possible way [but World Government] of eliminating
the most terrible danger which has ever threatened man."[28]

Despite Einstein's intense involvement with both Zionism and the
World Government movement, his FBI file reflects a lack of serious interest in either activity. The file's all-inclusive Correlation Report (1,160 pages
comprising Sections 2 through 6) does contain a few items on each issue,
but when Hoover and his people culled out the "subversive" stuff—
Einstein's activities they deemed most dangerous—for inclusion in the
142-page Summary Report of August 5, 1953, they completely omitted
both.[29]

A different book on Einstein's politics—not focused on his FBI file—
would devote at least a long chapter to each of these causes. But here, the
fact that Hoover did not consider Einstein's connection with them as
subversive—that neither "made the cut" to reach the FBI's most-menacing
list—reflects how completely anti-communism shaped the Bureau's policies. The Soviet Union and its supporters opposed* both of these causes.
That certainly did not mean the FBI had any sympathy for Zionism or
World Government—it was not a case where the good guys wore white
hats and the bad guys wore black hats. To Hoover, as to HUAC, the only
hats that mattered were red and made in Moscow. Without a Russian connection, you failed the FBI's "subversive test" and were not worth even a
mention in the Einstein file's Summary Report.

* * *

By contrast, Einstein's backing of Henry Wallace's third-party bid for the
White House in 1948 earned several pages in his FBI dossier. Wallace and
his running mate, Idaho Senator Glen Taylor, ran as candidates of the
newly formed Progressive Party. "A new and broader Communist front,"
was the way the California State HUAC described the Progressive Party.
It was no secret that the U.S. Communist Party had played a crucial role
in launching the Progressive Party, and the CP's organizers and supporters kept the Wallace campaign moving. But Wallace and Taylor themselves were far from communists, and the new party initially attracted

---

* The Russians initially supported the establishment of Israel (and part of the Zionist
movement), but by 1953, the romance had soured.

broad support as an alternative to the Cold War and loyalty-oath policies backed by both Democrats and Republicans. While Wallace had qualms about the CP, he refused to be maneuvered into Red-baiting and loyalty oaths within his own party; these were policies he viewed as far more destructive that having communists work in his campaign.

Einstein was a part of Wallace's broad support. But if the FBI was capable of analyzing such political diversity within the Wallace campaign (or any other group), you wouldn't know if from reading the Einstein file:[30]

> Newark Confidential Informant (Code# blacked out) advised that almost all Progressive Party candidates for public office in NJ are known to him as CP members....
>
> The Chicago Star...dated 10/4/47, page 2, contained a photograph of EINSTEIN together with Henry A. Wallace, Dr. Frank Kingdon of the Progressive Citizens of America, and Paul Robeson.
>
> An accompanying article stated that EINSTEIN had invited Wallace to his NJ home and expressed his "great admiration for Wallace's courage and devotion to the fight for world peace."

Other than "world peace," the file lacks any reference to the Progressive Party's program. In fact, Wallace and his campaign challenged the Truman Administration's policies not *just* on the arms race with Russia, but on a spectrum of issues, from the then-widespread strikes to racial segregation. In one speech early in his campaign, Wallace criticized the government's "use of force against [striking] coal miners through fines, jail threats and injunctions" as "a sorry way to deal with labor relations." Linking labor and foreign policy and advocating more trade with Russia instead of an arms build-up, he continued: "Just as guns won't take the place of food in our foreign relations, fines and jails won't take the place of solving the living and security problems of the coal miners and other workers."

But it was in the area of civil rights that the Progressive Party made its biggest impact. Besides challenging Truman to end lynching and establish equal-employment practices in government agencies, the Wallace-Taylor campaign refused to hold meetings in segregated halls. This meant that in most Southern cities, they met only in black communities. One exception occurred in Charlotte, North Carolina, when Dorothy Parker and Dwight MacDonald joined Taylor for a nationally broadcast forum at the city's five-thousand-seat municipal auditorium, but only after, according to one press report, "at Senator Taylor's insistence...the hall's management agreed to permit a non-segregated audience."[31]

By September, Truman, who had lost the conservative Southern Democrats—they split from the 1948 Democratic Convention to form the Dixiecrat Party behind Strom Thurmond's candidacy—adopted a liberal persona for the campaign. He also "adopted" a number of planks of the Progressive Party's platform-most notably ending segregation in the Armed Forces shortly before Election Day.

More than a million Americans voted for Wallace in 1948—the first substantial third-Party challenge from the left in twenty-four years (and the last in the twentieth century). Yet the vote count for FDR's former vice-president was far lower than Progressive Party leaders had hoped for.* Red-baiting and fear of communism had taken their toll, as well as Truman's dexterity at coopting Wallace's more liberal platform, which increased both the number of Truman's fans and those who voted for him as a "lesser evil" than Dewey.

Following the Wallace defeat, Einstein continued his counterattack, making another—this time, ideological—move. He accepted an offer from a new, small socialist magazine to make public his view that capitalism was a failure. "Why Socialism" by Albert Einstein was the lead article in the first issue of *Monthly Review,* May 1949. Here are a few excerpts:

> The economic anarchy of capitalist society as it exists today is, in my opinion, the real source of the evil....
>
> Private capital tends to be concentrated in few hands...[resulting in] an oligarchy of private capital, the enormous power of which cannot be effectively checked even by a democratically organized political society. This is true since the members of legislative bodies are selected by political parties, largely financed or otherwise influenced by private capitalists....The consequence is that the representatives of the people do not in fact sufficiently protect the interest of the underprivileged sections of the population. Moreover...private capitalists inevitably control, directly or indirectly, the main sources of information (press, radio, education). It is thus extremely difficult and indeed in most cases quite impossible for the individual citizen to come to objective conclusions and to make intelligent use of his political rights.
>
> The crippling of individuals I consider the worst evil of capitalism. Our whole educational system suffers from this evil. An exaggerated competitive attitude is inculcated into the student, who is trained to worship acquisitive success as preparation for his future career.
>
> I am convinced...the only way to eliminate these great evils [is] through the establishment of a socialist economy, accompanied by an educational system which would be oriented towards social goals....A planned economy would distribute the work to be done among all those able to work and would guarantee a livelihood to every man, woman and child.

---

* Wallace's 1,157,063 votes (2.38 percent) were even lower than Strom Thurmond's Dixiecrat vote of 1,169,032. Wallace's highest votes were almost all in predominantly black and Jewish precincts in New York and California.

Einstein obviously did not expect his article to spur a socialist upheaval in America. Yet, perhaps because of the rightward drift of the country in 1949, he felt it an important moment to make his views public. But "public" turns out to be a relative word: When *Time* completed the sanctification of Einstein, the only one of Einstein's elements, ideas, warts, and whims, totally omitted from the magazine's description of their "Person of the Century"—as we have noted—was his advocacy of socialism.

Hoover, of course, had no such problem:

> ... in April, 1949, a circular was distributed ... announcing a new magazine entitled "Monthly Review," "an independent Socialist magazine." The first issue was to corm out as the May, 1949 edition [and] would contain [an] article by Albert Einstein—"Why Socialism."
>   New York report dated 3-15-51
>   Re: "Espionage-CH"[for Chinese—the informant just happened to be an employee of the Chinese Consulate].[32]

Within two years, the escalating Cold War effectively squeezed out the Progressive Party. When Moscow broke into America's A-bomb club in 1949 with successful Soviet nuclear tests, the anti-communist arsenal acquired a major new weapon: fear of the Russian bomb. It was the same year that, as the media reported it, the United States "lost" China. And as Moscow stationed troops in the Soviet-controlled "peoples democracies" throughout Eastern Europe, Wallace, Taylor, and most of the Progressive Party's liberals split from the communists. The Russians said they were defending themselves and the East against "imperialist aggression." Washington and the new NATO military alliance argued they had to set up military bases around the world in order to stop the spread of communism.

To Einstein, who advocated a single World Government, they were both wrong. When Indian Prime Minister Jawaharlal Nehru visited him in Princeton in November 1949, Einstein encouraged Nehru's inclination toward a nonaligned policy. The Indian leader later said their conversation had strengthened his conviction "that India must stand outside the two big blocs and seek rather to…represent the millions in East and West who do not want a global war."[33] But despite Einstein's disagreement with both East and West, he saw the far greater danger from the growing signs of militarism and fascism in the United States and from NATO, which he called "a horror." As he wrote to the poet Christopher La Farge: "You are right in saying that the creation of a world government is the really important objective [but] I consider it most important to oppose the present almost hysterical trend toward complete militarization of this country and open conflict with Russia."[34]

The screaming near-violence outside the Waldorf Astoria during the Cultural and Scientific Conference for World Peace came on the heels of several threats of violence against the Wallace campaign. In one instance, the Veterans of Foreign Wars in New Jersey threatened to assault a Newark public school where left-wing Congressman Vito Marcantonio was speaking. The FBI's Einstein file adds:

> The WALLACE Committee…directed a telegram to Public Safety Director Keenan, Newark, NJ, charging that the avowed purpose of the VFW demonstration was to disrupt the peaceful meeting planned….
>
> …a statement signed by Professor EINSTEIN, along with numerous ,other NJ professors, ministers, lawyers, and other citizens was sent to Governor Driscoll requesting that the VFW permit be cancelled.
>
> The *Daily Worker*…contained an article which stated in part that more than 100 leading NJ professionals headed by EINSTEIN protested [the VFW] demonstration intended to "drown out" a WALLACE rally.

Governor Driscoll allowed the VFW counter-rally. But he also mobilized some two hundred police and state troopers, in uniform and plainclothes, to keep the two sides apart and prevent violence. The *Times* reported that nine hundred Wallace supporters inside the school heard Marcantonio declare that the two major political parties had merged virtually into one, so far as major policies were concerned. Outside, the veterans' counterdemonstration drew fifteen hundred people.

The New Jersey attack was stopped because the governor mobilized the state police to protect the school. But in Peekskill, New York, on Labor Day, 1949, the state police did nothing to stop a mob—also organized by veterans groups such as the American Legion—from attacking a racially mixed audience as it left a picnic-concert featuring Paul Robeson. The aim of the mob was to "get Robeson." Instead, they stoned cars and buses, smashing windows, dragging people out and beating them—more than fifty were hospitalized and one man lost an eye. State troopers stood by smiling—some were photographed joining the mob attacks. Following the Peekskill riot, bumper stickers appeared on cars in the area. One read: "Wake Up, America. Peekskill Did." And another: "Communism Is Treason, Behind Communism Stands—the Jew!"

Einstein saw a link between the growing violence in the streets and the militarization of America. Writing to Wallace in 1949, he described the political mood in America as "half fascistic."[35] It was the eve of McCarthyism.

PART III

Guilt by Associations

9

The List

"Had he gone fishing" for the last thirty years of his life, "his fame would be undiminished," wrote Einstein biographer Abraham Pais, referring to the fact that Einstein produced all his brilliant scientific theories before 1925.[1] Einstein could easily have "gone fishing" politically, too, resting on his scientific laurels, offering only an occasional pontification about the political state of the planet. The press and public would still have revered him, and his quotes would still adorn T-shirts, calendars, and coffee mugs around the world. But Einstein chose to use his celebrity as a political tool to help those he saw as voiceless or under attack because of race, religion, or radicalism. As Fritz Stern has so eloquently put it, Einstein "placed his scientific fame at the service of his moral indignation."[2]

As a result, at least two-thirds of his FBI file's eighteen hundred-plus pages comprise entries, often repetitious, on what the FBI considered his "Red fronts."* Hoover's Bureau dutifully recorded each political affiliation as proof of Einstein's dangerous character. The FBI's file, ironically, contains the most complete listing—the only listing—of the political causes Einstein supported.

---

* Toward the end of 1947, Attorney General Tom Clark issued a list of "subversive" organizations as a "guide" to the Truman Administration's loyalty program. Government employees were considered disloyal and could be fired—thousands were— if they belonged to any listed group or refused to answer questions about present or past membership. The AG could designate any organization as subversive without notifying the group or affording it a chance to refute the charges.

The first such "subversive" list was sent to all FBI field offices on Sept. 15, 1941— months before the United States entered the war. It listed eight groups: the Communist Party USA, the German-American Bund, the American Peace Mobilization, the Washington Committee for Democratic Action, the Michigan Federation for Constitutional Liberties, the National Federation for Constitutional Liberties, the American Youth Congress, and the National Negro Congress. (Whitehead, p. 351, fn. l.)

His political joining, as noted earlier, began during the First World War in Berlin, when, defying the widespread patriotic war fever, Einstein joined the New Fatherland League, which sought to create a "United States of Europe," and with a handful of others, he signed the anti-war "Manifesto to Europeans." Later, Einstein joined the pacifist War Resisters International and also became an advocate of World Government. But it was witnessing firsthand the rise of Nazi terror that primarily directed his choice of causes. After moving to the United States, Einstein, as we've seen, sided with the elected "Popular Front" government of Spain (which included socialists and communists) against Franco's Nazi-backed revolt, and joined Friends of the Lincoln Brigade and several other anti-Franco groups. In the late 1940s, he lent his prestigious name to several organizations defending the left, even communists with whom he disagreed, against what he saw as the far greater threat from the right. In all these cases, Einstein made his joining public. He felt his most useful contribution was to add the weight of his endorsement to anti-fascists and those defending immigrants, minorities, and political radicals he felt were unjustly persecuted. The whole idea was to make his affiliation as widely known as possible.

Indeed, the FBI's references to Einstein's "front groups" almost always cite published news reports or fliers put out by the groups themselves—and then sent in by the Bureau's paid informants. A good clipping service could have done at least as good a job at half the cost. One wonders whether the consciences of these informants bothered them when they submitted public documents as "Confidential Reports." For example:

> A highly confidential source on October 5, 1947, furnished a printed letterhead of the Detroit Jewish Committee to Aid Russian Rehabilitation, Incorporated, to the Detroit Office. This letterhead reflected that honorary chairmen of this organization were Rabbi Stephen S. Wise and Professor Albert Einstein.[3]

Hoover's FBI, to be sure, freely mixed fact and fiction in most of its files. Its methods of surveillance—spying on "suspects," opening mail, phone taps, etc.—as well as cramming its dossiers with reports from informers, whether accurate or not, have been well documented and widely publicized. In addition, the FBI "in some cases…creates a 'public' source by laundering false information* or surveillance-derived data through a planted press

---

* In Charlie Chaplin's case, for example, biographer David Robinson reports (p. 752) that the FBI would secretly feed unfounded stories about Chaplin to Hollywood gossip columnists Hedda Hopper and Louella Parsons, then turn around and cite those "press stories" in Chaplin's dossier: "…the FBI was not only using the gossip of these viperish ladies as evidence, but was also feeding information to them."

story."[4] The Einstein file, too, contains its share of false and fantastical allegations (see Chapter 14). But there should be no mistake about the fact that Einstein did—very deliberately—join, endorse, and sponsor the plethora of political organizations listed in his dossier. (Each group, quite naturally, publicized its Einstein connection.) Where the FBI cites his support for political causes, the Einstein file is not primarily lies, even if its underlying premise—that Einstein threatened to subvert America—is a lie.

Each time Hoover's agents drew up a summary of Einstein's "Red front" affiliations, they included more groups. For several years during the early 1950s, his "subversive" list grew at the rate of nearly one new "front group" per month. It wasn't that Einstein joined so many organizations during those waning years of his life, but that as McCarthy-Hooverism expanded its power, the Subversive Activities Control Board (SACB) and HUAC, the authorities on "subversive" groups, kept enlarging their lists.[5] The 1946 American Crusade to End Lynching, for example, was not included in Einstein's file until 1953. Like the ACEL, many of the later additions to Einstein's list were groups advocating racial equality.[*]

The Einstein file's most comprehensive listing includes seventy "subversive" organizations and fills ninety of the 143 pages in the FBI's August 5, 1953 Summary Report.[6] The items vary in length, but virtually every front-group entry follows a basic formula: first, quotes from the SACB, HUAC, or one of its state-committee clones to "establish" that the group is "subversive" or controlled or influenced by communists; second, Einstein's connection to the group, usually demonstrated through a news clipping, flyer, or letterhead submitted by a paid informant. For example:

NON-SECTARIAN COMMITTEE
FOR POLITICAL REFUGEES

This organization has been cited as a Communist front by [HUAC] and by the California Committee on Un-American Activities...as "among the more conspicuous Communist front groups in the racial, refugee, and alien sub-categories."

[Informant's name blacked out] disclosed that a leaflet issued by this Committee describing a New Years Ball to be held on 12/31/38 to benefit political

---

[*] Several historians have noted the link between McCarthyism and racism. Even as the Red scare was warming up in 1948, the NAACP complained of the "increasing tendency on the part of government agencies to associate activity on interracial matters with disloyalty." (Goldfield, pp. 270-271.)

The case of dismissed Labor Department employee Dorothy Bailey provides a telling example. In her hearing before the Loyalty Review Board, one Board member asked Ms. Bailey, an African-American: "Did you ever write a letter to the Red Cross [to protest] the segregation of blood?" (Schrecker, *Many Are the Crimes.* p. 282.)

refugees from Nazi terror at Hotel Riverside Plaza, New York City, set forth a list of sponsors of the...Ball. According to the informant, the name of EINSTEIN appeared as a sponsor.

As with many of the groups listed, the FBI gives no indication of the group's program or what it does, stating simply that it's "subversive" and that Einstein is connected to it.

Some of the longer items reveal more by quoting from a group's published reports or statements. On occasion, informants might take their own notes, although still reporting public information. Under AMERICAN COMMITTEE OF JEWISH WRITERS, ARTISTS AND SCIENTISTS, for example, the FBI's file includes five single-spaced pages of reports on banquets, benefits, and speeches by its co-chairmen Einstein and author Sholom Asch in support of the causes ranging from Jewish culture inside the Soviet Union to the establishment of Israel.

From the American Council for a Democratic Greece and the India League of America to the Society for Social Responsibility in Science, Einstein's "Red front" list indicates the extraordinary breadth of his social concerns. It would take a separate book to review in any depth the entire FBI roster of Einstein's alleged "communist fronts." But even a somewhat arbitrary listing of the kinds of causes these groups supported offers an insight into Einstein's priorities—as well as the priorities of this country's top law enforcement agency:

Organizations Aiding Victims of and Refugees from Fascism.[7] While most of these organizations offered relief assistance to victims of the Nazis, three groups focused on helping refugees from fascist Spain. One example: Einstein served on the Advisory Board to The Board of Guardians for Basque Refugee Children. In another case:

> Confidential Informant advised that in the latter part of 1941...he observed a list of anti-Nazi writers who had been assisted in reaching safety in this hemisphere by the EXILED WRITERS COMMITTEE.

Other Anti-Fascist Organizations.[8] Several of these were anti-Franco groups, such as Friends of the Abraham Lincoln Brigade, but they also included:

> Confidential Informant advised...that during the week of 12/27/46, the COUNCIL AGAINST INTOLERANCE sent a telegram to then President Harry S. Truman protesting the granting of permanent residence and citizenship to German scientists then working for the US Army...Among the signatures was ALBERT EINSTEIN.

Pacifist and Anti-Militarist Organization.[9] These groups included the Emergency Committee of Atomic Scientists, War Resisters International, and, among others:

> EINSTEIN and 20 other prominent figures, in a book entitled "The Militarization of America," distributed by the NATIONAL COUNCIL AGAINST CONSCRIPTION, issued a warning that America cannot remain democratic if the present trend toward military control of our institutions continues.

John Swomley, who headed the NCAC and put together *The Militarization of America* (1948), a year later put out a second booklet, *New Evidence of the Militarization of America,* endorsed by Einstein, Pearl Buck, Louis Bromfield, and fifteen others. Swomley, retired at eighty-four, but still active in anti-war causes, remembers Einstein's reluctance to endorse the second book. "He was extremely busy and felt it would be hard to take the time to read over. But," Swomley adds with a note of pride, "he did feel the book was very important, so after we talked for half an hour on the phone, he agreed he'd do it."[10]

Organizations Opposing McCarthy-Hooverism.[11] Among these are: Committee of One Thousand [to abolish HUAC], Dirk Struik Defense Committee, and, what really raised a red flag for Hoover, Committees to Defend the Rights of the Twelve [indicted] Communist Leaders, and to Protest the Sentencing of [their] Defense Attorneys.

Organizations for the Exchange of Views among Artists, Scientists, and Professionals.[12] Most of these groups had left-wing agendas, such as support for friendly relations with the Russians or opposition to McCarthyism. The biggest and broadest group in the cultural field was the League of American Writers with more than eight hundred members, including most of the wellknown writers in the country. Besides Einstein, the League counted among its honorary members the President of the United States. (Roosevelt's membership was never announced for fear it might be used by "his right-wing enemies" to attack him).[13] The League was torn apart by internal battles after the Hitler-Stalin pact of 1939, with the communists supporting the pact and most others opposing it.

The FBI's Einstein file targets three additional areas of his "Red front" activities for special attention: the Henry Wallace presidential campaign, discussed in a previous chapter; the Rosenberg case, discussed in a subsequent chapter; and Einstein's many civil-rights and anti-racist organizations.

10

Du Bois and Robeson

If W. E. B. Du Bois's most widely quoted insight—"The problem of the twentieth century is the problem of the color line"—is true, then when "the Person of the Century" speaks out about the problem of the century—speaks out not once but repeatedly, not haltingly but eloquently—it ought to be a significant event. At the very least, as my old City Editor would say, "It's a good news feature. Lots of interviews, profiles, celebrity photos." The problem is, the City Editor didn't agree with Du Bois about the seriousness of racism, or, like most media gatekeepers today, simply preferred not to think about it. As Anna Quindlen recently wrote, "Here's the riddle: why is our most important issue the one no one really wants to talk about?"[1]

Of all Einstein's little-known political and social causes, the least known is his support for civil rights and outspoken opposition to racism. Einstein is quoted on T-shirts, coffee mugs, posters, and calendars, yet nowhere in all this Einsteinia will you find his comment to the *Cheyney Record*, student newspaper at a small black college in Pennsylvania: "Race prejudice has unfortunately become an American tradition which is uncritically handed down from one generation to the next." Also missing are remarks Einstein made to an Atlanta conference of anti-racist educators—and cited in the *New York Times*—ten years before the civil-rights movement: "Every right-minded person will be grateful to you for having united to fight this evil that so grievously injures the dignity and the repute of our country."[2]

To Hoover, whose racial bigotry was not at all secret, every civil-rights group Einstein joined was yet another example of the scientist's unAmericanism to be recorded in his dossier. As a result, while the FBI file fails to mention any of Einstein's anti-racist essays, speeches, or interviews (see Appendix), it includes almost all his civil-rights affiliations. They comprise the largest category in the FBI's list of Einstein's "Red fronts"—twelve anti-racist, equal-rights organizations and campaigns.[3] Besides the American Crusade to End Lynching, here is the FBI's list of Einstein's "Red front"—associations guilty of advocating equal rights:

DEFENSE OF THE SCOTTSBORO 8 [Sic. There were actually 9.]

On July 5, 1931…EINSTEIN, THOMAS MANN, LION FEUCHT WANGER and several others [formed] a "German committee"…in support of "DREISER's committee…to save eight Negroes at Scottsboro, Alabama, from the electric chair.

"Dreiser's committee" refers to Nobelist author Theodore Dreiser, whose "subversive" activities included defense of the nine Scottsboro defendants. The last of the nine to go free was Hayward Patterson, who escaped to Michigan in 1948 after serving seventeen years in Alabama prisons on what the world knew were false charges. In 1950, Michigan's Governor G. Mennen Williams refused to extradite Patterson back to Alabama.

CAMPAIGN TO SAVE SAM BUCKHANNON

The Daily Worker of October 2, 1943, carried an article entitled "Final Hearing Set on Buckhannon Fight" with the subheading "Einstein Joins Defense to Halt Negro Extradition." The article stated in part that Professor Albert Einstein, the world-renowned scientist, was the latest to add his name to those battling to save Sam Buckhannon, 34-year-old Negro who *had served fourteen years on the chain gang* [in Georgia] *for stealing a package of cigarettes*…and that the National Federation for Constitutional Liberties was conducting the fight to save Buckhannan. [Emphasis added.]

After months of protests, a New Jersey judge freed Buckhannon. *(New York Times,* October 9, 1943.)

THE DEFENSE OF WILLIE MCGEE

The Daily Worker of 3/27/51 described WILLIE McGEE as a Mississippi Negro victim of a rape frame-up who was seeking an appeal of a death sentence before the US Supreme Court.

According to the Worker of 4/22/51…EINSTEIN stated in part: "In the face of the evidence, any unprejudiced human being must find it difficult to believe that this man really committed the rape of which he has been accused. Moreover, the punishment must appear unnaturally harsh to anyone with any sense of justice. [Informant blacked out] advised that WILLIE McGEE was a Negro convicted of rape and executed in the State of Mississippi for this crime.

In the eight years McGee spent in Mississippi jails before his execution, the Civil Rights Council won two new trials in his case and several stays of execution, despite death threats whenever their attorneys went to Mississippi. After Supreme Court Justice Harold Burton ordered a stay of execution in July 1950, a *New York Times* report from Laurel, Mississippi, stated: "Several small groups of men...gathered about the court-house building...during the afternoon, expressing resentment at Justice Burton's action and denouncing 'the damn Communists' and 'outside interference.'"

Despite Judge Burton's stay, the full Supreme Court refused—for the third time—to review Willie McGee's case. The night before he was electrocuted by the State of Mississippi, he wrote to his wife Rosalie:

"Tell the people the real reason they are going to take my life is to keep the Negro down.... They can't do this if you and the children keep on fighting. Never forget to tell them why they killed their daddy. I know you won't fail me. Tell the people to keep on fighting.

"Your truly husband, Willie McGee"[4]

After his death, *Time* and *Life* magazines directed angry editorial criticism—at the communists. Not a word about the case itself. But on May 14, 1951, *Time* did come up with an addition editorial target:

To Communists all over the world, "the case of Willie McGee" had become surefire propaganda, good for whipping up racial tension at home and giving U.S. justice a black eye abroad. Stirred up by the Communist leadership, Communist-liners and manifesto-signers in England, France, China and Russia demanded that Willie be freed....Not only Communists took up the cry. In New York, Albert Einstein signed a newspaper ad protesting a miscarriage of justice.

In strikingly similar language, five years earlier, the FBI—in its Einstein file—had called the American Crusade to End Lynching "another Communist attempt to instill racial agitation."

THE DEFENSE OF "THE TRENTON SIX"

The "Trenton Six" refers to the trial and conviction of six Negroes accused of killing William Homer, a Trenton, NJ merchant. According to [informant's name blacked out], the defendants were represented by the Civil Rights Congress and the case has been of interest to the Communist Party of New Jersey.

The Worker dated 6/5/50...: "EINSTEIN and 14 other individuals denounced the court attempts to deprive the Trenton Six of defense by naming attorneys of their own choice and advocated that the public help in the struggle to preserve the Bill of Rights."

DEFENSE FUND FOR NEGRO CITIZENS

A letter from the National Association for the Advancement of Colored People, Legal Defense and Educational Fund...dated August 14, 1943, addressed to

Mr. [Ernest] Hemingway…enclosed a statement signed by more than one hundred leaders in almost every field of American life, an appeal to the addressee to contribute to the establishment of a vitally necessary Defense Fund to safeguard the rights of the Negro citizens.

The signers of this petition included Albert Einstein.

CIVIL RIGHTS CONGRESS (CRC)

[An article in] the *Daily Worker* dated 12/15/48…entitled "Crusade to Capitol on 1/18 Will Urge Civil Rights Laws" [stated] the CRC had announced…that thousands of people would come to Washington…in a gigantic "freedom crusade" to demand payment of [Truman's] election campaign promissory notes on Civil Rights Legislation…sponsors included EINSTEIN.

From 1946 to 1956, the CRC, once called "the most successful Communist front of all time," led the national and international drives to save Willie McGee, the Trenton Six, and several similar campaigns (the Martinsville Seven, Rosa Lee Ingram). The CRC also published the landmark study *We Charge Genocide,* which detailed the lynchings and police shootings of blacks, year by year. The study was submitted as a petition to the United Nations. "Reprinted in many languages and many thousands of copies, this work was an international embarrassment for the US government…"[5] At the same time, the group organized protests in defense of communists arrested under the Smith Act and against what the CRC viewed as the main legal arms of McCarthyism—the Communist Control Act, the McCarran Act, and congressional investigating committees like HUAC.

NATIONAL COMMITTEE TO OUST BILBO

[Informants names blacked out] furnished the Bureau with literature distributed by the National Committee to Oust Bilbo, sponsored by the Civil Rights Congress…Included in this material was letter dated Dec. 4, 1946, signed by Quentin Reynolds and Vincent Sheehan….The names of 55 members of this Committee were set out including that of Albert Einstein.

THE FREEDOM CRUSADE

The conference would be held at the AFL Laborer's auditorium in Washington …sponsors of the conference and the "Freedom Crusade" included Dr. Albert Einstein and others.

SOUTHERN CONFERENCE FOR HUMAN WELFARE

The Southern Patriot of March, 1950…announced that the Southern Conference Educational Fund [will convene] a south-wide conference on discrimination in higher education in Atlanta University, April 8…the New Jersey sponsors of the conference [included] the name of Albert Einstein.

COUNCIL ON AFRICAN AFFAIRS (CAA)

According to the *Daily Worker* dated 4/22/47 in an article captioned, "EINSTEIN says Liberation of Colonies Urgently Needed," Professor EINSTEIN sent greetings to Max Yergan, Executive Director of the Council of African Affairs on 4/21/47 [and] said in part "no reliable or lasting peace will be possible without the political and economic emancipation of the subdued and exploited African and colonial people."

The CAA was founded in 1937 to "push de-colonization and antiapartheid."[6] Robeson became chairman in 1941 and DuBois honorary vice-chairman in 1948.

* * *

If Einstein's support for these organizations and civil rights has been only scantily reported, the legion of his biographers has totally ignored his close ties to W. E. B. Du Bois and Paul Robeson. Hens have more teeth than Einstein's biographies have references to these two giant figures.[7]

In early February 1951, a federal grand jury indicted Du Bois and four other officials of the Peace Information Center for failure to register with the Justice Department as Soviet agents (under the Foreign Agents Registration Act). It was two weeks before the renowned historian reached the age of eighty-three. Einstein's FBI file reports on his birthday party:

DINNER TO HONOR W:E.B. DUBOIS

Counter Attack, a weekly newsletter published by the American Business Consultants, Inc. of New York City, on February 16, 1951 stated…that accused "Foreign Agent DuBois" would be honored at a hotel banquet; that Dr. DuBois' "long record of pro-Communist activities had not deterred approximately 200 people (referred to as 'notables' in Communist Party press) from tendering him a banquet in honor of his 83rd birthday"; that the dinner was scheduled to be held at the Essex House in New York City on February 23.

Counter Attack stated further that the "notable" sponsors included Dr. Albert Einstein and others.

The paper "Freedom…dated February 1951…speaks of the DuBois testimonial dinner: "More than 200 prominent individuals from all sections of the US, among them Dr. Albert Einstein, Mrs. Mary McLeod Bethune, Dr. Kirtley Mather and Paul Robeson [are sponsoring the dinner] to honor Dr. W.E.B. DuBois on his 83rd birthday…in the Colonnades Ballroom of the New York Essex House on February 23.

The February 23 dinner was, obviously, a defense rally for Du Bois as much as a birthday party, and those who attended were making a clear— and bold—political statement. While Einstein's sponsorship of the dinner/ protest was recorded in the FBI's catalogue of "derogatory information," the scientist committed another act Hoover would have considered even more un-American had he known about it. Einstein planned to testify at Du Bois's trial. The prosecution's presentation was so weak that the judge dismissed the case in mid-trial—Einstein had been scheduled as the first witness for the Du Bois defense.[8]

* * *

The FBI's file on Du Bois, like other political dossiers, is filled mainly with lists of meetings, organizations, and other evidence to demonstrate the "danger" he posed to America. But one excerpt provides an interesting, if very sketchy, glimpse into his life during an earlier period, unintentionally relaying some of his insights on history:

> [Informant's name blacked out] stated that the subject is a Professor at Atlanta University and considered to be one of the most outstanding and prominent negroes [sic] in Atlanta...frequently called upon by negro [sic] lodges and Civic organizations to make addresses...
>
> [DuBois] according to this informant, while not a member of the Communist Party, is known to be in sympathy with the Southern Negro Youth Congress....
>
> In order to obtain some indication of [Du Bois's] foreign sympathies, informant read parts of [Du Bois book] "Dusk of Dawn"...On page 266 [Du Bois discusses] the Anti-Lynching bill of 1924 that died with the filibuster in the US Senate: "It was not until years after that I knew what killed that anti-lynching bill. It was a bargain between the South and the West... .lynching was let to go on uncurbed by federal Law, on condition that the Japanese be excluded from the United States."
>
> The writings in this book indicate that the subject is a socialist and does not claim to be a Communist.[*] He appears to favor equality between the white and colored races and the primary purpose of his efforts is the advancement of the colored people.[9]

For having the audacity to be both black and Red, Du Bois and Robeson faced a double-barreled assault from the U.S. government. Although Du Bois won his court case, the news photo of this venerated African-American scholar, at 83, in handcuffs during his arraignment, became a symbol for anti-American protests around the world, along with the denial of a passport to Paul Robeson. Perhaps more significant than Einstein's affiliation with any particular civil-rights group was his solidarity with these two worldrenowned figures—especially his enduring friendship with Robeson.

---

* In 1961, at the age of 93, Du Bois publicly joined the U.S. Communist Party.

Few targets of McCarthy-Hooverism faced so ferocious an attack, and, not unrelated, few had such broad popularity. Athlete, actor, linguist, concert performer, and political activist, Robeson was an authentic Renaissance Man, with devoted fans throughout America and worldwide. Born in 1898, Robeson was the youngest of seven children raised by their father, a former slave who became a minister in the black section of Princeton, the prosperous college town's working-class shadow and source of most of its manual labor.* By the time Einstein arrived in Princeton in 1933, Robeson was long gone (but not, as we have seen, the town's entrenched segregation).

With Princeton behind him, Robeson's star soared. At Rutgers University, despite intense and sometimes violent racism (only the third AfricanAmerican student in the school's history), "Robeson of Rutgers" made sports history as one of the nation's top college football players and was named All American in 1918.** Besides his success at sports—he won an astounding twelve athletic letters at Rutgers-Robeson was a member of the literary society, won several academic awards, and was elected to Phi Beta Kappa, the national honor society. After earning a law degree from Columbia University, he went on to a highly successful acting career, starring in the movie versions of *Emperor Jones, Show Boat* and *King Solomon's Mines*. In 1943, he was widely acclaimed for his portrayal of *Othello* on Broadway (with Uta Hagen as Desdemona and Jose Ferrer as Iago). But above all, it was Robeson's powerful singing voice—"full of

---

* Of his Princeton childhood, Robeson wrote: "I had the closest of ties with these workers since many of my father's relatives—Uncle Ben, Uncle John, Cousin Carraway, Cousin Chance and others—had come to this town and found employment at such jobs... domestics in the homes of the wealthy; cooks, waiters and caretakers at the university, coachmen for the town and laborers at the nearby farms and brickyards." *(Here I Stand,* p. xi.)

** There was no mistaking the reaction of his "teammates." "On the first day of scrimmage they set about making sure that I wouldn't get on their team. One boy slugged me in the face and smashed my nose. That's been a trouble to me as a singer every day since. And then when I was down, flat on my back, another boy got me with his knee, just came over and fell on me. He managed to dislocate my right shoulder." ("Robeson Remembers—An Interview with the Star of Othello," Robert Van Gelder, *New York Times,* January 16, 1944.)

For decades, Robeson's name was excluded from the official college football record book, which listed only ten names on the 1918 All American team (and the 1917 nationally picked team). He was omitted from Rutgers University's 1954 list of its top 65 athletes, and denied a place in the College Football Hall of Fame until 1995, 76 years after "Robeson of Rutgers" graduated. Although not generally known, Robeson played professional football on weekends while attending law school—one of the first black players in the National Football League. (The NFL banned African-Americans in 1934.)

thundering heaven and quaking earth"[10]— in concert and on records that won him millions of fans in dozens of countries. By the end of the 1940s, Robeson was the world's most renowned bass baritone.

He was also—although it was not yet public—near the top of J. Edgar Hoover's enemies list. FBI agents shadowed him, tapped his phone, opened his mail, and fed anti-Robeson allegations to HUAC and the Senate Internal Security SubCommittee.[11] His mammoth FBI dossier contains a long list of his "subversive" affiliations, and reports from informants on his public speeches. The G-men also scrutinized his movies and plays for signs of "subversion."[12] Early in 1943, while Robeson's *Othello* was drawing standing ovations on Broadway, Hoover placed him on the Custodial Detention list—those to be arrested in the event of war with Russia. (At the time, Russia was America's ally against the Nazis.) A few months later, the FBI file listed Robeson as "a leading figure in the Communist Party."

While he may never have actually joined the Party, Robeson was proudly political, and his politics were Red—even when it cost him his lucrative career. On the eve of the anti-lynching demonstration that Einstein co-chaired in 1946, Robeson told a Madison Square Garden rally: "The leaders of this country can call out the army and navy to stop the railroad workers and to stop the maritime workers [two recent strikes]— why can't they stop the lynchers?"[13] Robeson not only opposed racism and advocated the liberation of third-world colonies, he supported the Soviet Union, asserting that their system of socialism was the only way black people could achieve equality.[14]

Between watching Robeson and watching Einstein, Hoover's agents were able to report on a number of their cooperative "subversive" activities, besides the American Crusade to End Lynching in 1946. Earlier that year, the Einstein File records:

> Newark Confidential Informant [number blacked out] advised that the JAFRC [Joint Anti-Fascist Refugee Committee] had a meeting on 1/23/46 at Madison, Wisc., at which time PAUL ROBESON, National sponsor, spoke in behalf of the refugees in Spain. Literature distributed at this meeting set forth the name of EINSTEIN as a national sponsor...

And, in 1947, when Einstein and Robeson joined together in the presidential campaign of Henry Wallace:

> *The Chicago Star,* daily newspaper of Chicago, Illinois, dated 10/4/47, page 2, contained a photograph of EINSTEIN together with HENRY A. WALLACE, DR. FRANK KINGDON of the Progressive Citizens of America, and PAUL ROBESON.[15]

Both Paul Robeson and Albert Einstein supported Progressive Party presidential
candidate Henry Wallace in the 1948 election. From l. to r., Henry Wallace,
Einstein, radio commentator Frank Kingdon and Paul Robeson.

  But there is more to the Einstein-Robeson story. And despite his
extensive watchdog apparatus, Hoover appears to have missed the most
significant episode.

  The two men first met at a concert Robeson gave in Princeton during
the war. Einstein had gone backstage to proffer his congratulations, and
they discovered they shared both a love for music and a hatred for fascism. These were bonds that would grow stronger in the coming years.
In September 1947, there was relatively little risk for Einstein to invite
Robeson for tea—or even to share a photo-op with Henry Wallace. To
be sure, the Red-scare campaign against Robeson had begun, he had
been denounced as a subversive by HUAC and the American Legion and
barred from auditoriums in Peoria, Illinois, and Albany, New York. But he
remained one of the country's most popular figures,* and his concerts continued to sell out. The Peoria and Albany bans appeared as just a couple
of gray clouds, barely foreshadowing the coming storm.

---

* A 1947 Gallup poll found that Robeson was one of the America's "favorite people,"
finishing as one of 48 runner-ups to the top ten. (June 24, 1947, *Look* magazine.)

But things changed dramatically with the 1949 assault in Peekskill, where hundreds of New York State Police stood by, some smiling, as rock-throwing mobs shouting racist epithets attacked cars and buses leaving a Robeson picnic-concert. After Peekskill, Robeson was denied employment—stage and film offers vanished, commercial concert halls were shut to him, and even high schools and universities barred his appearances.[16] In 1950, the State Department decided that Robeson's travel abroad was "contrary to the best interests of the United States," and for the next eight years refused to issue him a passport. His friend Lloyd Brown reports that Robeson was even denied auto insurance, and whenever a black church invited him to appear, the minister received a stream of threatening phone calls.[17] Radio commentators and editorials regularly denounced Robeson as ungrateful to the America-that-gave-him-so-much. By the early 1950s, if you read the headlines and listened to news broadcasts anywhere in America, you might well have thought the unbending bass baritone was Public Enemy Number One.

In spite of—or more likely because of—that atmosphere, Einstein decided to invite Robeson to visit him again. What was relatively safe in 1947, when Einstein had arranged for the photo at his home with Wallace and Robeson, had become dangerous five years later. Friendship with Robeson was now enough to put you on Hoover's "un-American" list. So it was anything but a casual, off-hand gesture when Einstein sent him a message saying he'd be delighted if Robeson would drop by.

"Einstein's invitation was a definite act of solidarity, especially coming after Peekskill," Lloyd Brown remembers. A writer and Robeson's longtime friend and colleague, Brown accompanied him on the visit to Einstein's home in October 1952. Arriving at the house on Mercer Street after lunch, they were greeted by Helen Dukas, who led them upstairs to Einstein, who was reclining on a bed. His health was deteriorating but, Brown says, his mind was sharp and witty. Recalling how much he had enjoyed Robeson's concert years earlier, Einstein asked Robeson to be sure to let him and Helen Dukas know about his next appearance in Princeton so they could attend.

Brown thought it only right to advise Einstein that FBI agents were showing up outside Robeson's concerts to copy down the license numbers of all the cars parked outside.* Einstein turned to his secretary and indicated they could attend the concert without being identified since they didn't have a car. "Of course, we all laughed at the thought of Einstein

---

* "The FBI did that at all kinds of [left wing] events," Brown recalls. "Copied license plates, took pictures; it was something—even at funerals."

coming incognito," Brown says with a chuckle. But behind Einstein's little joke was a serious commitment—he would not be intimidated from supporting Robeson. It set the tone for their afternoon together.

If Einstein's invitation had been simply to make a political statement, only an act of symbolic solidarity, the scientist could have ended the discussion after an hour, quite gracefully. Instead, he and Robeson spent the entire afternoon together, engrossed in ideas. "We didn't leave until it started to get dark outside," Brown remembers. They talked about everything from music (Einstein regretfully said he was no longer able to play the violin) to what was happening in Africa (Einstein was eager to hear about how people were responding to colonialism), and, of course, they discussed resistance to McCarthyism at home. Robeson's description of the visit—the only written account—provides an insight into the mood of the two men and of the times:

> ...It was good, once again, to clasp the hand of this gentle genius. Recalling our previous meetings when I'd appeared there in concert and in *Othello*, Dr. Einstein asked about my life today as an artist, and expressed warm sympathy with my fight for the right to travel.
>
> We chatted about many things—about peace, for Dr. Einstein is truly a man of peace; about the freedom struggles in South Africa, which interested him keenly; and about the growing shadows...being cast over freedom of thought and expression here at home.
>
> Though he is physically frail and not in good health, one can feel the strength of his spirit and the glowing warmth of his compassion for humanity. There was a note of deep sorrow and concern underlying his comments on what is happening in our land.
>
> As he spoke, one could sense something of what this must mean to Einstein, the giant of science and culture, who was driven from his homeland by the Nazi barbarians and who felt the immeasurable tragedy that his people suffered at their hands...[18]

The two men obviously enjoyed each other's company. At one point when Robeson left the room, Brown remembers trying to make conversation by saying, "Dr. Einstein, it's really an honor to be in the presence of a great man." Einstein's response, with just a touch of annoyance, was: "But you came in with a great man."

11

How Red?

One of the most hotly debated of Einstein's political activities was his public appeal for clemency for Julius and Ethel Rosenberg. Arrested at the height of America's spy fever in 1950, they were charged with helping to pass U.S. atom-bomb secrets to the Russians. They were convicted, based primarily on the testimony of Ethel Rosenberg's brother, David Greenglass, who admitted stealing nuclear secrets himself but avoided the death penalty by testifying against his sister and brother-in-law. When he sentenced the Rosenbergs to death, Judge Irving R. Kaufman said they were responsible for the Korean War and American "casualties exceeding 50,000."

By the time Einstein issued his clemency appeal in January 1953, "the Rosenberg Case" had become an international *cause célèbre*. His friend and colleague, Nobel-winning chemist Harold Urey had publicly challenged the government's case, arguing that the hand-drawn designs atom-bomb components that Greenglass said he had made and passed on to the Russians were so primitive they would have been of no value to anyone. In a letter to the *New York Times* on January 5, Urey, one of only five Manhattan Project scientists awarded the Medal of Merit (the highest award the U.S. government can give a civilian), also charged that the couple had been convicted based "on perjured testimony" and called their death sentence "grossly unequal punishment."[1] Within a week of Urey's letter, Einstein wrote to President Truman (with copies to the press) asking him to grant the Rosenbergs clemncy.[2] His appeal cited many of the arguments "set forth by my distinguished colleague Harold C. Urey," but Einstein's primary focus was on the Rosenbergs' sentence: "My conscience compels me to urge you to commute the death sentence."[*]

---

[*] Einstein opposed capital punishment "only because I do not trust people, i.e., the courts." (Letter to Valentin Bulgakov, November 4, 1931: Einstein Archives.)

A month earlier, Einstein had not planned on a public statement. Instead, he had spelled out his position in a private letter to Judge Kaufman, apparently believing that away from the glare of publicity, he might persuade the judge to reverse the death sentence. He may also have believed his letter would have a special appeal to Kaufman as a Jew. But he surely never believed Kaufman would send his letter to J. Edgar Hoover. Yet that's exactly what Kaufman did.* Hoover added it to Einstein's dossier:

> Einstein stated that...the guilt of the defendants was not established beyond a reasonable doubt.
>
> He further stated...his conviction that the ROSENBERGS, in any event, played a minor role in the transmission...of a document prepared by DAVID GREENGLASS...hence it was incomprehensible that they should receive a more severe sentence than GREENGLASS whose crime was confirmed by his own confession.
>
> In addition, of all the individuals found guilty in the past of Atomic Espionage and who no doubt betrayed more important atomic information than the incompetent GREENGLASS, none...were executed.[3]

After more than two weeks with no answer from Kaufman, Einstein decided to "go public" and write to Truman—on January 11, while the President was still in office. Eisenhower had been elected in November and would be inaugurated on January 15, so commuting the Rosenbergs' death sentence could have been Truman's farewell humanitarian gesture. There is no report that Truman made any response to Einstein. The Rosenbergs were electrocuted five months later, despite mounting world-wide protests.

In the past few years, reports from the Venona decrypts—Soviet intelligence cables, intercepted and decoded by U.S. cryptologists—have caused many of the Rosenbergs' supporters to reconsider their innocence. According to Venona, Julius Rosenberg did spy for the Soviets, sending them mainly non-nuclear information, and he recruited others to the spy ring, including his brother-in-law David Greenglass in Los Alamos. The same papers indicate that Ethel Rosenberg played a lesser, primarily supporting, role. On the other hand, former KGB agent Alexander Feklisov tells a different story: On the PBS special, "Red Files," he said that Julius

---

* Kaufman adored Hoover, according to Daniel Yergen, quoting an unnamed former top FBI official: "Hoover was like Jesus Christ to him." (Yergen, *New Times*. May 16, 1975, in The Rosenberg File, p. 288.) In 1999, author Howard Fast, interviewed on WBAI radio, told a story of how Judge Kaufman did not really want to issue a death sentence but that President Truman somehow twisted his arm to make him to do it. But no one coerced Kaufman to send Hoover his private letter from Einstein.

was a spy but did not deliver any A-bomb secrets, just data about radar and sonar. The "atom-spy" charge is not true, he insisted. "America just wanted to kill somebody for the fact that the Soviet Union so quickly built an atomic bomb." Even Haynes and Klehr, whose book *Venona* describes the documents linking the Rosenbergs to espionage, acknowledge it is "unlikely, had the messages been made public... that Ethel Rosenberg would have been executed, [and Venona] would have made Julius Rosenberg's execution less likely." And espionage authority Ernest Volkman calls it "a tragic irony" that "the two most minor members of the [spy] ring, the Rosenbergs, were convicted...and executed [while] the more important assets were evacuated eastward by the GRU" [Soviet Military Intelligence]. Perhaps the most articulate and unflagging critics of the government's case against the Rosenbergs over the years have been Walter and Miriam Schneir. After having investigated the Venona files, the Schneirs are now convinced that Julius did, in fact, spy for the Soviets, providing information on primarily non-nuclear technology. But, they say, the Venona transcripts indicate that Ethel Rosenberg was not involved, and "none of the [trial] testimony so essential in convicting Julius is verified." Venona, therefore, "does not change our opinion of the political purpose of the trial and sentence one iota."[4]

On December 5, 2001, the Associated Press reported:

> Nearly 50 years after convicted Soviet spy Ethel Rosenberg was executed, her brother [David Greenglass] has admitted that he lied under oath to save himself, and says he is unconcerned that his perjury may have sent his sister and her husband to the electric chair.

And on the CBS program *60 Minutes II*, that same evening, Greenglass declared, "I don't care....I sleep very well."

If any single issue was the political lightning rod of America in the fifties, drawing the fiercest fire from both sides, it was the Rosenberg case. Fifty years later, it still roils the passions of both right and left. To the government and (polls showed) to most people in the United States, the Rosenbergs were traitors who stole America's atom-bomb secrets for the Russian menace. But for what was left of the left in America, their cause became a watershed issue, stirring thousands of people in the battered movement to write, speak, and picket, while in the rest of the world, the Rosenberg case—and communist organizers—galvanized mammoth protests.

To this impassioned, left-of-center movement, Einstein, the scientist star, quickly became a political hero as well. Yet he was a maverick even as a left-wing hero. In defending the Rosenbergs, he didn't seek to spur a public confrontation or a political campaign, but simply to convince the authorities to grant clemency. His private letter to Judge Kaufman and subsequent appeal to Truman, timed to arrive before the inauguration of Eisenhower, a Republican and a military man, reflect Einstein's hope that the case could be settled through private discussions. It is clear, too, that his sympathy for the Rosenbergs did not extend to their Clemency Committee. Three months after the execution, Einstein wrote that he felt the Rosenberg case had been "used as an instrument by the communists." In the same vein, veteran science writer Earl Ubell reports that while he was interviewing Einstein in Princeton early in 1953, a student came by to ask the scientist if he would sign a petition for clemency, which the Rosenbergs' Committee was circulating. Einstein answered tersely, "I've already made a statement." He also felt the Rosenbergs' trial defense had been woefully weak, calling it "lamentable" and even "bordering on treachery."[5]

Nonetheless, Einstein continued to advocate clemency for the Rosenbergs, and as the protests grew in size and multiplied in number, his name was held high on placards in a dozen languages and on virtually every continent. In the week before the Rosenbergs' execution, hundreds of thousands of demonstrators marched through the streets of London, Paris (four hundred jailed in clashes with police, one protester shot dead), Rome (a nation wide protest strike by Italian public-service workers), Toronto and Tel Aviv, as well as Moscow, Prague, Warsaw, and many other cities. Clemency pleas came from a remarkably diverse group of prominent figures, including, besides Einstein, Jean-Paul Sartre, Pablo Picasso, the president of France and four former French prime ministers, and Pope Pius XII, an unbending anticommunist.

Even within the United States, Einstein and Urey were far from alone. First hundreds, then thousands joined "Save the Rosenbergs" rallies in Washington* and other major cities. As the execution date neared, the protest campaign snowballed, with letters and telegrams deluging the White House—the number reached 21,300 in a single week, including one letter signed by 2,300 American clergymen. On the day of the execution—at the height of the Red scare-the *New York Times* reported more

---

* The nation's capital posed a special problem for the demonstrators: Save-the-Rosenbergs protesters were permitted to picket the White House, even to keep an all-night vigil there, but were denied service at most Washington restaurants—not because of their cause, but because of their color. They were a multiracial group, and in 1953, in the nation's capital, almost all restaurants, except in the black community, were for whites only. The Rosenberg organizing committee handed each protester who came to Washington a mimeographed list of the five or six downtown eating establishments that would serve black customers.

Front page of the *New York Daily News*, 19 June 1953. Under the headline
"Spies Get 1 More Day," a photo shows people picketing for
the Rosenbergs with signs citing Einstein's support.

than ten thousand protesters gathered in New York's Union Square and in front of the White House.

Demonstrations to save the Rosenbergs were by far the largest U.S. protests the left had mustered since the start of the fifties. They may even have been the first faint signs of a political turnaround in the country. But if so, they were very faint. For most people, anti-communism and fear of dissent were still The American Way. Nationwide, headline hysteria celebrated the execution.* The *New York Daily News* front page trumpeted

---

* In a nationally syndicated "news report" of Ethel Rosenberg's execution, veteran journalist Bob Consodine made no attempt to disguise his venom: "The deceptively softlooking, dumpy little woman, with the mouth of a minnow, walked to the chair with the smug air of a woman who has beaten another to a vacant seat under a dryer in a hairdresser's establishment." *(NY Journal American,* p. 1, June 20, 1953.)

SPIES DIE IN CHAIR. The day before, the *News* front page had displayed a photo of three placard-carrying women who were among "more than 1,900 organized supporters of the Rosenbergs [boarding) a special 16-car train for Washington…hoping to achieve clemency for the convicted atom spies." Their placards read:

THE ELECTRIC CHAIR CAN'T KILL DOUBTS ABOUT
THE ROSENBERG CASE!
"DON'T LET MY MOMMY AND DADDY DIE"—MICHAEL ROSENBERG

and

PROFESSOR EINSTEIN, DR. UREY URGE CLEMENCY

FBI memos alternately picture Einstein as a dangerous Red and an innocent dupe of conniving commies. Leaning toward dupe, one memo asserts:

Professor Einstein has been used by various Communist Front Organizations as a 'big name' 'innocent' [quotation marks in the original] sponsor.

And another:

Einstein has often been found among the ranks of deluded liberals who front for the Communists

On the other hand, in a few Bureau reports, he is a "suspected" member of the Communist Party; another calls him a "Communist adherent," and, as we've seen, one memo weighs in with "highly unlikely [to] become a loyal American citizen." But dupe or Red, what seems most to irk the FBI is Einstein's outspoken criticism of U.S. policies, or what Hoover would call his lack of patriotism:

Einstein…has opposed militarism and universal military training in the United States.…In 1948 he [stated] that the United States was no longer a free country…[6]

Overall, the FBI's dossier quotes remarkably little of Einstein's own opinions. Except for his 1947 pamphlet, "Atomic War or Peace," and a few scattered remarks, it contains virtually none of his published articles, essays, or interviews. Einstein's file bulges with what he belonged to rather than what he believed. While the two are obviously connected, the FBI's focus on affiliations means the dossier's definition of ideas is limited to attaching a pink or Red label to each group.

In fact, Einstein was neither Red nor dupe. Political maverick and individualist, he bowed before no edict simply because it carried a "government-approved" stamp. In a world totally consumed by nationalism and wars, he was an internationalist* and anti-militarist. It was a surefire formula for confrontation with autocracy. Einstein postponed that confrontation—and avoided serving in the Kaiser's army—by leaving Germany at the age of sixteen to live in Switzerland. But fifty years and two World Wars later, Einstein was again—or still—at odds with repression, this time in the United States.

There is a T-shirt, perennially popular among teenagers, that proclaims across its front: Resist Authority! It's not a quote from Einstein, but it could have been. And in the early 1950s, as the authorities running America's Red scare moved farther to the right, Einstein intensified his resistance, defending those most under attack. Just as he did not shrink from Robeson's red glare, Einstein supported several embattled groups that had leftist and communist leaders. Perhaps the most important example was the Civil Rights Congress. Like Robeson, the CRC had close ties to the Communist Party. Besides defending Willie McGee and other African-Americans it saw as victims of racist frame-ups, the CRC publicly supported the more than one hundred CP officials jailed under the Smith Act during the McCarthy/Hoover period.[7] The group's statements pointed to Hitler Germany, where the Nazis had first rounded up the Communists while most liberals shrugged from what they thought was a safe distance.** It was an example Einstein's memory agreed with.

But did Einstein's feeling of "obligation to do good for his fellow men" and "to help the underdog" make him a sucker for whatever group happened to come along with a quick pitch for the common man, as some have claimed? A number of his critics—and some of his admirers, fearing that a touch of red paint might besmirch the Einstein image—have charged he was simply naïve about the groups he backed. A few have suggested he was unduly influenced by some of the left-leaning people around him.[8]

It was in 1947, with the arrival of the Cold War, that the State Department's agent William T. Golden called Einstein "naïve in the field of international politics and mass human relations."[9] Discussing just such allegations, C. P. Snow later wrote: [Einstein] wasn't in the least naïve. What they mean was he didn't think the United States was always 100

---

* "Nationalism is an infantile disease. It is the measles of mankind." (Einstein in Dukas and Hoffman, p. 38.)

** Not all liberals shrugged. Einstein had signed an unsuccessful appeal, along with Kathe Kollwitz and Heinrich Mann, in 1932, urging the socialists and communists to unite behind a single slate of candidates, which would have been able then to defeat the fascists.

percent right and the Soviet Union 100 percent wrong." Ironically, when
Einstein's views, such as his call for World Government, conflicted with
the Soviet line, Moscow supporters, like Brecht,* joined the chorus calling
him naïve—"an eternal schoolboy with a penchant for generalizing about
politics."[10]

The historical evidence—including the FBI's Einstein file—fails to
support naïveté. In fact, it's quite the reverse. Anyone reading through
the scientist's letters finds numerous examples of Einstein turning down
endorsement requests, usually backed by detailed explanations. In 1945,
to cite one typical example, Einstein refused to authorize the American
Committee for Spanish Freedom to use his name in a fund-raising
campaign:

> Although I am convinced that justice is on the side of the Spanish loyalists
> and that the survival of Fascist Spain seriously endangers international sec-
> urity, I do not possess any firsthand information about the facts...attached to
> the fund appeal letter. It would hence not be honest and, indeed, unwise to
> use the popularity and advertising value of my name for the purpose of your
> appeal....I would very soon lose the confidence which many people have in me
> and which enables me to exercise some effective influence....

While Einstein's decisions at times seem to involve extra-fine hair-split-
ting, they leave no doubt about his serious approach. He did not select
groups to support by blindly sticking pins into a Yellow Pages of left-wing
organizations. As Otto Nathan recalls, "Einstein supported what he felt
deserved his support, never without having carefully studied the information...Despite the ever-intense preoccupation with his scientific problems
and the pressure of other work, he often spent many hours discussing a
political or social problem that had been submitted to him."[11] In Einstein's
words, "I have used every opportunity to help the underdog but, of course,
only [when] the person is within his rights."[12] Far from being naïve about
politics, as Holton has put it, "In retrospect, we can see that he had the
skill, at strategic periods of history, to lend his ideas and prestige to the
necessary work of the time."[13]

Einstein's position on Russia, like that of most Americans, vacillated
over the years from lukewarm to cool and back to warm during World
War II, especially when the Red Army broke the back of the Nazi war

---

* Brecht's attitude toward Einstein warmed after the playwright met with Leopold
Infeld in 1952. Shortly after Einstein's death, Brecht began to work on a drama he
intended to call *The Life of Einstein* (analogous to *The Life of Galileo*), and even
discussed plans for an Einstein opera with composer Paul Dessau. Brecht died
before either project could be completed. (Ernst Schumacher, *Drama und Geschichte*,
Henschel-Verlag, Berlin, 1965, pp. 320-322.)

machine. In October 1942—with Soviet Troops locked in the tide-turning battle of Stalingrad—Einstein, according to the FBI's file,

> made public statements lauding the scientific achievements of Russia and has indicated that it is the only country in which equality was not an empty phrase.

It was high praise in a world then, as now, racked by racial and ethnic "cleansing." Einstein's actual statement went farther. When the seemingly unbeatable Nazi juggernaut was stopped at Stalingrad, he, like most of the world, was euphoric. In remarks delivered over the telephone, he told the Jewish Council for Russian War Relief:

> Without Russia, the German bloodhounds would have already achieved their goal, or would achieve it very soon....We and our children owe a great debt of gratitude to the Russian people for having experienced such immense losses and suffering.
>
> [Russia's] conduct of the war has made obvious her great achievement in all industrial and technical fields...and in the limitless sacrifice and exemplary self-denial of every single individual, I see proof of a strong and universal will to defend what they have won... finally, a fact of particular importance to us Jews. In Russia the equality of all national and cultural groups is not merely nominal but is actually practiced...[14]

It was the closest Einstein came to the Russians. His praise faded after the war. On balance, he was decidedly less than cordial toward the Soviets, and grew increasingly critical of the Stalin regime's anti-Semitism. He never visited the USSR. During the 1920s, when the suddenly world-famous scientist traveled throughout the world from Japan to Africa, from Palestine to Latin America, he turned clown a number of invitations from Moscow. Over the years, he had many public disagreements with the Soviets—from 1918 in Germany, when he tried to convince a Berlin audience not to join the communist-led Spartakist uprising, to 1948, when he conducted the debate-in-print with leading Soviet scientists who had denounced his call for World Government.[15] In September 1933, the *London Times* quoted a press statement from Einstein: "I would now like to state that I have never favoured Communism and do not favour it now." He also dissociated himself from several organizations he had joined in Germany during the previous decade, such as the World Committee Against Imperialist War, and Friends of New Russia.[16]

His sharpest point of dispute with the Soviets was their anti-Semitism. On the same day that the *New York Times* reported Einstein's letter asking Truman to commute the Rosenbergs' death sentence, the paper's lead-headline announced:

MOSCOW ARRESTS 9,
LAYS MURDER PLOT
TO JEWISH DOCTORS

The "Doctors' Trial" immediately became a symbol, and nine days later, the *Newark Star Ledger* carried a United Press story stating: "Scientist Albert Einstein yesterday condemned the wave of anti-Semitic purges behind the iron curtain."[17]

The newly released pages of the FBI's Einstein file contain numerous allegations that many of Einstein's closest colleagues—Valentine Bargmann, Peter Bergmann, Leopold Infeld, and Otto Nathan, among others—were Reds, or at least they attended communist meetings. Presumably, therefore, Einstein had, or might have come under their nefarious influence. Here's a typical example (Section 8, p. 91):

> BARGMANN attended CP meetings m the home of Henry Leland Clark.... According to the Informant, Julia Clark had informed him that BARGMANN was a member of the CP [and] an assistant to Dr. EINSTEIN but that EINSTEIN did not know what was going on because "all he knew was mathematics."

The image of an otherworldly Einstein wandering through the world with his head in a far-off mathematical mist is clearly a myth. And if the FBI's implication is that Einstein's Red colleagues—also mostly mythical*—were casting a communist spell over him, their witchcraft certainly wasn't very successful.

Hoover and his Bureau were well aware of Einstein's differences with the Russians. The FBI's initial Ladd-to-Hoover memo on February 15, 1950 includes the fascinating, though unconfirmed, story of the Soviets' letter to Einstein just after World War II, inviting him to move to Moscow, and Einstein's response:

> Professor Kapitsa, under the direction of the Soviet Government, wrote a letter to Einstein inviting him to come and work with Kapitsa in the Soviet Union. Kapitsa stated "in a land of true democracy, free from selfish taint," where they could pursue their scientific research unhampered by restrictions imposed by capitalistic society. Einstein was assured that whatever funds,

---

* Nathan was friendly with the left, but not a CP member. Bergmann and Bargmann even less so. Infeld, who moved to Canada and then to Poland after the war, was the most Red of the group. Stachel's detailed article on their correspondence documents several friendly cautions from Einstein to lnfeld about the difficulties Infeld would face if he carried out his plan [which he did] to live in Eastern Europe. (See also note 8, this chapter.)

laboratories, buildings, equipment, books and assistants he might need would be immediately and completely placed at his disposal.

Einstein replied by a personal letter to Stalin...sent to Stalin through two Jewish members of a trade union delegation...expressed appreciation of the offer but stated that before he could consider it he must ask several questions. His questions in substance were: Why are Jewish scientists not permitted to hold prominent posts? Why are apparently unnecessary obstacles placed in the way of Jewish scientific and research workers? Why were certain Jewish professors of medical science...not elected to the recently created Medical Academy?[18]

Although it is described as a rumor, the story is supported by the fact that Kapitsa sent a similar letter to Niels Bohr in April 1944, after Bohr's escape from Nazi-occupied Denmark, inviting the Danish scientist and his family to settle in the Soviet Union.[19]

But none of these statements mattered to Hoover as long as Einstein supported groups and causes the communists also backed. Since the Reds made major issues out of racism and lynching, anyone, like Einstein, who supported civil rights struggles was at least suspect. This attitude continued into the 1960s, when FBI surveillance and harassment targeted civil rights workers far more than racist activists. That racism might actually *be* a major issue did not fit into Hoover's mind-set.

His only priority was to stop "the atheistic Communist dictatorship [that controlled] one fourth of the Earth's surface and one third of her peoples."[20]

Despite his clashes with Moscow, Einstein was more accurately a non-communist than anti. In January 1954, he wrote to left-wing activist Corliss Lamont, supporting witnesses who refused to answer the are-you-now-or-have-you-ever-been questions from congressional committees. "Party membership is a thing for which no citizen is obligated to give an accounting." Virtually all his life, Einstein viewed fascism as the main enemy, and during his last few years, saw the HUAC congressional investigations as...

an incomparably greater danger to our society than those few Communists in the country ever could be. These investigations have already under mined to a considerable extent the democratic character of our society.[21]

Einstein chose to defend the left publicly against the intensifying attacks from the right. More, he joined with the left to battle what he saw as a sharp and frightening turn toward militarism and unrestrained racism. And while he disliked the Soviet system, he was no fan of the free-market system. His essay "Why Socialism,"[22] as we have seen spells out his view that capitalism is dangerous to the health and welfare of working people:

This crippling of individuals I consider the worst evil of "capitalism."...the young individual...is trained to worship acquisitive success...only *one* way to eliminate these grave evils, namely through the establishment of a socialist economy...

If reading (other than memos and informants' reports) had been part of Hoover's regimen, he could have had a field day with Einstein statements such as: "The economic anarchy of capitalist society as it exists today is, in my opinion, the real source of evil."

Communism, Einstein told Peter Bucky, would—in theory—have been far better for the common people:

The philosophy behind communism has a lot of merit, being concerned with ending the exploitation of the common people and the sharing of goods and labor according to needs and abilities. Communism as a political theory is a tremendous experiment, but, unfortunately, in Russia, it is an experiment conducted in a poorly equipped laboratory.[22]

As conformity and fear choked the questioning out of America's intellectual life, especially ominous to Einstein was the way most Americans shrugged their shoulders at both history and the rest of the world:

Nothing astonishes me quite so much as the shortness of man's memory with regard to political developments.

The Red-scare tactics of the fifties worked on many American liberals,* but Einstein told a Chicago meeting:

The fear of communism has led to practices which have become incomprehensible to the rest of civilized mankind and exposed our country to ridicule.[24]

While "the actual influence of the Communists, and the extent of their infiltration," according to Sayen, "was...grossly exaggerated by the distemper of the times,"[25] Einstein was well aware that Robeson and Du Bois, for example, had close friendships with communists and advocated socialism as the only road to equal rights. But just as he had resisted joining Germany's bandwagon of patriotism during World War I, Einstein refused to let the American anti-communist stampede deter him from supporting what he considered just causes.

Einstein spelled out his position most clearly in a 1954 letter to the American Socialist Party leader Norman Thomas, who was intensely anti-communist:

---

* Morris Ernst, general counsel for the American Civil Liberties Union, secretly collaborated with the FBI for many years during the 1950s (Donner, pp. 146-147), and the ACLU refused to defend members of the Communist Party.

Here is the principal difference...between you and me....I believe: America is incomparably less endangered by its own Communists than by the hysterical hunt for the few Communists there are here (including those fellow citizens whose red tinge is weaker, a la Jefferson). Why should America be so much more endangered than England by the English Communists....No one there works with inquisitions, suspicious, oaths, etc...no teachers and no university professors have been thrown out of their jobs, and the Communists there appear to have even less influence than formerly.

It was an indelible lesson, he told Thomas, drawn from the Nazi horror:

In my eyes, the "Communist Conspiracy" is principally a slogan...which makes [people] entirely defenseless. Again, I must think back to the Germany of 1932, whose democratic social body had already been weakened by similar means, so that...Hitler was able to deal it the death-blow with ease. I am similarly convinced that these here will go the same way unless men with vision and willingness to sacrifice come to the defense.[26]

PART IV

Operation "Get Einstein"

12

"Eleanor Could Have Triggered It..."

Until 1950, the FBI's file on Einstein was really many mini-files—scattered reports and memos collected by the Bureau's local offices around the country and a few reports relayed to Hoover by other government agencies (such as the Woman Patriot diatribe forwarded by the State Department). To be sure, Hoover's agents had kept their suspicious eyes on the scientist and his activities, but their efforts were uncoordinated and unfocused. It wasn't until the start of the fifties—the decade when Hoover's power reached its peak-that the FBI chief decided to "get Einstein" and launched his top-secret vendetta aimed at sabotaging Einstein's popularity and undermining his influence. It started with Eleanor Roosevelt.

Hoover's anti-Einstein operation began on the morning after the former First Lady's initial weekly TV show. Premiering on Sunday evening February 12, 1950, on the NBC network, *Today With Mrs. Roosevelt* couldn't have made a bigger splash. For one thing, the former First Lady tapped into what was arguably the fastest-spreading technology in American history. The Cold War was just one of two phenomena sweeping America in 1950. The other was television. With Europe still reeling from World War II and the rest of the world raging in or near revolutions, Americans by the millions turned their eyes, ears, and rabbit-ears (indoor antennae on early TV sets) inward—tuning in on Tuesday nights to *Texaco's Star Theater* and the inane jokes of Milton Berle. Besides enriching Berle, Howdy Doody, and the World Series, television made the news more immediate and more dramatic than ever before.

But it wasn't the burgeoning TV technology that brought Mrs. Roosevelt's NBC debut international attention. It was the statement of her star guest, the world's most famous scientist. Just two weeks earlier, President Truman had announced America planned "to surge ahead of Russia in the race for military ascendancy" by building a hydrogen bomb "100 to 1000 times" more powerful than the bombs that destroyed Hiroshima and Nagasaki. Now Albert Einstein told millions of viewers that such a superbomb might well annihilate mankind. Einstein's warning was major news across America and around the world. *The New York Daily News* headline writers were as succinct as ever: DISARM OR DIE SAYS EINSTEIN.

The next day, a memo from Hoover to every FBI office in the country requested any and all "derogatory information" they had on Einstein. Did Einstein's public appearance with Mrs. Roosevelt prompt Hoover to launch his secret war against the scientist? At least one knowledgeable observer thinks it's a good bet. "Eleanor certainly could have triggered it," says former FBI official Neil Welch.[1] Hoover's loathing for President Roosevelt's wife was well known. "You know why I never got married?" he once asked a deputy. "It's because God made a woman like Eleanor Roosevelt." He didn't hide how he felt, calling her the "old hoot owl" and mimicking her high-pitched voice in front of senior colleagues.[2]

While his feelings about President Roosevelt were mixed, he and the President had generally gotten along—it was FDR, remember, who gave Hoover his expanded authority to go after subversives, specifically including communists. But Mrs. Roosevelt, the FBI chief was convinced, was a pinko, if not an out-and-out Red, trying to undermine the American Way of Life, doing everything she could to turn her husband against him and to interfere with the Bureau's operations against communism.

Mrs. Roosevelt did view the expanding political power of Hoover and his Bureau with alarm. In a note to her husband in 1943, she wrote about the FBI: "We are developing a Gestapo in this country, and it frightens me." Before he died in 1945, FDR—after years of virtually 100-percent support for Hoover—reportedly expressed similar fears.

To Hoover, Eleanor Roosevelt was not just Eve slipping her man the evil apple, but Eve and the Serpent combined into one vile being. He called her his "deadly enemy" and continued to describe her as "the FBI's most dangerous enemy" fifteen years after FDR's death.[3] Especially rankling to the FBI chief was her continuing support of black equality. "Whenever a black would speak out, he attributed it to Mrs. Roosevelt," one top FBI official said, and after a pro-civil-rights speech by one African-American educator, Hoover told his aides, "If she wasn't encouraging them, they wouldn't be speaking out." One Hoover memo said she was "in love with a Negro." Another attacked her for having given the commencement address at Gibbs Junior College (a historically black school). One Hoover biographer reports that he and Tolson privately called her a "n...-lover."[4]

The "n-word" does not appear in the FBI's Eleanor Roosevelt file, but the attitude does. In 1942, following a secret internal FBI report revealingly

Albert Einstein was the star guest on Eleanor Roosevelt's initial TV Show *Today with Mrs. Roosevelt* just two weeks after President Truman announced that the U.S. would be building a super hydrogen bomb. Einstein denounced it saying "Disarm or Die."

titled, "Survey Concerning Foreign-inspired Agitation Among the Negroes in This Country," the Bureau's Savannah and Birmingham field offices cited rumors "concerning the formation of Eleanor or Eleanor Roosevelt Clubs among the Negroes." FBI Assistant Director for Domestic Intelligence D. M. Ladd sent the following memo to Hoover on this "conspiracy":

> Such incidents as Negro maids allegedly demanding their own terms for working and at the same time stating they were members of an Eleanor Roosevelt Club are typical of the rumors reported to the Savannah Field Division. No substantiating information, however, has been received concerning these rumors. However, it is stated that complaints are received that the cause of the agitation among the Negroes in this area is largely attributed to the encouragement given Negroes by Mrs. Roosevelt. The Birmingham Field Division has received a report...that attempts in that area are being made to form Eleanor Clubs by a strange white man and a large Negro organizer traveling in an automobile. The unverified information indicates that only female domestics are desired for membership. The alleged slogan of the club is "A White Woman in the Kitchen by Christmas" inferring that Negroes [should] work only part of the day. Similar clubs are claimed to be in operation in other cities in Alabama.[5]

Despite the absence of any legal authority, Hoover ordered his men to pursue these rumors. He soon learned from another informer in New Orleans, that…

> practically every negro [sic] knows of these [Eleanor] Clubs and that they are places to patronize. As you know, the Bureau has made many inquiries in an effort to obtain specific information concerning the existence of such Clubs, which inquiries have met with negative results. [Ladd said he would press the informer to furnish more specific information concerning his allegation relative to the existence of the Eleanor Clubs.]

We can't be certain of course that it was Eleanor Roosevelt's TV show that prompted Hoover to make his move against Einstein, but we can certainly picture the FBI chief picking up his *Washington Post* the next morning and glaring at the front-page headline:

GIVES VIEWS ON VIDEO

EINSTEIN FEARS HYDROGEN BOMB

MIGHT ANNIHILATE "ANY LIFE"

(Picture on Page 3)

Hoover's well-known (and feared inside the Bureau) temper must have neared the boiling point as he read the *Post* story:

> Prof. Albert Einstein said today that if the H-bomb is developed "annihilation of any life on earth" is "within the range of technical possibilities."
>
> Einstein called the present armament race between the United States and Russia "a disastrous illusion."….He said a "supranational" body would be necessary…
>
> …Einstein's statement was part of Mrs. Franklin D. Roosevelt's first television show over the NBC network.
>
> ….Einstein said the fact that the United States first produced the atomic bomb had fostered the illusion that this country could achieve security through military superiority…led to establishment of military bases around the world [and] "concentration of tremendous financial power in the hands of the military…."
>
> ….Einstein said the armament race now "assumes hysterical character….In the end," he added, "there beckons more and more clearly general annihilation."

One can almost see Hoover seething—this was a typical pacifist-pinko call to surrender, to lower America's guard against the Russians. Hoover would surely have focused, too, on a small paragraph toward the bottom of the article in which Einstein warns against the increasing

> close supervision of the loyalty of the citizens [and] intimidation of people of independent political thinking.*

---

* Einstein's warning could not have been closer to the mark. One month later, on March 19, Paul Robeson became the first American to be banned from television when

To the FBI chief, words like that from such a popular figure with obvious headline-making power were not only un-American, they were a serious threat. What might be called "Operation Get Einstein" was launched the next morning.

But while the speech on Mrs. Roosevelt's TV show might have been the immediate trigger, the basic cause of Hoover's attack on Einstein was the changing political climate—the plunge into the Cold War. For most Americans, the fifties may have been the closest thing to living on Prozac—big cars, suburban lawns, and Lucy and Desi on TV—but happy days shared the decade with a long night of political fear. Einstein was one of the few individuals whose popularity spanned both cultures, suburban and subterranean, which made his dissenting politics particularly threatening to Hoover. To understand the FBI chief's anti-Einstein offensive, it's useful to review some of the events shaping America's political mind-set in early 1950.

Midway through what would later be proclaimed "The American Century," the nation suffered a severe case of spy fever. In September 1949, President Truman announced that the Russians had tested an atomic bomb and the United States was no longer the only nuclear power. The President assured Americans there was nothing to worry about. But Americans worried, their fears reinforced by banner headlines. The national mood may be at least partly imagined from a sampling of front-page spy stories during a single week in February 1950:

REDS GET OUR BOMB PLANS
BRITON HANDS ATOM SECRETS TO RUSSIANS

SPY ROAMED U.S. ATOM PLANTS

SMASH RED SPIES, CONGRESS DEMANDS IN H-BOMB LEAKS

540,000 REDS IN U.S., HOOVER TELLS SENATORS
Report Alarming, Says Senator Capehart

FUCHS ADMITS GIVING SOVIET
ATOM SECRETS FROM 1942 ON

ATOMIC SPIES SHIELDED
BY U.S. OFFICIAL LAXITY[6]

The 1950s began with the conviction of former State Department official Alger Hiss on two counts of perjury for denying he had relayed government secrets to the Russians. He was convicted largely on the

---

NBC barred his appearance on the very same program, *Today With Mrs. Roosevelt.* NBC Executive Vice-President Charles Denny declared: "No good purpose would be served by having him speak on the issue of Negro politics." (Stewart, p. xxxiii.)

testimony of ex-communist Whittaker Chambers, who claimed to have hidden microfilms Hiss had given him inside a hollowed-out pumpkin. American headline writers made "The Pumpkin Papers" a household term, and Chambers's book *Witness* became a best-seller. Hiss served a five-year prison term, but throughout his life he never stopped insisting he was innocent. Hiss was just the first of many "spies" who would soon be uncovered, promised HUAC's rising young Republican congressman from California, Richard Nixon.

Within weeks of the Hiss conviction, three separate events occurred that signaled America's political direction for the decade:

January 30: Truman announces America will launch a crash program to build a hydrogen bomb "more powerful by far than the atom bomb." The nuclear arms race is public policy.

February 9: Wisconsin Senator Joseph McCarthy, speaking to the Women's Republican Club of Wheeling, West Virginia, attacks the State Department for harboring communists:

> I have here in my hand [waving a piece of paper that was never shown to any-one] a list of 205 that were known to the secretary of state as being members of the Communist Party and who, nevertheless, are still working and shaping the policy of the State department.[7]

Although the Red scare had already begun, the senator's Wheeling speech is often cited as the beginning of McCarthyism.

February 2-10: Klaus Fuchs is arrested in London and confesses that during and after the war, he stole America's atomic-bomb secrets and passed them to the Russians.

"Red Spies" would be front-page stuff for months as Americans awoke to a new and more sensational "case" almost every week: Judith Coplon, Owen Lattimore, William Remington, David Greenglass, and Ethel and Julius Rosenberg. Meanwhile, magazine covers (pulp fiction as well as news weeklies) shouted cloak-and-dagger exposés from the nation's newsstands. The FBI's media people produced their share of such pieces over Hoover's byline, with titles such as "How Communists Operate," "Unmasking the Communist Masquerader," and "Underground Tactics of the Communists."[8] For Hoover, the Red-spy menace was a familiar refrain. The FBI chief had begun sending warnings to the White House about communist plots almost as soon as the war had ended. As early as February 1946, he told Truman that he had evidence the Soviets were planning war against America—he had heard from "American Communist sources" that Red-led uprisings were scheduled in France within six weeks as the first move of a Soviet operation aimed at placing Red Army troops on the Atlantic and Mediterranean seacoasts.[9] While Truman had ignored most of

Hoover's early memos, now that the Russians had the bomb, the President, as well as the press and millions of Americans, was beginning to listen.

Following Fuchs's confession, congressional committees and the media focused the spotlight of suspicion on scientists. While individuals such as Shapley and Condon had been singled out earlier, now virtually the entire scientific community was a target. The primary rationale was the specter of nuclear war. Russia had developed the atomic bomb sooner than expected, thanks at least partly to information supplied by several British and American scientists. Therefore, went the McCarthy-Hoover argument, scientists as a category must be closely watched. HUAC recommended that every applicant for a fellowship from the National Science Foundation be required to obtain security clearance, and Congress voted to require FBI checks on AEC fellowships, whether or not the research involved classified work. In a classic example of the McCarthyite mind-set, California's ultra-conservative Senator William Knowland declared: "There's always a chance that some student, even if engaged in non-secret studies, might hit upon a 'superduper' atom bomb and be off to Russia."[10]

In "security-sensitive" jobs or not, scientists continued to be fair game for Red hunters throughout—and beyond—the 1950s. The government's loyalty and security-clearance boards had a field day. In any single year during the 1950s, between twenty thousand and fifty thousand scientists, engineers, and technicians were not working, according to the *New York Times,* while they awaited security clearance.[11] At the Department of Health, Education and Welfare, some two hundred scientists, including Nobel laureate Salvador Luria, were victims of a secret blacklist that continued well into the 1970s. Every name suggested for an HEW advisory board was first run through the HEW Office of Internal Security's "National Agency Check"—a list of suspected radical scientists, supplied by the FBI and HUAC. If the name fit, that was it. HEW simply dropped the candidate without a word to him or her. There was no appeal—you can't challenge something you don't know about.[12]

"Fear!" is the one-word response from Leon Lederman, Nobel Prize--winning physicist, when asked what he recalls most vividly about the 1950s atmosphere among young scientists. "We were so scared at Columbia [University] in 1952," Lederman says, "that we were afraid to come out publicly for Stevenson" [Adlai Stevenson, Democratic Party candidate for President]. Other scientists echo Lederman's memories. "That's exactly right," says Sam Seifter, retired biology professor at Albert Einstein Medical College. "When General MacArthur came back from Korea after Truman fired him in 1951, there was a mammoth parade for him in New

York. At Downstate [then the Long Island College of Medicine], we were afraid to criticize the parade, to speak out in support of Truman. Afraid to support the President!* And that was in New York. Imagine what the fear must have been like in the M idwest."[13] The FBI file shows that Einstein frequently lent his support to scientists who resisted. Here is one example:

> DIRK J. STRUIK, Professor of Mathematics, MIT, was indicted during 9/51...
> for conspiracy to teach and advocate the overthrow by force and violence of
> the governments of...Massachusetts and the USA....
>   Informant advised that ALBERT EINSTEIN issued a check...[for] ten
> dollars ($10.00)...payable to the Struik Defense Committee...[14]

Nearly half a century later, Dirk Struik—at the age of 104—did not recall the ten-dollar check, but his memory of Einstein was clear:[15] "I first met Einstein when I was a student in Leiden during the war [World War I]. He was living in Berlin, but was a friend of our professor, Paul Ehrenfest, and would often come to visit him." Struik, an internationally eminent mathematician and avowed Marxist, said that following his arrest in 1951, "I went to see Einstein in Princeton to thank him for supporting my Defense Committee. I was still young, only in my fifties, Einstein was in his seventies. I remember exactly the first words he said as I walked in: 'So you are the man who is so dangerous!'" Struik chuckled: "Einstein was a good man—and quite witty."**

---

* Not without reason: When MacArthur, who had advocated bombing China during the Korean War, thus risking a world war, was fired by Truman, the general received a hero's welcome from a nation in the throes of the Red scare. New York City Schools Superintendent William Jansen organized "welcome-home" celebrations in all the city's schools to honor the returning general. Norman London, a teacher at Junior High School 52 in Manhattan, was reported by his principal for refusing to participate, and Jansen immediately announced he would take appropriate action. After two years of interrogations and hearings, London was fired.

** In the wit department, Struik held his own: When a reporter asked him to explain how he had managed to live so long, he replied: "I've lived this long because I didn't die." (Boston Globe, April 20, 1999.) The indictment against Struik was dismissed in 1955, and he returned to MIT. Did anyone ever apologize to him? "Not exactly, but when I was ninety-two, I got a special certificate from the governor of Massachusetts," he said matter-of-factly. "And when I was one hundred, they gave me another one." Dirk Struik died on October 21, 2000, at the age of 106.

13

Spy Hunt: Fuchs

While Hoover and his agents were shadowing Einstein's Emergency Committee of Atomic Scientists from 1946 to 1948, trying to lock America's barn door, the nuclear horse had already been stolen. Of all the certain and suspected Soviet spies making headlines in 1950, none did more to destroy America's nuclear monopoly than Klaus Fuchs. The Fuchs case also led to J. Edgar Hoover's first espionage allegations against Einstein.

Dr. Klaus E.J. Fuchs, a German-born naturalized British citizen, was one of some twenty scientists the British government sent to the United States in December 1943 to take part in the Manhattan Project. Intimately involved in the development of the atomic bomb, Fuchs remained in the United States until June 1946, attending a secret postwar conference on the projected hydrogen bomb. During his U.S. stay, Fuchs lived and conducted his research at the top-security nuclear laboratories in Los Alamos, New Mexico.

America's first gated community was built on a high New Mexican mesa. The guarded barbed-wire fence surrounding Los Alamos was designed to keep secrets in as much as to keep intruders out.* Besides

---

* "Several of the European-born [scientists and their families] were unhappy," Laura Fermi later wrote: "because living inside a fenced area reminded them of concentration camps." (*Atoms in the Family,* p. 201.) A second guarded barbed-wire fence—a wall within a wall-surrounded the research laboratory, "emphasizing," according to Richard Rhodes (*Atomic Bomb,* p.355), "that scientists and their families were walled off where knowledge of their work was concerned not only from the world but even from each other." Edward U. Condon, objecting to the tight restrictions, resigned after serving for just ten weeks as Oppenheimer's deputy at Los Alamos. The government had set up other barbed-wire "communities," most shamefully the "internment camps" where thousands of Japanese-Americans were imprisoned during the war years. But Los Alamos was the first gated community where residents moved in voluntarily.

guards at the fences, MPs patrolled the Los Alamos grounds, while Army security agents maintained constant surveillance, frequently interrogating Manhattan Project scientists, including (perhaps especially) Director J. Robert Oppenheimer. G-2 and the FBI also monitored all incoming visitors and outgoing trips.[1]

One physicist the FBI actively pursued and almost arrested during the war was Joseph Rotblat, who resigned from the Manhattan Project and left Los Alamos in December 1944 after learning from one of the Project's top military officials that the atom bomb was no longer needed to defeat the Germans—the original reason for building it—but was intended primarily to intimidate the Russians. Forty years later, Rotblat won the Nobel Peace Prize, but at the time, the G-men suspected he was a Russian spy.

It doesn't take a nuclear scientist to figure out that a man stealing atomic secrets doesn't walk away in the middle of the Manhattan Project. But the FBI "discovered" that Rotblat was an amateur pilot (something well known by his colleagues), and the Bureau seemed to fixate on that "due." While most spies, even before the Internet, managed to send secrets quite effectively with coded messages, shortwave radios, and undercover couriers, the Feds decided that the Polish-born Rotblat was planning to charter a small plane in London and fly to his native Warsaw and then to Moscow, carrying the A-bomb secrets with him. Apparently searching for evidence, Hoover's agents seized a wooden crate containing Rotblat's books and papers, including all his research notes. They never reported finding any evidence, but Rotblat never again saw his papers.[2]

(To a large extent, Rotblat has been carrying forward Einstein's political banner. The 1995 Nobel Peace Prize honored Rotblat, at eighty-seven, for his forty years of leadership of the international Pugwash Conference, the anti-war group first proposed by Einstein and British philosopher and educator Bertrand Russell. Signing the call for such an organization was Einstein's last political act before he died in April 1955. A few months later, the Russell-Einstein Manifesto was issued and the Pugwash Conference launched.)

While the FBI was rummaging through Rotblat's research and tailing him day and night, at Los Alamos, the extensive security measures were like a Swiss-cheese wall to Fuchs, who continued to collect and forward valuable information to the Soviets. (Although not publicly revealed until years later, a second master spy, Harvard-trained Ted Hall,* also had little

---

* Hall was on Hoover's spy-suspect list in 1950, but the FBI failed to find a smoking gun. The Hall story became widely known only in 1997 with the publication of *Bombshell* by Joe Albright and Marcia Kunstel.

trouble piercing the porous "protection" at Los Alamos and relaying top-secret A-bomb data to Moscow.) How much did Fuchs actually contribute to the Soviet atomic bomb? Although the question was debated for many years, by now there is little doubt that he saved the Soviets at least two or three years in producing their A-bomb. Markus Wolf, the former East German spy chief, citing Russia's top nuclear scientist, says that Fuchs "made the greatest single contribution to Moscow's ability to build an atom bomb."[3]

But how could Fuchs have known "details on Plutonium" since, as historian Greg Herken points out, "Fuchs worked primarily in the area of Uranium enrichment, not the chemistry of Plutonium"?[4]

A startling, previously unpublished explanation comes from Rotblat. Interviewed in the Pugwash Conference's London headquarters in 1996, the amazingly vigorous eighty-eight-year-old reported that immediately after the war:

> [T]he US, Britain and Canada set up a tripartite committee to review all the research produced by the Manhattan Project to see which of the valuable scientific papers could be released without compromising their national security. Each country assigned one scientist to the committee and for almost two years, 1946 and 1947, the three scientists reviewed *every single research paper* from the top-secret project. The U.S. scientist on the committee was Robert Marshak, the Canadians sent G. M. Volkoff, and the British representative on this top-security group was Klaus Fuchs.[5]

When he was arrested in February 1950, Fuchs was chief of the Theoretical Physics Division of the British Atomic Energy Research Establishment at Harwell. In his confession, he said he'd given the atomic-bomb secrets to the Russians because of his devotion to communism. On March 1, he pleaded guilty and received the maximum fourteen-year sentence under the British Official Secrets Act.

Whatever damage the Fuchs case did to U.S. national security,* some Washington officials seemed more concerned about America's wounded national pride. The biggest spy case in modern history, the theft of the atom bomb—America's bomb—had taken place right under America's nose, and now the spy who got away had been arrested by the British! Perhaps trying to shift the public blame overseas, some congressmen tried—publicly at least—to convince the British to send Fuchs to the

---

* MIT physicist Philip Morrison, who worked in the Intelligence section of the Manhattan Project monitoring the Nazis' science efforts, provides an unusual perspective: "The Russians had actually done better work themselves than what they got from the Americans via Fuchs, but they were too timid to implement their own work, so they copied the Americans and got second-rate." (Interview, July 22, 1997, at MIT.)

United States for trial. While Capitol Hill orations made good home-state headlines,* it's unlikely that even an American senator would actually have expected the British to extradite their prize catch of the century. Besides, with anti-U.S. sentiment on the rise among Western Europeans, increasingly turned off by America's obsession with catching communists, London was in no mood to share Fuchs with Washington. It was three months before the Brits would even allow FBI agents to interview Fuchs in jail.

But the Oscar for buck-passing was won hands down by General Leslie Groves, former military commander of the Manhattan Project. In a statement not designed to win friends in London, the general publicly blamed the British. "I would not have permitted British participation in the Manhattan Project," Groves told the *New York World Telegram* two days after Fuchs' arrest, adding that he would have allowed "Americans only."[6] (It's likely that no one appreciated Groves' flag-waving more than Ted Hall, the un-apprehended, all-American atomic spy from Harvard.) Groves' Monday-morning patriotism would have excluded not only the British, who played a key role in the Manhattan Project, but top physicists such as Fermi, Szilard, Teller, Bethe, Wigner, and more. Without foreigners, it's unlikely that the Manhattan Project could have produced a firecracker.

Hoover and his Bureau also faced a potential public-relations bit from the Fuchs case. The entire Manhattan Project, after all, had been under constant and intense surveillance by the FBI and G-2. The Bureau's official statements emphasized that it had provided Scotland Yard with vital information enabling them to nab Fuchs. Relying on intercepted and decoded Soviet messages (the Venona papers), the FBI and other agencies had, in fact, helped Scotland Yard zero in on Fuchs. But it was the British police who made the arrest and drew out his confession, and from there, Hoover knew, it could be just a short editorial jump to: Their cops outdid our cops. Behind the press releases, "All hell broke loose at Bureau headquarters" when Hoover heard about Fuchs, according to Robert Lamphere, the FBI's intelligence liaison officer for the military.[7]

When Fuchs signed his confession, he also implicated an unnamed American contact man, and Hoover pulled out all the stops, determined

---

* Headline in the *Boston Herald*, Feb.6: CONGRESS PONDERS FUCHS EXTRADITION. BRITAIN IS UNLIKELY TO TURN HIM OVER. *The Washington Star* on February 8 reported an effort by Michigan's Republican Senator Ferguson (an avid supporter of Hoover) to get Attorney General Howard J. McGrath "to try to extradite Fuchs from Britain for trial in an American court." (FBI Einstein file: Correlation Report 65-58805-A Jan. 1953, p. 1055.) The effort got nowhere with the British, but made headlines for Ferguson in Michigan.

to find Fuchs' accomplice, and quickly. With the media in a feeding frenzy for spies, the FBI chief mobilized special teams of agents across the country to launch a search. The Bureau soon had a list of more than five hundred suspects.[8] (The Venona messages showed that a number of Americans had been spying for the Russians, so even after Hoover's agents arrested a chemist named Harry Gold as Fuchs' accomplice,* the search for spies continued.)

Scientists, as we've seen, were especially suspect during the 1950 spy frenzy. To conservative, McCarthy-era congressmen, scientists were dangerous intellectuals, many of whom were also "foreigners" and/or Jews. It was a rationale that fit perfectly with Hoover's lifelong biases. Among the scientists he placed under close FBI surveillance for several months were two Manhattan-Project physicists (foreign-born, Jewish, intellectual), Hans Bethe and Edward Teller. Bethe, in a comment reflecting possible sympathy for Fuchs, had reportedly stated: "A scientist is of the world and works for the world." Most suspicious to Hoover was that Bethe made the comment "off-record" (it was nonetheless reported to the FBI). A few years earlier, Bethe had criticized the rising level of fear in America: "Perhaps the greatest impediment to the scientist...is the political climate of the country."[9]

Hoover had even more qualms about Teller, who, ironically, emerged as among the most politically conservative of the Manhattan Project scientists, testifying in the government's 1954 investigation of Robert Oppenheimer.** Hoover put Teller high on his spy-suspects list. Teller and his wife Mici had been close friends of Fuchs in Los Alamos, and in 1946, Teller had recommended Ted Hall for graduate work at the University of Chicago. On July 26, 1950, Hoover sent a memo to all bureaus: "Imperative to determine if Edward Teller is a Communist Party member or sympathizer." After several months, the investigations of both scientists were dropped for lack of evidence.[10]

In Einstein's case, on the other hand, Hoover had no shortage of leads. During the early spy-hunt months of 1950, a slew of accusations linking Einstein to Soviet spy operations arrived at FBI headquarters. And while allegations are not evidence, if it had been anyone but Einstein, the FBI chief would have had him subpoenaed and grilled by congressional committees. But Einstein had too much international support and sympathy—Hoover knew enough to wait until he had his pins lined up before making his move.

---

* "The Crime of the Century" Hoover called it in a *Reader's Digest* article, describing in none-too-modest terms how his men caught Gold. (RD, July 1951.)
** Known as "the father of the H-bomb," Teller was also the architect of President Reagan's costly and technologically dubious "Star Wars," or Strategic Defense Initiative.

If Monday, February 13, 1950—the day after Eleanor Roosevelt's television show—was like most workday mornings for Hoover, "James"* arrived as usual at 8:30 A.M. sharp to pick him up in the bulletproof black Cadillac. As usual, they swung by to pick up Tolson. And as usual, he and Clyde would stride into the office together at nine on the button. That gave them less than half an hour to discuss what to do about Einstein.

Clyde Tolson had been Hoover's number one deputy since 1931. The two not only spent much of their weekends and evenings together, they discussed virtually every case. (It was this closeness that first led to wide spread whispers that they were secret lovers.)

Born in Laredo, Missouri, in 1900, Tolson had come to Washington at eighteen to work as a clerk in the War Department. Within a year, he was confidential secretary to Secretary of War Newton D. Baker. Tolson replicated this phenomenal rise up the ranks when he joined the FBI in 1928. William C. Sullivan, the Bureau's number-three man before his falling-out with Hoover, described Tolson as "a man of unbelievable narrowness, provincial and reactionary...Nothing...would put him in the category of being a brain." He may not have been a deep thinker, but according to Assistant FBI Director Robert Wick, Tolson had "a photographic memory." Wick also reported that Hoover "never made an important decision without consulting Tolson," a point echoed by Hoover's friend George E. Allen: "[Hoover] discussed every decision with Clyde. Clyde had as much to do with running the FBI as Hoover did..."[11] If, as seems likely, Hoover decided on a counterattack against Einstein, it is a virtual certainty that he first discussed it with Tolson, probably on the drive into the office that morning.

Going after Einstein would not be easy, but if Hoover and Tolson needed a hook to hang their attack on, they didn't have far to look. Newspapers across the country, as well as radio commentators like Hoover's friend Walter Winchell, were rushing to join the national spy-

---

* Special Agent James Crawford was one of only six black FBI agents in 1950. Just as in 1946, as noted earlier, they included two other chauffeurs, one in La Jolla and one in Miami for Hoover's vacations there; a messenger, Worthington Smith; and Hoover's inoffice coat-taker, Sam Noisette. When World War II started, Hoover made all of them agents so they wouldn't be drafted. (Powers, *Secrecy and Power*, p. 323.) Crawford had never been the Boss's bodyguard, although some black publications seemed to prefer to describe him that way. When reporters, almost always from black publications, asked him, he said he was proud simply to be Hoover's chauffeur. According to Gentry (p. 19), he never carried a gun. For form's sake, he had gone through the FBI's Quantico training school—living in segregated quarters, alone. The sixth black agent, highly skilled veteran detective James Amos, was kept in the office supervising weapons inventory in the Bureau's New York district until his death in December 1953. (O'Reilly, pp. 29-30.)

hunt obsession, and editorials called daily for more arrests. The Hearst-owned *New York Journal American* had just run the first installment of a five-part series under the headline ATOMIC SPIES SHIELDED BY U.S. OFFICIAL LAXITY. The front-page story included a brief, undocumented allegation linking Einstein to Klaus Fuchs:

> In 1942, the British spy was in an alien detention camp in Canada, and according to his father "was released ...on the recommendation of Albert Einstein"... to work on the A-bomb in the United States.

The five-part series was written by Howard Rushmore,* who soon signed on as an investigator and speechwriter for Senator M cCarthy.[12] s Rushmore, the paper informed its readers that another staff member, former FBI agent Larry E. Kerley, had contributed to the series.

Whether or not Hoover and Tolson had already read the Rushmore article, Tolson's "photographic" memory almost certainly recalled several memos he had read over the past two or three years suggesting an Einstein connection to the Russians and to Fuchs. And unless you were Rip Van Winkle, you couldn't have missed the spy headlines shouting from every front page in America.

Shortly after arriving at his office, the man called "the Boss" by just about every agent in the Bureau summoned his chief of Domestic Intelligence, D.M. "Mickey" Ladd, and ordered a full report on Albert Einstein. Ladd was Hoover's man in charge of the Einstein case for five years. In Ladd, Hoover had a deputy director who would consider it quite natural, even likely, that the world's greatest scientist might be a Red agent. Ladd's political views were, if anything, farther to the right than Hoover's. Ladd's ultraconservative character comes out in his memo on Mrs. Roosevelt, cited earlier. But even more revealing is a comment from Russian superspy Kim Philby. When Philby, posing as a conservative, was posted to Washington as liaison chief for British Intelligence, Ladd became his fast friend. Twenty years later, during an interview in Moscow, Philby said: "This astonishingly dense person [Ladd] tried to convince me in all seriousness that FDR was a Communist agent."[13]

Above all, Hoover knew Ladd would understand the need for absolute secrecy in this case—the embarrassment it would bring to the Bureau (and to Hoover) if the world learned the FBI was investigating Albert Einstein.

---

* Rushmore was such a loose cannon that Hoover and Tolson never trusted him, and even McCarthy didn't keep him long. The next rung up (or clown) Rushmore's career ladder was a two-year stint as editor of the gossip-titillating publication, *Confidential*. In January 1958, Rushmore, in the back seat of a New York taxi with his ex-wife, took out a pistol and blew first her and then his own brains out.

He was not only the world's most popular scientist, he was America's most famous refugee from Germany, and World War II was still fresh in everyone's memory. From Ladd's memos, it's clear that Hoover gave his deputy director forceful instructions to use the utmost "discretion" in the Einstein case. Translation: If this gets out before we're ready, heads will roll. And if Ladd didn't understand, at least he wouldn't raise any questions. The son of Senator Edward Freemont Ladd of North Dakota,* Mickey was not known in the FBI for his intellectual agility. He had risen through the Bureau's ranks due primarily to his—to put a kind term on it—loyalty to the Boss.

But if he was Hoover's yes-man, Mickey Ladd was an important yes-man—with a good number of yes-men of his own to carry out instructions. Ladd was one of the top ten in the FBI's hierarchy. His title, Assistant Director for Domestic Intelligence, did not describe the full scope of his responsibilities. In a most respectful tone, Donald C. Moore, who directed the FBI's counter intelligence investigations beginning in 1956 (under Ladd's successor, Alan Belmont), explained, "Mickey was in charge of *all* investigations under Hoover-criminal, political, counter intelligence— all."[14] The Boss was not assigning the Einstein case to a low-level flunky.

We've seen that the FBI had been collecting information on Einstein, as on millions of others, in fragments—whenever something came up, it would be added to a file in one office or another. In addition, other government agencies had their own intelligence files, including the State Department and the counterintelligence branches of the Army (G-2) and Navy (ONI). Ladd's assignment now was to collect, compile, and then summarize the scattered items in one report. In just two days, he queried FBI offices around the country and collected Einstein material from various internal Bureau files and other government agencies. On February 15, 1950, Ladd handed the Boss a fifteen-page report, along with a two-page summary of "highlights." It was the beginning of the FBI's centralized Einstein file.

If President Roosevelt was a communist agent in Mickey Ladd's mind, it's not hard to guess what Hoover's Assistant Director for Domestic Intelligence thought of an anti-Nazi, anti-Franco, anti-racist, free-thinking, foreign, Jewish scientist. Ladd's February 15 report to Hoover was

---

* One of eight children born to Senator Ladd and his wife Rizpah, Mickey's ultraconservative politics and sycophantic yes-man-it is were totally unlike—a mirror image of—his father. The senator was a maverick Republican, associated with Wisconsin Senator Robert LaFollette and the liberal Populist group in Congress who were expelled from the Republican Party. Senator Ladd died in 1925 during his first term in office. There is no record of how many times he may have turned over in his grave.

predictably hostile. Whether Einstein was pink or Red—the report wavers—he was absolutely un-American. The second sentence of Ladd's "highlights" sets the tone:

> In December 1947, [Einstein] made the following statement: "I came to America because of the great, great freedom which I heard existed in this country. I made a mistake in selecting America as a land of freedom, a mistake I cannot repair in the balance of my life."

No source is cited for this statement anywhere in the summary, or for that matter, in the FBI's entire Einstein file. But the bulk of Ladd's report, although it includes a few other falsehoods,* is not so much wrong as it is far-right-labeling as "subversive" Einstein's left-of-center political ideas and organizational affiliations. As you would expect in a document thrown together in two days, the report is mostly a rehash. In a section subtitled EXPRESSION OF IDEOLOGICAL SYMPATHIES,** the Ladd report repeats several old items, including that Einstein—

- supported the anti-Franco forces and stated that he "felt ashamed that the democratic nations had failed to support the Loyalist Government of Spain."
- advocated "World Government" and the outlawing of atomic energy as a means of war; opposed "the increasing militarization of America."
- was listed as a sponsor of the National Non-Partisan Committee to Defend the Rights of the Twelve [indicted] Communist leaders.

Ladd also re-lists a number of Einstein's "Contacts and Associates since 1938," who, the report claims, are "known members and sympathizers of the Communist Party." The FBI had monitored most of these through its phone and mail intercepts, described in a previous chapter. Ladd then repeats Einstein's 1948 statement criticizing the government for invading his privacy:

> In 1948, [Einstein] indicated to the Polish ambassador that the United States was no longer a free country and that his activities were carefully scrutinized.

---

* Grudgingly, in two brief sentences, Ladd acknowledges Einstein's well-known letter to Roosevelt that led to America's atomic-bomb project, followed by a totally fictitious "account" of a meeting between Einstein, Szilard, and Roosevelt:
"Einstein accompanied [Szilard] to Washington, where they conferred with President Roosevelt. This conference resulted in the [Manhattan Project]."
** "The FBI is concerned with acts and deeds, not thoughts or beliefs," Hoover wrote just two months after this report with its revealing subtitle. "A man is entitled to think and to believe what he desires." (*New York Times Magazine*, April 18, 1950, pp. 30-31.)

The report even digs out the old Woman Patriot Corporation slanders, citing Mrs. Frothingham's totally fabricated accusations...

> that Einstein believed in or was affiliated with Communist groups which advocate the overthrow by force or violence of the Government of the United States; that he admitted his attitude was revolutionary and his position illegal, and that he believe in or advocated a system of organized sabotage against ail preparations of the United States to defend its existence.

But by far, the largest section of the Ladd report is subtitled AFFILIATION WITH SUBVERSIVE AND OTHER ORGANIZATIONS, citing Einstein's affiliation with "at least 33 organizations"* cited as subversive or Communist fronts by the attorney general or HUAC or California's state HUAC.

It was only the first of several such listings in Einstein's file—as the Red scare intensified, many more groups were labeled "subversive"—but it reflected how far McCarthyism had already reached in early 1950. The diversity of groups also gives some indication of the breadth of Einstein's social concerns.

EINSTEIN'S AFFILIATIONS WITH ORGANIZATIONS CITED AS SUBVERSIVE

American Committee of Jewish Writers, Artists, and Scientists:	Honorary President
Ambijan Committee for Emergency Aid to the Soviet Union:	Honorary President
American Committee for Protection of the Foreign-Born:	Sponsor
American Committee for Spanish Freedom:	Supporter of protest
American Council for Democratic Greece:	National Petitioner
American Friends of the Chinese People:	Signer of letter
American League Against War and Fascism:	Endorser
The American Pushkin Committee:	Sponsor
Civil Rights Congress:	Sponsor
Committee of One Thousand [to abolish HUAC]:	Original sponsor
Committee for Peace Through World Cooperation:	Endorser of meeting
Congress of American-Soviet Friendship:	Sponsor and patron
Council on African Affairs:	Message of Greetings
Friends of the Abraham Lincoln Brigade:	Member
German-American League for Culture:	Member
Hollywood Anti-Nazi League:	Sponsor

---

* Besides these 33, some 50 other groups are not listed (most are included in later FBI reports) but simply described as "either scientific, cultural, pacifist, anti-discrimination or Russian [World War II] relief."

Independent Citizens Committee of the Arts, Sciences and Professions:	Director
International Labor Defense: Message of Greetings	
International Workers Aid:	Endorser
Joint Anti-Fascist Refugee Committee:	Sponsor
League of American Writers:	Affiliate
Medical Bureau and North American Committee to Aid Spanish Democracy:	Advisory Committee
Motion Picture Artists Committee:	Sponsor
Musicians Committee to Aid Spanish Democracy:	Sponsor
National Council of American-Soviet Friendship:	Sponsor, patron
National Federation for Constitutional Liberties:	Signer of Letter
Nat'l Reception Committee to the Russian Delegation:	Honorary National Chairman
Non-Partisan Committee of Artists and Scientists:	Member
Non-Sectarian Committee for Political Refugee:	Sponsor
Progressive Citizens of America:	Sponsor
Reichstag Fire Trial Anniversary Committee:	Signer of Declaration
World Congress Against War:	Delegate

A single sentence in the fifteen-page document, buried in the paragraph on Einstein's "contacts and associates," drew a response from J. Edgar Hoover. The sentence read:

> Information not yet fully developed indicates [Einstein] may have had some contact with Emil Klaus Fuchs, who was recently arrested in England as a Soviet espionage agent.

At the bottom of the page, Hoover scrawled two notes—his only written comments on Ladd's report. In the first note, he wrote:

> *We should develop this: I have seen somewhere Einstein was the one who requested Fuchs assignment* [to work on the atom bomb]. *What about this?*

The second Hoover note said:

> *Also, 1 recently saw a statement to the effect that a member of his family was in Russia. 1 think it stated it was his son.*

Taken together, the two notes suggest that Einstein might be involved in the Klaus Fuchs spy case, perhaps connected in some way because his son was in the Soviet Union, possibly a hostage of the Russians.

As significant as what Hoover wrote is what he didn't write: The Boss made no comment whatsoever on the pages of details on Einstein's political affiliations, virtually ignoring the entire report Ladd and his staff had collected, the report Hoover had just rush-ordered two days earlier. Not

that Hoover didn't appreciate a good list of "subversive organizations"—
most of his political dossiers on Americans contain little or nothing else.
But, to put it directly, that approach simply would not work with Einstein.
His popularity was so universal that his connection with a group like the
Friends of the Lincoln Brigade would primarily serve to help the group's
public image. Any plan Hoover and Tolson devised to nail Einstein would
have to focus on something much more sinister—like espionage.

Both of Hoover's handwritten queries, it turned out, referred to internal FBI memos on Einstein, written in previous years. Hoover was not
known for remembering such items, but they were precisely the kind of
things that Tolson's "photographic memory" would have recalled. Hoover
and Tolson no doubt expected Ladd to find the memos and include them
in his report. But Ladd, eager to be prompt, completely missed them. He
well knew that Hoover's notes were Hoover's orders: His Einstein investigation would now concentrate on the espionage angle.

Ladd's first task was to locate Einstein's son, "Albert, Jr."—a task made
more difficult by the fact that no such person existed. Albert Einstein's two
sons were named Eduard and Hans Albert. But the FBI's earlier memos
had misidentified one (the possible Russian hostage), and the misnamed
"Albert, Jr." continued to appear in the Bureau files for five more years.
Whatever his name, Ladd's assignment was to find him, and if he was in
the Soviet Union, determine whether he was being held as a hostage to put
political pressure on Albert, Sr.

For those who don't remember life before the Internet, the process
of locating someone in those days required interviewing people. In this
case, interviews posed a problem, since the FBI had to keep news of their
Einstein investigation from getting out to the world. Ladd determined
that someone in Princeton, Einstein's home, would probably know where
"Albert, Jr." was. But how could agents ask people about him without
explaining why? Ladd put Alan Belmont, his chief assistant (and eventual
successor as assistant director), on the case, strongly advising him to be
"discreet." Belmont discreetly approached the Newark FBI office. It took
two weeks, but Belmont finally got back to Ladd:

> On the afternoon of March 3, 1950, I called SAC [Special Agent in Charge] of
> the Newark Office to ascertain whether he had a discreet contact at Princeton
> University through whom he could ascertain the present whereabouts of
> Albert Einstein Jr., who allegedly is in Russia. Mr. McKee advised that the
> Newark Office has an excellent contact in this respect and that he believed the
> information could be obtained discreetly. I advised Mr. McKee that we did not
> want to make any open inquiries indicating an interest in the Einstein family.

But despite his promising memo, a few days later, Belmont informed Ladd that the "excellent contact" at Princeton not only didn't know where Einstein's son was, but had "never heard that Einstein has a son."

In fact, the Newark FBI office's inability to locate Einstein's son may have resulted as much from their own incompetence as from the hush-hush nature ("discretion") of their operation. Newark FBI SAC Sam McKee reported that his agents had been asking about "Albert, Jr." at Princeton University, "where the father Professor Albert Einstein is currently located." An earlier memo from McKee referred to "Professor Einstein's position on the staff at Princeton University and his residence on the campus at Princeton."[15] Einstein, of course, worked at the Institute for Advanced Study, located in the town of Princeton but separate from Princeton University. And, as almost anyone living in Princeton could have told McKee, Einstein lived in the town, not on the campus.

Eventually, Ladd found the information himself—by looking through the FBI's own files. What he discovered was that less than a year earlier, on April 25, 1949, the FBI's Los Angeles office was approached by a man named Kimbrough, who said his sister was the wife of Upton Sinclair (described in the FBI file simply as "the famous writer"). According to Kimbrough, his sister Mrs. Sinclair was "quite friendly" with Mrs. Albert Einstein and:

> The Einsteins had stated to Mrs. Sinclair that all their present activities were influenced by the fact that Albert Einstein Jr. was presently in the Soviet Union....that particularly Mrs. Einstein was "scared to death" over the fact that her son was in Russia and might be held as a hostage to force some particular action on the part of Professor Einstein.

The only problem with that report was that there is no Albert Einstein, Jr. Well, maybe not the only problem.

Ladd's investigation "discovered" that Einstein's two sons, Eduard and Albert, Jr. (he continued to get Hans Albert's name wrong), were children of his first wife, Mileva, whom he had divorced in 1919. His second wife, Elsa, who came to the United States with Einstein, had no sons and therefore could not have been "scared to death" about her son even if she didn't know his name. One other problem: Elsa died in 1938 and so could not have told the "quite friendly" informant anything at all in 1943 or 1944, the date of the alleged conversation. One more problem with Kimbrough's story: Neither of the Einstein sons were or had been in the Soviet Union. Ladd finally uncovered the whereabouts of both sons. Albert, Jr./Hans Albert was a college professor in California, and Eduard, who suffered from schizophrenia, had for years been in a Swiss psychiatric hospital.

Indeed, we don't really know whether Kimbrough *was* Mrs. Sinclair's brother. He advised the Los Angeles FBI office not to question her because "she was not aware" that he was talking to the Bureau. It's likely, then, that Upton Sinclair, socialist and muckraking author of industry exposés like *The Jungle*, which revealed the inhuman conditions in Chicago's meat-packing plants, did not know what his brother-in-law (if Kimbrough was his brother-in-law) was up to.

The Einsteins actually did meet the Sinclairs, although it's not clear they ever became close friends. During their visit to the United States in 1931—before the FBI started keeping tabs on him—Einstein and Elsa visited the Sinclairs at their California home.* After the visit, Einstein wrote about Sinclair in his diary: "A splendid idealist and at the same time a man with a gay temperament. Favorable opinion of Russia because, he says, they educate the masses and bring them to life...." (It was not a view Sinclair would continue to hold.)

Despite the fact that the L.A. office had concluded a year earlier that Kimbrough's story failed to hold up, the "hostage" story didn't die. Ladd's memo to Hoover again reported that neither of Einstein's sons was or had been in the Soviet Union.[16] Though the FBI had now checked and doublechecked and twice refuted it in less than a year, the Albert, Jr.-as-a-possiblehostage story continued to reappear in FBI reports, including the Summary Report (p. 5)—which supposedly had filtered out ail frivolous and false allegations—more than three years later.

But it was Hoover's other handwritten note about a reported link between Einstein and atomic-spy Klaus Fuchs ("I have seen somewhere Einstein...requested Fuchs' assignment.") that had the most explosive possibilities. If Einstein had helped Fuchs get past the top-security nuclear door, it would be a short step to "aiding and abetting" the Soviet spy. Ladd located a report in the FBI's files (probably the one Hoover/Tolson had remembered seeing "somewhere") from an informant who stated that after the war, "Einstein had sent for Fuchs to help work on the atom bomb." The informant gave no details or evidence to support the claim. Ladd also found several recent news reports claiming that in 1942, Einstein had helped get Fuchs released from detention in Canada, where he had been

---

* During the 1931 visit, Einstein agreed to an interview with Sinclair for the socialist weekly *The New Leader*. Sinclair asked him to comment on the economic depression—"the misery and starvation in a land which has such enormous power to produce." Einstein: "The present grave crisis in consumption is a clear indication that the existing economic organization, as far as one can call it an 'organization,' is not suitable to provide adequately for needs of the population." (Interview and Einstein's diary excerpt: Nathan, pp. 120-121.)

held as a suspected enemy agent. The report first ran on February 6 in the *Newark Evening News,* the *Clevland Plain Dealer* and the *Washington Sun Times,* with a Berlin dateline. All three papers cited Fuchs' 75-year-old father, who reportedly told a reporter that Einstein's recommendation had been the key that released his son Klaus from Canadian detention. Fuchs's father was also reported to have said that Klaus was a lifelong communist, although Einstein hadn't known it.

The report appeared again on February 7 in *The Chicago Tribune* (in a Page 3 story by its staff-writer specialist on communism, William Moore) and in the *Chicago American* on February 14, as well as in Rushmore's series in the *New York Journal American.* Such repeating news stories tend to feed one another, with each new report citing one printed earlier. Yet Ladd never tried to investigate where the first story (on February 6) came from. It was just one of many leads Mickey Ladd failed to pursue in his "investigation" of Einstein's reported intervention for Fuchs:

- He never tried to contact former FBI Agent Kerley at the *New York Journal American,* or reporters at any of the other papers that ran the story, to see where their information came from or what supporting evidence, if any, they had.
- He made no attempt to contact the British Foreign Office to see if they had ever received such a letter. (Einstein's secretary Helen Dukas told the press that as far as she knew, no such letter had ever been written.)
- Perhaps most telling, he made no attempt to contact or even to locate Klaus Fuchs' father in Germany to see if he would confirm his statement about Einstein's letter.

It's almost as though Ladd was satisfied to allow the unsubstantiated newspaper reports to stand as the only record. In three months of "searching," he was unable to come up with anything other than those news stories to indicate that Einstein had any connection with Fuchs. In response to his memos to several FBI offices around the country, the Boston office reported to Hoover on March 11, 1950, that they could find no link between the two men. If Ladd balked at checking out the newspapers' account, it may have been because he knew what he'd find. While the FBI (Ladd) sat on its hands, the *Washington Post* contacted Fuchs' father in Germany on February 9, only three days after he had been quoted by the *Washington Sun Times* and the Newark and Cleveland papers. He denied that his son was a communist or that he had ever told that to any reporter. He made no mention whatever of Einstein.

Despite the lack of tangible results from Ladd's initial investigation, Hoover was not discouraged. Even as his first leads petered out, new reports reached his desk linking Einstein to Soviet atom spy Fuchs.

Unlike General Groves's buck-passing, Hoover used the Fuchs case primarily to build his Bureau. With the international-tension index soaring and hostility between the West and the communist world nearing the boiling point, the FBI chief must have heard opportunity pounding. In the week following the atom spy's arrest in London, Hoover held three meetings with the Senate Appropriations Sub-Committee to urge more FBI funding, primarily for additional agents. Instead of the-spy-who-got-away story, the senators emerged from these sessions with the-FBI-needs-more-money-and-men, telling the press that only Hoover and his Bureau could protect America, now virtually under siege by communist spies and the growing Red menace.

"I am flabbergasted," Indiana Republican Senator Capehart told the *Chicago Tribune* on February 8. "It is the most alarming thing I have heard in a long time." Capehart said Hoover had reported that "there are hundreds of thousands of Communists and fellow travelers in the United States." Adding to the alarm, the *Tribune* headlined, 540,000 REDS IN U.S., HOOVER TELLS SENATORS, although the article itself said that one-tenth of that number were actually "members of the Communist party." The rest were "fellow travelers." One senator told the *Tribune* that in view of the spy danger, Hoover can get "just about anything he wants."

While revving up the engine of McCarthyism, Hoover kept a wary eye on his critics. Eleanor Roosevelt and Einstein were not the only ones warning that the FBI had too much power and was threatening to turn America into a police state. In a lengthy article in the *New York Times Sunday Magazine,* Hoover served up his response. It was in no way a defensive article—the author was clearly confident of his power. Still, a façade was needed:

> The responsibility of the FBI is to secure the facts. We do not make decisions as to prosecutive action or recommendations as to whether an individual is suitable or unsuitable for Federal employment. The FBI is concerned with acts and deeds, not thoughts or beliefs....I would not want to be a party in any action which would "smear" innocent individuals for the rest of their lives.
>
> Investigative files are not maintained on anyone, in or out of Congress, unless there has been a complaint coming within the purview of our investigative responsibilities.

In a later interview, Hoover added even more yeast: When the FBI investigates someone, he told a *Times* reporter,

Favorable information and comment is recorded as fully as derogatory data. The words of a neighbor who praises will be jotted down just as dutifully as those of an associate who disparages.[17]

But while covering his rear with platitudes about civil liberties and fictional accounts of a hands-off-Congress policy (even as he built up files on virtually every member of both Houses), Hoover kept the big anti-communist artillery booming. After meeting with the FBI chief, South Dakota Senator Karl Mundt, Hoover's brother-in-conservatism,* told the *New York Journal American* that Russian spies "are after the hydrogen-bomb secrets just as surely as they tried for, and succeeded in getting, the A-bomb." He reported: "Between 4,000 and 4,400 Communists are under constant watch" by the FBI, adding that Hoover's Bureau was ready to herd them into "concentration camps" within "24 hours if war breaks out."

The spy-case headlines no doubt were largely responsible for the increased number of tips and leads on "spies" flowing into the FBI in early 1950. Among these, a letter from a woman in Berlin caught Hoover's attention. He would have routinely passed Emma Rabbeis' letter on to a subordinate, but the first words of the translator's summary made his G-man antenna crackle: "In connection with the espionage case of Dr. Klaus Fuchs and the references in the press concerning Dr. Albert Einstein…" For all Mickey Ladd's initial dead-end leads, a possible link between Einstein and Fuchs was still very much alive on Hoover's agenda. He just needed something more substantial, another piece of evidence—the Rabbeis letter couldn't have arrived at a better moment. It seemed quite logical that since both Fuchs and Einstein were German, information connecting them might well come from a woman in Germany:

> Since the announcement of the espionage affair of Dr. KLAUS FUCHS, I have read with growing concern all newspaper reports pertaining to Prof. ALBERT EINSTEIN….I am no informer and would not make such statements if it did not concern such weapons as atom plus hydrogen which can exterminate nations….
>
> The accusations made against [Einstein] by American politicians are not unfounded….If a man who is an active RED such as EINSTEIN, as I positively know, can look into the research status of such horrible [atomic] weapons, one must not remain silent….

---

* Coauthor of the Mundt-Nixon Communist Control bill of 1948 that would have made it a crime to belong to any "Communist-front" group that failed to register with the government. Although Congress failed to pass it (approved overwhelmingly by the House but died in the Senate), the bill was a harbinger of political repression to come just a few years later, specifically the 1952 Internal Security (McCarran) Act.

Maybe if Einstein had answered her letter, things would have been different. But after months with no word—and after the headlines about Fuchs and other possible atom spies—Emma Rabbeis, until then simply a dressmaker for some of Berlin's most prominent ladies, wrote to the U.S. State Department (which forwarded the letter to Hoover). Declaring her aim was "preventing spies from doing any harm," she did not have the tone of most crank-mail writers.

A few sentences may have sounded a little strange, like Rabbeis' implication that Einstein was involved in the recent fire in Princeton University's cyclotron, but most of her letter promised just the kind of news Hoover was looking for. Rabbeis said she was in a position to give "very positive statements" about Einstein's political activity, adding:

> I can also give you most exact information about…a woman with whom Einstein collaborated internationally.[18]

Hoover didn't hesitate. Since Germany was outside the FBI's jurisdiction, he immediately sent the Rabbeis letter to Army Intelligence for investigation. He knew these things needed checking out. But Emma Rabbeis' finger wasn't the only one pointing at Einstein and espionage.

No less a source than the younger sister of confessed atom spy Klaus Fuchs, a woman named Kristel Heineman who lived in Boston, had reportedly said that Albert Einstein had "sent for her brother to help build the atom bomb."[19] From Hoover's point of view, this was a live wire. It would be three months before the FBI managed to get permission from the British to interview Fuchs in prison,[20] and in the meantime, an accusation against Einstein from the atom spy's sister was the next best thing to hearing it from Fuchs himself.

There was just one small fly in Hoover's ointment: Kristel Heineman was suffering from a degenerative form of schizophrenia and dementia praecox, and had been confined to the Massachusetts State Mental Hospital at Westboro. But this news did not cause Hoover to reconsider, or even to hesitate. The nation's number one G-man ordered the FBI's Boston office to press Kristel Heineman for "all information in her possession regarding any relationship between Fuchs and Dr. Albert Einstein."[21]

Doctors initially told the Boston FBI agents there might be a problem arranging the interview because of Mrs. Heineman's deteriorating medical condition. Hoover instructed his Boston agents to talk to her doctor about the rising menace of Russia and Communism, and appeal to his patriotism. It seemed to work. Dr. Rollins Hadley, director of the Westboro hospital, clearly wanted no questions raised about *his* loyalty. Whether driven by patriotism or fear, he eagerly cooperated with the

Boston agents becoming—according to the FBI file—a virtual part of their team.

The medical reports on Mrs. Heineman said she was "mentally going backward...beginning to forget her children and remember only her childhood. [She has] no apparent hope of recovery." Yet, in the twelve days from February 2 to 14, 1950, a team of Boston FBI agents, headed by Special Agent Brenton Gordon, interviewed the deranged patient for over an hour *on four separate occasions*. Dr. Hadley was present at each session. During these interviews, Kristel repeated her claim about Einstein having "sent for" her brother Klaus, although she was unable to offer any details.[22] In fact, she gave fuzzy and contradictory responses to most of the agents' questions and "appeared to be generally confused." Agent Gordon's report on the February 5 interview noted also that Mrs. Heineman was "receiving treatment because her mental illness had caused confusion in her mind as to times, persons and places." Nonetheless, Gordon's team continued to return to Westboro and conduct more interrogations.

As for Dr. Hadley, apparently eager for official approval, he became the FBI's Confidential Informant T-1 in this case. (T-1, according to former agents, is the Bureau's symbol for the "most reliable" informant in each case.) Even when Kristel Heineman's condition deteriorated to the point where she could barely talk and further FBI visits would clearly be unproductive, the patriotic physician assured Agent Gordon—in a private memo—"should there be any change in Mrs. Heineman's condition which would warrant her leaving the hospital under any circumstances whatsoever," he would "advise the agent before permitting such to occur."[23] But Dr. Hadley came up with no new information on the alleged Einstein-Fuchs connection.

FBI agents quizzed the confused and mentally ill woman about possible contact between Fuchs and several other scientists besides Einstein. They showed her photos of ten leading physicists, including Hans Bethe, Philip Morrison, Robert Marshak, Victor Weisskopf, and Richard Feynman, but Kristel didn't recognize any of them.[24]

Agent Gordon also interviewed Kristel's husband Robert, who was known to the FBI as a communist. Possibly shaken by his brother-in-law's confession as a Soviet spy, as well as America's new anti-communist atmosphere, Robert Heineman was "extremely cooperative" with the FBI. The final memo on this case to Hoover reported that Robert "renounced his former association with the Communist Party...identified Party members with whom he was affiliated and [expressed] willingness to testify against those persons in a court of law."

But despite his quick conversion, he did little to support his wife's story:

Robert Heineman stated that he knew of no direct relationship between Fuchs and Albert Einstein.[25]

Only Kristel Heineman "knew" about her brother and Einstein. True, she had a hard time describing any details to Agent Gordon about when or how Einstein had "sent for her brother." But she definitely knew the name Albert Einstein.

Klaus Fuchs' sister Kristel, it turned out, would be a shaky eyewitness in Hoover's hoped-for arsenal of evidence against Einstein. Still, she might be useful as backup, together with what Army Intelligence (G-2) reported from Berlin after interviewing Emma Rabbeis. By the end of July, the Rabbeis interview was on Hoover's desk, telling a tale of sex, politics, and even a little mystery. But would-be Hollywood producers will be disappointed. For drama and excitement, her interview doesn't quite measure up—not even to the standards of Tinseltown. Here are some of the highlights:

- In the early 1930s, prior to the Nazi assumption of power, Rabbeis operated a dress salon in Berlin and numbered among her customers a certain Baroness von Schneider-Glend, wife of a former German consul in Japan and mother of Elli von Schneider-Glend, who was also a client of Fraulein Rabbeis. The entire von Schneider-Glend family were "known as Communists."
- On one occasion, possibly in 1930, Elli von Schneider-Glend mentioned that she was working with Professor Einstein and that she might be going to America...A short time later, she ordered a great many clothes from Rabbeis and said that...she would soon be leaving [for America]. Rabbeis later learned from the Baroness that her daughter had gone to America in the company of a "Professor" who was not further identified...that her daughter had been involved in an incident that caused talk among...fellow passengers. The Baroness said her daughter and the "Professor" had remained seated during the playing of the German national anthem and this had been taken by other passengers as an indication that Elli and the "Professor" were communists.
- Elli returned to Germany a year or so later with an illegitimate infant son. [Rabbeis] believes the "Professor" may have been the father of this child.
- [Rabbeis] believes that the information...indicates that Mr. Einstein is a communist.

The report from Army Intelligence where interviews of Germans who had stories to tell about their wartime and pre-war lives still took place fairly often—concludes:

...it appears evident from the information contained in the above report that Rabbeis knows nothing other than hearsay information regarding Einstein.

Rabbeis "does not make a favorable impression as to her reliability," the report states. By way of explanation, the interviewer adds:

> Prior to volunteering her hearsay information, she stated that she is an amateur mathematician and some few months ago wrote to Mr. [sic] EINSTEIN at "PRINCETON" asking his opinion of a system she had worked out to win the Berlin "Toto" gambling pool. She had not received a reply to her letter [to Einstein] and wishes to be furnished Subject's correct address so that she may communicate with him regarding her system. She also feels that if it is permitted to contact Mr. Einstein, she may be able to gain other information to "prove" that he is a Communist.[26]

Once again, as with the Albert, Jr. "hostage" report, Hoover's hopes outreached his grasp. The FBI chief could not come up with a credible case when the key piece of evidence identifying Einstein as a communist was that he reportedly refused to stand up for the German national anthem.

The FBI finally dropped the Einstein-Fuchs story, but only after Special Agents Hugh H. Clegg and Robert Lamphere interviewed Fuchs in May in his London prison cell and reported:

> In reference to Professor Albert Einstein, Fuchs said that he never met Professor Einstein. He said that he knew of no activity on the part of Einstein in his behalf.[27]

But dropped or not, and despite the shaky "witnesses" and Fuchs' own refutation, the story of an Einstein-Fuchs connection—like the "Albert, Jr." hostage tale—would be cited again in the FBI's August 5, 1953, "Summary Report" (p. 93).

Hoover might have been discouraged by the Army Intelligence report on Rabbeis except that the cover letter, signed by G-2's General John Weckerling included a new and potentially explosive lead: G-2's European Command had just obtained information "about Einstein's past activities...from former well-placed KPD [German Communist Party] members." Weckerling assured Hoover that it is "presently being checked" and promised to send "a detailed report" as soon as it was ready.[28] The Boss did not have long to wait. The new report turned out to have far more historical heft than the imaginative creations from Emma Rabbeis and Kristel Heineman. It would provide the meat of the Einstein file for the next five years.

Hoover's Einstein spy hunt was just getting started.

14

Far Out

If witch-hunts attract screwballs, it's probably because when you're hunting witches, the line between zealous and zany is so very fine and easy to cross. It was a line crossed several times in the FBI's Einstein file. The dossier is replete with far-out allegations, several of which were given the Bureau's serious attention.

The FBI started receiving crank, or crackpot, mail about Einstein as early as 1934 (if you don't count the Woman Patriot Corporation's 1932 treatise sent to the State Department), and his file is peppered with letters and postcards such as the handscrawled card postmarked Philadelphia, July 8, 1947:

> ALBERT EINSTEIN. Are we safe with Atomic Energy as long as we have men like Einstein on our list? Watch out for him. (P.S. Flying Saucers are SMALL experiments by Russia for disks 1000 times larger—later on).
> (signed) American

The messages are often anti-Semitic and almost always shrilly anti-Communist. One begins: "I THINK IT LONG PAST DUE TO PROSECUTE THIS COMMUNIST FELLOW TRAVELER AS BEING AN UNREGISTERED SPY AND AGENT OF THE COMMUNIST." The lengthy letter, typed in capital letters and sent to the attorney general (then forwarded to Hoover) on June 12, 1953, concludes: "THE COMMUNISTS ARE TEACHING THE...TEENAGERS HOW TO ATTACK—THE STREET FIGHTS IN NEW YORK ARE COMMUNIST PROMOTED...WHO ELSE BUT A COMMUNIST, WOULD SHOW THESE TEENAGERS HOW TO MAKE AND USE A MOLOTOV COCKTAIL?" Many of these far-out missives made up in imagination for what they lacked in stability. In one case, a caller to the FBI office announced that he had solved the kidnapping case of the century:

On September 28, 1951, Mr. William E. Henry, Washington, DC, called [and] claimed he had solved the Lindbergh Kidnapping Case. He stated that Professor Albert Einstein...had framed Bruno Hauptmann, who was convicted and electrocuted for the kidnapping of the Lindbergh child.

When the Bureau decided the complaint against Einstein was from a crank or a crackpot—as it did in most of these cases—the caller or letterwriter was essentially dismissed. With the sleuth who solved the Lindbergh kidnapping case, for example, the Einstein file notes: "Mr. Henry was very incoherent...and was referred to the Complaint Desk in the Old Post Office Building."

When there was a return address, Hoover sent a cordial-sounding note—"Thank you for writing and let us know if you get any new evidence"—and that was the end of it. It was not assigned to any district office for further investigation. And even though most of the Einstein crackpot mail was virulently anti-Semitic and often threatening, the FBI almost never referred it for investigation to other federal, state, or local law-enforcement agencies.*

Four of these far-out missives, however, must have touched a nerve or triggered a loose cannon in Bureau headquarters, each was assigned for follow-up investigation, and two were cited in subsequent reports. In one instance, the Hollywood Caper, the FBI launched a special, year-long investigation (mid 1953 until August 1954), resulting in a twenty-page report. More important, all four remained in Einstein's dossier over the years, were repeated in the Bureau's Summary Reports, and included in the "derogatory information" the Bureau sent out to state and federal agencies. And, like the man who "solved" the Lindbergh kidnapping, all four of these cases showed considerable creativity.

On February 24, 1938, Mrs. Lucy Apostolina of Jersey City, N.J. writes to the FBI about an electrical robot invented by "Professor Albert Einstein of Germany" that can read and control the human mind. When that letter reaches Bureau HQ in Washington, HQ orders the New York SAC to assign a Special Agent to interview the letter-writer. Six weeks later, the New York office reports back to headquarters on what Mrs. Apostolina has told him:

---

* The only exception occurred during World War II. In May and June 1944, at least 20 threatening postcards were received by "various people of Jewish extraction" around the country, including Einstein, all from the same source in Kansas City. The Kansas City FBI office collected many of the postcards and sent them to the FBI's forensic lab in Washington for processing. No further action was reported. The postcard sent to Einstein read: "Why don't you lousy Jews keep your traps shut? If Roosevelt is re-elected, we'll put all the Jews in concentration camps. You ought to have stayed over in Europe. We'll get *you*."

The aim and purpose of this monstrous invention by Professor Einstein is to enable the communication to Germany of all contemplated plans of the American military authorities in the event of war with that nation.

Mrs. Apostolina knows this because "for the past three years," she has been under the influence of that device. She reports that a "German" neighbor in the house where she and her husband live has the device in his thirdfloor apartment. He invited her to his rooms three years ago, and ever since, has been using her "as a human experiment." The interviewing agent concludes it is

> apparent that the utterances of Mrs. Apostolina were those of a person suffering from a deranged mind, she having admitted being for two years an inmate of an insane asylum.[1]

The second such report arrives in July 1942. The FBI receives an anonymous report from Beaver Falls, Pennsylvania, urging the Bureau to investigate a secret organization called the "Music Boys." The letter, with anti-Semitic overtones, describes an alleged meeting on November 1, 1938, at New York's Biltmore Hotel, with "Rabbi Stephen Wise presiding," at which the group was plotting to take over this country. The letter continues:

> Louis Lipsky [a Zionist activist] was the next speaker. He said Einstein is experimenting with a ray which will help us to destroy armed opposition— aircraft, tanks and armored cars. He hopes that with it a dozen men could defeat 500. Through it 5% could rule a nation.

What appears to be this same death-ray shows up again nearly eight hundred pages later:

> A dipping from the Arlington (Virginia) *Daily* of May 21, 1948, indicated that Professor Einstein and ten "former Nazi research brain-trusters" held a secret meeting and watched a beam of light melt a block of steel 20 x 29 inches. It was indicated that this new and secret weapon could be operated from planes and destroy entire cities.[2]

The *Arlington Daily* story above is sent to the Research Branch of Army Intelligence, which advises the Bureau that such a death-ray machine has "no foundation in fact." But there is no evaluation or opinion from either Army Intelligence or the FBI on the "foundation in fact" for reports that both Nazis and Jews are plotting to take over the world with the same secret death ray. And Einstein is collaborating with each of them. The death-ray story reappears on February 15, 1950, as part of Mickey Ladd's report to Hoover, summarizing Einstein's most serious subversive activities.

With the arrival of the 1950s and McCarthyism—much like the com-ic-book heroes who found new Red villains to battle*—the far-out allega-tions against Einstein become Communist plots: "As a result of the trial of Alger Hiss," states a memo to Hoover on February 10, 1950, from the head of the FBI's Phoenix office, an informant has remembered an incident that "might be used for the denaturalization and deportation of Einstein as an undesirable alien." The Phoenix SAC's report to Hoover continues: The informant, James S. Sheafe, a seventy-four-year-old retired railroad engin-eer, has reported that he heard from a friend of his in Los Angeles who heard from an unnamed couple that either the husband or the wife (Sheafe doesn't remember which) "had found out that the other was a Communist and had secretly been meeting with Dr. ALBERT EINSTEIN." The report from Phoenix, from Sheafe, from his Los Angeles friend, from either the husband or wife, continues:

> EINSTEIN was...a personal courier from Communist Party Headquarters, relaying messages orally to selected sources throughout the United States... the messages were of too great importance to be trusted through the mails, telephone, telegraph or other means...EINSTEIN being a trusted Communist, was selected as the personal Courier for the Party.

To demonstrate Einstein's communist affiliation, Sheafe quotes an entire page from Elizabeth Dilling's far-right catalogue *The Red Network* (see "Why Einstein?": p. 42), denouncing relativity and Einstein. The Phoenix FBI office recommends that the LA office immediately interview Sheafe's good friend Fred Bunnell, who, Sheafe says, will confirm his story about Einstein, the Red courier. The LA office assigns a special agent to the interview, and reports back to Phoenix. The memo's final paragraph eerily echoes the closing of the story about Mrs. Apostolina from Jersey City:

> In July 1943...the police at Casa Grande Arizona reported that Sheafe had a growth on the brain and has been a patient in a private mental hospital in Chicago...[3]

As the Red scare moves into high gear, it spawns another tale of Einstein intrigue that might be titled, "Einstein Does Hollywood," except it was not intended as a comedy. On April 21, 1953, Hoover receives a letter from a Garritt J. Lloyd in Tulsa, Oklahoma, claiming he was an advertising and story executive with the David Griffith movie studios in Hollywood from 1919 until the mid 1930s.

---

* "Beware, commies, spies, traitors and foreign agents! Captain America, with all loyal, free men behind him, is looking for you." *(Captain America* comic strip, 1952.)

Lloyd claims that during "the early thirties," Aaron Tycko,* a photographer friend, invited him to his portrait studio in the lobby of the Ambassador Hotel in Los Angeles and there tried to recruit him as director of propaganda for "the Bolsheviks." When Lloyd refused, Tycko said, "Well, I can see that Dr. Einstein has got to take you in hand. He...never fails with the big shots." Tycko then took him upstairs and knocked on the door of a suite, and Einstein opened the door. According to Lloyd:

> He said he was too busy but would see me the next day. I got a glimpse into his rooms and I thought the man I saw there was Charlie Chaplin.
>
> Going downstairs Tycko told me that Einstein was organizing all the big studio figures, Schulberg at Paramount, stars like Freddie March, Walter Huston, [Katharine] Hepburn, etc. and ail the leading directors and writers. He said: 'We've got them in our hand, and the Dr. has never failed on one; give him an hour and he convinces you.' [and] that through Einstein they were getting control of every studio...[4]

Lloyd later adds that Tycko described Einstein as...the brain that was setting up Hollywood in the l930's for the big Communist push...he was one of the most dangerous and powerful figures in what has become the Communist movement."

Hoover considers this letter important enough to order the FBI's Los Angeles office to open an investigation. Agents from the LA office spend fifteen months—at taxpayers' expense—checking out this twenty-year-old story and then issue a twenty-page report that includes the following points:[5]

- The archives of the *Los Angeles Times* show that Einstein and his wife Elsa did visit Southern California (and Caltech) during the winters of 1930-31, 1931-32, and from January 10 to March 10, 1933.
- During the first visit, he and Elsa became friends with Charlie Chaplin, whom they had met on the boat coming over. They were his guests of honor at the opening (January 31, 1931) of Chaplin's new film *City Lights*. The *Times* files also show that Einstein spoke at two evening events at the Ambassador Hotel during February 1931.
- When agents re-interview Garritt Lloyd, his story has changed. He now claims he saw Einstein and Chaplin at the Ambassador Hotel "in the mid-thirties," not the early thirties as his letter states. He is sure of the date because Franklin Roosevelt had been President "for several years."

---

* Tycko's name (like Lloyd's) was blacked out of the Einstein file released by the FBI in 1983. It did appear however in the version of the same report released by the Defense Department. But in the newly released pages of The Einstein file, the FBI has "revealed" the identities of both Tycko and Lloyd, as well as the more celebrated names in this episode.

- There is no record of any visit by Einstein to Southern California after March 1933, when Roosevelt became President.
- Employment records show that Garritt Lloyd worked at Griffith Pictures for only six months, not the fourteen years he claimed (Griffith Pictures moved to New York in 1920), and for nine months as a writer at RKO in 1931 ("reason for termination not shown")...Extensive interviews—with Lloyd's former friends, his ex-wife, and others who worked at the Griffith—contradict almost all the specific details in his story. It is not known where else, if anywhere, he worked in the movie industry.
- Interviews with the photographer Tycko and his wife show that he has always been a vehement anti-Communist (although he once seemed interested in Leon Trotsky after Trotsky had split with Stalin and gone into exile). He barely knew Lloyd and never would have asked him to join the Communists. He met Einstein only once, briefly, when he took his photograph, and never met Chaplin.
- Finally, the records of the Ambassador Hotel "fail to indicate that either Albert Einstein or Charlie Chaplin ever had rooms in their own names."

...[I]n their own names. Is the FBI hinting at a possible subterfuge here? Albert Einstein and Charlie Chaplin, probably the two most recognizable figures in twentieth-century America, using assumed names in Hollywood? ("Welcome to our hotel, Doctor Einstein. What name would you like to register under?")

15

Spy Hunt 2: Operation Cable-Drop

Outside the building at 5 Haberlandstrasse in Berlin, where Einstein lives in the spring of 1929, the street is busy. Besides the usual traffic of strollers and shoppers, a steady stream of foreign and German sight-seers stop briefly to stare up at the fourth-floor apartment that is the home of the world's greatest scientist, and since the apartment is also Einstein's office, deliverymen from the central post office enter the street-level door several times a day, along with visitors from around the world and, from time to time, a reporter seeking an interview. Only a few of the passersby wear red armbands with black swastikas—it is still nearly four years before the Nazis will seize power. In the midst of all the activity, Richard Grosskopf glances quickly over his shoulder as he steps into the doorway, but otherwise appears to be just one more visitor.

At the apartment door, Helen Dukas, Einstein's secretary, lets the visitor in and shows him to the foyer. "Wait here." She turns and walks to another room. Grosskopf takes off his hat and stands there, fidgeting nervously, waiting.

In a few minutes, Dukas returns carrying a small packet of cablegrams. She hands the packet to Grosskopf, who puts it in his jacket pocket, gives her a good-bye nod, and leaves.

Walking from the house, Grosskopf again blends in with the bustle of visitors, gawking tourists, and passersby. In a minute, he is gone.

Half an hour later, Grosskopf reappears in another section of Berlin. Glancing over his shoulder again, he enters an official-looking building through its wrought-iron gate, which is held open for him by a uniformed guard. Atop the flagpole just inside the gate is a bright red flag with a yellow hammer-and-sickle in one corner. Above the gate, large metal letters announce: "Embassy of the USSR."

Meanwhile, back in the Einstein apartment, Helen Dukas enters the scientist's study, where he is jotting down some figures on a small, wall-mounted blackboard. Einstein turns halfway to greet her and asks, "Did everything go well with your visitor?"

Dukas begins arranging some papers on the cluttered-looking desk in one corner of the room, then looks directly at Einstein: "Everything's fine." Einstein nods knowingly.

It's not a scene from a new Hollywood hit movie *Einstein the Spy*. It is, essentially, the version of events alleged in the espionage sections of the FBI's Einstein file.

To recapitulate the earlier chapters of this spy story: Hoover's first leads to an Einstein-the-spy scenario did not pan out. They were based on vague recollections—"someone said" Einstein *might* have helped get Fuchs his atom-bomb assignment, or Einstein's son *might* be a Soviet hostage. Then came the wispy allegations from those less-than-totally-stable accusers, Kristel Heineman and Emma Rabbeis. These were short-lived efforts, although perhaps not as short as they deserved to be.

But in September 1950, far more substantial espionage charges against Einstein reached Hoover, compiled by U.S. Army Intelligence (G-2) agents in Germany and sent to the FBI in two reports in 1950 and 1951. Despite some variations, each report told essentially the same story; Between 1929 and 1932, before Einstein moved to America and before Hitler and the Nazis took over Germany, Russian spies in the Far East used Einstein's home in Berlin as a cable-drop to relay double-coded messages to Moscow. Einstein's secretary received the cables and passed them on to couriers— German communists working for Moscow's spy network—who came to the apartment on Haberlandstrasse to make their pickups. Einstein at the very least knew about the arrangement and did nothing to alter it.

What seems most impressive about the G-2 story is its detail. Any good detective will tell you that all else being equal, the more detailed an accus-ation, the more likely it is to be true. When you come upon an extensively detailed case, your reaction tends to be: "No one would make up such a complicated story." The G-2 spy charges, recorded in the FBI's Einstein File, include page after page of dates, places, and especially names of con-tacts, couriers, and collaborators in the alleged spy network:[1]

- Prior to 1933, the Comintern [Communist International] and other Soviet Apparati were very active in gathering intelligence informa-tion in the Far East. Many International Communist functionaries were stationed in SHANGHAI and CANTON....One means of communication...to Central Headquarters in MOSCOW was...telegrams. However, these telegrams, which were always in code, were never sent directly to Moscow, but... to agents in other countries such as Egypt or France, where they were recopied and forwarded to telegram addresses in Berlin. One of these addresses was the [home/office] of EINSTEIN which proved to be very successful since EINSTEIN received a great quantity of mail, telegrams, cablegrams, etc., from all over the world.

- EINSTEIN's personal secretary (her name cannot be recalled) turned over the telegrams to a special Apparat man whose duty was to pick up such mail....

The 1951 report adds a little spice:

- This secretary had close personal relationships, probably of an intimate nature, with an international Apparat [Communist] functionary whom Source cannot identify.
- EINSTEIN's Berlin staff of typists and secretaries...were recommended to him (at his request) by people...close to the "Klub der Geistesarbeiter" (Club of Scientists) which was a Communist cover organization....
- EINSTEIN was closely associated with [that club] and very friendly with Fritz EICHENWALD, Dr. BOBECK, Dr. CARO, Dr. HAUTWERMANN, and Dr. KROMREY...who later became agents of the Soviets. Also associated with this Club were the two FUCHS brothers.
- EINSTEIN's telegram address was for some time under the supervision...of Richard GROSSKOPF, who...was in charge of the KPD's [German Communist Party] passport falsification program.

The G-2 reports claimed that a total of sixteen Germans—all of them on the Gestapo's list of "Communists"—knew about the Einstein cable drop. Five of these, including Grosskopf, were listed as couriers who visited Einstein's house to pick up the coded cables.[2]

For his case against Einstein to work, Hoover had to show not only that Einstein's house was used as a drop by Russian spies, but that Einstein knew about it. (Someone else could have been handling the coded cables from his house while he was out or upstairs sleeping.) How much did Einstein himself know? A key paragraph in the G-2 allegations provided the answer Hoover needed:

EINSTEIN must have become aware of what was going on in the summer of 1930 when his personal secretary went on leave...he was given a large amount of telegrams which he kept until his secretary returned....When the girl [sic] returned...all cables were turned over to her by EINSTEIN and there were no unpleasant repercussions. The use of the cable address by the Soviets continued as in the past.[3]

It wasn't stealing the atom bomb, but it *was* Russian spies, and even in a twenty-year-old case, Einstein's name would guarantee the biggest story of the year, maybe of the decade.

The impact of the new Einstein spy connection, and especially what it could do for the FBI's prestige and budget, had to be among Hoover's first thoughts on the day G-2's 1950 report reached his desk—by coincidence the same day as his testimony before the Senate Appropriations Committee.

In Hoover's forty-six years as FBI director, he never had any serious trouble when it came to approval of his annual budget by Congress. (Hoover may have run the Bureau, but Congress paid the bills and—theoretically— could have affected its operation.) He probably could have sent a subordinate to testify before the House and Senate Appropriations Committees every year, but he preferred to appear himself to make the presentations, which were usually laced with dramatic warnings of the perils in store for America without an increased FBI budget. Hoover seemed to relish the role. In photos of his testimony, he assumes an almost identical pose year after year (only the color of his suit is different), painting a warning finger as he testifies, his square jaw jutting out at an angle that emphasizes stem determination. The same unyielding figure appeared in all the film clips of Hoover introducing Hollywood's FBI movies of the 1950s. His fixation on that tough-cop image—like his belligerent homophobia—may have been a macho mask for insecurity about his own alleged homosexuality, but if you were a victim of his venom, you had more to worry about than Hoover's personal psychodrama.

In the early 1950s, congressional committees were keenly interested in hearing how many hard-core communists Hoover was prepared to put into "detention camps" in case of a war with Russia. This was the "Detention of Communists"—or Det-Com—list. While the FBI had millions of security files, "only" several thousand were slated for such emergency camps. The purpose of Det-Com, David Wise explains, was simply "to determine which of us to lock up in the event of war or a presidentially decreed 'emergency.'"[4] On September 7, 1950 (the day G-2's first Einstein spy-memo arrived), Hoover told the senators the FBI had targeted twelve thousand Reds to be rounded up "in the event of war with Russia." The *Washington Post* reported the next day that he also requested funding for 835 new agents and 1,218 new clerical workers.

Never a stickler for statistics, each time he went before a congressional budget group, Hoover increased the reported number of communists he claimed the FBI was ready to put into detention camps in the event of war. In the six months since he had told a senate subcommittee there were four thousand on the list (following the Klaus Fuchs arrest), Hoover had tripled the number. By April 1951, his Det-Com figure escalated again:

FBI SET TO SEIZE
14,000 REDS IN WAR

Washington, April 27 (1951) (UP)—J. Edgar Hoover, director of the FBI, considers the Communist Party in this country more dangerous than the Nazi Fifth Column during World War II and is ready to arrest 14,000 "dangerous" Reds in event of war with Russia.

...the House Appropriations Committee is considering a proposal to spend $775,000 to prepare four abandoned military camps as places of detention for suspected subversives...[5]

How many people were actually in Hoover's Det-Com file? It wasn't a small number. Former FBI official Neil Welch says there were "thousands," but that when Hoover periodically went before Congress to get his appropriations, "He told them any damn thing they wanted to hear about how many he had on his list," adding with a laugh, "I'm sure that damn list kept growing."[6]

Maybe Hoover allowed himself to dream of making history with a blockbuster Einstein spy case—it would be just the ticket to win approval for his plan to set up FBI offices in Europe—but his well-honed survival instinct told him G-2's first report alone wasn't enough. He had just been through a series of fizzled leads that had first seemed to promise espionage evidence against Einstein. This time, while the 1950 report's details were certainly impressive, the supplier of virtually all those details was a single, unnamed informant sometimes referred to in the report as *Source*. Hoover needed that informant to come forward publicly—if possible, to testify. He had to know the identity of G-2's *Source*.

G-2 was unlikely to let their key witness come to Washington. But the FBI chief had just sent two agents to interview Klaus Fuchs in jail in London; sending someone to the American zone of Berlin to interview *Source* would be no problem. After consulting with Tolson, he wrote to G-2 asking for more details on their Einstein allegations. But the first report, as we've seen, was spilling over with details. The real reason for Hoover's letter was almost certainly his request—

that the information include, if possible, legal evidence and the identity of informants who can testify to the information furnished if the need arose in connection with any action taken against Dr. Einstein by the United States Government.[7]

Asking another agency to reveal an informant's name was, Hoover knew, unusual. But then, "action...against Dr. Einstein by the United States government" wasn't exactly your routine employment check. The FBI chief had reason to expect G-2 to cooperate.

But it wasn't G-2 he needed to worry about. It was the unnamed witness. *Source's* reaction to Hoover's mention of testifying was like a potential witness against the Mafia emerging from a private "sit-down" with Lucky Luciano. Not only didn't he volunteer to testify, *Source* insisted he was through talking to anyone. The bottom line was G-2's "recommendation"—

that no further exploitation be made of *Source* in this case.

Before clamming up, *Source* had reaffirmed to G-2's investigators his basic story about Einstein's spy connection. He changed a few particulars—no longer citing a "staff of secretaries" but now only one or two—and generally distanced himself as a witness, emphasizing that most of what he knew was "hearsay." Nonetheless, he stuck to his story linking Einstein to Soviet espionage, and most of the details were the same. G-2 continued to back him up-primarily because, as discussed earlier, his account was so detailed:

...the information given by *Source,* as far as it goes, is probably accurate. On all points, every effort was made to avoid generalities...

Hoover had to have been disappointed by *Source's* backing out. But apparently eager to leave the scene on good terms, *Source* pointed out a possible substitute supplier of Einstein information: former officials of the *Reichssicherheitshauptamt* (RSHA), the Nazis' central police (state security) agency.

Source told G-2 he'd been a member of the German Communist Party (KPD), working for Grosskopf, before Hitler. But when the Nazis took over in 1933 and started rounding up KPD members, *Source* seems to have had a sudden change of heart-and allegiance. It is evident from his statements to G-2 that he developed a close working relationship with the Nazi internalsecurity apparatus. He reported that an "unnamed person" told RSHA officials "that Einstein's cable address had been used by the Soviets and/or Communists." He also knew "for certain" that as late as 1935, RSHA officials were still "working on" the Einstein case. If Hoover and G-2 wanted to pursue the matter in Germany, *Source's* parting recommendation was—

that former RSHA personnel now available be queried regarding the identity of those officials who, shortly after 1933, worked on the case built up around the cables received by Einstein's office.[8]

Without its informant, the FBI's investigation of Einstein flounders for more than a year. Searching for new sources of information, the Bureau, briefly, resorts to reading. But even reading, in Hoover's FBI, isn't so simple. Like everything else they do on the job, agents need prior approval. In a memo to the Boss on May 16, 1951, the Newark office respectfully submits a "suggestion…that perhaps a review of available biographies or writings concerning EINSTEIN would reveal some of his European associates."

Two weeks later, Hoover gives his permission:

> The Bureau has no objection to a review of available biographies or writings concerning Einstein by Newark for the purpose of determining his former associates in Europe and thereby identifying the unknown personal secretary …who according to G-2 reports allegedly assisted the Soviets during their use of Einstein's Berlin office as a cable address.

At least one Newark FBI agent must have impressed his neighbors and fellow beachgoers that summer by spending his days reading books about Einstein. From these—primarily *Einstein: His Life and Times* by Philipp Frank—by the end of August, the Newark office "discovered" the fact that Helen Dukas "was connected with EINSTEIN since 1928 as a secretary and later as his housekeeper."

In Germany, G-2 was skeptical about any Einstein spy connection and not at all happy about pursuing what they saw as Hoover's project—they probably use another word for it. Pressed by Hoover to come up with some information, G-2 sent a pair of agents door-to-door in Einstein's former neighborhood, asking old-timers for any memories they might have about Albert and his family, especially their political opinions.

GIs in uniform were the law in what was still the American-occupied zone of Berlin in 1951. Only six years after Hitler's defeat, Germans knew that when an American soldier asked a question, no matter how far-fetched, it was best to answer respectfully, if not always honestly. In

---

* In a MEMO FOR RECORD (not sent to the FBI) on October 30, 1950, G-2 chief John Weckerling wrote, "G-2 files reflect considerable support by Einstein of CP fronts but no evidence to support active participation w/Soviet agent activities in Germany." Weckerling notes that he has agreed to Hoover's request to pursue the case, but adds that he will notify Hoover "as a courtesy…inasmuch as it is believed that EUCOM [European Command of G-2] will not be able to provide material needed by Dept/ Justice without considerable expenditure of time." The final, telling line of Weckerling's private note, all capital letters, says: ALTERNATE CPY NOT NECESSARY. (G-2 files, National Archives, not in FBI's file.)

that atmosphere, picture U.S. Army counterintelligence agents traipsing around West Berlin in search of surviving residents and merchants who had lived or worked in Einstein's neighborhood twenty years earlier and might remember something, anything, related to G-2's spy story. The comic-opera nature of the investigation is best illustrated by the agents' own reports from "the field."[9]

First, the G-2 men had to locate the Einsteins' former home. They found the street, but the building had been destroyed during the war. Most of the former residents were gone. They did turn up one former neighbor, Tetzlaff, who remembered that the Einsteins were "friends of the Auerbachs." It didn't exactly break the case wide open, but now the door-to-door gumshoes could pursue the Auerbachs as well as the Einsteins. Their next stop was the grocery store:

> Interrogation of former residents of this area disclosed the existence of Max Krueger, the former grocer of this area. An interview with Krueger on Feb. 24, 1951, disclosed that he knew Frau Auerbach and her daughter Lotte. Krueger praised the character of these two women but could not give any further information.

All in all, G-2's questioning of neighbors discovered:

> The Auerbachs' daughter Lotte married a man named Schiffer and moved to London where they still lived ... The Auerbachs' former housekeeper Marie Kulkoska continues to be a good friend of Einstein and "still receives food packages from him...."

And perhaps more relevant:

> The Auerbachs and the Einsteins "were anti-Nazi because of the persecution of the Jews..." In 1941, Frau Auerbach was arrested by the Gestapo "and has not been heard of since."

G-2's work was handicapped by Hoover's decision to keep the Einstein case secret. Early in the investigation, G-2 Assistant Chief of Staff Paul Guthrie reported: "The prominence of Einstein requires extreme discretion, and possible knowledgeable sources have been deliberately avoided." Even in its door-to-door interviews, G-2 was guided by caution:

> The one possible lead which might be considered capable of further exploitation concerned Marie Kulkoska. Since Marie Kulkoska is considered to stand in close contact with SUBJECT [Einstein], no attempt was made to interview her because of the possibility of compromise of the investigation of SUBJECT.[10]

Ironically, Hoover's secrecy prevented G-2 and FBI investigators from questioning the most logical potential witnesses—Einstein's friends and colleagues. The same cloak of secrecy that made Hoover's dossiers so frightening to so many in high places ("What's he got on me?") was now suffocating his own investigators in the Einstein case.

Gossipy interviews didn't alter the deadly serious goal of the FBI/G-2 investigation: to find someone or something Hoover could use to defame and undermine Einstein. By far, the most intriguing aspect of the G-2 operation in Germany is what they did not investigate. G-2's *Source* had pointed to others who knew about his allegations against Einstein—specifically, former members of the Nazi state security agency RSHA, who had "worked on" the Einstein case as late as 1935 and were "now available." The next step for investigators should not have been hard to figure out. But it didn't happen. G-2 completely ignored this one group of people who, if they believed their own *Source,* knew the Einstein spy story. We can only guess at the reason for this glaring gap in what should have been standard police procedure. But we do know that most former Nazis avoided discussing their past lives—maintaining a silence that eased their way into new jobs and often influential positions in postwar Germany. This was doubly true for former members of the Nazi police or security operations such as RSHA. Also, former Gestapo officers not in prison, many of whom had changed their identities to hide past crimes, were not about to rush forward to talk about the Einstein case.*

Meanwhile, two United States Army counterintelligence agents spent at least several weeks pounding the pavements of West Berlin, knocking on doors, asking questions, taking notes. Seeking evidence of espionage, they ended up with neighborhood gossip. It would be laughable if it hadn't been so time-consuming and expensive, and the purpose—to defame Einstein— so serious.

While he didn't know about Hoover's effort to link him to espionage, the chill in the political air was unmistakable, and Einstein had to have been quite aware that he was the target of increasing Red-baiting flak from the media-Time's sniping at his defense of Willie McGee, *Life's* "Dupes and Fellow Travelers" piece, and, one of the earliest, a 1947 *Newsweek* article, "Paean from Pravda" (duly noted in his FBI file, Section 1), that quoted

---

* We're fairly sure the Gestapo had an Einstein file, because after they raided Einstein's Berlin apartment three times in 1933, they called in the Einsteins' housekeeper, Herta Wallner, for questioning, and she later reported that on the Gestapo interviewer's desk was a sheaf of papers in file marked "Einstein." The file was "quite possibly" destroyed by the Gestapo before the Nazi surrender, according to one authority on Nazi police operations, Robert Gellately, who explains, "The Gestapo destroyed ninety percent of their files on individuals." (Phone interview with Gellately, June 1998.)

at length from the Soviet Communist Party newspaper *Pravda* that had included Einstein on a list of "Russia's many warm friends in the United States."[11]

Most anti-Einstein attacks came from right-wing groups and media. High on the FBI's most frequently cited list was conservative columnist George Sokolsky:

> Sokolsky stated that these conferences—the World Congress of Intellectuals in Defense of Peace held at Wroclaw, Poland and the second one which was held in New York City—were designed to mobilize intellectual propaganda against the United States. He quoted the following message sent by Albert Einstein to Wroclaw: "I hope with all my heart that you will succeed in assembling open-minded personalities with real courage..." (Section 6, p. 986.)

Einstein also continued to be a favorite target for diligent defenders of the flag such as the American Legion and Daughters of the American Revolution, who upheld the mantle of Mrs. Frothingham and the Woman Patriot Corporation:

> On August 19, 1950, Mrs. W.H. Noel, Harlan, Kentucky, [wrote] to the FBI on stationery of the Daughters of the American Revolution of Kentucky...[and] set out a list of names which... the DAR magazine had listed as Communists. Mrs. Noel stated she was going to visit all the Kentucky DAR districts and make a talk on Americanism and inquired if it would be alright to mention their names to be boycotted. The list of names included Professor Albert Einstein. (Section 6, p. 1106.)

Thirty-six years of such sniping had immunized him—Einstein truly seemed indifferent to attacks against him, whether from cranks, editorials, or congressmen like Rankin. As long ago as 1936, he had stated, "Arrows of hate have been shot at me...but they never hit me, because somehow they belonged to another world."

What is more remarkable is how little these attacks affected his popularity—especially considering the widespread fear wrought by the Red scare of the fifties. (In 1951, a newspaper found that the majority of people it surveyed would not sign their name to the Bill of Rights, even after they were told that it simply consisted of the first ten amendments to the U.S. Constitution.) Somehow, Einstein's image and near-universal popularity was immune to such attacks.

Despite the tense times, Einstein continued to receive oceans of mail, and his archives show that with the help of Helen Dukas, he answered many, if not most, of the letters. During the height of the Korean War, to cite one example, he exchanged several letters with Gene Sharp, a twenty-five-yearold conscientious objector and Ohio State graduate who—a generation before Muhammad Ali—had been indicted for defying the draft law and refusing to report for induction. Sharp later received a two-year prison sentence.

With the defeat of the Nazis, Einstein had returned at least partway to pacifism. (He never questioned his support for the anti-fascist fighters in Spain or the Allied anti-Nazi forces during World War II.) Besides his antibomb activism as chairman of the Emergency Committee of Atomic Scientists, and his articles and interviews calling for a World Government as the only solution to war-clashing publicly with bath U.S. and Soviet policies—he urged young people to resist going into the army. He responded to Mr. Sharp:

> I earnestly admire you for your moral strength and can only hope, although I really do not know that I would have acted as you did, had I found myself in the same situation.... The state adheres to the written law; only with great-re-luctance does it take into account the unwritten law of conscience [which] was unmistakably established in the Nuremberg trials [and] is a precious tool in the fight against slavery resulting from the civic duty to kill.[12]

Hoover's fear of a public backlash if word of his anti-Einstein campaign got out was well founded. Despite the anti-Einstein editorial attacks, Einstein remained a favorite among journalists. He almost always had a friendly and usually witty word for the reporters and photographers who turned up at every event, private or public, when they heard he would be present. An Einstein interview, even just a picture, was almost always good for the next morning's front page. One such event spawned a historic news photo. It was Einstein's seventy-second birthday, March 14, 1951 (six weeks after G-2's second secret spy-allegation report), and a group of friends and colleagues had gathered for a party at the Princeton Club. After the party, Einstein patiently posed for news photographers who had heard about the event. As he was getting into a car to leave, Art Sasse, a photographer for International News Photos, called out: "Ya, Professor, shmile for your birthday picture, ya?" It had been a long day. Whether out of fatigue or annoyance at Sasse's use of dialect, Einstein turned and stuck out his tongue at the photographer. Sasse's photo of that moment has become a classic. But before distributing it, INP's editors, worried that the scientist might be offended, almost decided to kill the photo. Instead of being annoyed, Einstein characteristically enjoyed the joke and wrote to INP ordering nine copies of the print. Today, it's one of the world's best-known photos—on T-shirts, coffee mugs, calendars, and posters everywhere, as a symbol of Einstein's maverick spirit.

For popular appeal, Einstein was a hard act to match, but at least within the United States, Hoover was becoming quite a media star himself. While the CIA operated in almost total secrecy—its "achievements" included the overthrow of popular, left-leaning governments in Iran in 1953 and Guatemala a year later—the FBI relished public attention. *As* Korean War casualties mounted and the number of people called before congressional investigating committees grew to hundreds and then to thousands, the FBI became a big-screen feature for millions of American moviegoers. Perhaps to prove their patriotism, Hollywood studios produced a flood of anti-communist feature films, most of which glorified Hoover and his Bureau. In 1951, Frank Lovejoy played a Pittsburgh undercover agent, Matt Cvetic, in *I Was a Communist for the FBI,* and the next year, *My Son John* featured Helen Hayes turning in her communist son to the FBI. As she contemplates her decision, the movie's main FBI agent, played by Van Heflin, spells out the film's message: "That's going to be quite a test. God and country—or her son, John."

Although neither film was a critical success,* anti-communism made up in volume for what it lacked in talent. Hollywood bombarded the public with more than forty such films between 1948 and 1954. Production peaked during the election year of 1952, when no less than twelve Red-menace movies hit the screens. Besides *My Son John,* they were mostly small-budget and small-audience flops, including such sizzlers as *Red Snow, The Steel Fist, Big Jim McClain* (with John Wayne as a HUAC investigator) and *Walk East on Beacon.*[13] Also that year, *I was a Communist for the FBI* became a radio series, and *I Led Three Lives,* the book by under-cover FBI agent Herbert Philbrick, was serialized in hundreds of news-papers. (Five years later, it was repackaged as a prime-time TV show.)**

By the end of 1952, the Republicans, under Eisenhower, had recaptured the White House after twenty years, and all signs pointed to an even more conservative and anti-communist period ahead. Joe McCarthy was the most publicized man in America and seemed to be on an unstoppable

---

* The American Board of Review of Motion Pictures panned *My Son John*, stating it would make the U.S. look ridiculous abroad (Films in Review, 5/52). American Mercury (6/52) said, "What is being upheld here is purely stupidity." And Bosley Crowther's *New York Times* review said, "It seethes with the sort of emotionalism and illogic that is characteristic of so much thinking these days."

** The popularity of pro-FBI films and books is open to much question. Besides the movie box-office flops mentioned above, there's the case of two books on the 1966 "best-seller" list: *The FBI Story* and *Hoover's Masters of Deceit*. In fact, the ultraconservative Dorothy H. and Lewis Rosenstiel Foundation purchased 25,000 copies of each book, making them instant best-sellers. Lewis Rosenstiel, chairman of the board of Schenley's, was also a leading supporter of the J. Edgar Hoover Foundation and the American Jewish League Against Communism, whose founder and president was Roy Cohn. Cohn was not only Joe McCarthy's top aide, he was "the apple of Hoover's eye."(Nash, p. 109.)

power trip—who could predict how far he might rise? More than a hundred officials of the U.S. Communist Party were in jail under the Smith Act, and many states were enforcing their own anti-communist and sedition laws. In Connecticut, the state sedition act outlawed publication of "scurrilous or abusive matter, concerning the form of government in the United States, its military forces, flag or uniform"; under Tennessee's law, anyone guilty of unlawfully advocating the violent overthrow of the government could be executed;[14] and Texas approved the death penalty for anyone convicted of membership in the Communist Party. The following June, the Rosenbergs would be electrocuted.

There could not have been a time more ripe for an Einstein spy exposé. But G-2 in Germany had so far come up with nothing to support the story from *Source*. With no help from the Army, Hoover needed a credible witness willing to testify to Einstein's connections to the Russians or the Reds—a witness who would give some relevant detail from pre-war Germany. In a Hollywood courtroom drama, this would be the moment for the "mystery witness" to make a surprise appearance. Once in a while, life does seem to imitate the movies.

MYSTERY WITNESS

Miami was drizzly on Friday morning, September 4, 1953, when the dapper, well-dressed, sixtyish man walked into the FBI office and in a clipped German accent, informed the receptionist that he had important information about Albert Einstein's Communist activities. During the night, Hurricane Carol had curled away from the mainland, leaving Miamians relieved and eager to get an early start on the long Labor Day weekend. But there was something about the poised way the man carried himself, perhaps his distinguished European manner of speaking, perhaps his reference to the famous Einstein, that convinced the receptionist to call the SAC's office right away.

In the late summer of 1953, Miami's FBI office was a relatively quiet assignment. The city was still small, segregated, and thoroughly Southern. (Besides cheering Hurricane Carol's turn toward the open sea, some Miamians were celebrating the capture in New York of George "Limpy" Anderson, who had escaped from a Dade County jail in May while awaiting trial on charges of killing a motorcycle patrolman. *The Miami Herald* described Anderson as a "35-year-old Negro" and a "trigger-happy desperado.") It was five years before Castro's band of guerrillas came to power ninety miles away and started the flow of refugees who transformed the city, and another five years before it became a center for the billion-dollar business of illegal drugs. In the early 1950s, the Miami SAC's most nerve-rattling job may have been hosting Hoover's annual Christmas-vacation visit.*

The unexpected arrival of the suave German, bearing information about Einstein's "subversive" past, had to make for an extraordinary day at the office for the FBI's Miami SAC, who rushed off an urgent memo to the Newark office, which was coordinating the Einstein investigation. The Newark SAC immediately sent a copy to Hoover. The walk-in witness told an unusual story (with an unusual slant on science):

> ...an individual of German origin who has been in the United States but a few years, stated that he has known of [Einstein] for many years and that in 1905 EINSTEIN developed a hypothetical theory of relativity...in 1919...the German Left-wing press hailed EINSTEIN as a great scientist...[However] Einstein...was not a scientist or a philosopher, but was a politician who would bring the German people to anarchism and Communism....

For Hoover's efforts to pin something serious on Einstein, the most important comment from the "individual of German origin" was:

> ...in an article that appeared...sometime between August 20 and 25, 1920 in the "Berliner Tageblatt...*Einstein admitted that he was a Communist* [emphasis added].

The witness told the Miami SAC that he had tried to get a copy of Einstein's 1920 article from the Library of Congress and the New York Public Library, but couldn't locate it...

> because of his unfamiliarity with library procedures in this country and, due to his unfamiliarity with the language in making himself clearly understood.[15]

The FBI censors who blacked out the Miami witness's name in their 1983-released version of the Einstein file, did not count on two German scholars, Klaus Hentschel and Andreas Kleinert, who, besides studying history, enjoy solving puzzles. After considerable research, each of them concluded that the Miami walk-in witness was a seedy character named Paul Weyland. In his detailed biographical study, Kleinert reports that Weyland was in Miami in August and September 1953, and knew about the Berlin newspaper thirty years earlier. Hentschel, too, was convinced it was Weyland, but to be certain, he carefully measured how many

---

* The Boss came down with Clyde Tolson for two weeks every Christmas, but they had almost no contact with local agents, keeping to the beach and the track. Miami Special Agent Tim O'Malley, known for his horse handicapping, apparently had no other assignment except to squire Hoover and Tolson around on their annual visits. (Welch, pp. 68-69.)

letters would fill the space of the FBI file's blacked-out name. The letters in Paul Weyland's name were a perfect fit.[16] (It will come as no surprise to Hentschel and Kleinert, but they may be reassured to hear that in the "un-redacted" pages the FBI released in 2000, the Bureau censors have removed their black-out, "revealing" Paul Weyland's name.)

To understand Weyland's role in this case, it requires going back to Berlin in the chaotic days following Germany's defeat in World War I. Most Einstein biographies briefly mention Weyland as the organizer of a series of public meetings in Berlin in 1920, held to denounce the Theory of Relativity and to attack Einstein with thinly veiled anti-Semitic insults. The meetings were organized by the Working Party of German Scientists for the Preservation of Pure Science—a mouthful of a title that Einstein scornfully renamed "Anti-Relativity, Inc." Weyland was not only the president of that "organization," he was its entire membership. As the public face for the anti-relativity crowd, Weyland was energetic but lacked scientific credentials. Einstein had tried in vain to determine his background. "Doctor? Engineer? Politician? I was unable to find out," Einstein wrote in *Berliner Tageblatt*.[17] While Weyland's public speeches were too shrill to be taken seriously at that time, for nearly a year, he mobilized significant support and publicity for a major anti-Einstein, anti-Semitic, Germany-First campaign. It was an ominous preview.

Who was behind this effort? Alone, it seems highly doubtful that Weyland could have organized his way out of a paper bag, let alone put on public meetings. He had no money of his own, yet his "organization" rented the Berlin Concert Hall and provided hefty fees to anti-relativity speakers. Who paid this piper—and called his tune?

The most prominent star in Weyland's anti-relativity show was Nobel Prize-winning physicist Philipp Lenard, who had secretly and successfully lobbied the Nobel Prize Committee in Stockholm for several years to withhold the award from Einstein.* Years later, as Hitler's chief scientist,

---

* Before winning the 1921 Nobel Prize, Einstein had been nominated and rejected ten times in the previous twelve years. Some years later, Irving Wallace (The Prize) interviewed Dr. Sven Hedin, one of the Nobel judges. Wallace writes in The Writing of One Novel that Hedin acknowledged Lenard had had great influence with many of the judges, convincing them to keep the prize away from Einstein. Lenard probably didn't have to work terribly hard, as Hedin himself later publicly supported the Nazis and was a close friend of Goering, Himmler, and Hitler. To readers familiar with official explanations, it will probably come as no surprise that in the records of the Nobel Committee for Physics, among the many explanations the committee provides for having rejected Einstein ten times between 1910 and 1921, anti-Semitism is not included. For a detailed account of the Committee's official comments, as well as the nomination process, see Pais (*Einstein Lived Here*), pp. 68-76.

Lenard wrote "Science, like every other human product, is racial and conditioned by blood."[18] While Lenard, in 1920, led the public attack on relativity and Einstein, one of Weyland's secret financial backers reportedly was the notoriously anti-Semitic, American industrialist Henry Ford.[19]

It was still a bit early, however, for such widespread *public* anti-Semitism in Germany. Virtually the entire war-weary world was celebrating Einstein; he was an honored guest at universities and civic and scientific societies in almost every continent; and crowds cheered him everywhere—except at home, where he was attacked by anti-Semites. As noted earlier, the antiEinstein campaign embarrassed Germany's postwar Weimar Republic, which put the brakes on the attackers, and by mid 1921, Weyland had left Germany. Also gone was a right-wing magazine he edited, *German Peoples Monthly,* which ceased publication after just one vitriolic issue aimed at "cleansing Germany of Jews."

Thanks to Kleinert, we know that Weyland's Berlin scam was just one in a long series. After his flash of notoriety as Berlin's anti-relativity entrepreneur, Weyland showed up in New York on Halloween (October 31, 1921) and managed to arrange an interview with the *New York Times.* Learning from his past omissions, this time he gave himself a Ph.D., and as "Dr. Paul Weyland, President of the Association of German Natural Scientists," told the *Times* (January 2, 1922) that German chemists had discovered how to make motor fuel from water and calcium carbide. Asked about politics, "Dr. Weyland" proclaimed that the German people favored a monarchy over democracy. No doubt figuring that if you can

---

* In 1923, when Henry Ford announced he might become a candidate for U.S. President, a little-known Nazi Party leader in Germany named Adolf Hitler told the *Chicago Tribune:* "I wish I could send some of my shock troops to Chicago and other big American cities to help." (Higham, Trading with the Enemy, p. 155.) Hitler was a fan of Ford's booklet *The International Jew: The World's Foremost Problem.* The booklet first appeared as a series of articles in Henry Ford's newspaper, misnamed *The Dearborn Independent.* "At the peak of its popularity, the Dearborn, Michigan paper, owned by Ford, boasted a circulation of 700,000. It first attacked Jews in its May 22, 1920, issue and continued to do so in its subsequent 91 editions." (Anti-Defamation League: "Anti-Semitism from the Roaring Twenties Revived on the Web," available on-line.) In *Mein Kampf,* asserting that the Jews were the "controlling masters" of American production, Hitler added: "Only a single great man, [Henry] Ford, to their [the Jews'] fury, still maintains full independence." Ford was a financial backer of the ultraright anti-Semite, Elizabeth Dilling (Higham, American Swastika, p.60), and in 1938, the year of Kristallnacht, Ford accepted the Grand Cross of the German Eagle, the highest Nazi award given to non-Germans. (For a detailed account of how Ford's company collaborated with the Nazis even as late as August 1942, well after the United States entered the war, see "Ford and the Fuhrer" by Ken Silverstein, *The Nation,* January 24, 2000.)

fool 'em there *(New York Times)*, you can fool 'em anywhere, Weyland spent the next seventeen years traveling the world—Sweden, Switzerland, South America, North Africa, Spain, and Belgium—trying to hustle loans, grants, and investment capital from German consulates, banks, and businessmen to support his "research." But sooner or later, "Dr. Weyland" was almost always spotted as a charlatan and had to move on. In 1938, he unsuccessfully tried to embezzle money from his ideological allies, the Nazis, who put him in prison. After the war, Weyland hustled a job with the U.S. occupation forces in Germany—first as an interpreter and then in the Berlin Document Center, where he had access to all the records of the Nazi Party. The opportunity was simply too tempting for an old con-artist like Weyland to resist, and he began extorting money from people by threatening to reveal their past Nazi connections. But in 1946, he was exposed, and facing a major lawsuit for extortion, moved again. With thousands of other Germans, Weyland and his wife Kate had no trouble in immigrating to the United States in 1949.[20]

Weyland's polka-dotted past—even if Hoover had known about it—in no way diminished the potential value of his story for the FBI chief's case against Einstein. After receiving the Miami report, Hoover immediately ordered his Washington field office to track down and translate the 1920 article in *Berliner Tageblatt*. Although it wasn't espionage-related, if the article showed that Einstein had declared he was a communist in Germany, his failure to report that membership when he became a United States citizen would undermine his credibility. Besides tarnishing Einstein's image, it was grounds for revoking his citizenship, grounds Hoover could send to the Immigration and Naturalization Service. (See Chapter 16.) In Weyland, Hoover had finally found a witness willing to come forward and publicly denounce Einstein as a communist, a witness who had been doing it for years.

* * *

Weyland's walk-in testimony was, assuming it checked out, an unexpected bonus for. Hoover, but his agents had also located another informant, someone potentially more valuable than Weyland to the Bureau's anti-Einstein campaign—a man whose experience and knowledge seemed to assure his qualifications as an expert at identifying communists and their fellow travelers.

In the three years following Eleanor Roosevelt's first TV program, the FBI had amassed 1,160 pages of "derogatory information" on Einstein. But the file was repetitious, unvetted, and too big to circulate to other government agencies (not known for their ability to digest long reports) or even to "leak" to the press when the time was right. Hoover ordered the Newark office to put together a "comprehensive summary," selecting the most important items from the mammoth Einstein dossier, and on August 5, 1953—forty-three months after Hoover began his secret antiEinstein campaign—he approved a 143-page "Summary Report on Einstein," prepared by Newark Special Agent Vincent E. Murphy. (FBI censors blacked out Murphy's name in both the 1983 release and the "unredacted" version of Einstein's dossier released in 2000, but other sources confirm that he was the report's author, and Murphy himself, when asked, did not deny it.*)

Far more than a summary, Murphy's report levels the FBI's most serious accusations against Einstein, including several new, espionage-related charges. From its opening note, it has the tone of an indictment:

> NOTE: This memorandum is classified "Security Information-Secret" inasmuch as secret information from G-2 is included. Albert Einstein is the subject of a pending Internal Security-R investigation….[R is FBIese for Russia.]

Besides listing Einstein's "Red-front" affiliations and repeating the claim that Einstein's Berlin office had been a cable-drop for Soviet spies in the Far East, Murphy's summary, for the first time, alleges:

> The Fuchs brothers, one of whom was Klaus Fuchs…were members of the same club as EINSTEIN.

This appears to be a very loose adaptation—not really new—of a point made by G-2's *Source,* but *Source* never claimed that Einstein was a member of Fuchs' club, and in fact, *Source's* second G-2 report of January 13, 1951 specifically stated that Einstein was not a member.

> PAUL RUEGG… Comintern agent and head of the Fareastern [sic] Bureau … at one time had a large amount of intelligence information and [used] EINSTEIN'S address and another cover address to forward this information. RUEGG was…arrested on 6/15/31 by the Shanghai Municipal Police.

> Among those individuals active in the successful espionage ring headed by RICHARD SORGE was one GUNTHER STEIN, a British Journalist… phone calls were made from STEIN's residence to Dr. ALBERT EINSTEIN AND HELEN DUKAS.

---

* When I called Murphy at his home in Gillette, NJ, he first said the Einstein case was "so long ago" he couldn't remember anything about it. When I offered to read sections of his 1953 Summary Report to him as a possible memory refresher, he said he didn't want to discuss it. He did not respond to a second call or two letters requesting an off-the-record discussion.

234 THE EINSTEIN FILE

If the charges were true, the names of two top Soviet agents in the Far East, Paul Ruegg (alias Hilaire Noulens) and Moscow's superspy Richard Sorge, would add inches to the height of Hoover's headlines when he was ready to release his Einstein "spy case." The cameo appearances of Sorge and Ruegg lend Einstein's FBI file a touch of James Bond (Volkman calls Sorge "the greatest [spy] of them all"), but more important, suggest that Murphy had a source familiar with the workings and history of the international communist apparatus (Comintern).[21] In fact, one of Murphy's confidential informants (code number T-136) was just such a person: Louis Gibarti. (Gibarti's name, like Agent Murphy's, was blacked out by FBI censors in both the old 1983 and newly released 2000 versions of the Einstein file.*) A Hungarian-born communist whose real name was Laszlo Dobos, Gibarti spent fifteen years of his life, from 1923 to 1938, as a Comintern agent, with several assignments in the United States, before getting caught in an intense factional battle with Moscow.

Here, a brief historical detour may be helpful (for those who were born in the past sixty years): The Comintern (Communist International) was organized shortly after the Russian revolution of 1917, under Lenin's leadership, to ensure that the Communist Parties in all countries followed a common, or at least coordinated, revolutionary strategy. Delegates from CPs around the world met regularly and, theoretically, determined that strategy, although in most cases, the line came from Moscow. CP members from many countries served as Comintern agents and, often holding other jobs such as journalists or academics, traveled the world to ensure that the line was being followed. They also picked up information—and local people who would supply information—that was useful to Moscow. But a major part of their job was, in fact, to see to it that the Comintern line was carried out.

Gibarti was assigned to work with the U.S. Party at the start of America's Great Depression. In 1930, he sent an official message to the Party leaders in New York "urging" that they and their front group, the Unemployed Councils, immediately set up "soup kitchens to feed large unemployed families, the long-term unemployed, and pregnant women." (Some leaders of the U.S. Party had objected, arguing that such soup kitchens would contradict their demand that the government provide unemployment

---

* It's usually difficult to track down informants when the FBI has withheld their names, but in this case, J. Edgar Hoover himself made it easier by sending Gibarti's name to six other government agencies. Although Hoover's memo, too, was blacked out by the Bureau's classifiers, several of the other agencies, including Army Intelligence (G-2), identified Gibarti (Confidential Informant T-136) in their files as a key contributor to Murphy's Summary.

insurance. But after receiving Gibarti's missive, the Party did set up soup kitchens.) In 1934, he arrived in the United States, officially representing a group called Workers International Relief. One of his Comintern assignments was to oversee the Party's work with the unemployed.[22]

After Lenin's death, Stalin became increasingly preoccupied with what he believed were anti-Soviet conspiracies orchestrated by Western powers. He was especially mistrusting of foreigners, suspecting and accusing many of them (including loyal communists from other countries) of being agents of imperialism. This culminated in the widely publicized "purge trials" of the mid 1930s. At the same time, Stalin began to rely less on the Comintern and more on his own network of Soviet KGB (then called NKVD) agents. In a major struggle inside the communist movement, a number of Comintern agents became disheartened, some criticized Stalin and the "trials," and many left—or were expelled from—the Party. One of those who left in 1938 was Louis Gibarti.[23] (Stalin's 1939 nonaggression pact with Hitler drove out more Comintern agents, and Stalin finally dissolved the Comintern in 1943.)

Picture Gibarti in 1938: his whole adult life devoted to the communist movement and now, suddenly, if not alone, at least lonely—a man without a Party. He has been not just a loyal follower, but also a dedicated cadre, devoting his life, full time, to helping the Comintern remake the world into a sharing place, an egalitarian society. The belief has not died, but the leadership, and especially Stalin, has betrayed the goal. What's left is a handful of friends also expelled, or self-expelled, and now "enemies of the working class," which means enemies of the Party, which means on the run—yet still fiercely anti-Nazi and hoping somehow to build a new socialist movement. In Paris, the little group publishes a magazine, The Future, in 1939, but the future ends the next year when the Nazis march into Paris.[24] Gibarti moves south, and when the Nazis get to Southern France, he crosses the border into Spain, which is officially neutral but is really neutral for Hitler, and it doesn't take long before Franco's police arrest him. He spends the war years in a Spanish jail. After the war, Gibarti continues his search for an antiStalinist, left-wing movement, and some years later, he approaches the newly formed Congress of Cultural Freedom, one of whose leaders is another Hungarian-born ex-Comintern agent, Arthur Koestler, to ask about writing for their journal Encounter. But trust is scarce in this group, already fraught with factions and riddled with rumors about the source of its fonds,* and they turn Gibarti down.

---

* Although some critics saw the hand of the CIA pulling the purse strings, it was decades before the Agency acknowledged its role as the group's secret sponsor. The CIA

Politically homeless, Gibarti appeared to be if not a symbol of his times, at least a sympathy-deserving victim, caught between two sides...until the summer of 1950, when he decided to become an informant for the U.S. government. We don't know what spurred him that July to approach the American Embassy and its legal attaché in Paris. (Or did the legal attaché approach him?) If he was out of work, it may have been the twenty thousand francs (equivalent to a year's pay for a skilled worker in the United States) the Embassy official paid him for filling out a questionnaire. Whatever the cause, Gibarti had to know the Embassy's questionnaire was just the first slip down the slope. Within six months, he gave an interview to the FBI, and six months later, the Senate Internal Security Subcommittee (chaired then by McCarthy's Democratic Party clone and Senate ally Pat McCarran) sent a subcommittee to Paris to question him. In both interviews, Gibarti cooperated fully, naming names, identifying people he had known during his Comintern work, and providing other details. The McCarran Committee promptly sent a copy of his testimony to the FBI.[25]

If Weyland's charlatanism was as easy to spot as a three-dollar bill, Louis Gibarti was far more successful in concealing his duplicity. Keeping quiet about his cooperation with the FBI and the McCarran Committee, he managed to land a position as a public-relations consultant to India's Prime Minister Nehru, and even accompanied Nehru to the 1955 international conference of nonaligned nations in Bandung, Indonesia.* As Comintern historian Helmut Gruber put it, "Gibarti played both sides of the political aisle."[26]

Included in Gibarti's secret testimony to the FBI in 1951 were allegations against Einstein. Besides mentioning Sorge and Ruegg—Gibarti had known Sorge in Berlin in the 1920s—the ex-Comintern agent added a new name to the list of Einstein's international communist contacts. Juergen Kuczynski, whose father Robert, a prominent economist in Berlin, had been a friend of Einstein's before they both became refugees from Hitler. Citing Gibarti as its source, Murphy's report states:

---

document, "Secret Cultural Cold War: Origins of the Congress for Cultural Freedom, 1949-1950," is available over the Internet, with some parts "redacted for security considerations."

* The nonaligned nations, whose leaders in Bandung included Indonesia's Sukarno, Yugoslavia's Tito, and Nehru, welcomed China's foreign minister, Chou En Lai, to the conference but gave a decidedly suspicious reception to U.S. Congressman Adam Clayton Powell, Jr., who attended their meeting without State Department approval. We can imagine how fast the conference organizers would have ousted Gibarti if they had known he was an informant for the FBI and the McCarran Committee.

JUERGEN KUCZYNSKI arrived in the US in the late l920's or early 1930's. Due to the fact that Professor EINSTEIN was acquainted with the father, he took a strong interest in his son, JUERGEN...[They] are very close friends and KUCZYNSKI has frequently visited EINSTEIN in Princeton....

According to Murphy/Gibarti, Juergen Kuczynski was "probably a member of the CP in Germany [and] possibly a member...in the US."

In 1922, when Robert Kuczynki (Juergen's father) saw the front-page news photo with the announcement that Einstein had won the Nobel Prize, he said to his wife, "Oh, that's the little physicist I sometimes take the train with, coming home from meetings of the Liga [League for Human Rights]." Like Einstein, Kuczynski was a Jewish intellectual who supported Germany's struggling Weimar Republic after World War I. And like Einstein, he leaned toward socialism. What Kuczynski liked most about Einstein was his "wise unpretentiousness."[27] When the Nazis took power in 1933, they both became refugees, the economist in London and his "little physicist" friend in Princeton.

The Kuczynski family illustrates the segue, seen frequently in the decades before and during World War II, from anti-fascism to communism, and in some cases, to espionage. Robert Kuczynski was not a communist, but according to the FBI, the KPD "utilized him in...campaigns attempting to improve German social legislation."[28] Another version of the story is that as the Nazi threat became ever more frightening inside Germany, Kuczynski saw the communists battling Hitler's gangs in the streets and quite consciously decided to work with the KPD. As he moved closer to the Party, so did his son and daughter, who became communist cadres, and in the cause of saving communism, which they equated with saving the Soviet Union from the Nazi assault, agreed to collect information for Moscow.

In the world of spies, the most important Kuczynski was Juergen's sister Ursula—better known by her adopted name, Ruth Werner—described by one espionage authority as "the most brilliant Soviet intelligence agent in all of Great Britain."[29] Breaking in with the Sorge spy ring in China, she was eventually assigned to England, where she became the "handler" for Klaus Fuchs, relaying his nuclear information to Moscow for two years before he joined the Manhattan Project in Los Alamos. At the time, Fuchs was working at the British atomic research facility, innocuously named the Tube Alloys Project. With the nuclear "squiggles" Ruth Werner transmitted from Fuchs, the Soviets were able to start working on their atomic-bomb project in 1942, saving them years and possibly helping as much as anything Fuchs later sent from Los Alamos. Ruth also enlisted the help of two economists she knew well—her father, then teaching at

Oxford, and her brother Juergen, who worked at the British Air Ministry and had access to strategic military data. While never as celebrated as his sister, Juergen was "an active GRU [Soviet Intelligence] agent throughout the war," and it was he who introduced Fuchs to Soviet intelligence officers in London.[30]

In the fall of 1953, Hoover's case against Einstein had never looked so promising. Weyland's statements in Miami pointed to a possible Einstein cover-up of a communist past, and Murphy's Summary Report, supported by testimony from former Comintern Agent Gibarti, connected Einstein to Kuczynski and suggested a link, albeit twenty years earlier, to the top Soviet spies in the Far East. The charges still needed checking out, of course, but Hoover certainly must have hoped that so much smoke signaled at least a little fire. In October, the FBI chief sent a copy of Murphy's Summary Report to G-2 headquarters in Washington—going over the heads of the officers in Germany. Noting that the G-2 in Germany had not sent even an update on their Einstein investigation since January 8, Hoover concluded:

> It will be appreciated if the Department of the Army will complete its investigation at the earliest possible time and forward the results to this Bureau.[31]

The Newark office also sent copies of Murphy's Summary Report with Gibarti's input to twenty-two FBI offices around the country. In addition, Hoover sent it to the intelligence divisions of the Army, Navy, and Air Force, the CIA, the State Department, and the Atomic Energy Commission. He also sent it to the Immigration and Naturalization Service, where it added to an effort, already underway, aimed at deporting Albert Einstein.

16

"Undesirable Alien"

Americans are proud that he sought and found here a climate of freedom in his search for knowledge and truth.

—*President Dwight D. Eisenhower on Einstein's death, May 1955*

When he wrote that eulogy to Einstein, President Eisenhower's speech-writer possibly didn't know it, but for five years—under Eisenhower, and President Truman before him—the government's Immigration and Naturalization Service (INS), with help from the FBI, had been conducting a secret effort to take away Einstein's citizenship and then deport him as "an undesirable alien."

On March 8, 1950 (Einstein file, section 1), FBI Director J. Edgar Hoover received an unusual request from the INS:

Please furnish a report as to the nature of any derogatory information contained in any file...your Bureau may have concerning the following person:

Name: Einstein, Albert
Date of birth: March 14, 1879
Birthplace: Ulm, Germany
Marital status: Widower
Name of spouse: Elsa Einstein
Race: Hebrew
Color: White
Sex: Male
Occupation: Professor of Theoretical Physics

A follow-up INS memo explained:

"...this naturalized person, notwithstanding his world-wide reputation as a scientist, may properly be investigated for possible revocation of naturalization" [the first step in the deportation process for a naturalized citizen].

It is tempting to see the deportation effort as another example of one or two crazies who wormed their way into the federal woodwork—if not the White and Red Queens from Wonderland, perhaps the ghost of the Woman Patriot Corporation. But interviews of present and former INS employees, a search through archives, and an examination of that part of their Einstein file that the Agency's officials were willing to release,* tell a different, more ominous story.

One evening in May 1951, the Philadelphia district director of the INS, Karl I. Zimmerman, and his wife walked into a restaurant for dinner, only to be greeted by eighty-six INS employees who had gathered for a surprise party in honor of what the INS *Monthly Review*[1] newsletter called "40 years of distinguished service" by "their chief" (Zimmerman). The most newsworthy aspect of the dinner party, the same newsletter reported, was the congratulatory greeting sent to Zimmerman by incoming INS Commissioner Argyle R. Mackey. INS commissioners, of course, like all politicians, frequently sent greetings to benefit events honoring key employees. But Mackey, a Virginia politician connected to the Byrd machine, had just been appointed that month and was still moving into his Washington office. No one would have thought poorly of him if he'd missed a dinner party for one district director. Yet Mackey made sure to send his greeting, and the INS newsletter made sure everyone else knew he'd sent it.

Zimmerman was one of the few employees at that dinner party who could remember the old Immigration Bureau when it was still part of the "Commerce and Labor Department." He'd been on the job for about eight years when the bureau took part in the "Palmer raids," organized by a young Justice Department go-getter named J. Edgar Hoover. Although they rarely receive "recognition" for it, Immigration agents had teamed up with Justice Department deputies on those raids, helping to make the ten thousand arrests of suspected foreign-born communists in cities across the country. Several arresting agents reportedly used unnecessary violence, and many of those arrested were paraded through city streets

---

* "The INS has not always played it straight with freedom of information. When Professor Richard Schwartz submitted a FOIA request to INS in 1983 for their file on Einstein, the INS responded (Nov. 8, 1983) that "the investigation was never conducted." This response turns out to have been less than truthful. In fact, the INS amassed what the FBI described as "a rather extensive file on Professor Albert Einstein"(FBI Einstein File, Section 3, p.300). Of the nearly 500 pages in the INS Einstein File, 395 were sent to the Agency by the EBI, ten pages came from Naval Intelligence (ONI), and a small (still undisclosed) number from Army Intelligence and the State Department. In addition, in response to my FOIA request, INS released 62 pages "which originated with the INS." (Letter from Ave M. Sloane, Chief, FOIA/PA Unit, INS, Aug. 31, 1998.)

in chains. "A number...were badly beaten by the police...their heads wrapped in bandages," The New York Times reported. "Most of them also had blackened eyes and lacerated scalps..."[2]

Some 6,500 were released immediately after questioning—many were U.S. citizens, arrested "by mistake." Of the rest, most were released within weeks. Nonetheless, as a result of the raids, more than five hundred non-citizens were deported with only a smattering of protest from the rest of the country. In David Caute's words:" A nation of immigrants developed a great fear of the immigrant."

Later, the raids were denounced in Congress and the press as violations of human rights and the U.S. Constitution.* Montana Senator Thomas Walsh called the searches and seizures without warrants "the lawless acts of a mob."[3] But not everyone had such negative memories, and from what we know of Zimmerman, deporting "undesirable aliens" might well have been in his thoughts thirty years later, when he submitted the INS request to the FBI for "derogatory information" on Einstein.

To explain why the INS has decided to go after Einstein, Zimmerman sends the FBI a five-page memo that reveals at least as much about the immigration agency as about Einstein. Two aspects of this INS/Zimmerman "indictment" of Einstein are unusual. First, the report focuses almost all its fire on a single "subversive activity"—Einstein's support for groups fighting the Nazi-supplied fascist forces of Francisco Franco during and after the Spanish Civil War.** Under the 1940 Alien Registration Act, a naturalized citizen like Einstein could have his citizenship revoked if it could be proved that he had failed to reveal past membership in any group that advocated the violent overthrow of the U.S.

---

* The New York Times, which became one of the sharpest critics of the Palmer raids, had originally reported the roundup with front-page praise, including this unsubstantiated headline: EVIDENCE SHOWING CAMPAIGN TO FORM SOVIET COUNCILS AND OVERTHROW GOVERNMENT.

** Besides denouncing Einstein's support for the Spanish Republic, the INS/Zimmerman memo briefly cites as a possible reason for deporting Einstein the old charge that he was in "the leadership" of the First World Congress Against War and Fascism held in August 1932 in Amsterdam. The charge was no more true in 1950 than when Hoover sent it to the War Department ten years earlier.

Labeling Einstein "a pacifist and Communist sympathizer," the INS memo also mentions Einstein's sponsorship of the 1949 Scientific and Cultural Conference for World Peace. HUAC listed 49 names of sponsors of the conference, and according to Zimmerman's memo, "Among those listed is Albert Einstein." Although the conference had some 500 sponsors, HUAC's list of 49 sponsors is quite similar to Life magazine's photo display (April 4, 1949) of 50 "Dupes and Fellow Travelers" reportedly attending the same conference.

government. In Einstein's case, this meant the allegations focused on his pre-1940 (the year he was naturalized) affiliation with anti-Franco groups. These groups did not advocate overthrowing the U.S. government, but the attorney general had put them on his official "subversive" list, which made them fair game for the INS. As we've seen, few twentieth-century conflicts polarized the right and left as publicly, dramatically, and widely as the Spanish Civil War. Conservative groups consistently supported Franco. After World War II, right-wing forces in the United States used Franco's technical neutrality during the war to advocate increased support for the Spanish dictator and denounce his opponents. Remember, Mississippi's Rankin attacked Einstein just three months after the war's end for having endorsed the American Committee for Spanish Freedom. (RANKIN WANTS FBI TO CURB EINSTEIN, declared a *Detroit News* headline.[4]) Others who continued to hail Franco and Red-bait his opponents included HUAC, the officialdom of the Roman Catholic Church, and the American Legion, which gave its 1951 Award of Merit to Generalissimo Francisco Franco.

On the other hand, popular American culture sided with the elected Spanish government and its Loyalist supporters, no matter that they were mainly on the left. Millions read Hemingway's *For Whom the Bell Tolls* or saw Gary Cooper in the movie, and millions more admired Picasso's *Guernica*, honoring the Spanish civilians massacred by Franco's (German and Italian) planes.

Not yet five years after World War II, therefore, it was unusual for a U.S. government "indictment" to make anti-fascism the cardinal sin, the litmus test for disloyalty—if you oppose Franco, your litmus paper turns red.

The second atypical aspect of the Zimmerman/INS memo is even more revealing. The primary source Zimmerman cites to certify Einstein's subversive character is *The Tablet*, which he describes simply as "a paper published in Brooklyn, New York." Attached to the memo is a long article about Einstein reprinted from *The Tablet* of February 25, 1950, which *"might justify the filing of a suit to cancel citizenship"* [emphasis added]. First, Zimmerman quotes *The Tablet* quoting HUAC*:

> [*The Tablet*] stated that a report of the House Committee on Un-American Activities…shows that Albert Einstein was an endorser of the North American

---

* On those occasions when the various anti-communist agencies, journalists, and organizations felt a need to cite "authoritative" sources, HUAC was their favorite. Other Red-scare congressional investigating committees, such as the Senate Internal Security Committee and McCarthy's Permanent Sub-Committee on Investigations were also frequently quoted, but HUAC was the most prolific, and of all the Red-scare productions on the Washington circuit, had by far the longest (more than twenty-five years) run.

Committee to Aid Spanish Democracy [and] was named a sponsor of [its] Medical Bureau...In reports of the Special Committee on Un-American Activities dated Jan. 3, 1940 and March 29, 1944, the North American Committee to Aid Spanish Democracy was cited as a Communist-front organization.

Next, Zimmerman cites *The Tablet* citing the attorney general: "In a list furnished the Loyalty Review Board by Attorney General [Tom] Clark which was released to the press...April 25, 1949, the committee [to Aid Spanish Democracy] was cited as Communist." And finally, Zimmerman simply quotes *The Tablet*:

> Dr. Einstein was a sponsor of the Spanish Refugee Relief Campaign as shown on a letterhead of that group, dated Nov. 16, 1939, and a pamphlet entitled "Children in Concentration Camps..."
> Albert Einstein contributed a manuscript for Spanish aid to the League of American Writers...Both Attorney General Francis Biddle and Attorney General Tom Clark have cited the League of American Writers as a Communist-front organization.

If it seems less than likely that Karl Zimmerman in Philadelphia would have read a newspaper from Brooklyn, *The Tablet* was not just any paper. When the publishers of *The Tablet* first named their weekly in 1840, they were not thinking of the little pill most commonly associated with aspirin, but something far more potent—the two fiat stones engraved with the Ten Commandments that the Bible tells us Moses brought down from Mount Sinai. Like its namesake stones, *The Tablet* for more than a hundred years had provided its readers with guidelines on morality. In addition, each week, the paper presented an analysis of world events as seen through the righteous eyes of its publishers, the Roman Catholic Church.

By 1950, *The Tablet* was America's largest Catholic newspaper. As the official publication of the Brooklyn Archdiocese, the paper consistently reflected both the puritanical moralism and the archconservative views of the right wing of the U.S. Catholic Church, which included leading churchmen such as Francis Cardinal Spellman in New York and Bishop Fulton J. Sheen.*

Occasionally, an article would stand out for deftly combining puritanism and politics. Two weeks before the Einstein attack cited by Zimmerman, a *Tablet* article attacked "bad books" under the headline: BISHOP SAYS PERVERTS, ANTI-AMERICANS ARE SOLELY RESPONSIBLE FOR

---

* Sheen once reportedly said to his close friend J. Edgar Hoover, "Edgar, I'm used to pomp and ceremony, but I'm always impressed when I'm around you. Your FBI exceeds anything the Pope has ever done!" (Welch, p.24.)

IMMORAL PUBLICATIONS. The following week, the paper praised Bishop John F. O'Hara of Buffalo, New York, who "has forbidden Catholic children in the city's public schools to see the sex-education film, 'Human Growth.'" Another story reported disapprovingly that "film actress Ingrid Bergman and film director Roberto Rossellini are living in a state of public adultery...."[5]

In politics, *The Tablet* was an early booster of Senator McCarthy well before he launched his Red-scare campaign. Its editors even printed an editorial of congratulations on McCarthy's wedding. The publication's love affair with the Wisconsin senator was true-blue, enduring the toughest times, even after the Army, then Congress and the rest of the media, dropped him. But with or without the senator, McCarthy's ism was *The Tablet's* ism. Early in 1950, a *Tablet* article urged readers to protest to CBS because the radio network's Philharmonic Concert program had interviewed "pro-Red guests"—radio writer and director Norman Corwin and actor Jose Ferrer.* Not surprisingly, *The Tablet* frequently featured the FBI and its chief. J. EDGAR HOOVER CITES RED THREAT, a typical *Tablet* headline declared.[6] In the opinion of some observers, *The Tablet* was also anti-Semitic.[7]

As the voice of the Roman Catholic hierarchy, which supported the fascist regime of Hitler's ally Franco, *The Tablet* had long targeted Einstein for special editorial attacks because of his outspoken stand against Franco and fascism. Were these anti-Einstein articles also motivated by anti-Semitism? *The Tablet's* editorial of May 14, 1938, leaves little doubt. Einstein and a group of Princeton University professors had just issued an appeal to lift the U.S. embargo blocking aid to the Spanish (anti-fascist) government. Here is *The Tablet's* editorial:

> Professor Einstein...was given sanctuary in this land. Now he is... telling our government how to run its business. This is sufficiently impertinent and arrogant but what is worse is to have him indorsing [sic] a move to shoot down and continue the persecution of Christians in Spain....
>
> In reference to persecution the only ones worthy of assistance are apparently the Jews, in fact the only ones capable of being persecuted are the Jews....
>
> The Einsteins think every government, every country is particularly theirs, that it is to be run for their benefit and the devil with the rest....

----

* Corwin and Ferrer hardly burned up the airwaves with communist ideology. During the concert intermission on January 1, *The Tablet* (Feb. 11, 1950) reported, Corwin "delivered New Year's greetings to the musical world." The next week, Ferrer "largely talked about himself." However "pro-Red" Ferrer was in February 1950, a year later he begged HUAC to forgive him and urged the outlawing of the Communist Party.

...the Gersons, Isaacs, Rabbi Steven Wises, Einsteins, etc...are causing more widespread anti-Semitism here than all Hitler's hirelings together. As suggestion number one toward good will, we suggest...*Einstein be sent back to Germany where he may fully realize how to mind his own business.* [Emphasis added]

While editorially spitting on Einstein and proposing he be turned over to Hitler, *The Tablet* turned to tenderness when it came to describing Franco. The Spanish dictator was "shy, retiring, pleasant and friendly." This description appeared on February 18, 1950, under a front-page headline hailing the HEROIC FIGHT OF SPAIN. One week later, *The Tablet* published another attack on Einstein—the article cited by Zimmerman in his INS memo.

To be sure, not all Catholics, and not the entire Catholic leadership, were so ultraconservative.* But the right wing had long been a major force within the church, and during the 1950s, as might be expected, these conservatives gained even more power. While various Catholic factions shifted positions in the church's internal debate over McCarthyism and other key issues of the day, *The Tablet,* in the words of one analyst," was always right."[8]

That Zimmerman's anti-Einstein memo did not say any of this but instead, passed *The Tablet* off as just another newspaper, leads one to suspect at least ulterior motives. One likely motive—consistent with quoting but not identifying *The Tablet*—lies in anti-Semitism. A small detail may be telling: INS form G-59, the request for the FBI's "derogatory information" on Einstein, begins with standard identification lines. Next to *Name:* the words EINSTEIN, ALBERT have been typed; *Date of birth:* March 14, 1879, *Place of birth:* Ulm, Germany, etc. The word typed on the line next to *Race:* is "Hebrew."

The use of the term "race" to describe Jews, as well as the concept of the "Hebrew race," did not generally appear on government documents in this country, or just about anywhere—except in Nazi Germany and those lands occupied by Germany during World War II. And on INS form G-59, requesting the FBI's Einstein files, the form signed by Philadelphia District Director Karl Zimmerman.

But the INS's attempt to deport Einstein was not just a one-man effort. If Zimmerman came from out of political right field, the INS made him feel quite at home. Targeting "foreigners," with little opposition

---

* After decades of denial, many leading Catholic officials, including New York's then Cardinal O'Conner, marked the new millennium by acknowledging the Church's past anti-Semitism and publicly apologizing to Jews around the world.

from a xenophobic American public, the INS was able to out-McCarthy McCarthy in waging war against radicals and dissidents who had the misfortune of having been born in another country. Like HUAC and its congressional-committee clones, the INS, during its deportation hearings, refused to let foreign-born "subversives" know who their accusers were, and badgered witnesses to name names, bringing contempt charges against several "uncooperative" witnesses. But the INS's war on "foreigners" went farther. The McCarran-Walter Immigration and Nationality Act of 1952, described by veteran American diplomat Averell Harriman as "short sighted, fearful and bigoted," allowed the INS to arrest "aliens" without a warrant, detain them indefinitely without bail, and deport them—often without a hearing—to any country that would accept them. It is truly the Mad Hatter of Wonderland shouting "No room! No room! No room!" ("'Why, there's plenty of room,' said Alice.")

While relatively few political deportations and denaturalizations actually occurred,* the "success" of INS political terror cannot be measured simply by its court record. The Justice Department's aim, as Caute explains, "was to harass and frighten radicals to the point where the light was no longer worth the candle." In 1953, Attorney General Brownell declared that "10,000 naturalized citizens suspected of subversive affiliations were under investigation," and in 1956, the immigration agency reported investigating 8,226 "subversives."[9] By no coincidence, INS management personnel were generally in political tune with the agency's anti-immigrant, Red-hunting policies. One Texas congressman—praising the INS—said the agency "looks upon all aliens as wicked people and constantly fights them." At the district director level, Zimmerman was just one of a group Caute describes as "often bigoted, destructive and arrogant."[10]

Most decisively, the INS commissioner at the time of Zimmerman's 1950 Einstein memo was Watson Miller, who had developed his expertise on immigrants as an official of the American Legion. Besides its love affair with Franco, the Legion had extensive experience in reporting on the activities of possibly subversive immigrants. Under the Legion's Contact Program, Legion members in most of the organization's 11,700 posts around the country served as secret FBI informers. Begun at the start of World War II, the Contact Program was designed to "help" the FBI monitor "communities where groups or settlements of persons of foreign extraction or possible un-American sympathies are located...learning the identity of the leaders of these groups, the locations of their meeting

---

* Caute reports that "only" 163 "subversives" were actually deported between 1945 and 1954, although the INS arrested hundreds more.

places, the identity and scope of operation of their social clubs, societies, language schools, etc." After the war, Hoover and the Legion officials continued the secret operation, broadening the Contact Program's goals to monitor leftists, radicals, and dissidents in each Legion Post's community. According to Theoharis, by October 1943, "approximately sixty thousand Legionnaires had been recruited as informers." The Legion's "arrangement" with Hoover continued until 1966, when presumably most of its members were simply too old.[11]

The Legion had been an ideal training camp for Commissioner Miller, who, if he did not order, certainly approved District Director Zimmerman's denaturalization effort. Either way, the INS anti-Einstein initiative had wide, high-level approval. Besides Miller, it was also okayed by both INS Chief of Investigations W. W. Wiggins and Assistant Commissioner W. F. Kelly.[12]

Which brings us to Zimmerman's surprise party a year later and in-coming INS Commissioner Mackey's telegram of congratulations—a sign of approval from the new chief.

The idea of deporting Einstein must have stoked Hoover's memories. It was thirty years earlier, but not the kind of thing a man like Hoover forgets. To Hoover, Emma Goldman, the anarchist and feminist pioneer, had been a communist Jew—and an opportunity.

It had been relatively easy. First, the denaturalization. Since she was a citizen due only to a previous marriage, Hoover simply had her former husband denaturalized and that automatically revoked Goldman's citizenship. Then her trial—he made sure all the old charges were brought up again, though the courts had dismissed them, even the disproved story that she had helped with President McKinley's assassination. Then he arranged to put her (and the others) on the old Navy ship at 4:30 A.M., which went steaming off to Russia before anyone had a chance to contact families, friends, or lawyers. The journalists he had invited called it the "Soviet Ark," and hailed Hoover's forceful action against the anarchist aliens.

The liberal backlash against the Palmer raids had soured some of Hoover's recollections, but getting past it or around it had left him with a sense for survival, which continued to serve him well. Given that survival sense, Hoover must have seen that the initial Zimmerman/INS memo was a weak foundation on which to build a case for deporting the world's most renowned scientist. The Spanish Civil War was long ago, and besides, they would hardly get much public support by accusing Einstein of being on Gary Cooper's side. Something more—and more incriminating—was clearly needed.

Once he resolved to cooperate,[13] Hoover sent the immigration agency virtually everything he had on Einstein. In January 1952, a five-page memo gave INS the FBI's version of "Einstein's life and pro-Communist views," as well as a two-page list of his "subversive organizations." A few weeks later, Hoover sent a more extensive summary of "derogatory information," this time including a detailed report on the espionage allegations against Einstein. A secret past connection between the scientist and Russian spies, if it could be proved, would surely be a basis for revoking his citizenship and spurring his deportation. Neglecting to mention that they were far-from-certain allegations, Hoover stated as if it were fact that—

> Prior to 1933, the Comintern and other Soviet Apparate, were active in gathering intelligence information in the Far East; the agents who gathered this information sent it to agents in other countries in coded telegrams. These agents then re-coded the telegrams and forwarded them to addresses in Berlin, one of which was the office of Albert Einstein…Einstein's personal secretary turned the coded telegrams over to a special apparat man, whose duty it was to transmit them to Moscow by various means.

Apparently trying to make it appear that the FBI had bolstered its case against Einstein with more than one anonymous allegation, Hoover's memos to the INS even revived three items the Bureau itself had already discredited:

- The old story that "in about 1944 or 1945," Einstein had feared his son "Albert" was being held hostage in the Soviet Union;
- The fiction that Einstein had "a staff of typists and secretaries" in Berlin, all of whom were communists or sympathizers;
- The suggestion that Einstein had known Klaus Fuchs in Berlin.[14]

INS investigators also obtained Einstein files from Army and Navy Intelligence (G-2 and ONI) and from HUAC—all of which essentially rehash the same "Communist front" affiliations listed in the FBI's file.[15] HUAC's file was little more than a stack of index cards, each with an undocumented allegation and a reference to a previous HUAC hearing. One card cites Einstein's sponsorship of the "National Civil Rights Legislative Conference in Washington D.C., January 1949," something even the FBI had missed. Another charges Einstein with having signed "an open letter to the Mayor of Stalingrad, June 1943" (a few months after the Nazi defeat in that city had changed the course of the war). Perhaps most revealing of all, one HUAC card says Einstein was "a supporter of Communist Bookshops." During the entire five-year INS investigation, not a single reference to Einstein's achievements and not one quote from his published articles or biographies managed to intrude into the immigration agency's file.* The clerks and secretaries copying and filing pages might well have wondered who this Einstein person was with the same name as that famous scientist.

But a conservative columnist named Jimmy Tarantino did earn a place in the INS file on Einstein. An undated column begins with Tarantino's name in huge, half-inch letters at the top, followed—in smaller type— by the topic of the piece, RED-FRONTING EINSTEIN SHOULD BE DEPORTED:

> The Senate Internal Security Committee would most likely discover that Einstein's Commie connections have been so wide, and vast in scope that it may be safer to this nation's security to DEPORT him to his native Europe.
>
> So who needs this Einstein? Not the American people, and that's for sure... [Einstein] may know what he's talking about, but I'll be darned if I do.[16]

One by-product of the INS Einstein investigation provides a glimpse of that agency's mind-set. The immigration agency publishes an orientation booklet called *Gateway to Citizenship,* which is given to prospective citizens. Originally issued in 1943, it was revised in 1948 and then re-revised in 1953. In the booklet's "Freedom of Expression" section, the 1943 and 1948 editions contain quotes from a number of famous people, including the French philosopher Francois Voltaire (1759), the abolitionist Wendell Phillips (1855), an unnamed Chinese philosopher (2000 B.C.), editor Horace Traubel, and the following:

> "Political liberty implies liberty to express one's political opinion orally and in writing, and a tolerant respect for any and every individual opinion."

> —ALBERT EINSTEIN (1933)

The 1953 revision contains the same section with exactly the same quotes from Voltaire, Phillips, the unnamed Chinese philosopher, and Traubel.

Only the Einstein quote has been deleted.**

---

* Only after Einstein's death did the INS add to its file a number of newspaper articles praising Einstein: his obituaries.

** INS Historian Marian Smith reports that the Editorial Committee for the 1953 revision cross-checked all the names in the booklet against an index of people cited as "subversive" by HUAC: "If they were on the HUAC list, they were taken out of the JNS booklet." (Interview, INS headquarters, Washington, D.C., February 5, 1998.)

PART V

Denouement

17

Turning Tides

At the cutting edge of the McCarthy/Hoover anti-communist crusade were the congressional investigating committees led by the House Committee on Un-American Activities (HUAC) and its clone, the Senate Internal Security Sub-committee (SISS). In addition, several states, like California and Massachusetts, set up their own loyalty-checking mini-HUAC's, which imitated and cooperated with their federal big brothers.

Then there was the Mother of All Committees: Though it operated for only a few years in the early 1950s, Senator McCarthy's Sub-committee on Government Operations created by far the biggest and most hysterical headlines. McCarthy himself was (and still is) the most widely known of all the congressional inquisitors. During his heyday in the Senate, the McCarthy committee made major news stories almost daily—a witness "confessing" to former left-wing ties, or another "Red" uncovered in another corner of American life. Congressional hearing rooms were the bleeding ground where witnesses either "cooperated" or faced the prospect of losing their jobs, and sometimes jail sentences for Contempt of Congress. Those subpoenaed were not allowed to cross-examine their accusers, or even to know who their accusers were. While many capitulated to McCarthyism, many others defied the committees, refusing to name names. For their principles and refusal to become informants, the defiant ones knew the likely price: The number of "uncooperative" witnesses who were fired is hard to confirm, but Schrecker says the best estimate is from Ralph S. Brown of Yale, who reported "roughly ten thousand people lost their jobs" but admits "the figure may be low" as it does not include thousands who quit before being subpoenaed, were dismissed under other pretexts, or whose firings were simply not reported. It doesn't count scholarships and promotions lost, careers ruined, and even suicides.* Moreover, it doesn't count the pervasive fear.

As a "service" to employers and a sword over the head of witnesses, HUAC made its records available to any company requesting them. According to Caute, during the McCarthy period, the committee provided data on sixty-thousand people to inquiring employers.[1] In a quite typical example, on June 19, 1953, Helen Lewis refused to answer Senator McCarthy's questions about her past political ties. As a result, the U.S. State Department immediately cancelled the Fulbright Scholarship that had been awarded to her husband, Professor Naphtali Lewis of Brooklyn College. "'I believe [the scholarship cancellation] is an excellent idea,' the Senator asserted at the end of a 37-minute hearing," the New York Times reported (front-page) the next day: (PROFESSOR LOSES FULBRIGHT AWARD AFTER WIFE BALKS AT RED INQUIRY).

Altogether, the committees subpoenaed thousands of Americans, demanding they not only confess their own political witchcraft, but also name names of other witches they knew or might have heard about. During the 83rd Congress (1953-54), its investigating committees conducted fifty-one separate anti-communist investigations, and from February 1953 to March 1954, the McCarthy committee alone held more than one hundred hearings.[2]

And the committees reached well beyond the walls of the hearing rooms on Capitol Hill. McCarthy and his counterparts were in the news day after day, and despite several rules and rulings baring TV cameras,[3] congressional hearings were frequently televised. Turn on the news or glance at the morning paper and you were immediately bit with the latest charge of infiltration of Reds into some segment of society. This pervasive media coverage served as a megaphone for the congressional finger-pointers; it magnified the fear and fed the hysteria. Like everyone else in the country, Einstein could not avoid the media barrage. Thirteen years earlier, just before becoming a citizen, he had told a national radio audience, "In this country, it has been generations since men were subject to the humiliating necessity of unquestioning obedience."

* * *

---

* As early as 1948, a first-grade teacher in New York's Staten Island public schools, Minnie Gutride, was called out of her classroom to be questioned about her political views by Nicholas Bucci, the law secretary of New York's Board of Education and Assistant Superintendent of Schools John F. Conroy. Ms. Gutride committed suicide that night. ("New York's Subversive Teachers," Adler and Zelman, The Nation, April 9, 1977.)

"You are very right in assuming that I am badly in need of encourage-ment," the man who had revolutionized mankind's view of the universe to become the century's most celebrated thinker wrote in November 1950, responding to a letter from a friend in Indiana. "Our nation has gone mad." America's obsession with anti-communism and the rising tide of political fear, Einstein's letter continued, "reminds me of the events in Germany since the time of Emperor William II: through many victories to final disaster."

The first few years of the 1950s were not a happy time for Einstein. With American boys dying in the Korean War, the country was caught up in a frenzy of patriotic anti-communism, fed by fear of a Russian nuclear attack. As schoolchildren in classrooms across America cowered under their desks during "take-cover" drills, enterprising American business-men turned that fright into profits by selling family bomb shelters for "protection" against atomic bombs and radiation. In the early fifties, many families spent thousands of dollars hoping to save themselves from the agony and death Hersey had so vividly described in *Hiroshima*. Whether or not such shelters could have saved anyone, they had the effect of inten-sifying fear and shifting public attention from joining with others to ban nuclear weapons—as Einstein and the Emergency Committee had advo-cated—to each family trying to survive alone.

Einstein's letters spoke his sadness, and everywhere he heard German echoes; "...the dear Americans have vigorously assumed [the Germans'] place," he wrote in January 1951 to his friend, Belgium's Queen Mother Elizabeth.* "The German calamity of years ago repeats itself...People acquiesce and align themselves with the forces of evil, and one stands by, powerless." But beyond despair and dejection about McCarthyism, Einstein felt more politically alone and isolated than ever before in his iconoclastic life. He wrote to friends in Europe: "I hardly ever felt as alienated from people as right now....The worst is that nowhere is there anything with which one can identify. Everywhere brutality and lies...." By the start of 1952, he seemed to have almost lost hope: "Saddest of all is the disappointment one feels over the conduct of mankind in general."[4]

We don't know what prompted Einstein's turn from despair to defiance in 1953, but it was the same year that McCarthyism developed a new focus: book-banning. As one observer noted, "The purge, especially distressing Mann and Einstein, was that of books and of teachers."[5]

---

* One of Einstein's closest letter-friends since they met in 1929, Elizabeth shared both his love for music and hatred for Nazis.

Robin Hood was denounced as communist propaganda before the end of the year by a member of the Indiana Textbook Commission, who demanded the book be removed from the state's school libraries. The Lord-turned-outlaw "promoted Communist doctrine," according to Mrs. Thomas J. White—apparently by stealing from the rich and giving to the poor. Indiana Superintendent of Education Wilbur Young "said he would re-read *Robin Hood* to consider the merits of the charges." Governor Craig had "no comment."[6]

Protests from around the world managed to save Robin Hood from being outlawed for a second time. (The current sheriff of Nottingham, interviewed in England, said, "Robin Hood was no Communist.") But during the 1953-54 frenzy to safeguard the minds of American school-children from insidious Red influences, local libraries, school boards and textbook publishers around the country removed a host of authors, from Mark Twain to Booth Tarkington, as well as more obviously "subversive" writers such as Sinclair Lewis and Theodore Dreiser.

Reading the morning papers must have been haunting to Einstein. Each day's headlines reported new incidents of anti-communist book-banning—spearheaded by Senator McCarthy's campaign to remove "un-American" books from the overseas libraries operated by the U.S. Information Service (USIS). In February, the State Department ordered the USIS to permit "no material from books or other works by Communists or other controversial authors under any circumstances." On February 20, the *New York Times* headline declared:

VOICE [OF AMERICA] MUST DROP
WORKS OF LEFTISTS
Agency Reveals Dulles Order
And Declares Its Libraries
Will Ban Books

By the beginning of May, State Department officials had "blacklisted a number of composers, artists, and writers." And while McCarthy's attack on the USIS overseas programs made the biggest news splash, many publicschool officials at home interpreted the writing on their political walls as a signal for them to join in the outlawing of reading material that might possibly plant "dangerous" seeds in young minds.* In one widely reported case, two members of the Shaftsbury, Vermont, School Board

---

* "Some states are taking a closer look at textbooks for any taint of Communism," the United Press reported in January 1953. "Textbooks have been banned in some places and ordered rewritten in others." The same UP dispatch reported that "teacher loyalty oaths appear to be gaining acceptance."

resigned rather than go along with a decision to ban from the school library *Our Neighbors to the South,* a book about the peoples of Latin America. The majority of the Shaftsbury Board voted to outlaw the book because its authors allegedly (according to anonymous sources) had communist sympathies.[7]

By May, the California Un-American Activities Committee—perhaps the most active blacklister of all the mini-HUAC's—charged that "Communists had infiltrated the San Francisco public school system," and declared it would also investigate textbooks in San Rafael schools for "Communist influence." In Marin County, State Senator Jack McCarthy (no family relation to Joe) announced he would hold hearings to investigate "the use of subversive books" in local schools. *(New York Times,* May 2, 1953.)

A month later, banning became burning. Rumors had circulated for months that local libraries and individuals were trashing, and even burning, books they thought might be "incriminating." On June 16, it was no longer just a rumor. At the top of page one, the *New York Times* headlined a statement by Secretary of State John Foster Dulles:

> Some Books Literally Burned
> After Inquiry, Dulles Reports

Six days later, the *Times* reported that works by forty authors had been banned and that "many" banned books had been burned by USIS officials overseas.

It was almost exactly twenty years earlier, on May 10, 1933, that Nazi gangs tossed "dangerous" books into bonfires in the Unter den Linden Square facing Berlin's opera house. With all the hysteria of a Mississippi lynch mob, the young Aryan *Übermenschen* danced around the flames, shouting *"Brenne* [Burn] Karl Marx! *Brenne* Freud!"—burning also the works of Thomas Mann, Stefan Zweig, Erich Remarque, André Gide, Heinrich Heine, and others on Goebbels's list of "Communist" literature, including books on the "Jewish theory" of relativity by a man named Einstein.[8]

Even when he had felt most isolated in 1950 and 1951, during those early months of the Red-scare hysteria and the Korean War, Einstein knew that a few people, most of them on the political left, were in fact resisting, refusing to name names or sign loyalty oaths, usually losing their careers. But the vast majority of Americans—aptly dubbed "the Silent Generation"—stayed busy building split-level suburbia and deaf to dissenting voices. In January 1951, Einstein had written ruefully of America: "Honest people constitute a hopeless minority."[9]

But by 1953, the number of those refusing to "cooperate"—even at the cost of lost jobs and ruptured lives—was beginning to multiply. Einstein's decision to challenge the congressional "inquisitors," as he later called them, drew strength from that resistance—and added strength to it.

If Einstein was seeking a platform from which to reach the widest audience, the congressional committee hearings themselves were a logical choice. In retrospect, these are-you-now-or-have-you-ever-been hearings today may seem like the theater of the absurd—Salem witch-hunts where the only way to "prove" you weren't a witch was to name names of those who were*—but the media gave national coverage to virtually every fear-filled scene. For an act of defiance, there was no stage more public.** But Einstein was never summoned by McCarthy, HUAC, or any of the committees, who no doubt could figure out that in a public confrontation with the scientist, they would be the big losers. No subpoena came, but Einstein found another way to publicly take on the investigators.

William Frauenglass wrote to Einstein in May 1953. A high-school English teacher in Brooklyn, Frauenglass had been subpoenaed by the Senate Internal Security Sub-committee and refused to be a "cooperative" witness, though it meant the New York City School Board would fire him. Six years earlier at a Board of Education-certified seminar for teachers, Frauenglass had given a talk on "Techniques of Intercultural Teaching in the Field of English as a Means of Overcoming Prejudice Among School Children." That "overt act" led SISS to subpoena him for questioning about possible communist affiliations and associates. He had heard Einstein in a recent radio broadcast twitting congressional investigators, describing himself as "an incorrigible nonconformist whose nonconformism in a remote field of endeavor [theoretic physics] no senatorial committee has as yet felt impelled to tackle." In his letter, Frauenglass suggested

---

* Arthur Miller, whose play The Crucible exposed the historical parallel between McCarthyism and the 1692 witch-hunts in Salem (where some 20 people were executed as "witches"), was subpoenaed by HUAC in 1956. When he refused to answer the committee's questions, citing his rights under the First Amendment, he was indicted for Contempt of Congress. The indictment was later thrown out by the courts.

** Congressional hearings actually provided an ideal setting for opposition demonstrations—the confrontation was ready-made. On one side, sitting high up on a platform several feet above the hearing room, were the Goliaths—old white men who made up in arrogance what they lacked in intelligence. Below, at the witness table, sat the little Davids, and the nature of the hearings required that they respond to the questions. The room could be filled with spectators—or demonstrators—and the media were already there, eager to cover a clash. But it was the 1960s before the New Left movement discovered this opportunity, and several years of widely publicized demonstrations finally led to the end of HUAC.

that a statement of support from Einstein "at this juncture would be most helpful in rallying educators and the public to resist this new obscurantist attack."[10] It was a bold idea that meshed with Einstein's outrage over the unchecked congressional "inquisitions."

The result was Einstein's letter to Frauenglass, which they agreed to send to the *New York Times*.* On June 12, the letter appeared as part of a front-page story, under the headline:

'Refuse to Testify,' Einstein
Advises Intellectuals Called In by Congress

The letter, which has since been included in *Bartlett's Anthology of Familiar Quotations,* declares in part:

Reactionary politicians have managed to instill suspicion of all intellectual efforts into the public by dangling before their eyes a danger from without. Having succeeded so far, they are now proceeding to suppress the freedom of teaching and to deprive of their positions all those who do not prove submissive, i.e., to starve them out.

What ought the minority of intellectuals to do against this evil? Frankly, I can only see the revolutionary way of non-cooperation in the sense of Gandhi's. Every intellectual who is called before the committees ought to refuse to testify, i.e., must be prepared for jail and economic ruin, in short, for the sacrifice of his personal welfare in the interest of the cultural welfare of this country. . . .

If enough people are ready to take this grave step, they will be successful. If not, then the intellectuals deserve nothing better than the slavery which is intended for them.

Einstein's name—and his call for civil disobedience—made the letter a major news story around the world. In the coming weeks and months, it was acclaimed and attacked by press, politicians, and public. Also, as resistance often does, it encouraged further resistance.

Senator McCarthy immediately labeled Einstein "an enemy of America."** Echoing McCarthy's attack, other ultraconservatives took

---

* After they had discussed it, Frauenglass sent Einstein's letter to the Times. Einstein had explained that he didn't want to be in the position of asking the Times to publish his letter (Richard Frauenglass reports). Besides drawing media coverage because of his celebrity, Einstein had an unusual instinct for what we now call "good public relations." He never asked reporters to do a story—the initiative always came from them, which ensured better and more coverage. (It's an approach that will work every time—if you're Einstein.)

** "Anyone who advises Americans to keep secret information...about spies and saboteurs is himself an enemy of America," McCarthy charged, adding that Einstein's statement was "nothing new. That's the same advice given by every Communist lawyer that has ever appeared before our committee." (New York Times, June 14, 1953.) In a second

a more threatening tone: Former Democratic senator from Maryland, Herbert O'Conner, declared that Einstein "should not be permitted to impede the efforts of officials of our nation to uproot subversive activities...." And the California Republican State Committee denounced him as a refugee "freeloader" who "has received from the United States far more than he has given," who considers himself "above the laws of nations." (That Einstein ought to be thankful for the blessings America had bestowed upon him was the theme song of America's conservative chorus until the day he died—and beyond: Just four days after his death, far-right commentator Gerald L. K. Smith urged a Senate sub-committee to stop admitting refugees so that America would not "get another Einstein," who, he added, typified the "undesirable" type. And three months later, columnist Westbrook Pegler denounced Einstein as an "ingrate immigrant" for urging people "to refuse to comply with our laws."[11]

While most of the letters to Einstein supported his Frauenglass statement, some of the others ("You should be shipped back to your homeland and a camp!")—even though he dismissed them as "bigoted" and "illiterate"—were enough to revive frightening memories. But it wasn't simply the far right and the cranks who attacked Einstein's Frauenglass letter. Virtually all the major media, including the liberal *New York Times* and *Washington Post,* joined in. Following, if not setting, the anti-communist agenda, the *Times* and *Post* fixated on Einstein's call for intellectuals to "be prepared for jail and economic ruin."

Sounding quite Salemesque, the *Times* editorial of June 13, 1953, assailed the "forces of civil disobedience" as not only "illegal," but "unnatural." In an ironic choice of adjectives, the editorial denounced Einstein as "most unwise." (Three years later, the *Times* would conduct its own internal purge of "Red" employees.)[12] *The Washington Post* called Einstein "an extremist," and warned that if "citizens generally followed Dr. Einstein's advice and went to jail in preference to testifying...our representative system would be paralyzed.... If we are going to have orderly government, each summoned witness must be required to speak...."

Less than ten years later, both the *Post* and *Times* hailed the civil disobedience of Martin Luther King and others in the Civil Rights movement, no longer finding it "unnatural." (One is tempted to say, the *Times* had changed.)

But if the media were an attack pack in their anti-Einstein editorials, letters to the editor were fairly evenly divided. One notable response to

---

blast a week later, he "modified" his label, calling Einstein a "disloyal American." (*Times,* June 22.)

the *Times* editorial came from Bertrand Russell, which the paper, to its credit, reprinted in full on June 26:

> In your issue of June 13, you have a leading article disagreeing with Einstein's view...You seem to maintain that one should always obey the law, however bad. I cannot think that you have realized the implications of this position. Do you condemn the Christian Martyrs who refused to sacrifice to the Emperor? Do you condemn John Brown? Nay, more, I am compelled to suppose that you condemn George Washington and hold that your country ought to return to allegiance to Her Gracious Majesty, Queen Elizabeth II. As a loyal Briton, I of course applaud this view; but I fear it may not win much support in your country.

The second partner-in-protest Einstein took up with that summer was not new to resisting. In fact, his role in resistance had earned him one of the nation's highest honors.[13] His story offers another window onto the way the Red scare worked....

It was nearly midnight on November 15, 1943 when George Wuchinich jumped from the low-flying British Royal Air Force Halifax bomber into the moonlit night sky over German-occupied Yugoslavia. As his chute opened above him, Wuchinich looked down at the bonfires set by the anti-Nazi guerrilla fighters to outline his landing area. He worried that they might be Nazi decoy signals, which had lured several other OSS agents to their capture and death. But not this time. The partisans rushed forward with handshakes and embraces as soon as he hit ground, and took him to their mountain hideaway.[14] For eight months, Wuchinich shared the rugged, guerrilla-war life of the Yugoslav partisans—including the daily threat of capture and execution by the Nazis. Constantly on the move from one mountain hut to another, he and his small team of OSS agents radioed vital information on German troop movements to listening-posts in North Africa (Cairo and Tripoli). Acting on that information, OSS "Operations Agents" quickly moved in to blow up key bridges, railroad tracks, and Nazi troop transports, saving lives of Allied soldiers and helping to shorten the war.

In 1944, Wuchinich was awarded the Distinguished Service Cross—the nation's second-highest military honor—for "extraordinary heroism behind enemy lines in the Balkans, from 20 November, 1943 to 26 July, 1944." Several years later, with the onset of the Cold War, the newly formed CIA offered Wuchinich the Medal of Honor (the highest military award) if he would become a spy for the Agency, posing as a salesman on a trip to Russia. The partisans Wuchinich had shared his life with for eight months were among the most successful anti-Nazi guerrillas in World War II. Led by Josip Broz (Tito) and the Yugoslav Communists, they drove out the

Germans and after the war, set up the regime that governed Yugoslavia for forty years.* Wuchinich, whose parents were immigrants from Yugoslavia and spoke their native language at home, developed lasting, forged-in-battle friendships with many of the guerrilla fighters, along with sympathy for their cause. He turned down the CIA offer. Years later, he explained to his son David that he had come to believe that Washington had turned against popular wars of liberation such as those in Yugoslavia.

After the war, his experience with Tito's partisans encouraged Wuchinich toward the left. Returning to Pittsburgh as a war hero, he hosted a weekly radio show, *Keep America Free,* and was executive secretary of the American Slav Congress, which sought support for left-wing movements in the Balkans. But as the American Red scare developed, steel-and-coalproducing cities such as Pittsburgh were primary targets of the government's campaign to purge militant leftists from the labor movement. Although he never joined the Communist Party, he was attacked as a "dangerous Communist" by local hunters of subversives. Unable to find a job, Wuchinich and his family moved to New York in 1949.

On June 11, 1953, ten years after he had parachuted into Nazi-occupied Yugoslavia, George Wuchinich (along with another former OSS officer) was called before the SISS, headed by Indiana Republican Senator William Jenner, which was investigating alleged "Communist infiltration and influence in the military."

* * *

This is a good moment to pause in our story to review how the Red-hunting congressional investigating committees "discovered" such "plots": Just as the government—the Army's G-2 and the FBI—knew the left-wing leanings of many of the scientists they recruited for the Manhattan Project, so the OSS knew that many of its recruits had "Reddish" resumes. If it had been up to Hoover, of course, you would have had to sign an anti-communist loyalty oath to get into the OSS. But when the FBI chief warned ("advised") OSS Director Bill Donovan that several candidates for the secret agency were "Reds," Donovan hired them anyway. Infuriated, Hoover, who envied Donovan's job and influence with Roosevelt, dropped several suggestions that the OSS director was "soft" on communism. It was beyond Hoover's ability to grasp, but Donovan, like the men behind

* After publicly breaking with Stalin in 1948, Tito did not join the Western Alliance, but became a leader of the nonaligned group of nations. In 1955 as previously noted, Tito and India's Nehru co-chaired the first world nonaligned conference in Bandung, Indonesia.

America's atomic-bomb project, realized that many of these leftists were dedicated anti-fascists, and—especially important for the OSS—shared the same political wavelength as the anti-Nazi guerrilla groups in Europe and Asia (often led by communists) that the OSS worked with behind enemy lines.

But after the war, America's foreign-policy horse had a different color—the anti-Soviet strategists took charge. As early as 1945, well before Donovan's secret agency became the CIA (with the help of "former" Nazis), the OSS began discharging its left-leaning agents because "with their political backgrounds, there was serious doubt they could fit into our Post-war German operation."[15]

"Infiltration" of the OSS by these battle-tested and often medal-earning commandos who had been known all along as leftists was "uncovered" by McCarthy, Hoover & Co. in the fifties, when it suited their Red-scare strategy—just as they targeted many openly left-leaning Manhattan Project scientists who were no longer needed for their technical skills.

Before the Jenner Committee, Wuchinich was not just defiant, he boldly challenged the senators with his war record. When Committee Counsel Morris called him "Mr. Wuchinich," he snapped back, "It's *Captain* Wuchinich, and I earned it—where were you during the war, behind some desk at home?"[16] Refusing to answer questions about his political affiliations, Wuchinich instead read his DSC citation:

November 6, 1944: The Distinguished Service Cross is awarded to George S. Wuchinich, 0519816, Captain U.S. Army, OSS, for extraordinary heroism with a secret military operation in the Balkans against an armed enemy, 28 November, 1943-26 July, 1944.

Captain Wuchinich's descent by parachute into enemy-occupied territory, his leadership and his resolute conduct in the face of great peril throughout an extended period in the successful accomplishment of an extremely hazardous and difficult mission, exemplified the finest traditions of the armed forces of the United States.

The SISS was clearly not used to such defiance—especially from a war hero. Wuchinich's citation seemed to fluster Senator Jenner, who may not have known before the hearing about the DSC award. The committee dismissed the witness after just a few questions. The next morning's banner headline in the *Indianapolis Star* announced: EX-OFFICER DEFIES JENNER.

Before his testimony, Wuchinich had been offered a new job selling machinery for General Motors. The day after his appearance before the committee, GM told him the job was not available. Einstein's letter arrived a few days later, expressing "admiration for your devotion to the common cause of democratic rights" and offering "to help in any way I can." Wuchinich had written to ask Einstein for support after reading about the scientist's letter to Frauenglass. Einstein received many such requests and almost always turned them down. He felt the way to be most effective lay in "restricting myself to having publicly and clearly stated my position" and to let others use that public statement in their struggles. But Wuchinich's militant stand, at the cost of his job, caught the spirit of Einstein's new, public challenge to McCarthyism. That, as well as the former OSS captain's heroic anti-Nazi war record, undoubtedly prompted Einstein to reach out in this case. By sheer coincidence, Wuchinich's defiance of the Jenner committee was reported in the *Times* on the same day (June 12, 1953) that the front-page story on Einstein's letter to Frauenglass appeared. The Frauenglass story was continued on page 12, directly beneath a photo of Wuchinich captioned: SAYS HE WAS SPY, BUT FOR THE U.S. Einstein could not have missed it.[17]

After the 1953 Senate committee hearing, the FBI continued to harass Wuchinich, "convincing" several of his employers to fire him or face losing government contracts if they kept him on.* Finally, in 1956, he found a lasting job with a company in which one of the top executives was an OSS veteran and willing to stand up to FBI threats. "George knew he'd be fired if he refused to cooperate with the Committee," Sarah Wuchinich recalls with a mixture of anger and pride in her husband. "But he lived by his principles. He would not become an informer." The letter from Einstein not only boosted his spirits, but was sent by Wuchinich—with Einstein's complete agreement—to prospective employers.**

Six months after Einstein's "Frauenglass letter" made worldwide headlines, Al Shadowitz drove to Princeton. In the early evening of December 8, 1953, he pulled his car over to the curb and called to a young man passing by, "Say, can you tell me where Doctor Einstein lives?" Without hesitation, as if he'd been asked for the time of day, the young man gave him directions to the house on Mercer Street.

---

* The FBI's PR machine did its best to paper over the Bureau's harassment role: "The responsibility of the FBI is to secure the facts. We do not make…recommendations as to whether an individual is suitable or unsuitable for…employment."—J. Edgar Hoover in the *New York Times Magazine*, April 16, 1950.

** "As an epilog to these tribulations," David Wuchinich writes, "my father, having formed his own business selling industrial chemical process equipment, later participated in the anti-Vietnam War movement along with the rest of the family and actively campaigned door to door in staid Mt. Kisco for…George McGovern in 1968."

Shadowitz had just received a subpoena to appear before Joe McCarthy's Senate investigating committee. One of McCarthy's many targets that year was communist "infiltration" into defense plants during World War II, and particularly a left-of-center union, the Federation of Architects, Engineers, Chemists and Technicians. An electrical engineer on government contracts since 1941, Shadowitz had helped organize FAECT at the Federal Telecommunication Labs of IT&T, as an alternative to the in-house union that barred black workers from membership.

Shadowitz knew there was no way he would answer the committee's questions, but he was still shaken by the subpoena: "I was positive I'd wind up in jail."[18] He remembered news accounts months earlier about Einstein's letter advising a Brooklyn schoolteacher not to answer committee questions, and thought Einstein might be willing to help him, too. When he discovered the scientist's phone number was unlisted, he drove from his home in northern New Jersey to Princeton.

"You can't just come in to see Professor Einstein without an appointment!" Helen Dukas told Shadowitz at the scientist's front door.

"I must have looked really disappointed, because then she asked me what I wanted to see him about," Shadowitz remembers. "When I told her about the subpoena from McCarthy, she took a good long look at my face and then said, 'Come in.'"

As a lover of physics and the son of Jewish immigrants, Shadowitz revered Einstein. "When he came downstairs wearing his baggy pants and sweatshirt, I was overawed just being in his presence. But he just made you feel comfortable right away." Einstein agreed to support Shadowitz's refusal to answer McCarthy's questions and told him to feel free to use his name. He was especially pleased that Shadowitz planned to rely on the First Amendment—pointing out that the committee was violating his rights of free speech and association—rather than the Fifth Amendment.

Einstein believed that "taking the Fifth"—refusing to answer because it might "incriminate" you—made a witness seem to be guilty, to be hiding something "self-incriminating." He thought witnesses should refuse to answer without using "the well-known subterfuge of...the Fifth Amendment." Nonetheless, when Frauenglass "took the Fifth" and argued (as did Supreme Court Justice William O. Douglas) that it was an important Constitutional guarantee against tyranny and should not be abandoned, Einstein had agreed to go along.[19] (Wuchinich, besides citing his heroic war record, also "took the Fifth.") The only way a witness could avoid "naming names" and still *be sure* of staying out of jail was "the Fifth." (Such witnesses could still be fired from their jobs...and often were.) When witnesses refused to become informers based on their First

Amendment rights (freedom of speech, press, and association), the committees could issue indictments for Contempt of Congress. Several "First
Amendment" refuse-niks served jail time.

Shadowitz agreed with Einstein that "taking the Fifth" was "like an
admission of guilt."[20] When he went before the McCarthy committee, he
cited the First Amendment as his reason for not "cooperating." McCarthy
told him, 'I'm giving you good advice" and warned he could "spend considerable time in jail" unless he took the Fifth Amendment. "I told him,"
Shadowitz recalls with a smile, "It's up to me who to take advice from, and
I prefer to take my advice from Doctor Einstein." (Shadowitz was, in fact,
indicted for Contempt of Congress, but the case was eventually dismissed
after the Senate voted to censure McCarthy.[21]

Before his hearing, Shadowitz and his attorney met for a preliminary
discussion in closed session with McCarthy and Committee Counsel Roy
Cohn, who usually asked the questions. But as soon as Shadowitz cited
Einstein's name, McCarthy himself "did all the questioning." Almost all
his questions were about Einstein, Shadowitz recalls. "When did I meet
him? How did I meet him? And so on. He couldn't believe I just went to
Einstein's house." Shadowitz got the definite impression that McCarthy
was "out to get" Einstein.

At his public hearing on December 16, Shadowitz refused to answer
questions, citing the First Amendment, but also "because Professor
Einstein advised me not to answer." Einstein's name—as with the letter to
Frauenglass—turned the event into a major news story across the country.
Under a front-page photo of Shadowitz, the *New York Times* headlined:

WITNESS, ON EINSTEIN ADVICE,
REFUSES TO SAY IF HE WAS RED

It's hard to overstate the electrifying impact of Einstein's defiance on
the morale of young teachers and scientists, among others, facing the terrifying choice: your job or your self-respect. Twice in six months, Einstein
had very publicly challenged the congressional investigators. The battle
had been joined.

Considering the worldwide press coverage of Einstein's letter to
William Frauenglass, and the front-page treatment the agenda-setting
New York Times gave both that letter and, six months later, Einstein's
public support for Al Shadowitz in defying McCarthy, it's surprising how
little space the FBI's Einstein file devotes to these events.

Under the heading "Protest of Congressional Hearings," the file
(Section 8, pp. 77-78) contains only copies of press reports, including the
complete Frauenglass articles (June 12, 1953) from the *New York Times* and
Daily News, as well as the following excerpts:

—The *Newark Star Ledger* dated 6/12/53 contained an article captioned "EINSTEIN RAPS LOYALTY PROBES." [In his letter to Frauenglass] Einstein accused "reactionary politicians" of "proceeding to suppress the freedom of teaching and deprive of their positions all those who do not prove submissive.".... Einstein urged witnesses called before Congressional "inquisitions" to refuse to testify even if they face jail for their silence.

—The *New York Journal American,* dated 6/15/53, also disclosed that Dr. EINSTEIN wrote a letter to WILLIAM FRAUENGLASS, a High School teacher who was facing dismissal because he refused to testify before the Senate Internal Security Sub-Committee...which stated, "every intellectual who was called before one of the committees (of Congress) ought to refuse to testify," and "be prepared for jail and economic ruin" as the penalty.

—On December 17, 1953, the *Newark Sunday News* reflected an article concerning a hearing conducted by Senator JOSEPH McCARTHY at which one ALBERT SHADOWITZ...stated he had personally consulted EINSTEIN at his home in Princeton, NJ, and was using his advice in defying the probe by the committee. SHADOWITZ refused to answer questions put to him by Senator McCARTHY on the basis of his rights under the First Amendment. ... Through his secretary [Einstein] stated "I advised him not to cooperate with the investigating committee on the basis of First Amendment..."

To demonstrate the "subversive" character of Einstein's position, the FBI file also reprints an editorial from the Yiddish-language communist newspaper, the *Morning Freiheit,* which, according to the Bureau's translation, hailed "Prof. Einstein's Proud Call to American Intellectuals," declaring:

> "Professor Einstein has placed himself at the head of the growing number of those who protest against the witch-hunts. He has made it the urgent and noble job of American intellectuals to protect their own honor and liberties together with the honor of democratic America."[22]

Perhaps the most intriguing entry in this section of the FBI's Einstein file is its reference to Wuchinich. Under the heading: EINSTEIN'S CONGRATULATIONS TO GEORGE S. WUCHINICH FOR REFUSING TO TESTIFY BEFORE SENATE INTERNAL SECURITY COMMITTEE, 1953, the FBI's Einstein dossier (Section 9, 11/23/53 memo) contains a page and a half entirely blacked out-even in the new, "un-redacted" version the Bureau released in the spring of 2000. One of the official reasons the FBI cites for blacking out these pages is that the information "could reasonably be expected to disclose the identity of a confidential source...."[23] Yet we know, despite the blackout, that the main informer against Wuchinich was Max Cvetic, Pittsburgh's most celebrated anti-Communist, who parlayed his finger-pointing career into movie money *(I Was A Communist for the FBI).*

"Do you think I have to go to jail?" Einstein asked his close friend Otto Nathan a few days before the letter to Frauenglass was to appear on the front page of the *New York Times*. To Nathan, Einstein seemed frightened.[24] They seriously considered withdrawing the letter from the *Times*.

Hard as it may be today to imagine that the U.S. government would even consider jailing the world's most famous scientist (at seventy-three, and in failing health), such fears were not irrational. Hoover's repeated testimony before Congress that the FBI had identified and was ready to put thousands of "Communists" in "detention camps" in the event of a war, had been headlined across the country. And remember that only two years earlier, world-celebrated historian W. E. B. Du Bois was arrested and brought to court in handcuffs—at the age of eighty-three. Closer to home, Nathan himself had recently been denied a passport because of his left-leaning political views. As he became more active in anti-McCarthy protests, Nathan faced a very real threat of prison. He was cited for Contempt of Congress when he refused to answer questions about others in that resistance; instead of taking the Fifth Amendment, he simply declared, "No Congressional Committee has the right to inquire into the political beliefs of American citizens."[25]

But if Einstein was worried about possible retaliation for speaking out against the congressional "inquisitors" in the Frauenglass case, remaining silent was more onerous. He might well have quoted his own words, written seven years earlier, about racism: "I can escape the feeling of complicity...only by speaking out."[26] McCarthyism had become an epidemic in America. After "dangerous" books, the loyalty agencies aimed their anti-Red artillery at "dangerous" teachers. The subpoena to Frauenglass and his subsequent firing by the New York City Board of Education was not an isolated case. He was one of twenty-five New York City high-school teachers subpoenaed by SISS.* Thirteen of them were dismissed without a hearing after they took the Fifth Amendment. Altogether, between 1950 and 1953, 156 teachers were "removed" from the City's schools. In 1953 alone, 84 City teachers were fired, with another 189 under investigation.[27]

Once the *Times* ran the Frauenglass letter on page one, the publicity left little time for fear. Overnight, Einstein became the center of a growing public debate—a symbol of what was perhaps an awakening national conscience—about the Red scare. His call to resistance was a lightning rod for pro and con statements by columnists, politicians, and ordinary

---

* In light of the link between McCarthyism and anti-Semitism, it's noteworthy that 24 of the 25 subpoenaed teachers were Jewish. "The great majority of New York teachers purged in the fifties were Jews." (Caute, pp. 437-38.)

citizens sending letters to news media around the country. Fresh political winds were beginning to stir in America, and Einstein's letter was at least a contributing gust.

The Korean War truce in July brought a widespread sense of relief. With war casualties steadily climbing—forty-five thousand American troops killed, and no victory in sight—the public mood had clearly shifted toward peace.[28] Moreover, many U.S. officials viewed the death of Stalin in March, followed by a struggle within Russia for control, as an opening for the West to establish more contact with and influence on that country. At home, resistance to McCarthyism, which had been limited mainly to a small, besieged, organized left wing, was stirring among many previously silent: In April, New York Senator Herbert Lehman denounced "creeping McCarthyism," and by July, he reported the demand for copies of his speech was so unexpectedly large that all twenty thousand printed copies had been sold and a second printing would soon be issued. In May, the Methodist Conference of New York attacked Senator McCarthy and HUAC Chairman Harold Velde (Illinois Republican), and even the International Ladies Garment Workers Union, still steeped in anti-communism, spoke out against McCarthy.

In July, coordinated sermons from a group of influential Protestant church leaders in New York denounced McCarthyism as a "threat…to intellectual freedom." Dean James A. Pike of the Cathedral of St. John the Divine warned that "if this systematic smearing of our fellow citizens continues, more than the Rosenbergs will have died in our land," while Adam Clayton Powell told his Abyssinian Baptist Church congregation: "This is the hour of the antichrist." Moreover, in other countries where McCarthyism had never been popular, protests were getting louder. In Paris, the chairman of UNESCO warned that the United States faced international wrath for its book-burning policies, and the chairman of the British Trade Union Council sarcastically advised the United States to replace the Statue of Liberty with a statue of McCarthy.[29]

To be sure, the Red-scare days Stefan Kanfer called "the Plague Years" were a long way from over. And while McCarthy himself had become such a mental case (and an alcoholic) that he was embarrassing even to his former conservative allies[30] congressional hearings, loyalty oaths, and teacher firings continued. It was another five years before the State Department gave back Paul Robeson's passport.*

---

* The policy change actually moved like a snail across America's political map. Although McCarthy was censured by the Senate and dropped out of public life by the end of 1954, his ism endured at least another decade. Throughout the 1950s, movies and prime-time TV shows like I Led Three Lives continued to make Hoover and his

Still, the volume of protests against McCarthyism grew louder as 1954 began, and media coverage both reflected and promoted this shift. In February, when Edward R. Murrow demolished the senator on *See It Now,* viewer response was overwhelmingly positive. Six weeks later on *Meet the Press,* Einstein's old friend Eleanor Roosevelt denounced McCarthyite congressional committees as "not legitimate," and charged they "have endangered the freedoms and rights of some of our people."

But of all the liberal critics of McCarthy, only Einstein publicly urged civil disobedience—refusal to cooperate with the investigators. If he had simply wagged a disapproving finger at the McCarthyites, the *New York Times,* the *Washington Post,* and other liberal media would no doubt have cheered him on. Instead, he called for disobeying the law, in effect, challenging the system. His was not just criticism, it was a plan of resistance. Because he was Einstein, his call for defiance made front-page headlines twice in six months, and cast him into the forefront of the growing protest against the Red scare. Despite his insistence that he would not be a political activist,[31] Einstein's public challenge to the committees was a political bombshell.

The house on Mercer Street was bustling with calls from reporters, requests for TV interviews,* cables of congratulations, messages from others who had received or feared subpoenas and wanted help, and a flood of letters—most supporting Einstein's stand. With his newfound upbeat activism, Einstein also intervened to find a job for another blacklisted victim, Alex Novikoff. A biochemist and cancer researcher, Novikoff wrote to Einstein in June, after the University of Vermont fired him for refusing to answer questions about his politics before the SISS. With Einstein's help, Novikoff was soon hired by a medical school in formation at New York's Yeshiva University, which opened in 1956 as the Albert Einstein School of Medicine.** Einstein also wrote to Novikoff expressing "my respect for your upright position."[32] For thirty-three years, Novikoff remained at the

---

FBI into superpatriotic good guys saving America from godless communism. Political blacklists, loyalty oaths, and HUAC hearings continued into the mid-1960s.
* For reasons of health and also because he thought "economy" best when it came to media exposure, Einstein declined interview requests from both ABC and NBC. On Sept. 13, 1953, he turned down ABC's Martin Agronsky (see Nathan, pp. 594-5), and on March 29, 1954, he declined an offer from his friend, broadcaster Raymond Graham Swing to appear on Murrow's See It Now. (Princeton Archives.)
** Originally intended as a center for Jewish pre-med students barred by the quota system from other universities, Einstein Medical School was a haven not just for Jews, but for many blacklisted researchers (e.g., Helen Deane Markham, anatomy professor fired by Harvard) and others who didn't fit the approved mold and so couldn't find work elsewhere. This is partly why the school immediately became a first-class research facility-it had no problem attracting top talent, such as Novikoff, from around the country.

Einstein Medical College as researcher and Professor of Pathology. "His research into how living cells are chemically changed by cancer brought him within a whisker of the Nobel Prize in 1974," the *Boston Globe* reported on March 12, 1989, adding: "Perhaps he would have won if it had not been for the controversy." Thirty years after firing him, the University of Vermont in 1983 gave Novikoff an honorary degree.

As such acts often do, Einstein's letter to Frauenglass encouraged and inspired others to join the resistance. Just as Wuchinich and Shadowitz read about Frauenglass, others read about Einstein's support for them. Near the end of 1953, two more high-school teachers in New York, Irving Adler and Norman London, cited Einstein's letter to Frauenglass in support of their refusal to answer questions about alleged "subversive" activities. (Nearly fifty years later, Adler still remembers the letter as a definite booster, "good for our morale.") As the new year began, the War Resisters League announced that some one hundred pacifists had taken a pledge to follow Einstein's advice if they were subpoenaed.[33]

How much Einstein helped hasten the shift of public opinion against those he called "reactionary politicians" is, of course, impossible to measure. Many factors, including the statements by Murrow and Mrs. Roosevelt, the continuing defiance of people like Robeson and Du Bois, as well as hundreds of witnesses who refused to name names for the committees, contributed to the decline of McCarthyism, but there can be little doubt that Einstein's very public stand against the "inquisitions" helped turn that tide.

Whatever the political effect of Einstein's challenge, there is no question about its impact on his own life. Einstein's sense of despair and isolation vanished once the first public punch was thrown: the publication of his Frauenglass letter, June 12, 1953. While support from the famous scientist certainly heartened the three defiant witnesses, paradoxically it was Frauenglass, Wuchinich, and Shadowitz whose resistance bolstered Einstein's spirits and provided the "encouragement" that, a few years earlier, he was "badly in need of." Despite the intensifying political activity, he found time to keep up with his new friends. Besides his usual, heavy schedule of correspondence with contacts and colleagues around the world, Einstein now wrote enthusiastically to all three, along with numerous letters of recommendation to prospective employers. William and Tillie Frauenglass came for a visit with their thirteen-year-old son Richard, and later, Al Shadowitz brought his wife Edith and his immigrant father, who worshipfully gave Einstein a kiss. (He also sent photos of the rest of the Shadowitz family—his mother Sarah and the three girls, Naomi, Deborah, and baby Rebecca.)

William and Tillie Frauenglas visit Einstein at Princeton two weeks after
Einstein wrote to Frauenglas urging him not to cooperate with congressional
investigating committees. (Photo: Courtesy of Richard Frauenglas)

A rare picture of Einstein's lifted spirits, as well as some of his political
views, comes from Tillie Frauenglass's unpublished notes on the family's
visit to him on June 30, 1953. While most of the scientist's views expressed
through the notes are not new, they provide a unique insight into the
relaxed mood in the Einstein home. "He was very soft-spoken, mild-man-
nered and self-effacing—a humble human being," Richard Frauenglass
remembers. "He made you feel comfortable. It's rare for a teenager to feel
that way about any adult-and this was Einstein!"[34]

The Frauenglass family spent an hour and forty minutes chatting with
Einstein, his stepdaughter Margot, and Helen Dukas in their house on
Mercer Street in Princeton. On the drive back to Brooklyn, Tillie, who,
like her husband, was a schoolteacher, had the family write down everything they could remember from the visit. Here's a sampling from those
remarkable handwritten accounts:[35]

At the very beginning, he asked Bill, "Have you a job? Can I help you?" We
brushed it aside. "It's all right, you needn't worry, people are helping." At the

end of the visit, he came back to this and said, "I insist on helping you. Tell me to whom to write."

We said we didn't want to bother him and it would be more than enough if he would write a simple "To Whom It May Concern" recommendation. He said, "Oh no, that's no good—each one will think it concerns someone else. I want to write to specific people about you."

He asked me [Tillie] what I do. When I told him I'm a teacher, he asked if I had suffered from all of this and if my job was in danger.

We talked a lot about schools: "Students given long lists of books to read-too much, too fast. Should digest slowly."

"Overcrowding in schools is very bad....Schools and society too competitive; competition breeds hate ... marks in school destructive tochild ... love and interest are the best motivation, not duty as in German schools...."

Opposed to stress on speed: "People should ponder, meditate ... nature especially needs a slow approach...."

"Degrees not needed for doing a good job.... IQ tests are not truthful."

Rich was offered Coca-Cola and social tea biscuits. We were given grape juice and cookies we had brought.

As a boy, E said, he was not a good student ... asked Rich, "What's your favorite subject?" Rich said math. I said, "But Rich is not so good at French irregular verbs." E said, "Me, too. I never could memorize foreign languages. A lot of trouble with Greek—verbs had to be memorized in certain sequence...."

He was kept after school for "Arrest." His father laughed when the teacher wrote home in red ink about him. So did his mother.

Secretary [Helen Dukas] said talking about how he had not been a particularly good student was "undermining Richard."

I laughingly referred to the myth that he did not know how to fill out own income tax return. Helen Dukas said, "Is there anyone who *does* know?" I said, "Maybe it's a way Americans have of comforting themselves that even Einstein can't understand a tax return." Richard's comment: "It would be a bigger comfort if there was no income tax at all!" Everyone laughed. Helen Dukas commented, "Out of the mouths of babes!"

Richard wrote in his notes—"Thought that people who wanted to learn should go to colledges [sic], not to go just so they could get better jobs.

Warm, gentle man. Good sense of humor. Likes children. Talks slow but has a lot to say.

Liked the cookies we brought from Brooklyn."

E said he felt his letter had done some good—most of the letters he'd received had been positive—two-thirds favorable, one-third against. Those against seemingly illiterate and bigots. He was told that President Eisenhower and others in Washington had been affected by the letter. "But the American people must not depend on a few 'great' men."

As we were leaving, E thanked Bill "for giving me the opportunity to express myself." He said writing the letter "gave me one of the deepest satisfactions of my life."

His friend Erich Kahler observed that after Einstein's decision "to stir the conscience of the public," he underwent a dramatic mood change: "I have never seen him so cheerful and sure of his cause."[36] Barely two years after he'd written to Queen Mother Elizabeth about how "powerless" he felt, the uplifting impact of his confrontation with the McCarthy/Hoover committees was obvious. Now he told Elizabeth:

> I have become a kind of enfant terrible in my new homeland, due to my inability to keep silent and to swallow everything that happens there. Besides, I believe that older people who have scarcely anything to lose ought to be willing to speak out in behalf of those who are young and who are subject to much greater restraint. I like to think it may be of some help to them.

It was two weeks after his seventy-fifth birthday.[37]

Einstein kept up his resistance to McCarthy-Hooverism until his death on April 18, 1955. In November 1954, the editor of *The Reporter* magazine asked if Einstein would comment on the magazine's recent articles by Theodore H. White ("US Science: The Troubled Quest"), which dealt with McCarthy-style policies toward science and scientists, including the government's denial of security clearance to J. Robert Oppenheimer. Einstein's response, in the November 18 *Reporter,* was typically feisty:

> If I were a young man again…I would not try to become a scientist or scholar or teacher, I would rather choose to be a plumber or a peddler, in the hope of finding that modest degree of independence still available under present circumstances.[38]

In his last letter to Frauenglass, on March 9, 1955, six weeks before he died, Einstein wrote: "It seems that resistance to this kind of stupid tyranny is slowly developing."

18

The Unraveling

Entering its fifth year in early 1954, Hoover's spy case against Einstein began to unravel. Had Hoover known of Paul Weyland's history as a hustler, he would not have been surprised at the result of the Bureau's check of Weyland's charge that Einstein, in a 1920 newspaper article, had publicly acknowledged being a communist. It took the Washington office less than three months to get a translated copy of Einstein's *Berliner Tageblatt* article to Hoover, and unfortunately for the FBI chief's anti-Einstein effort, Weyland's story was one more that didn't check out. In his four-page 1920 article, Einstein dismissed Weyland contemptuously in a brief paragraph: "Mr. Weyland, who does not seem to be any kind of an expert...has not brought out anything realistic...simply indulged in gross rudeness and base accusations." But the article said nothing at all about being a communist. The only reference to his own politics in the entire four pages was Einstein's opening paragraph referring to himself as "a Jew with liberal, internationalist views..."[1]

It's possible, of course, that Weyland misremembered the article. But it's at least as likely that he was hoping the FBI in Miami would simply believe his story, or not be able to come up with a thirty-three-year-old German newspaper. Weyland's claim that his poor English had prevented him from finding the *Berliner Tageblatt* in American libraries, while no doubt sounding reasonable to the Miami G-men, simply wasn't true. Besides having been an interpreter for the Americans in postwar Berlin, Weyland, Kleinert tells us, "could express himself in a sophisticated style...and was fluent in English, French and Spanish."

What was in it for Weyland? What prompted the old charlatan to bring his Einstein story to the FBI? He had never liked Einstein, of course, but of more immediate self-interest, just three months earlier, Weyland and his wife had applied to become U.S. citizens. No government document has surfaced (nor has Kleinert cited any evidence) reporting that Weyland offered to trade his testimony for the FBI's "assistance" in speeding the citizenship approval. But it is a matter of historical record that Mr. and Mrs. Paul Weyland were granted United States citizenship in January 1954, an amazingly short seven months after they applied—and four months after Weyland walked into the Miami FBI office to discuss Einstein and his "hypothetical theory of relativity."

The second part of Hoover's Einstein case to come unknit was the August 5, 1953 Summary Report composed by Newark Agent Murphy, with help from former Comintern operative Louis Gibarti.[2] Linking Einstein to Soviet agents Sorge, Ruegg, and Juergen Kuczynski should have revitalized Hoover's hopes for a headline-making spy case, but for all its namedropping, the Summary Report barely held together. Among its loosest threads was its alleged Einstein-Sorge connection: two phone calls to Princeton from British journalist Guenther Stein, who had been part of Sorge's anti-Japanese spy ring during World War II. But the calls occurred on January 30, 1948, when Stein was in New York, and the war, Sorge, and his spy ring were all but memories. FBI phone monitoring showed that one of Stein's calls was placed to "Princeton 2580," which Murphy's report tells us "was listed for the Institute for Advanced Study, of which institute Einstein was in charge."[3] It is perhaps a small error—by 1953, the FBI should have learned that Einstein was not and had never been director of the IAS—but it doesn't help the credibility gap in Agent Murphy's Summary Report.

Then there is the Kuczynski connection. On page 97 of Murphy's report, ex-Comintern Agent Gibarti describes Einstein's long-standing friendship with the Kuczynski family, adding that Juergen Kuczynski "has frequently visited Einstein" in Princeton and was "possibly a member of the CP in the US."

When the Einsteins moved to the United States in 1933, Juergen Kuczynski was working in New York as a researcher for the American Federation of Labor. At twenty-nine, he had already begun writing his forty-volume opus on workers' living conditions throughout the world. His work provided any number of reasons—other than a communist conspiracy—for visiting his father's old colleague in Princeton. "We discussed God and the world, his first marriage, the role of math, and the Princeton Institute [for Advanced Study]," the younger Kuczynski later wrote of his visit to Princeton in May 1938. Far from having "frequently visited Einstein in Princeton," his memoirs describe that 1938 visit as the only time he saw Einstein in America.[4]

An avowed Marxist, Juergen Kuczynski joined the German Communist Party (KPD) in 1930. Shortly after Hitler came to power in 1933, the Nazis began arresting communists and outlawed the KPD; surviving Party members scrambled to set up an underground apparatus, and in 1936, Kuczynski returned to Berlin to help organize the anti-Nazi underground. It was his most dangerous assignment; it also launched his career as an intelligence officer—he'd been recruited for the Berlin job by the GRU. He returned to the United States briefly in 1938, and according to his memoirs, it was then that he made his one visit to Einstein. If during their conversation, Kuczynski tried to "pump" his old family friend for information about the U.S. military or the state of nuclear research, he wouldn't have come up with much. Einstein, at least until Szilard visited him the following year, was completely out of the strategic-research loop.

Just weeks after visiting Einstein, Kuczynski moved to London, where he spent the war years as both a leader of the underground KPD and a spy for Moscow. He also had a third job: In 1944, the American Embassy in London recruited him to help evaluate the impact of Allied bombings on Germany's war machine and made him a lieutenant colonel in the U.S. Army.[5] Considering this history, Juergen Kuczynski's single visit to an old family friend in Princeton was, at best, a weak foundation for Hoover's hoped-for spy case against Einstein.

But Murphy's Summary Report went from weak to worse when, at the end of 1953, Hoover made it clear (within the Bureau) he didn't trust Gibarti. The FBI chief may have learned that Gibarti had been jailed by Franco during World War II or that Gibarti had begun doing public-relations work for Indian Prime Minister Nehru and the nonaligned nations. Either would have been more than enough to convince Hoover that despite Gibarti's complete cooperation in testimony to the FBI and the McCarran Committee, Confidential Informant T-136 was still pink, if not Red. Hoover put the word out that Gibarti was an "alleged former Comintern member" whose "credibility is not known"—an FBI euphemism for snake in the grass. (The relevant pages of Gibarti's FBI file are so heavily censored—some 80 percent blacked out or withheld by the Bureau—that they provide no due to Hoover's reasoning.[6]

Initially, the August 5 Summary Report was distributed to a select group of FBI and other government offices, including the INS and G-2[7]—but then, silence. Murphy's document disappeared from the case. And Louis Gibarti? He became a nonperson. Neither his name nor number would be mentioned again in connection with Einstein...until after the case was closed.

Meanwhile, if Hoover had hoped that the wave of postwar German immigrants would produce credible anti-Einstein witnesses, he was disappointed again. To be sure, many in that group had anti-Semitic and anti-communist pasts, often including barely concealed Nazi activity. And when they saw America's political winds gusting to the right, quite a few rushed forward with allegations against one or another political or personal enemy. But eager ex-Nazis, as might have been predicted, made less than credible witnesses against Einstein.

In one such case, a newly arrived German told the Newark FBI office that he had a friend whose "aunt or great aunt had been a cook for Einstein in Germany in 1917 [and] had heard him make speeches in favor of Communism." More important, she "could prove [Einstein] was [then] a member of the CP underground in Berlin."* The former cook, Miss Gung, was now living in Lynbrook on New York's Long Island. Interviewing her, two of Hoover's agents found that she had indeed been Einstein's maid and cook in Berlin, but…

> Miss Gung stated he was never affiliated with or active in the Communist Party. She stated that she never heard him speak about or praise Russia or communism. [He] was anti-Monarchist and did not have sympathy for the Kaiser. She said that he did favor better conditions for the working people.
>
> Miss Gung knew nothing of an unfavorable nature about the subject and placed him very highly. She described him as "a human being of the purest humanitarianism."[8]

For Hoover, it was another fizzled lead, one more dead end. The other German expatriates who volunteered anti-Einstein stories were no more accurate than Paul Weyland. Most had only hearsay anecdotes to offer—like the man with the friend with the aunt or great-aunt on Long Island.

In Germany, too, the Einstein investigation was running on empty, despite Hoover's intensified efforts to press G-2 to find someone besides their publicity-shy *Source* to talk about Einstein's alleged twenty-year-old Soviet spy-ring connection. The FBI chief bombarded G-2 with memos, sending four letters in less than a year requesting, almost pleading for, a usable witness or piece of evidence:

> It will be appreciated if the Department of the Army will complete its investigation at the earliest possible time and forward the results to this Bureau.

But G-2 couldn't—or wouldn't—come up with anything other than what they'd already reported. In one typical response, W. A. Perry, chief of G-2's Security Division, stated simply: "Investigation is pending."[9] In the summer of 1953, Soviet and East German troops crushed violent antigovernment protests by workers in Berlin and other cities, and G-2 in

---

* In 1917, there was no CP in Germany—under or over-ground—only the Spartacus League, led by Rosa Luxemburg and Karl Liebknecht.

Germany was busy fanning the flames of discontent.[10] Einstein's activities more than twenty years earlier were low on Army Intelligence's priority list.

At Hoover's request, G-2 did finally interview Einstein's old friend and colleague Max von Laue. Now seventy-four and living in West Berlin, von Laue was one of the few German scientists who had stood up to the Nazis and supported Einstein in Germany during the Hitler years. While he had not seen Einstein since Christmas of 1932, von Laue had nothing but good words for his old friend, and certainly he knew of no espionage connection. In the language of spy chasers, this translated into "von Laue...had no new information."[11]

In five years, the FBI had failed to find a single credible witness against Einstein. But it was not the scarcity of witnesses that caused Hoover's cooling to the Einstein chase. His G-men often kept after suspects for far longer before coming up with tangible evidence. What's more, the FBI still had several un-checked leads suggesting a possible Einstein-espionage connection.

FBI phone taps and mail interception, unauthorized and possibly illegal, had identified calls and letters between several alleged Comintern agents and Einstein and Dukas. Besides the two calls from Guenther Stein in 1948, other contacts included Otto Katz and Pavel Mikhailov, the latter the Soviet consul general in New York and a former Red Army intelligence operative. FBI surveillance reported that during the early 1940s, Dukas "corresponded with" Katz, a Comintern representative (who later returned to his native Czechoslovakia, only to be executed during the 1952 purge of the mostly Jewish "Slansky group").[12] Also, the FBI noted that on one occasion, Einstein visited the Soviet Consulate to meet with Mikhailov.* Another FBI memo, this time from the Newark office "in the latter part of 1951," claimed, without any supporting explanation, that:

> Albert Einstein, scientist and mathematician, was a contact of Vladimir Pravdin, former KGB agent...[13]

Once again, a lot of smoke but no fire. Several other-than-espionage explanations are possible for those contacts. Pravdin, for example, was a correspondent for the Soviet news agency Tass, and might well have wanted to interview Einstein for a story if, in fact, they had any contact at

---

* The newly released FBI pages note that Margarita Konenkova helped arrange the meeting between Einstein and Mikhailov. Also that she visited Einstein's house on several weekends. In June 1998, love letters between Einstein and Konenkova, who had allegedly been involved in espionage, received world-wide, albeit brief, media coverage. (See "Post-script.")

all. (The FBI dossier includes only the one assertion, with no date or other specifics cited). Guenther Stein was a British journalist, and Otto Katz was a writer and publisher of anti-Nazi magazines and books, and "according to the files of the NY [FBI] Office," at the time of his correspondence with Dukas, was "writing for the *Freies Deutschland...* in Mexico City."[14] Nonetheless, if you're looking to put together a spy case against Einstein, these contacts are doors asking to be opened.

But by mid 1954, Hoover had decided not to pursue any more leads. In the end, it appears to have been politics more than evidence or witnesses that persuaded the Boss to abandon his Einstein chase. McCarthyism had become a prime target for anti-American sentiment on the rise around the world. In France and Italy, public dismay at the U.S. "Red scare" was fueling the growth of left-wing groups, especially the communists, who garnered close to a third of the vote in each country. Behind the scenes, after the death of Stalin in March 1953 and the Korean truce in July, Washington was inching toward less rigidity with Moscow as the new Soviet leaders opened first Russia's windows, and later, her doors to the West. A team of congressmen began arranging a trip to the previously off-limits Soviet Union, and White House strategists planned for a 1955 summer summit with Russia's new chiefs. At home, a more liberal Supreme Court, headed by Earl Warren, outlawed school segregation; resistance to congressional inquisitions was stiffening; and President Eisenhower—only after the anti-Red crusaders had driven communists and other leftists from most unions and schools in America—warned right-wing Republicans not to go too far.* When McCarthy ignored the warning and attacked the U.S. Army for "harboring Communists," it was his last attack. In the spring of 1954, the Army-McCarthy hearings on national television exposed the senator as a political goon, leading to his censure by the Senate in December and his rapid disappearance from the political scene.

It was only a slight shift in the political winds. The end of McCarthy was far from the end of the *ism*. The Red scare would continue for years, with HUAC hearings, loyalty oaths, and blacklists. If America's anti-communist crusade was ebbing, it was going to be a very slow ebb. For his part,

---

* Eisenhower's "Dartmouth speech" in June 1953, denouncing "book-burners," drew national headlines, but two days later, he "clarified," telling a press conference he did not support the distribution of books advocating communism. A more meaningful signal came on March 1, 1954, with the dismissal of McCarthy's ally Scott McCleod from his job overseeing State Department personnel. The next morning's *New York Times* called it "a thrust by the Administration at the McCarthy wing of the Republican party."

Hoover kept up both his secret "security files" and his public torrent of anti-communist speeches and articles, with no hint of mellowing.*

But the FBI chief was remarkably agile politically. Washington insiders usually pick up signals of policy changes well before they make The Evening News, and Hoover's network of eyes and ears picked them up before most insiders. The FBI chief could sense even a slight political wind shift, and in the summer of 1953, months before the Army-McCarthy hearings opened, Hoover emphatically broke off his partnership with the Wisconsin senator. McCarthy had violated their secrecy agreement by blurting out on the Senate floor that he had an FBI document in his possession; that gave Hoover a reason to cut off the senator's supply of secret FBI reports. At about the same time, Hoover discovered that McCarthy was involved in a secret plot to undermine President Eisenhower. The plotters, a group of wealthy, far-right Catholics, led by Joseph P. Kennedy and New York's Cardinal Spellman, planned to run McCarthy for President in 1956. Hoover reported the conspiracy to Eisenhower's Attorney General Herbert Brownell. Obviously, the plot thinned and then vanished with McCarthy's fall from grace.[15]

The dramatic events from the death of Stalin in March 1953 to McCarthy's demise twenty-one months later produced what Theoharis calls "a new phase of the Cold War with an attendant muting of the fear of Communism."[16] With that muting, for Hoover—the master survivor—the Einstein chase was no longer worth the risk to the FBI's (or his own) reputation.

Also, by 1954, the FBI had learned that Einstein did not have long to live. Memo after memo in Einstein's dossier repeats—as if it were a coded message—"He is in poor health and his activities are limited." If Hoover's political barometer told him it would be tough to sell the public a spy

---

* The FBI's PR office placed scores of anti-communist articles with Hoover's by-line in publications around the country. Typical titles included: "The Communists Are After Our Minds" in *American Magazine*, October 1954; "God, Country or Communism?" in the *American Legion Magazine* three years later; and "22,663 Red Spies" in the Shreveport (Louisiana) Times, April 15, 1955. For a comprehensive list of Hoover's articles, pamphlets, speeches, films, radio, and TV shows, see Donner, pp. 468-477. "Hoover had a fixation...about Communism," according to former FBI official Welch. "No one could tell him anything." Wekh, who has no sympathy for the left, but believes in America's Constitution, added, "Hoover's whole anti-Communist thing suffered from a lack of proof, an absence of challenge. No adversarial confrontation so vital to our legal system. Hoover should have devoted more time to catching criminals." (Interview with Welch, June 16, 1998.) Former Deputy FBI Director Oliver "Buck" Revell has reportedly (Kessler, FBI, p. 4) said: "Hoover would be prosecuted [today] for the money he kept from the books he supposedly wrote but didn't write."

charge against Einstein the scientist living in Princeton, the FBI chief knew it would be impossible against Einstein the saint.

When Hoover finally agreed in January 1955 to authorize Newark agents to interview Helen Dukas, the game was already over. In fact, his permission for the interview with Einstein's secretary signaled his surrender. For five years, he had kept the Einstein investigation secret by diligently avoiding face-to-face confrontations with anyone at all friendly with Einstein, and especially Dukas, as one FBI memo spelled out.

> ...because of her close association with Albert Einstein...and his known tendency to make public statements concerning matters with which he personally disagrees.[17]

Besides risking the security of his secret investigation, Hoover had little or nothing to gain from such an interview. Dukas had devoted the last twenty-five years of her life to Einstein, as his secretary and housekeeper. From all accounts, she was virtually a member of the family. You didn't have to be Sherlock Holmes to figure out how she would respond to FBI questioning. After a quarter-century of loyalty, even if she did have any incriminating information, she wasn't about to tell the FBI. She certainly wasn't going to say the man she was devoted to had been a Soviet spy.

Months before the Dukas interview, FBI memos make it clear the Einstein case was all but over and the Bureau was simply tying up loose ends. In a memo to Hoover on November 9, 1954, the Newark office confirmed:

> ...further investigation into this matter is not warranted after the completion of present outstanding leads [interviewing Dukas], and upon completion of these leads, the Newark Office will consider closing the case concerning Dr. EINSTEIN.

On February 23, 1955, with Einstein only weeks from death, two Newark FBI agents finally interviewed Helen Dukas, pretending—on Hoover's instructions—to be seeking her help in an investigation of German communists in prewar Berlin. The agents found Dukas "extremely friendly... quite sincere...and not...evasive in any manner." She offered to meet with the FBI again if they needed her help with any other investigations. Based on the Dukas interview, the FBI agents reported they were certain that neither she nor Einstein knew anything about a Soviet spy connection in Berlin, that no cable-drop ever existed in Einstein's home/office, that she did not know any of the sixteen Germans listed as co-conspirators by G-2's *Source*, and that no other secretary had worked for Einstein since she took the job in 1928:

Dukas...was the only employee of Dr. Einstein since 1928 and that in itself tends to discredit the allegations by G-2's Source...that Einstein's office had a staff of secretaries and typists...

The agents concluded:

It is not believed that additional investigation in this matter is warranted.[18]

No one, not the Newark agents conducting the Dukas interview, not the Newark SAC, and most significantly, not Hoover, questioned her credibility. Dukas had denied knowing Otto Katz or Guenther Stein, for example, despite FBI records showing they had called or written to her. Perhaps she had forgotten—so many people called and wrote to Einstein's office—but no one even asked her. Once Hoover decided that the political climate would no longer welcome an Einstein spy case, it made little difference what she said. The chase and the case were over.

On April 18, 1955, Einstein died at the age of seventy-six. A few days later, Hoover officially closed the case.

It ended not with a bang but, from Hoover, a whimper. He still had tracks to cover up—Louis Gibarti's tracks. Hoover considered Gibarti so disreputable, dangerous, or both that he wanted no trace that the FBI had once relied on his information in the Einstein case. Hoover made it clear that all of Gibarti's testimony should now be disregarded. For six months after the Einstein file was officially closed, Hoover's SACs in Newark and New York scrambled to change the FBI's records, advising their offices around the country that "at the direction of the Bureau..."

all information furnished by LOUIS GIBARTI in all letters and reports be attributed to him by name.[19]

In the topsy-turvy, top-secret world of the FBI, if you want to end the career of a Confidential Informant, instead of deleting his or her name, you make the name as widely known as possible. This meant adding Gibarti's name—in ink—to all the Bureau's records that had previously quoted him simply as a Confidential Informant or T-136. Besides the flurry of letters and memos to FBI offices, Hoover sent a "suggestion" to G-2, with copies to the CIA, Navy, and Air Force Intelligence, and the INS:

Subject: ALBERT EINSTEIN
INTERNAL SECURITY- R
Reference is made to the report of Special Agent Vincent E. Murphy dated August 5, 1953, at Newark, New Jersey ...
Your attention is directed to ... information ... furnished by Confidential Informant T 136. This informant is Louis Gibarti, an alleged former Comintern representative whose credibility is not known since he has in the past furnished both reliable and unreliable information.

It is suggested that the agencies receiving copies of this communication may desire to make an appropriate notation on the copy of Special Agent Murphy's report...*

Hoover's letter was an appropriate finale to five years of false leads and unconfirmed anti-Einstein allegations (all distributed to seven other federal agencies) from unstable or unidentified informants.

---

* Hoover's letter, October 4, 1955, like the entire Gibarti episode, is blacked out in the file released by the FBI, even in the new version released in the spring of 2000. The records cited here were obtained from other government sources.

19

Einstein the Spy?

With the arrival of the new millennium, official U.S. government documents continue to report—with not a hint that it may be untrue—an Einstein-espionage connection: In 1999, the same year Einstein was named "Person of the Century" by *Time,* and A&E TV selected him as the eighth most important person of the entire millennium, if you submitted a FOIA request to Army Intelligence (G-2) for their security file on Einstein, you would have (eventually) received ten heavily blacked-out pages with the following readable paragraph:

> ...with reference to Einstein's Berlin residence prior to World War II... Einstein was aware that his Berlin Office was used as a telegraphic address by Soviet agents....The Soviets and Communist International Apparats [sic] used the subject's [Einstein's] Berlin office as a letter drop for conspiratorial correspondence, primarily from the Far East, and...the subject must have been aware of such use of his office.[1]

Is it possible Einstein did assist a Soviet spy ring while living in Berlin from 1929 to 1932?

During Einstein's last years in Berlin, the dying years of the Weimar Republic, with Germany's unemployment rampant, more young people swaggering around in swastika armbands, and stepped-up violence by Nazi street gangs going unpunished, for many democrats, the "New Russia" seemed to promise hope in a frightening world. The Western political scene hardly offered a progressive alternative: U.S. troops in Washington tear-gassing a ragtag, unarmed "army" of World War I veterans camped in the capital to demand the bonuses they'd been promised. Meanwhile, the Japanese army invaded Manchuria with barely a scolding from the League of Nations. Einstein would not have been the first anti-Fascist to go to work for Moscow.

But did he?

J. Edgar Hoover's failure to confirm or refute the detailed espionage connection alleged by G-2's anonymous *Source* doesn't really prove or disprove anything. As we've seen, a combination of shifting political winds and Einstein's death in 1955 left Hoover little choice but to close the case.

In 1991, an article by Frederick Litten in the prestigious *British Journal for the History of Science* argued that *Source* basically had it right in the FBI's file, that Einstein's Berlin office had indeed serviced a Soviet spy network from 1929 to 1932. Litten's *BJHS* piece claims, however, that Einstein had a second office at the headquarters of the League Against Imperialism and *that* office, not Einstein's home, was a cable-drop for the Noulens (a.k.a. Ruegg) and Sorge spy rings.[2] Greeted when it appeared by a great shrug from the academic community, Litten's theory nonetheless deserves a response. More important, the entire Einstein espionage allegation detailed by *Source* has remained unanalyzed—and kept alive at least in the G-2 files (also in the INS files) on Einstein.

There is really no dramatic, colorful, action-packed way of reading through old reports. Yet, with no surviving eyewitnesses, no fingerprints, no DNA, and no recoverable hard drives, playing historical detective requires scrutinizing documents for dues and contradictions. In this case, the FBI's Einstein file itself—including the espionage accusations from G-2's *Source*—is a treasure trove of previously unanalyzed evidence. Remember, it was the extensively detailed nature of those allegations that G-2 officers said made the charges so believable.

But the allegations from *Source*—that Einstein allowed his Berlin office to be used as a cable-drop for Russian spies—simply don't hold up under careful examination. The very details G-2 found so believable actually provide conclusive evidence that Einstein didn't allow it.

First, *Source* lists sixteen people who knew about Einstein's alleged cable-drop. Telling sixteen people is not exactly a secure way to keep a secret, but there's more: All sixteen were in the Gestapo's "Wanted" files as Communist espionage agents.[3] Surely even the Russians, who knew a little about spying, could have found at least one unknown (to the Gestapo) mailman, dogcatcher, cook, or newsboy to serve as courier to and from Einstein's house—if it had actually been a cable-drop.

The G-2 report also decisively knocks out Litten's thesis that the espionage cables were sent to Einstein's second office—there is no record that he ever had one—in the headquarters of the League Against Imperialism. In the Einstein file, *Source* states unequivocally: "The office [which allegedly served as the espionage-drop] was SUBJECT's [Einstein's] private office, which had no connection with any organization or ins titution."[4]

Even if a Soviet spy ring did somehow use Einstein's home office as a cable-drop, the evidence cited by *Source* (and still reported in G-2's files) that Einstein knew about it is simply false. Remember that the key paragraph in *Source's* reports alleged:

> EINSTEIN must have become aware of what was going on in the summer of 1930 when his personal secretary went on leave…he was given a large amount of telegrams which he kept until his secretary returned…When the girl [sic] returned…all cables were turned over to her by EINSTEIN and there were no unpleasant repercussions. The use of the cable address by the Soviets continued as in the past.[5]

But Einstein was not in Berlin in the summer of 1930. In April, he and Elsa moved to their new vacation home in Caputh and spent the entire season there. In mid July, the renowned Indian poet Rabindranath Tagore came to Caputh by train to visit them. "Einstein was so fond of his rural existence [that summer] that he stayed away from the physics Colloquium and even the weekly meetings of the academy.…"[6] (News reports of police attacking and arresting leftist demonstrators in the streets of Berlin that summer did nothing to increase Einstein's desire to return home quickly.[7])

Then there is the small matter of a cable address. The *G-2/Source* report leaves no question:

> …the actual address of SUBJECT's [EINSTEIN's] office was not used as a letter drop. What was used was the authorized international cable address.…This cable address is believed to have been EINSTEIN BERLIN or ALBERTEINSTEIN BERLIN. (The exact address can be determined by consulting a German cable address book from 1929 to 1930.…[Sentence in parenthesis is included in *Source's* report.]

This is the kind of specific detail that makes *Source's* report seem believable. But a check of the International Cable Directory from 1915 to 1931 shows *no listing* for Albert Einstein.[8]

Other evidence also refutes the cable-drop story: *Source* reported that Einstein's cable address was an ideal "drop"—

> since EINSTEIN received a great quantity of…cablegrams, etc., from all over the world.[9]

But if ever an occasion would have drawn such cablegrams, it was Einstein's fiftieth birthday in 1929, when his home in Berlin was deluged by greetings from friends and admirers throughout the world. Yet among the more than 150 birthday greetings Einstein received on that occasion, there is not a single international cable. Indeed, no such cable is to be found anywhere among the archive's thousands of letters and messages Einstein received during his eighteen years in Berlin.[10]

Without a cable address, without cablegram traffic, even Soviet master-spy Richard Sorge would have had a hard time using Einstein as a cable-drop. This flaw in *Source's* ointment not only discredits his entire allegation against Einstein, it also effectively undermines the possibility that someone else—a building superintendent or a postman—might have used Einstein's address as a "safe-drop" without the scientist's knowledge.

But the most persuasive argument that Einstein was not involved in espionage is that he didn't share the political commitment to the Soviet Union and communism that motivated virtually all the successful Soviet spies during the first half of the century. Unlike today's spies such as Aldrich Ames and Robert Hanssen, who are driven by money and ego, Soviet spies such as Philby, Fuchs, Sorge, Ted Hall, George Blake, Ruth Werner, Lona and Morris Cohen, to name a few, did their deeds out of dedication to the egalitarian society they believed the Soviets were creating. That they turned out to be wrong about Moscow doesn't mean they were any less committed. Interviewed in 1999, Melita Norwood, the eighty-seven-year-old British grandmother who had been a successful Soviet spy for years, declared that even without the Russian model, she had not given up the ideas and ideals originally inspired by the Soviets. But that was not Einstein. He was far too much a maverick, a rebel against authority, and as we've seen, not a fan of Stalin's Soviet Union.

If *Source's* Einstein espionage charge wasn't true, who would have gone to all the trouble to make up such an elaborately itemized story? And why? Two incidents reported in the German press provide a clue. The first, reported by Einstein biographer Philipp Frank, occurred in the fall of 1923, when, if you read certain Berlin newspapers, you would have learned about Einstein's first trip to the Soviet Union. It was initially revealed by the conservative *Deutsche Allgemeine Zeitung,* which on September 15 told its readers, "From Moscow we learn that Professor Einstein is expected there at the end of September [and] will speak on the theory of relativity." The paper added, "Russian scientists are looking forward to the lecture with great interest."

Although Einstein didn't get to Moscow by the end of September, on October 6, the *Berliner Tageblatt* reported he was on his way: "Professor Einstein has left for Moscow [where] preparations are being made [for] an imposing welcome." Three weeks later—there was no commercial airline travel in 1923—he was expected to arrive in Petersburg the next day, according to the *Berliner Borsenzeitung,* and would speak on the relativity theory "to a group of scientifically trained workers." On November 2, the *Kieler Zeitung* reported: "Einstein is staying in Petersburg for three days."[11] The Nazis were still a decade away from state power, but it was a period of increasing right-wing nationalism in Germany, and the reports of Einstein's Moscow trip brought him a slew of threatening letters.

Just one additional point: Einstein never went to Moscow. The trip was totally fabricated, as was each "report" in the series. It's theoretically possible that each newspaper made up its own story, but it's far more likely they were all fed pieces of the tale by one, probably right-wing source. (After the first piece was printed, the rest would be simply "updates.")

The second incident occurred in the summer of 1941. Nazi officials then occupying Paris issued a warrant for several French Jews, charging them with conspiracy to assassinate the Sudeten Nazi leader Konrad Henlein. According to the Gestapo, the group had held several secret meetings at night inside *Asyle de Jour et Nuit,* a Paris shelter for destitute Jews, where they designed their assassination plot. Henlein would have been killed, the warrant stated, except that the murderer's weapon failed to go off.

The story, widely reported in the Nazi-controlled Paris press, was totally invented-with all its who-what-when details—by the "Jewish Desk" of the Nazi Security Service. We now know, thanks to Saul Friedlander's thorough research, that the Nazis frequently concocted "very precise— and totally imaginary—Jewish plots."[*] (Before Americans become too self-righteous at such German dirty dealing, remember that Hoover and his Bureau didn't hesitate to fabricate evidence and more—plant false evidence, send forged letters, break into homes and offices—against many targets during the FBI's "Cointelpro" operation and the civil rights movement of the sixties, including Martin Luther King.)

Einstein was at or near the top of the Hitler regime's enemies list. As mentioned earlier, within two months of taking power, the Nazis raided the Einstein's house in Caputh, claiming they were looking for a cache of weapons. They found nothing, but nonetheless announced: "The property was obviously going to be used [in] a Communist revolt." Remember, too, that the Nazi press offered a reward for Einstein's assassination, and a U.S. government official reported seeing his name on the Nazis' "dead or alive" wanted list. Einstein's achievements and worldwide reputation totally undermined the Nazis' Aryan superrace propaganda. He was a prime target for one of the Gestapo's "very precise—and totally imaginary—Jewish plots."

---

* "The most astonishing aspect of the system...was its concreteness." The Nazis' Jewish Desk (SD II-112) considered themselves the top "Jew experts" in Germany, holding conferences several times a year to hear updated "information." SD Il-12 compiled a massive file of index cards on "every Jew" in the Third Reich. (Friedlander, *Nazi Germany and the Jews,* 1933-1939, pp. 199-200.)

If the Nazis manufactured the Einstein spy story, how did it get to G-2 (where it became the lynchpin of Hoover's anti-Einstein campaign) in 1950? To understand that, we have to go back to the closing days of World War II, when the Third Reich that Hitler had predicted would "last a thousand years" was collapsing under the Allied military assault. With Russia's Red Army at the gates of Berlin, several U.S. agencies were already laying plans to recruit "former" Nazis into America's fight against international communism. Following the war, Washington brought over thousands of "ex"-Nazi scientists, military officers, and intelligence operatives who had been part of Hitler's anti-Soviet network. The Russians were not completely averse to recruiting "former" Nazis either, but with a few significant exceptions, most of the defecting Nazis rushed to join the American side, where they could continue their anti-communism (and other anti-isms).*

"Operation Paperclip," a top-secret project run by the U.S. Joint Chiefs of Staff, brought some sixteen hundred "former" Nazi scientists to America between 1945 and 1968 (that date is not a typographical error) to work for the U.S. military and NASA. The best-known was rocket scientist Wernher von Braun, who helped build NASA's space program, but there were at least *hundreds* more. Many were assigned to work on projects similar to the gruesome experiments they had conducted on prisoners in Nazi concentration camps.** (A number of these "scientists" also took part in the radiation experiments that—decades later—the U.S. government admitted conducting.) Despite government efforts to avoid publicity, the arrival in America of so many ex-Nazis was not a secret for long. In March 1946, Einstein joined Eleanor Roosevelt and several other former FDR associ-

---

* Some mind-boggling statistics indicate the frantic race westward by deserting German troops: Between April 11 and 20th, 1945, with the war's end imminent, 25,823 German soldiers were reported missing on the Eastern front (fighting the Russians) while 268,229 German officers and men were "missing" in the West! (Bialer, p. 621.)

** Among the former Nazi scientists working in the United States under Operation Paper Clip were (to cite just one example) space-medicine "expert" Hubertus Strughold and a group of "doctors" who had worked under him at the Dachau concentration camp, who were brought to the Brooks Air Force Base School of Aviation Medicine in San Antonio. In one "survival experiment" at Dachau, Nazi "doctors" had given a group of 40 Gypsies no food and nothing but seawater to drink until "the people were crazy from thirst and hunger," according to testimony of one survivor. Under Operation Paperclip, "scientists" who had authorized or planned such experiments were put in charge of space-medicine research in San Antonio in the early 1950s on projects like the effects on man of extreme heat, oxygen deficiency, and rapid decompression. See "In the Name of Science: San Antonio's Nazi Connection" by Linda Hunt, *San Antonio Current*, June 22, 1995.

ates at a meeting in New York of the National Conference on the German Problem. But the problem the group protested was American more than German. They demanded the Truman Administration immediately stop the immigration of Nazis, and especially denounced Operation Paper Clip.[12]

The FBI was quick to monitor this suspicious activity—the protests, not the federal welcome wagon for former Nazis. A memo in Einstein's dossier from Mickey Ladd to Hoover cites a *New York Times* report:

> In December 1946, Einstein joined a group of "more than 40 scientists, educators, clergymen and other persons" who signed a protest against the granting of permanent residence and citizenship to Nazi scientists then working for the US Army.

Ladd's memo also mentions briefly a federal program innocuously named the *Protective Custody of the Joint Intelligence Objectives Agency*.[13] Under this "Protective Custody," hundreds, perhaps thousands, of former Nazi police and espionage agents were welcomed into the rapidly expanding U.S. Intelligence operation. And just as quite a few of the German scientists often continued the work they had been doing under the Nazis, only now for a new employer, many of these former intelligence agents simply renewed their previous anti-Soviet operations under the banner of the U.S. CIA.

While Einstein and other holdover anti-fascists protested, America's spymasters and strategic planners mapping the nation's anti-Soviet policy celebrated. Recruiting the old Nazi spy network—with their undercover agents around the world, as well as their information—was considered a definite asset for the U.S. in the global balance of postwar power. In such an atmosphere, one more espionage allegation from one more "ex"-Nazi would hardly seem unusual—even if it was aimed against Einstein.

By now, it is thoroughly documented that the CIA was set up in 1947 with the cooperation and participation of former Nazi agents, including Hitler's spy chief Reinhard Gehlen. And the merger was far from a hostile takeover. How totally the anti-communist atmosphere permeated America's intelligence operations is clear from the open-armed welcome extended to these "ex"-Nazis:

> [After US troops captured him in 1945] Gehlen found a high-ranking US Army intelligence officer and offered a microfilmed set of his files on the Soviet Union-and his agent network. He was one of scores of Nazis who were accepted by the West as good prospective ASSETS to use against the Soviets.[14] [Emphasis in the original.]

The FBI, too, tapped into this newfound, eager-to-cooperate manpower supply for its share of "former" Nazis. Valerian Trifa, for example, the Romanian fascist who led the bloodthirsty, anti-Semitic mobs during that country's "Malaxa pogroms" in 1941, made postwar broadcasts on Radio Free Europe from the United States to Romania, broadcasts that he bragged were arranged by "my good friend J. Edgar Hoover." With U.S. leaders and media focusing on the Red Menace, "ex"-Nazis were not excluded from America's criminal justice establishment just because they had blood on their hands. "Instead of arresting them, the FBI promptly [in 1950] recruited every White Russian Nazi it could find in the New York-New Jersey area."[15]

In Germany, the U.S. Army's Counterintelligence Corps (G-2) actively recruited "former" Nazi agents. While some G-2 officers who had helped track down and arrest Nazis after the war were anti-fascists, others welcomed the transfusion of new, vehemently anti-communist blood. G-2 didn't even have to pay moving costs for its new "network of recruited informants and agents consisting of former Nazis...."[16] How many "ex"-Nazis followed the well-traveled trail from German to American intelligence agencies bearing tales of real or imagined Red spies is anybody's guess. But if one was the informant code-named *Source*, releasing the Einstein-espionage story into the anti-communist atmosphere of G-2 would have been as simple as pulling a trigger.

Source's detailed account includes inadvertent arrows pointing to his possible Nazi past. First, there's that list of the sixteen people allegedly in on Einstein's cable-drop who just happen also to be in the Gestapo's files of Communist espionage agents. Who but someone inside the Nazi State Security apparatus would know the German police records—essentially, the descriptions included in *Source's* report—on all sixteen names? And who but a Gestapo insider would have known that Nazi police officials—

> shortly after 1933, worked on the case built up around the cables received by [Einstein's] office... and] the [Einstein] case was being worked on in 1935.[17]

(Even *Source's* choice of words may be revealing: "...worked on the case built up around..." could easily imply the invention, manufacture, and elaboration of a fictitious story.)

But here's an interesting twist in the search for *Source*: G-2's first letter (July 31, 1950), promising to send Hoover "a detailed report...about Einstein's past activities" in Europe, said the information came "from former well-placed KPD (German Communist Party) members."[18] *Source*, it seems, was sources. And they had been well-placed KPD-ers. Yet Markus Wolf, former head of East Germany's foreign intelligence operations (you can't get any more well-placed), says he has never heard even a hint of an Einstein-espionage connection.[19] However, the Einstein spy-story could have come from German communists who defected to the Nazis in 1933 when the SS started rounding up Reds, union activists, homosexuals, Gypsies, and Jews. Many ex-KPD members worked with the Gestapo and other anti-communist police agencies, and could easily have helped concoct the tale of the cabledrop. After the war, many of these rather-switch-than-fight operators switched again, this time to the Americans—either as agents of the U.S. Occupation authority or simply as sources of anti-communist information, true and otherwise.

Several were working with G-2 in Germany in 1951, the date of *Source's* second and last report on Einstein, and the list of *Source's* possible identities includes, but is not limited to, a number of the sixteen names cited in that report.[20] A Hitlerite background would also explain why *Source* quit the case as soon as Hoover asked for someone to testify against Einstein in public—where media meddlers rummaging through closets might uncover who knows what Nazi skeletons.

But the significant question is not who but how—how Hoover could have based his five-year Einstein spy hunt solely on such an impeachable source or sources. Hoover may not have known where the anti-Einstein spy allegations came from, and he (presumably) did not have access to the Gestapo files. But it's hard to believe the powerful FBI director couldn't have obtained information about a friendly potential witness. It's even harder to believe he would have spent five years conducting the anti-Einstein campaign based on the testimony of someone he knew nothing about. It's far more likely that Hoover at least suspected the Nazi nature of G-2's anti-Einstein informant. With the postwar stream of "former" Nazis into the FBI (as well as the CIA and other agencies), it was hardly unusual for the Bureau to include reports from "ex"-Nazis in its security dossiers.

"During the McCarthy era," writes historian Klaus Hentschel, "the FBI accepted statements picked up from extreme right-wing [German] newspapers...as politically incriminating material against troublesome left-wing scientists like Einstein."[21] If extreme right-wing German newspapers are good as anti-Einstein sources, extreme right-wing Germans are better.

Conclusion

1

It is tempting to laugh at the often inept and sometimes ludicrous practices of Hoover's FBI (also those of G-2 and the INS). In Einstein's case, these included, among other things, playing Keystone Kops on the streets of Berlin, following a totally fictitious "hostage" tale about Einstein's son (whom they misnamed), and seriously pursuing fantasies invented by an array of obviously deranged and dishonest informants.

But it wasn't just Einstein. Charlie Chaplin's file was full of "sloppiness and stupidity" as well as falsehoods, according to biographer David Robinson,* and Franklin Folsom tells of how, when he was chairman of the League of American Writers in the 1930s, the FBI for years mixed up his file with another person with the same name but no other similarities. Such "wrong man" (and woman) stories abound among those who were targets of the McCarthy-Hoover Red hunts. One report from a classified Justice Department study found a 50-percent error rate in a sampling of FBI data bases. That means one out of every two FBI facts were not.[1]

But chortling misses the point. McCarthy, Hoover, and their crew did not *aim* for accuracy. They had a two-pronged goal: first to isolate and cripple the hard-line leadership of the organized left—driving com-

---

* Besides the "alarming...degree of sloppiness and stupidity" in the FBI's Chaplin file, Robinson adds: "Nothing, however negative, was disregarded...A soldier charged with a security offense snapped, 'Sure I'm a Communist...so is Charlie Chaplin.' It was reported by the Army to the FBI, and stayed on Chaplin's record to the end; for no detail, however meaningless or insubstantial, was ever erased, once it was on the files. In April 1943, Chaplin was seen at a showing of the Soviet classic Baltic Deputy. He attended a Shostakovich concert. It was recorded as a sign of undesirable radical views that he was signatory to a letter from 800 labour, religious and social leaders who urged Roosevelt to prevent racial outbreaks and lauded his stand against discrimination." (p. 750.)

munists and those close to them out of positions of influence in unions, schools, academia, and entertainment—and second, perhaps even more important, to intimidate the remaining population into silence, bath verbal and mental.

Arresting the wrong man, harassing people based on false leads— bumbling or not—actually helped implant fear of government into the American mind-set. The frightening effect of the FBI's "mistaken identity" harassment was much like that of the police who sometimes smash through front doors of the wrong apartments while searching for reported criminals. Even when the victims of such frightening "mistaken" attacks on rare occasions receive an apology and a new door, no number of new locks can keep out their terror. Hoover's method of intimidating the population was what Ron Kessler has called the "vacuum cleaner approach"[2]— sweep up everyone in the room, or the meeting hall, or the organization. According to former Attorney General Tom Clark, Hoover...

> admitted himself that only about one percent of these people were really bad, but in public I think he said ten percent. You have to remember that it was a small group that overthrew the Russian government. That was his attitude.[3]

While Hoover had no qualms about the ethics of this approach, its appearance was something else. Ever eager to put his best face forward, America's number one G-man clearly saw the need to construct a more democratic façade-millions of Americans, even frightened, still believed in the Bill of Rights. In April 1950, in the Sunday *Times Magazine,* Hoover (or his ghostwriters) pictured a kinder, gentler FBI, ever vigilant to protect Constitutional rights-the Boy Scouts (at least the public image of the Boy Scouts*), with Hoover as chief Scoutmaster dedicated only to the well-being of his troops and the greater good of his country. Nothing demonstrates this as clearly as his classic statement, cited earlier: "I would not want to be a party in any action which would 'smear' innocent individuals for the rest of their lives."

We have already seen that Hoover was not beyond an occasional "misstatement," as with his adamant denial that he ever fed secret information to congressional committees, but in the *Times Magazine* piece, the FBI chief outdid himself in storytelling—solemn, dignified, bordering on indignant, and dissembling all the way.[4]

But even as his public-relations people polished Hoover's democratic veneer, the FBI's role as shock troops for McCarthyism was just beginning—following radicals and suspected radicals, paying "visits" to their

---

* The Boy Scouts' policy of barring homosexuals fits perfectly with Hoover's homophobic policies, never mind whatever he may have kept in his closet.

employers, privately pressuring people to become informers on friends and political associates, and investigating the backgrounds of current and prospective government workers for any possible pink tinge. The FBI "vacuum cleaner" often caused more damage than just a smashed-in door. "Out of the first 7,667 full field investigations performed under Truman's executive Order 9835," according to Schrecker, "nearly five hundred had been based on information that related to another person."[5] Since the FBI's accusers remained anonymous, the result of such a mix-up was often the loss of one's job. If the FBI were bumblers, they were terrifying bumblers.

The core of McCarthyism, however, was not the FBI's mistakes but their non-errors, targeting people who *did* have left-wing ideas. In the case above—just one of hundreds of such examples—firing the seven thousandplus people with radical ideas or associations was the fundamental injustice underlying America's fearful society of the fifties. Einstein chose to speak out not about the easy-to-protest mistaken identity cases, but about the thousands subpoenaed, fired and jailed because they *were* radicals, socialists, sometimes communists—people like Bill Frauenglass, Al Shadowitz, and George Wuchinich—those who refused to abandon their views or become informers. In Einstein's case, despite their bumbling manner, Hoover's Bureau knew exactly whom they were pursuing and why. Einstein's maverick and left-leaning politics combined with his almost universal popularity made him a major threat to those trying to turn America into a nation of political sheep.

II

Most Americans today have no idea that Einstein supported so many—or any-political groups. Here is a giant of history—"Person of the Century"— a man the whole world knows, and yet virtually nobody knows him.

Einstein's political legacy has been caught in a historical double whammy: For Hoover, Einstein's left-ism was a potential embarrassment. After collecting a ton of evidence to "prove" what Einstein would readily have told anyone—that he supported a large number of radical organizations—Hoover realized that he couldn't use that information publicly. Without something more, like a spy connection, Einstein was simply too popular and unapologetic about his principles. For almost any other FBI target—a schoolteacher or labor organizer who refused to sign a loyalty oath or name names—a "Red front" exposé could, and often did, cost them their job. But in Einstein's case, the reason he had joined most of those groups was not to go out on Saturday mornings and hand out fliers at a supermarket. His contribution was precisely to add the prestige of his name to their programs—as publicly as possible.

When you've spent decades, like Hoover, splashing Red paint on hundreds of organizations to scare people away from them, you don't want to hand a microphone to one of the most respected men in America so he can endorse those very groups. Einstein threatened to undo the Red-Menace image that Hoover, McCarthy & Co. had so diligently created. When a little boy in the crowd shouts out that the emperor in the passing parade has no clothes on, that's bad enough. But when the message comes from Einstein....Understandably, then, for all the FBI's compiling, listing, and cataloguing of Einstein's "Communist-front groups," Hoover showed not the slightest *interest—unless* he had been able to come up with an espionage connection—in publicizing, or even leaking, any of these affiliations to the media.

The twist, the second part of the double whammy, is that most Einstein scholars and biographers seem to have been more frightened by Hoover's Red-baiting than Einstein was. Apparently fearing it would scandalize Einstein's name if the world learned that he stood left of center, they have muzzled Einstein, minimizing or omitting his "controversial" connections—especially his anti-racist and left-wing organizations such as the Civil Rights Congress and the Friends of the Lincoln Brigade. For their part, the mass media as well as the leading scientific societies and academies have done little or nothing to correct this omission. Despite his giant's stature in history, Einstein *was* hurt by Hooverism. To the extent Einstein's political activities and insights-especially his eloquent anti-racism that might lend some sanity to today's wounded society—have been deleted by his historians and silenced by scientists who fear attacks from the right, to the extent his image has been "sterilized," to that extent, Hoover has won.

Political controversy might tarnish the iconized Einstein—*Time's* "...kindly, absentminded professor...wild halo of hair, piercing eyes..." "(When the 1996 *Nova* Special, "Einstein Revealed," called him "the otherworldly genius," it revealed more about *Nova* than about Einstein.) Einstein would probably laugh at the irony, even while finding it bewildering and sad, that he is world-renowned for theories most people don't begin to fathom, yet his extensive advocacy of disarmament, civil rights, and political dissent—which everyone can understand—is virtually unknown. Perhaps with the end of the Cold War, the time is ripe for a change in what is biographically acceptable. If the *New York Times* can report that Groucho Marx was "proud of" being a "subversive," perhaps Einstein can get a public hearing for his political activism in defense of unpopular causes, a commitment, after all, that earned him a place of honor on Hoover's enemies list.

It would be history's poetic justice if Hoover's once-secret files create a new awareness of Einstein's "dangerous" thought, enabling today's students to discover the words Einstein addressed to Caltech students in 1931:

> Concern for man himself and his fate must always form the chief interest for all technical endeavors, concern for the great unsolved problems of the organization of labor and distribution of goods—in order that the creations of our mind shall be a blessing and not a curse for mankind. Never forget that in the midst of your diagrams and equations.[6]

III

That it could have happened at all—the government's secret campaign to defame and deport Einstein—is a jolt to our common sense. That it could have continued for a full five years and included a serious effort to denaturalize and deport Einstein defies rational explanation. But the most frightening aspect is that of the scores, possibly hundreds, of people who knew of the anti-Einstein effort—FBI memos were shared with G-2 and INS, as well as with Navy and Air Force Intelligence, the CIA, the State Department and, in some cases, the Atomic Energy Commission—not one person was concerned enough or brave enough to speak out, even anonymously, and blow the whistle on the Einstein file. We would like to believe that such a fearful age will never happen again.

Lately, a small group of conservative historians has been raising signals that it wants McCarthyism reevaluated and restored to historical grace, that it wasn't really such a bad time and, in fact, did America a lot of good with its political cleansing, ridding the country of all those subversives. More serious signs that the corpse of McCarthy-Hooverism still stirs have also begun to appear. The most notable—and ominous—is the case of Wen Ho Lee. The Chinese-American nuclear scientist was imprisoned, shackled, and locked in solitary confinement with no bail for nine months, based largely on false FBI testimony (the agent later admitted his testimony was untrue) that he had given American nuclear secrets to China, and (also false) that he had flunked a lie-detector test. Government prosecutors declared that his release on bail might pose "a grave threat [to] hundreds of millions of lives." When he was finally released, after the government dropped all but one of its fifty-nine charges, Federal Judge Parker apologized to Lee for the government's misconduct in the case. Was the Wen Ho Lee case an exception, a once-only throwback to the frightened fifties? Perhaps.

But in a less publicized (and therefore perhaps more ominous) case, the government recently tried to silence MIT physicist Theodore Postol,* a critic of the Bush Administration's missile-defense program. An unclassified document Postol sent out over the Internet contained evidence that Pentagon claims of successful missile shots had been based on doctored data. The Pentagon threatened to withdraw lucrative contracts from MIT if the university didn't stop Postol from circulating the unflattering (to the Pentagon) information. The charges had been published previously in a frontpage *New York Times* story by Pulitzer Prize-winner William J. Broad (MISSILE CONTRACTOR DOCTORED TESTS, EX-EMPLOYEE CHARGES), but the government's Ballistic Missile Defense Organization claimed it had to protect national security by stopping the dissemination of "potentially damaging information"—even when that information was publicly and widely available.[7] Two months before "9-11," before "America's New War" and "Homeland Security" became this country's code-words for silencing dissent, Victor Navasky, citing the Wen Ho Lee case among other evidence, noted: "There is something in the national mood that is a stark reminder of the ugly underside of the McCarthy era."[8]

Whether or not McCarthyism is making a comeback—perhaps cloaked as a war on terrorism**—Einstein, if he could see today's world, would recognize an array of other old ghosts. On the whole, the victims of social injustice haven't changed much: the immigrant whose dream book ends in a horror story of forced servitude; the mother denied Medicaid for her children unless she agrees to work for poverty wages; the casualty (dead or alive) of racial profiling by police. Virtually all the demons he opposed—from racism, nationalism, and war to unquestioning accept-

---

* After the first Gulf War, Postol publicly exposed as false many of the Pentagon's widely televised claims that its Patriot missiles had shot down Iraqi Scud missiles. Turns out, it was a missile show made for TV.

** "Those who provide support, financing and inspiration to terrorists are as guilty as the terrorists themselves," said Henry Kissinger, echoed by President Bush and his enforcers. To which, Eduardo Galeano replied: "If that's how it is…Kissinger…provided 'support, financing, and inspiration' to state terror in Indonesia, Cambodia, Iran, South Africa, Bangladesh, and South American countries that suffered the dirty war of Plan Condor….There is much common ground between low- and high-tech terrorism. They all share a disrespect for human life: the killers of the 5500 citizens under the Twin Towers…and the killers of 200,000 Guatemalans, the majority of whom were indigenous, exterminated without television or newspapers…paying any attention. Those Guatemalans were not sacrificed by any Muslim fanatic, but by the terrorist squads who received 'support, financing and inspiration' from successive U.S. governments." (*La Jornada*, September 21, 2001.)

ance of authority—are still here, and he would be painfully aware of how little, if any, progress has been made.

But what emerges most vividly from Einstein's political life—even if one disagrees with some of his tactics or arguments—is the picture of a man who never stops trying, never stops working to help bring about liberty, equality, and fraternity for everyone, not just for those who can afford to pay. A year before his death, he explained:

> A large part of history is...replete with the struggle for...human rights, an eternal struggle in which a final victory can never be won. But to tire in that struggle would mean the ruin of society.[9]

Postscript

In June 1998, newspapers around the world featured a story about secret love letters Einstein had written to Margarita Konenkova, and claims that she had been involved in espionage. The story was planted with the *New York Times* by Sotheby's auction house, where a sale of the love letters was to be held a few weeks later. Former Soviet KGB Agent Pavel Sudoplatov had identified Mrs. Konenkova as a Soviet spy, and the Sudoplatov-Sotheby-*Times* story hinted that the Einstein letters "revealed" the scientist had been lured by love into an espionage entanglement.[1]

While there is little doubt that Einstein had an amorous liaison with Mrs. Konenkova, it is far from clear that she was a Soviet spy, as Sudoplatov claims, or that Einstein had anything but amour in mind. Sudoplatov's spy-and-tell book *Special Tasks* has been thoroughly debunked by scientists and historians alike. Roald Sagdeyev, former head of the Soviet space program, now a research scientist at the University of Maryland and a critic of the Soviet regime, called the book "a complete fabrication."[2] (Sudoplatov also claimed that the conniving Konenkova had attempted to seduce J. Robert Oppenheimer into espionage. But during the period she was in Princeton, Oppenheimer was more than two thousand miles away directing the Manhattan Project in Los Alamos. He didn't move to Princeton until 1947, two years after Mrs. Konenkova had left.) Unfortunately for Sotheby's, the story didn't hold together long enough to attract a big enough bid at the auction. The letters—like the spy story— went unsold.[*]

Even then, the story didn't quite die. On June 13, 1998, Sudoplatov's U.S. promoters, Jerrold and Leona Schecter, wrote to the *Times*, asserting it "thus far appears to be the case" that Einstein was "used without

---

[*] In February 2000, Sotheby's top officers resigned after the renowned auction house was accused of price-fixing collusion with its arch and equally upper-class rival, Christie's.

being aware" by Soviet Intelligence. The Schecters cited no evidence to support their claim. The most recent revival of the myth comes in a book called *The Venona Secrets,* by Eric Breindel and Herbert Romerstein, the latter a longtime informant for and employee of HUAC and other congressional committees. "New information that links Albert Einstein to Soviet Intelligence ..." proclaims the book's dust jacket. It is, in fact, neither new nor true. It is partly the same Sudoplatov/Schecter tale of the affair between Einstein and Mrs. Konenkova, trying to twist their trysts into espionage. The book then quotes from the FBI's Einstein file an excerpt containing the Berlin cable-drop spy story, but fails to mention that Hoover and his Bureau finally decided the charges didn't hold up.[3] *The Venona Secrets* also does not mention that the Venona files do not mention Einstein.

Appendix

Einstein's Anti-racist Statements (partial list)

"To American Negroes," *The Crisis,* Feb. 1932, vol. 39, p. 45.

"Minorities," *Querido Verlag,* Amsterdam, 1934. Reprinted in *Mein Weltbild,* 1953, edited by Carl Seelig, and *Ideas and Opinions,* 1954.

Address at the 1940 World's Fair Wall of Fame, Einstein Archives, copy in Special Collections Library, Princeton University.

"The Negro Question," *Pageant,* Jan. 1946, reprinted in *Out of My Later Years,* 1950.

Address to students at Lincoln University, May 1946, only briefly described in *The Lincolnian,* v. 17, No. 4, June 4, 1946 (Langston Hughes Memorial Library Special Collections, Lincoln University); even more briefly mentioned in *New York Times,* May 4, 1946, p. 7.

Message to National Urban League Conference, Sept. 16, 1946: Einstein Archives, Princeton. This message includes his statement that "racism against the Negro is the worst disease under which ... our nation suffers." (*New York Times,* Sept. 25, 1946, p. 38.)

Comment on an article by Walter White in *The Saturday Review of Literature,* Oct. 11, 1947, reprinted in *Albert Einstein, The Human Side,* 1979.

Interview with the *Cheyney Record,* student paper at Cheyney State Teachers College, Oct. 1948, Nathan, pp. 501-502.

Message to the Southwide Conference on Discrimination in Higher Education, Atlanta University, 1950, sponsored by the Southern Conference Educational Fund:

> If an individual commits an injustice he is harassed by his conscience. But nobody is apt to feel responsible for misdeeds of a community, in particular, if they are supported by old traditions. Such is the case with discrimination.

Every right-minded person will be grateful to you for having united to fight this evil that so grievously injures the dignity and the repute of our country. Only by spreading education among all of our people can we approach the ideals of democracy.

Your fight is not easy, but in the end, you will succeed.

—from *Discrimination in Higher Education*, SCEF, New Orleans, 1951.

Replies to questions on "the uncomfortable situation of the Negroes" and "relations between anti-Negro sentiment and anti-Semitism," in *The Private Albert Einstein* by Peter A. Bucky, 1992, pp. 46-47.

The "clash of giants" narrative appealed to all, and particularly Hollywood, when the *New York Times* framed the *The Einstein File* that way on the front page of the Science Section, May 7, 2002.

Author's Update

"I Am A Revolutionary" – Albert Einstein

The first edition of this book appeared in spring 2002. When the *New York Times* devoted almost the entire front page of its science section to the story, life changed in the Jerome family…for about a week. The large story essentially provided the approval of the establishment media. The article was framed by photos of Einstein on one side and Hoover on the other. It seemed like a great story for the movies, a clash of giants: the bad giant (Hoover) versus the good giant (Einstein). That it was also a clash of cultures—the culture of conformity and compliance versus the culture of challenge and change—was hardly noticed. But the movie companies obviously loved "the Clash of Giants" narrative.

Just a few days after the *Times* story on my book was printed, the phone call came from Hollywood:

> Hello Fred, this is Susan Rocklow—I don't know if you remember me, but we were both in Professor Rosen's history class at CCNY 40 years ago (ohmygod was it really?) I sure remember you, asking questions all the time. Anyway, I'm now with XYZ Film Productions in Hollywood and we just read the *New York Times* story about your book and we want to offer you a movie deal, in fact we'd like to option the book…how soon can my boss and I come there to meet with you?

When my eyes stopped popping out of my head and I'd taken a couple of gulps of the black coffee I'd been sipping, I realized that, as luck would have it, the following morning I was scheduled to fly to Southern California to visit my wife's cousin and his family in Oxnard…and yes, I could certainly stop by XYZ offices which were on the way to Oxnard.

That was the first of three Hollywood movie company calls I received within a week of the *New York Times* article. They all wanted to meet right away; one even came to my wife's cousin's house to make his offer.

Meeting with movie companies, including Suzie Rocklow and her boss, was a trip! I don't believe any of them knew about the other two. They each had different actors in mind to play Einstein and Hoover, and each had a somewhat different storyline, but at some point fairly early in our conversations, *they all had the same thing to say*:

"Uh, listen Fred, there's only one thing we need to change in the story, one character we need: an FBI Agent who is on Einstein's side, who doesn't like Hoover."

"But," I protested, "I don't believe there was any such agent. In talking with many folks in Washington, including former FBI agents (some did not like Hoover) and the authors of several books about Hoover and the FBI, I never even *heard* of any such agent."

"Well, but it's only a story," they said. "How will it hurt? It will make it easier for us to do the film. In fact, if we can't make that change, we can't do the film."

I was not persuaded. It was an exciting but short week. Readers will note that the subtitle of the new edition is now "The FBI's Secret War Against the World's Most Famous Scientist."

* * *

Jumping from Hollywood to television, a brief look at *Genius*, the 2017 ten-part series on Einstein that aired on the *National Geographic* cable channel, provides another reason for producing this new edition of *The Einstein File*. Indeed, since it brought thousands of viewers a new outlook on the great scientist, it might have been called *TV's New Edition of Einstein*.

"[A]n errant lover, a draft dodger, an adulterer, a clueless rebel, an arrogant, self-centered dreamer and a stubborn, curious soul," is how the TV series portrays Einstein, according to a *New York Times* review.

Is it possible that the producers of *Genius* didn't like Einstein—or didn't like his politics? It's hard to imagine any other reason for remaking the great scientist as "a clueless rebel." To a be soap opera 'genius.'

Or it might have been called a fairly standard TV soap opera: man meets Woman #1; marries her; meets Woman #2; leaves Woman #1; marries Woman #2. All with much pulling of heartstrings.

In *Genius*, Einstein's first wife, Mileva Maric (Woman #1) is portrayed as the victim, a theme repeated in almost every one of the ten episodes, while Einstein is portrayed as not being a very nice guy. *Genius* does include a couple of brief references to Einstein's political views—Einstein speaking at a historically black university (Lincoln) and Einstein at odds with J. Edgar Hoover—which are more than most folks have ever seen. But for most of the ten episodes of *Genius*, it's soap opera time.

"I liked the program because it showed Einstein as a real person, not just an icon," was the way one friend of mine reacted—along with probably thousands of other TV viewers. To be sure, making an icon into a human being is almost always a popular show business technique. But there remains the small issue of accuracy. Einstein was indeed a human being, but was he *that* human being?

The hot-button theme that makes this soap opera different from all other soap operas is its repeated claim that Einstein's first wife Mileva Maric, who had a degree in physics, provided him with scientific insights and information to help him become the world's most famous genius—yet he gave her no credit. She was, as portrayed in this TV series, almost his co-genius.

But wait! Read this:

> What was Mileva's role?…There is no evidence that [Mileva] came up with any of the mathematical concepts. None of their many letters, to each other or to friends, mentions a single instance of an idea or creative concept relating to relativity that came from Maric.

These words come from—you will never guess—Walter Isaacson.

Very strange indeed. For we are told again and again on the TV screen that *Genius* is based on the Einstein biography by this very same Walter Isaacson. Yet, in that biography, Isaacson says just the opposite of what the TV series claims:

> For both the sake of colorful history and the emotional resonance it would have, it would be fun if we could [say that she did]. But instead we must follow the less exciting course of being confined to the evidence.…None of their many letters, to each other or to friends, mentions a single instance of an idea or creative concept relating to relativity that came from Maric. Nor did she ever—even to her family and close friends while in the throes of their bitter divorce—claim to have made any substantive contributions to Einstein's theories.[*]

(The last TV episode even has Einstein telling his son and grandchildren—*in a totally fictitious conversation*—that he "couldn't have" come up with his theories if it weren't for Mileva.)

For the record, several other historians have raised the same point, contrary to the TV show. John Stachel, a founder of the Einstein Papers Project,

---

[*] Walter Isaacson. *Einstein: His Life and Universe*, New York: Simon & Schuster, 2007, 126-37.

director of the Center for Einstein Studies (Boston University) and author of dozens of historical studies on Einstein, has written several articles on the topic, all of which appeared well before Isaacson's biography. After carefully examining the so-called evidence, Stachel concluded: "There is no evidence at all that [Maric] contributed any ideas of her own."

Could it be that Einstein, as a human being and not an icon, was a human being who didn't behave in such a selfish, anti-social manner? Might even have been a nice guy? As I've said, perhaps the TV-program's producers wanted to paint a not-very-nice portrait of Einstein because they didn't like his politics. In any event, it is clear—in the TV business as in the movie business (as in just about all business)—whoever pays the screenwriter calls the plot.

To be sure, Einstein's relationship with, and attitude towards, Maric was far from perfect. He "failed to encourage her to pursue an independent career or to involve her in serious collaboration," observes John Stachel in Einstein from 'B' to 'Z'. But that is a far cry from depicting her (as in the TV series) as his unacknowledged "co-genius."

The overall effect of *Genius*—if it were unchallenged—would be to undermine public sympathy for Einstein. There is not room here for a full discussion of *Genius*, but that will come. In that light, I would welcome— and do my best to circulate—comments from readers of this book.

* * *

It is a challenge to "update" a book about the FBI's file on Albert Einstein, considering that, in the 16 years since the book's initial publication in 2002, the FBI has not changed a single line in their file. Yet, as readers will see below, this update will add much that was not included in the first edition, including some material not previously published anywhere. But first a brief recap of the FBI's file.

- Much of the FBI's Einstein dossier is fiction—a weird variety of fabricated allegations from an even weirder variety of 'allegat-ers' (if you will permit me to coin a word). One claimed that Einstein helped kidnap the Lindbergh baby; another that Einstein was working on a secret weapon that could blow up the world; yet another came from Klaus Fuchs' sister who was at the time a patient in a mental institution in Massachusetts, and claimed she had seen Einstein helping her brother commit espionage—although she couldn't identify a photo of Einstein (Chapter 14).
- Most of the dossier focuses on a list of some 70 "subversive" organizations (in Hoover's opinion)—anti-racist, anti-fascist, anti-war groups

that Einstein endorsed (Chapter 9). All were groups Einstein supported *publicly*—he *wanted* people to know about his endorsement. As he put it, "If a man has such esteem, it is his obligation and duty to use this power to do good for his fellow men." Collecting this list didn't require Hoover's network of G-men. A good clipping service could have done a better job at half the cost.

- The rest of the FBI file records Hoover's attempt to link Einstein to a Soviet spy ring, during the period in in the 1920s in which Einstein had lived in Germany. If you read the book, you will know it was simply one more harebrained fantasy.

- Reading through the Einstein dossier, it becomes clear that Hoover, despite his 'me first' mentality, realized the potential public outrage if word got out that the FBI was pursuing the world's wisest scientist. So he kept the Einstein dossier secret, not only from the media, from scientists and from the public, but even from most of his own FBI agents. Sam Papich makes this very clear in the Introduction to this book. [p. 27]

If the question is, then: What's new in the FBI's file on Einstein? the answer should probably be: What's old is new.

Sixteen years ago, the first edition of this book revealed that the FBI under J. Edgar Hoover spent more than 20 years collecting nearly 2,000 pages about Einstein's politics. These revelations sparked shock and outrage in the national and international media, as well as among scientific organizations, colleges and universities, labor unions and teachers' organizations, and in letters and email from readers around the world.*

Here's an excerpt from a media report, taken from *Public Citizen*:

The file on Einstein details how the FBI sought [unsuccessfully] to connect him to a Soviet spy ring and...assisted the INS...to determine whether to revoke his citizenship because of his political beliefs...The FBI believed Einstein [had contact] with a list of scientists, Hollywood stars and educators—including Charlie Chaplin, Bette Davis and Katharine Hepburn and Nobel Prize winners Linus Pauling and Harold Urey who, according to FBI sources, had 'subversive' connections to or were under the 'subversive' influence of Einstein.

The shock has faded today, Thanks to *Wikileaks*, we know that Washington has been spying on just about everyone. NSA eyes in our laptops and NSA ears in our cell phones, those are today's Surveillance Society. What seemed extreme 15 years ago was a sign of things to come.

---

* For a listing of reports, reviews and interviews by newspapers, magazines, radio and TV stations, world-wide, as well as universities in many countries that sent invitations to speak, see www.theeinsteinfile.com.

While upset about Hoover "going after" Einstein, the media for the most part have not been nearly so upset—if upset at all—that the FBI has collected similar investigative "reports" on the meetings, associations and friends of thousands of people, mostly (but not all) on the Left in the United States over the past half century.

Twenty years earlier, in 1983, the FBI had released a heavily "redacted" version of Einstein's dossier—"redacted" in FBI-ese means blacked-out. The blacked-out sections in 1983 included the names of informants. In 2001, after a five-year effort, with help from Erica Craven of the Public Citizen Litigation Group, I was able to get the FBI to release most of the 1800-page file. I obtained the rest of it—including names of inform-ants—by searching other government documents (e.g. CIA, Department of Defense) in the National Archives and from interviewing former FBI Agents (who had no love for Hoover).

Some years later, the FBI announced that many of their files—espe-cially those on well-known people—would be available online to the pub-lic. I expected they would include the Einstein dossier they had released to me. But no, it was still only the redacted/blacked-out, 60-percent version they had released in 1983. I immediately made the entire 1800-page file available on this book's website: Theeinsteinfile.com.

As a result, you can now click into the entire 1800-page file and read it yourself. Hard to beat for summer beach read!

WHAT'S NEW?

We have considered what's old in this book, now let us look at what's new. For, despite the FBI policy of making No-Change in their files—there is a good deal of new material, not included in the original edition, that needs to be added.

As a work of investigative reporting, this book is a two-pronged report. The first prong exposes the FBI's long-secret file on Einstein. That's the prong that got all the publicity—"The Clash of the Giants" Hoover vs. Einstein, as mentioned above. The second prong of investigative reporting seeks to bring to light Einstein's many rarely-or-never-reported political views and activities in support of people of color, immigrants, the under-dogs and underclass (working people).

The FBI dossier is used here as a scaffold on which to hang Einstein's politics. The *double entendre* is apt. Hoover and the FBI wanted a scaffold from which Einstein and the Einstein reputation would be left hanging. For me, it is a scaffold to showcase his politics.

Hoover did his best to have his agents collect a list of all Einstein's political views, as well as activities that he considered subversive, un-American and communistic. These included Einstein's associations and friends who opposed racism, including W. E. B. Du Bois, Paul Robeson, Horace Mann Bond, and anti-fascist groups, such as supporters of volunteers in the Lincoln Brigade who fought Franco in the Spanish Civil War, and groups or individuals against nuclear war, such as Irene Joliot Curie, John Hersey, and the Emergency Committee of Atomic Scientists.

But for all their experience at opening mail and tapping telephones, FBI snoopers missed a number of important aspects of the political Einstein. Ergo, this update: which contains what you probably don't know about the politics of "the world's most famous scientist," even if you read the first edition of this book.

EINSTEIN THE ANTI-RACIST AND THE PEOPLE OF WITHERSPOON STREET

As most Americans have by now come to know, Hoover not only hated Martin Luther King Jr., but tried to frame him on a series of fabricated charges. Indeed, by now most Americans ought to know that Hoover hated just about everyone who wasn't a White Anglo-Saxon Protestant like him. So it shouldn't really be surprising that Hoover didn't like Einstein. Moreover, he enjoyed the support and the blessing of a long series of presidents and administrations despite those attitdes. Or is it because of them?

In the first edition, reference is made to Einstein's 1946 visit to Lincoln University in Pennsylvania (the oldest historically black university in the Western hemisphere) and his friendship and collaboration with W. E. B. Du Bois and Paul Robeson. This included: the 1946 American Crusade to End Lynching, co-chaired by Robeson and Einstein (20 pages in the FBI's Einstein dossier refer to that "dangerous" Crusade); Einstein's offer to testify in Federal Court in 1951, as a defense witness for Dr. Du Bois; Einstein's invitation to Marian Anderson—when the great diva was denied a room at the Palmer House, the main Princeton hotel—for her to stay at his house with him, his step-daughter and housekeeper.*

But the FBI's file contains not a single word about Einstein's many long-lasting friendships with folks in Princeton's Witherspoon Street African-American community. It is my firm belief that you cannot understand Einstein if you do not know about his strong friendships with the people of the Witherspoon Street community.

---

* Fred Jerome and Rodger Taylor, *Einstein on Race and Racism,* (New Brunswick: Rutgers University Press, 2005,) pp. 42-43.

Princeton street signs today, a hint of a history that was not such a tranquil scene.
(Photo: Fred Jerome.)

Here are but a few comments from Einstein's Witherspoon Street
friends that will give readers an overview.

Henry Pannell: "I remember seeing Einstein when we were kids. He'd come
by—white sneakers, no socks, a loose-fitting sweater—and: I guess everybody my age in this community remembers—he'd give nickels to us kids.
I remember him coming up and sitting on my grandmother's porch and
chatting with her. My grandmother, Carrie Dans Pannell, was a founding
member of the Friendship Club. She lived on Jackson Street right at the edge
of the Witherspoon community. Like if Einstein was walking from his place
on Mercer Street to the hospital which was and still is in the Witherspoon
community, Jackson Street (it's now Paul Robeson Place) was the first street
he would have come to, maybe a chance to rest before continuing on, maybe
a chance to chat with friends, most likely both. My grandmother worked as
a chef in the Nassau Club and was active in the Friendship Club, along with
Emma Epps, Bertha Hill Brandon, and others. Einstein used to talk to everybody in our community. He didn't just come and sit on my grandmother's
porch, but on the Wilsons' porch and others. He'd talk with everyone."

Albert Hinds: "My brother Paul had a garbage company and he picked up
Einstein's trash. Einstein would invite him in often to talk."

Timmy Hinds: "My father [Paul Hinds] would talk with Einstein's sister Maja when he went by to pick up the trash."

Paul Hinds, interviewed in *The Packet,* a local Princeton paper, July 16, 1985, said, "I speak to everyone in the same way, whether he is another garbage man or the president of a university. I have lived among the eggheads. I sat down and talked to Dr. Einstein when I used to pick up garbage from him. I didn't just pick up the garbage and leave. I had to talk to the people—sit down and have a cup of coffee."

Albert Hinds: "My sister Violet Hinds Jones frequently worked for a family who were Einstein's neighbors. My sister and Einstein would hold hands and walk up Mercer Street daily. I learned that from my niece, Shirl Gadson who was Violet's daughter."

Shirl Gadson: "My mother [Violet] was a member of the Friendship Club. Her father was from British Guiana and worked at the university as a valet for the class of 1923. His picture is in that yearbook. Violet's mother was a Princetonian. They had five girls. My mother didn't tell me much about Einstein. She just said, 'I knew him.' Once, talking about him, she said he was 'a great friend.'

"She did tell me they used to meet each other after she got off from work. He was standing there waiting at a certain spot. Then he'd say, 'We seem to meet at the same place every day.' Sometimes he would say, jokingly, 'We've got to stop meeting like this.' Violet would answer. 'Yes, we do,' and Einstein would say, 'Well, we can walk together.'

"'What did you talk about?' I asked my mother.

"'We talked about the students, about the town. Well, maybe not every day but frequently. Sometimes we only walked a block or two together.'

"'What did you call each other?'"

"'I called him Mr. Einstein. He called me Miss Hinds. Then he started calling me Violet.'

"Violet moved to Philadelphia; that's why they stopped seeing each other, she told us.

"When my mother died, we had a memorial service at the Episcopalian Church. Uncle Albert [Hinds] spoke there. He said: 'Violet was a—I'll use the term buddy—of Albert Einstein.'"

Alice Satterfield: "I worked in the kitchen at the Institute for Advanced Study in the early forties for three to five years, and got to know Einstein. Shirley was in school and I would be leaving the Institute to walk home. If I didn't get the bus and Professor Einstein would be walking, we'd walk together until we got to his residence. I'd bid him goodbye and continue home. We didn't talk a lot—on a couple of occasions he held my hand without saying anything. He would just walk in a silent and wonderful way in which you knew everything would be all right. You felt good walking with him. He did not look down on people. He was inspirational."

[short pause]

Alice Satterfield

Shirley Satterfield

"You didn't have to be a scientist to be invited into Einstein's house. He was just very down to earth. Too bad they made that absent-minded image of him. [short pause] He *was* inspirational."

Some of Ms. Satterfield's friends say she is pretty inspirational herself. When she was younger, she decided to sit in the whites-only section of Princeton's movie house, the Garden Theatre.

Alice Satterfield: "I just felt I'm gonna do it anyway. We talked about breaking the taboos of racist seating and such, so I just sat where I wanted to in the Garden Theatre. I remember it was Friday afternoon, they had programs for kids and that day it was Rin Tin Tin, the movie dog. Colored were supposed to sit on one side. Instead, I sat in the white section. Nothing happened to me—maybe I was lucky. I remember not being allowed into Balt Bakery. We weren't supposed to go in. Heck, there were lots of other stores on Nassau Street that were segregated too. I didn't like that kind of thing, so I'd go into Balt anyway.

"The Institute for Advanced Study had its own private bus that brought the workers, black and white, back to town. I took that bus and sometimes Einstein was on the same bus. He was a man of great warmth. Too bad there aren't more people like him. On those buses, you could sit where you wanted to sit. The Institute itself was filled with people from all over the world. A gentleman from India and I would sit together and ride until we got to Nassau Street. The Institute was integrated as far as foreigners and everyone; it was different from the university, which was segregated.

"Still, the Institute wasn't all that integrated. There was a definite class structure—clearly they didn't want people to mingle with the help. Dr. [J. Robert] Oppenheimer would have a big party every year—I remember one professor got reprimanded for dancing with me. He said to me, 'I don't understand why I cannot dance with you.' I don't recall Einstein going to these parties."

Alice Satterfield's story is not the only one about Dr. Oppenheimer and the Institute frowning on fraternization between its scientists and those in lower-level positions (usually nonwhites). "I can tell you a true story about

Griggs [black-owned] restaurant in the late 1940s," recalled **Freeman Dyson**, the world-renowned theoretical physicist at the Institute, in a conversation he had some ten years ago with Rodger Taylor, myself and my wife Jocelyn in his Princeton office:

> I ate supper there regularly with David Bohm* who was then at Princeton University. The food was good and cheap. Ham and cabbage was my favorite dish. I received a letter from Kay Russell, who was Oppenheimer's secretary, saying it was inappropriate for a member of the Institute to be eating at Griggs. Of course, I ignored the letter and continued eating at Griggs. I never found out whether Oppenheimer instigated the letter or whether he knew about it. But I rather suspect that Kay would not have sent it without his approval.

> **Shirley Satterfield**: "Einstein didn't look down on people. I would often be with my mother in the Institute kitchen. Einstein would come in at lunchtime...I remember this man with all of this white hair. He was so nice. He'd take me for walks. I remember playing on the balcony and walking around the Institute with Einstein. I'd also go in his office with him. I'd say I was about six years old. I just remember he was very kind and his hair was always, well, like he never combed his hair. He would take me by the hand, walking with a cane in his other hand, and talk to me. I can't remember anything of what he said, but I remember that accent and that he spoke really soft. He looked different because he had all that hair and wore sandals in all weather. He used to eat raw eggs. And I used to eat all the olives—they had big jars of olives in the Institute kitchen. They also fixed a bread pudding in that kitchen that I loved—I always used to eat in the kitchen and the cafeteria. My mother worked real hard, but when I came home, I would talk to my family, sometimes about Einstein."

EINSTEIN, A CULTURAL ZIONIST OPPOSED TO POLITICAL ZIONISM AND THE FOUNDING OF A JEWISH STATE

The FBI's dossier contains virtually nothing about Einstein on Zionism or Israel. The first edition of *The Einstein File* just mentions it, noting that one of the reasons Einstein gave for turning down the offer to be President of Israel in 1952 was, "I would have to say to the Israeli people things they would not like to hear." Moreover, when Israeli Prime Minister Ben Gurion had made the offer to Einstein, he told a close associate, "Tell me what to do if he says yes. I've had to offer the post to him...but if he says yes, we are in for trouble."

---

* Bohm, a brilliant physicist, was fired by Princeton president Harold Dodds in 1950 after Bohm refused to name names before Senator Joseph McCarthy's inquisitors. Dodds's well-known anti-Semitism might well have been a factor in the ouster of Bohm, who was Jewish.

Any serious research will find dozens of public statements by Einstein—before Israel was established—opposing such a state, opposing even the *idea* of a Jewish State. Much to the chagrin of a long string of Israeli leaders and Zionist organization, which have tried to describe Einstein as their supporter, the record is clear. Here are but a few examples:

> "I should much rather see reasonable agreement with the Arabs on the basis of living together in peace than the creation of a Jewish state. My awareness of the essential nature of Judaism resists the idea of a Jewish state with borders, an army, and a measure of temporal power. ... I am afraid of the inner damage Judaism will sustain," quoted in 1938 in *The Guardian*.

> "The state idea is not according to my heart. I cannot understand why it is needed. It is connected with many difficulties and narrow-mindedness. I believe it is bad," testimony to the Anglo-American Committee of Inquiry in January 1946, also reported in *The Canadian Changer*.

> "I am in favor of Palestine being developed as a Jewish Homeland but not as a separate State. It seems to me a matter for simple common sense that we cannot ask to be given the political rule over Palestine where two thirds of the population are not Jewish" from a letter to Henry J. Factor in Indianapolis, January 1946 (courtesy of the Shappell Manuscript Foundation).*

Perhaps even more significant is a letter to Louis Rabinowitz, a Zionist in Brooklyn who had written to Einstein praising the continued Israeli colonization in Palestine. Einstein compared Israeli treatment of Palestinians to the the way U.S. settlers ("Pilgrims") treated Native Americans:

> "Did it not come you your mind that 'the Pilgrims' who came from England to colonize this country, came to realize a plan very similar to your own? Do you also know how tyrannical, intolerant and aggressive these people became after a short while? Being Baptized in Jewish water is no protection either."

Einstein wrote that letter on March 17, 1952, five years *after* the establishment of the State of Israel.

Indeed, Einstein made so many statements opposing the establishment of a Jewish state, that the *New York Times* did not describe him as pro-Israel—until he was dead! It was in Einstein's obituary, published on April 19, 1955, that the *Times* first said that Einstein "had championed" the establishment of Israel "as a state."

In fact, Einstein's opposition to the Israeli Zionists' oppression of Palestinians has been reported in the past. As early as 1994, Abraham Pais, probably the most widely acclaimed of Einstein's many biographers, wrote:

---

* See Fred Jerome, *Einstein on Israel and Zionism* (New York: St. Martin's Press, 2009) for scores of such statements including letters never before published.

"Einstein hoped for full cooperation of Jews with Arabs, but realized that for the time being that would not come to pass. ... I am sure he would have been disgusted with the later governments of Begin and Shamir had he lived to see their methods—and would have said so publicly."*

When I later (1999) met with Pais in his office at Rockefeller University, his view had grown only more critical of Israel's anti-Arab policies. He expected those policies to become more repressive, and added "Disappointing but not surprising." Indeed, Pais might well have anticipated this recent report: "In 2016 alone, Israeli authorities demolished or seized 1,093 Palestinian homes in the West Bank, including East Jerusalem, and 2017 is on track to exceed that number."**

"Disappointing but not surprising." Pais was convinced Einstein would have felt the same way.

One of the last Einstein comments to be published during his lifetime was quoted by Dorothy Schiff, publisher of the *New York Post*, who reported in her "Dear Reader" column on March 13, 1955, that Einstein had told her: "We had great hopes for Israel at first. We thought it might be better than other nations. But it is no better."

EINSTEIN'S GOT MAIL (AND THERE'S A LOT TO LEARN)

Although FBI snoopers seemed to relish opening people's mail—including Einstein's, somehow they missed quite a lot. I have collected copies of dozens of letters Einstein wrote over more than 30 years to a wide array of cultural and political figures around the world. So far they have been not been published but all express Einstein's sympathy with and support for radical and sometimes revolutionary politics.

In an often told but possibly untrue story about Einstein, he was walking in Princeton and stopped to ask a neighbor, "Excuse me, but am I going east or west?" When the neighbor replied that he was going east,

---

* Abraham Pais, *Einstein Lived Here,* (Oxford: Oxford University Press, 1994), p. 254. A Dutch-born American physicist and science historian, Pais (1918-2000) served as an assistant to Niels Bohr in Denmark and was later a colleague of Einstein's at the Princeton Institute for Advanced Study. During World War II, Pais lived in Amsterdam, hiding from the Nazis for two years. He later wrote: "One of the things I learned, one of the strangest things, is how to think. There was nothing else to do. I couldn't see people, or go for a walk in the forest. All I had was my head and my books, and I thought a lot. I learned, because there was no interruption....I was just short of twenty-two then."

7. The report on Israeli housing demollition: www.ochaopt.org/content/record-number-demolitions-and-displacements-west-bank-during-2016

Einstein, the story goes, declared, "Then I've had my lunch." The absent-minded professor image is probably the most frequently repeated myth in the mass media, especially television.

The myth of the fuzzy-wuzzy genius, so absorbed in physics formulae that he had no time for the real-world worries of the rest of us, has lately been joined by a cartoon-character myth. The Walt Disney Company paid millions of dollars to the Hebrew University of Jerusalem for the "rights" to manufacture and market (for many more millions than they paid) their porcupine-haired Einstein cartoon. Despite several recently published reports to the contrary, the mainstream media continue to sell their funny-but-false Einstein.

In the game of Concentration (I say "ice," you say "cold"; I say "library," you say "books"), were I to say "Einstein," most people would probably say "genius" or "scientist." Some might say "E equals MC squared," others, "the hair." Practically no one would say "social activist" or "anti-racist," and nobody at all would say "socialist."

Yet Einstein's mostly unpublished correspondence leaves no doubt about his social and political conscience—his opposition to racism, colonialism and classism, as well as his commitment to building a society based on economic, social and political equality.

Einstein's cultural and political correspondence will surprise, perhaps amaze, those who see him as the absentminded genius-scientist totally absorbed in squiggly figures on his blackboard. Perhaps more important, virtually all of the writers, musicians and artists with whom he corresponded were outspoken critics of the inequality and racial bigotry so widespread then (and still).

The letters are a book waiting to be published. Here are just a few examples, followed by the list of correspondents.

To WILLIAM O. DOUGLAS, Justice of the US Supreme Court, June 23, 1953 (after Douglas had unsuccessfully voted to stop the execution of Ethel and Julius Rosenberg).

Einstein: "You have struggled so devotedly for the creation of a healthy public opinion in our troubled time."

Handwritten reply from Justice Douglas, June 30, 1953: "You have paid me a tribute which brightens the burdens of this dark hour—a tribute I will always cherish."

To MAXIM GORKI on his 65th birthday, September 29, 1932: "How greatly I rejoice that there is such a man as you in the world. Few creative masters of the first rank have remained, to the degree that you have, both servants of their own society and fighters for the improvement of mankind's lot.... Destiny will always be decided by what the individual feels, wills and does. That is why, in the long run, the education of man will always be far more the task of creative minds than of political leaders."

To THOMAS MANN, April 29, 1933: "The responsible and conscientious attitude shown by you and your brother [Heinrich Mann] has been, in the recent past, one of the few cheerful events in an otherwise dark Germany....Once more, it becomes clear that the fate of a community is primarily determined by the level of is moral standards. Any leadership worthy of the name will crystallize and develop only on the basis of the values and ideals which you and your brother represent. Even if you should not live to see such leadership materialize, this hope should give you real solace in these cruel times and in the bitter days yet to come."

To MORRIS RAPHAEL COHEN, December 16, 1933: "I was pleased to note that in your book [on the philosophy of law] you properly defend reason which has been so discredited in our time of decay."

From YEHUDI MENUHIN, March 14, 1934: [Historical Note: After Hitler came to power in Germany, Einstein felt that stopping the Nazis was the world's—and his own—most important challenge. Realizing that this almost certainly meant a military conflict, he moved away from his earlier pacifism and wrote to several people, including Menuhin, explaining his views.]

"Dear and beloved friend Prof. Einstein: It was like a dream coming true the idea of counting Albert Einstein among my friends!...I understand your reasoning perfectly—namely that one cannot act like an ostrich and believe that by shutting one's eyes and ears one thereby also shuts off the peril....

However, it seems terrible to start the race for armaments again and let the big munitions, iron and coal manufacturers gain power and prestige. If at least France, England and the rest were saints whom we could trust, but they are not! However, as you said, one must choose, and, as terrible as it is, one must face facts and act accordingly!

Would it be possible for you to attend my concert this Sunday in New York? Your loving friend,
    Yehudi

To JOHN HERSEY, August 6, 1944: "I have to thank you from the bottom of my heart for the indescribable pleasure your Italy-book [*A Bell for*

Adano] has given me. I enjoyed equally its human veracity and your art of concise characterization. I also appreciated very much the considerable service you have rendered to equity and justice....One evening, after having worked till midnight, I began reading *A Bell for Adano* and could not stop until 5 o'clock in the morning."

From JOHN HERSEY, March 3, 1945: "[Reading your letter was] one of my greatest pleasures....I'm only sorry for one thing: that I made you lose some sleep."

* * *

Many if not most of Einstein's letters to political figures, especially to presidents and prime ministers, expressed his political opposition to particular policies.

To MRS. FRANKLIN D. ROOSEVELT, July 26, 1941: [Historical Note: Until the US entered World War II against Germany and Japan (in December 1941, after the Japanese bombing of Pearl Harbor), Washington maintained diplomatic relations with Germany. Under Secretary of State Cordell Hull, immigrants from Germany were required to present what might be called "good-conduct" notes from the German police, a policy that automatically excluded Jews and anyone accused by the Gestapo of "Communist sympathies." In an (unsuccessful) effort to convince Washington to change its policy, Einstein wrote to Eleanor Roosevelt.]

Dear Mrs. Roosevelt:

I have noted with great satisfaction that you always stand for the right and humaneness even when it is hard. Therefore in my deep concern, I know of no one else to whom to turn for help. A policy is now being pursued in the State Department which makes it all but impossible to give refuge in America to many worthy persons who are the victims of fascist cruelty in Europe. Of course, this is not openly avowed by those responsible for it. The method which is being used, however, is to make immigration impossible by erecting a wall of bureaucratic measures alleged to be necessary to protect America against subversive, dangerous elements. I would suggest that you talk about this question to some well-informed and right-minded person such as Mr. Hamilton Fish Armstrong. If then you become convinced that a truly grave injustice is under way, I know that you will find it possible to bring the matter to the attention of your heavily burdened husband in order that it may be remedied.

Yours very sincerely,
Albert Einstein

ELEANOR ROOSEVELT's reply, August 9, 1941:
My dear Professor Einstein:
   I have read your letter with much interest, and I am bringing it to the President's attention.
   Very sincerely yours,
   Eleanor Roosevelt

To PRESIDENT HARRY S. TRUMAN, January 11, 1953: "My conscience compels me to urge you to commute the death sentence of Julius and Ethel Rosenberg. This appeal is prompted by the same reasons which are set forth so convincingly by my distinguished colleague Harold C. Urey in his letter [*New York Times*] of January 5, 1953."*

From BERTRAND RUSSEL, June 20, 1953: "*Dear Einstein:* I am in whole-hearted agreement with your contention that teachers called before McCarthy's inquisitors should refuse to testify. When the *New York Times* had a leading article disagreeing with you about this, I wrote a letter to it supporting you. But I am afraid they are not going to print it. I enclose a copy, of which, if you feel so disposed, you may make use in any way you like.
   Yours very sincerely,
   Bertrand Russell

Here is Russell's letter to the *New York Times.*
In your issue of June 13 you have a leading article disagreeing with Einstein's view that teachers questioned by Senator McCarthy's emissaries should refuse to testify. You seem to maintain that one should always obey the law, however bad. I cannot believe that you have realized the implications of this position. Do you condemn the Christian Martyrs who refused to sacrifice to the Emperor? Do you condemn John Brown? Nay more, I am compelled to suppose that you condemn George Washington and hold that your country ought to return to allegiance to Her Gracious Majesty, Queen Elizabeth II. As a loyal Briton, I of course applaud this view; but I fear it may not win much support in your country.
   Bertrand Russell

---

* Urey's letter to the *Times* had argued that the Rosenbergs' conviction was based on «perjured testimony» and called their death sentence «grossly unequal punishment.» Despite worldwide protests, the Rosenbergs were executed in the electric chair on June 19, 1953.

From W. E. B. DU BOIS, November 29, 1951:

[HISTORICAL NOTE: At the start of 1951, the Federal Government indicted W. E. B. Du Bois, then chairman of the Peace Information Center, and four of the group's other officers, for failing to register as "foreign agents." The government's principal charge was that the Peace Information Center—described by historian Robin D. G. Kelley as an "antinuclear, anti-Cold War" group—had committed the "overt act" of circulating the Stockholm Peace Petition. Thus, W. E. B. Du Bois in 1951 was brought before a judge in a Federal courtroom—the world-renowned scholar, at the age of 83, goateed, short in height but standing unbent, wore a pinstriped, three-piece suit and handcuffs.* Like Paul Robeson,** Du Bois had refused to go along with Washington's anti-Soviet, anti-Communist policies, refused to cooperate with congressional investigating committees, and had his passport suspended.

Shortly after the Federal indictment, Einstein sent Du Bois a copy of his just-published book, *Out of My Later Years*. In April, Du Bois wrote back and included information about his upcoming court case. Einstein volunteered to testify as a defense witness for Du Bois and to give Einstein's appearance in court the maximum impact, defense attorney Marcantonio*** held the announcement until the last minute. In a rare, first-hand account, Shirley Graham Du Bois, describes the judge's response: "The prosecution rested its case during the morning of November 20 [1951]... Marcantonio...casually told the judge, 'Dr. Albert Einstein has offered to appear as a character witness for Dr. Du Bois.' Judge [Matthew F.] McGuire fixed Marcantonio with a long look, and then adjourned the court for lunch. When court resumed, Judge McGuire ... granted the motion for acquittal."****]

---

* Kelley, quoted in Mari Jo Buhle, Paul Buhle and Dan Georgakas, *Encyclopedia of the American Left*, (Oxford: Oxford University Press, 1998), p. 204. "The venerated Du Bois...handcuffed, fingerprinted, bailed, and remanded for trial." Caute, p. 176.

** While no letters have (yet) been found between them, Einstein's little known (virtually unreported) 20-year friendship with Paul Robeson will be included here by reprinting Robeson's description of his last visit with Einstein, published in the Harlem newspaper *Freedom in* Nov. 1952.

*** Vito Marcantonio, a popular, independent, fiery, left-wing congressman from New York's East Harlem, with support from both the Italian and Puerto Rican communities there. Among his many distinctions, he was the only member of Congress to vote against sending U.S. troops into the 1950 Korean "Police Action."

**** Shirley Graham Du Bois, *Du Bois: A Pictorial Biography*, (Chicago: Johnson Publishing Company., Chicago, 1978).

"My dear Dr. Einstein:
I write to express my deep appreciation of your generous offer to do anything that you could in the case brought against me by the Department of Justice.

I am delighted that in the end it was not necessary to call upon you and interfere with your great work and needed leisure, but my thanks for your generous attitude is not less on that account.

Mrs. Du Bois joins me in deep appreciation.

Very sincerely yours

W. E. B. Du Bois

Here's a partial list of other well-known cultural and political figures who were among Einstein's correspondents

- Musicians and composers include Ernest Bloch, Adolph Busch, Pablo Casals, Herman Keyserling, Arnold Schoenberg (on Verdi) and Jaromir Weinberger.
- Writers and artists include Mann, Hersey, Brecht and Kazantzakis, Sholom Asch, Benedetto Croce, Anatole France, John Gunther, Diego Rivera (in French), George Bernard Shaw, Stefan Sweig, Rabindranath Tagore, Ernst Toller, Edward G. Robinson, Dorothy Thompson (on Wallenberg), Fritz von Unruh, Hendrik Willem Van Loon, Ernst Waldinger, and H.G. Wells.
- Among the more political people, Jane Addams, Hannah Arendt, Leon Blum, W. E. B. Du Bois, Mahatma Gandhi, Dag Hammarskjold, Sidney Hook, Cordell Hull, Trygve Lie, Maxim Litvinov, Ramsay MacDonald, George C. Marshall, Thomas Masaryk, Jawarhalal Nehru, Romain Rolland, Adlai Stevenson, and Henry Wallace.

2018 AND GOING FORWARD

Let us briefly consider the evolving political picture in the U.S. and the world since the first edition of this book was published—and what the world's most famous scientist might say about it today.

In 2002, it didn't take an Einstein to figure out that the George W. Bush Administration was about to launch yet another war in the Middle East. In his "State of the Union" address that year Bush declared: "Whatever it costs to defend our security, we will pay....We will win this war, we will protect our homeland, and we will revive our economy....North Korea, Iran and Iraq are an axis of evil....Our war against terrorism is only beginning."

Yet even Einstein would not have predicted sixteen years (so far) of expanding, nonstop wars through three Administrations, with a rapidly increasing number of U.S. troops and mercenaries ("Contractors") on the ground* and U.S. planes and drones dropping death from the skies over Iraq, Syria, Libya, Pakistan and—in America's longest and losing-est war—Afghanistan, as the U.S. and other western powers seek to colonize (or recolonize) the Middle East and Africa.

Although virtually unreported by America's mainstream media, US military forces are now stationed in many African countries. During its second term, the Obama Administration sent troops to at least 19 African nations, with no publicity.12 "I had no idea we had troops in Niger," at least one US Congressman declared in 2017, after 4 soldiers were killed in a firefight (possibly with Niger villagers). Other members of Congress echoed the I-didn't-know statement, and most of the U.S. public was equally uninformed.

We don't have to wonder in this case what Einstein would say:

> "Without the political and economic emancipation of the now subdued and exploited African and colonial peoples," Einstein declared in April 1947, "no reliable or lasting peace will be possible." He added that, "emancipation is one of the most urgent needs of our time."**

Relatively speaking, Einstein might say, the political picture is not a pretty one. Indeed, he would no doubt be dismayed. But dismay would be nothing new for Einstein. Consider that, in January 1951, as the US population was (mostly) caught up in a patriotic war fever and the media whipped up a semi-hysterical fear of a Russian A-bomb attack, Einstein's letters spoke of his sadness, and everywhere he heard German echoes: «The dear Americans have vigorously assumed the Germans' place. The German calamity of years ago repeats itself.»

Indeed, 1951 was an especially dismaying time for Einstein and for millions more, as Cold War fears and the Red Scare hysteria spread across the country, with thousands of folks—teachers actors, journalists and trade union activists losing their jobs and worse for refusing to become political informers.

---

* The Pentagon is not telling, but according to the Defense Manpower Data Center, run by the Department of Defense, there were 25,910 U.S. active-duty, national guard, or reserve military personnel in three Middle Eastern countries as of September 30. That is over 11,000 more than the 14,765 personnel that the Pentagon has said are deployed in those three countries.

** See Einstein's letter to the Council on African Affairs, chaired by Paul Robeson. The Vice-chairman was W. E. B. Du Bois. (See also, Section 8 of the FBI's Einstein file.)

And just as Einstein was dismayed at how much 1951 and the rise of McCarthyism echoed his memories of the rise of Nazi Germany, today's America reminds many of us the 1950s. Again, one can't help but wonder: what would Einstein say about today's politics?

At the conclusion of *The Einstein File*, I wrote the following:

> Whether or not McCarthyism is making a comeback—perhaps cloaked as a war on terrorism?—Einstein, if he could see today's world, would recognize an array of other old ghosts. On the whole, the victims of social injustice haven't changed much: the immigrant whose dreambook is a horror story of forced servitude; the mother denied Medicaid for her children unless she agrees to work for poverty wages; the casualty (dead or alive) of racial profiling by police. Virtually all the demons he opposed—from racism, nationalism and war to unquestioning acceptance of authority—are still here, and he would be painfully aware of how little, if any, progress has been made.

That was then, this is now. Besides his sorrow at seeing "the old ghosts of injustice," here are but a few of today's events that would add to Einstein's dismay:

- Pro-Nazi organizations marching throughout Europe—not to mention Charlottesville, Virginia!
- Millions of people across the U.S. waking up every morning worn with worry that their healthcare, their jobs, and their homes will be *trumpled* by the current regime in Washington.
- The murders of unarmed black men by police across the U.S.—murders continuing and continuing to go unpunished. As early as 1946, Einstein told the Urban League, racism is America's "worst disease." (See *Einstein on Race and Racism*, Rutgers University Press, 2005).
- The expansion of NATO and NATO bases, now including bases in Eastern Europe, bringing NATO (and the U.S.) that much closer to Russia—and to World War III. (NATO "is a horror," Einstein wrote to Henry Wallace.) NATO bases now form a military ring (some observers call it "a military noose") around Russia and are developing a similar pattern of bases around China.
- Einstein, who devoted so much energy to helping immigrants from other countries (see his letter to Eleanor Roosevelt, above) might have been *greatly* dismayed by the repeated Trump-eting of racist, anti-immigrant noises (and policies) coming from the White House, but *most* dismayed today by the rounding up and deporting of *tens of thousands* of immigrants—mostly from Latin America and the Middle East.

The U.S. today, Einstein might well say, has achieved a new dimension of dismay.

But dismay was not despair for Einstein. If one can choose a single most important point in this book, let me repeat it here. For Einstein, dismay was never despair. It is a part of Einstein often mssed even by sympathetic observers. No less a writer than the great Uruguayan poet-historian Eduardo Galeano declared in *Century of the Wind*: "Einstein believed that science was a way of revealing the beauty of the universe. The most famous of sages had the saddest eyes in human history."

But despite his moving poetry, and despite his usually accurate historical insights, Galeano got Einstein wrong.

Certainly—if he were here now—today's Trumped-up world would not be the first disappointment for Einstein. Throughout the first half of the 20th Century, he was often disappointed—the worldwide rise of racism, anti-Semitism and anti-immigrant-ism were clearly disappointments to him, but perhaps nothing was more tragic in this eyes than the U.S. bombing of Japan.

Yet even after this most tragic event, Einstein did not despair. His answer was to organize for change. With other similarly dismayed nuclear scientists, Einstein helped to organize—and served as chairman of the Emergency Committee of Atomic Scientists—and to educate the public on the dangers of nuclear weapons, and to organize a campaign against nuclear war.

EINSTEIN AS ORGANIZER

"'Though everybody knows me, there are very few people who really know me,' Einstein told his friend Johanna Fantova toward the end of his life. He added, 'I am a revolutionary.'" *(New York Times*, 24 April 2004). He might have added: "I am an organizer."

The multitude of Einstein biographies—even those few that focus on "the political Einstein"—are all collections of his writings—his words, but not his deeds.

Besides his scientific genius, which helped change the way we understand and approach our universe, besides his unfrightened political insight, his commitment to "speak truth to power," Einstein believed in action. He believed in organizing—and lived his belief.

Most of these examples have been cited earlier, but listed together they underscore the scope of Einstein's organizing efforts during the last ten years of his life:

In 1945, after the U.S. dropped atomic bombs on the civilian populations of Hiroshima and Nagasaki, Einstein helped to organize the Emergency Committee of Atomic Scientists and served as the group's chairman.

- In 1946, as lynchings spread across the U.S., aimed mainly at black GI's returning from the war, Einstein helped to organize the American Crusade to End Lynching, serving as co-chairman along with Paul Robeson.
- In 1947, as the Democratic Party and President Truman embraced Cold War policies, Einstein hosted a photo-op in his home with Paul Robeson and Henry Wallace (and himself) in support of the newly formed Progressive Party and Wallace's 1948 Presidential campaign.
- In 1950, as the Cold War intensified and the U.S. announced they would build a hydrogen bomb much more powerful than the atom bomb (the Russians had developed their own atom bomb), Einstein went on TV—on Eleanor Roosevelt's first nationwide TV program—to urge Americans to reject the H-bomb.
- In 1952, Einstein twice urged witnesses called before congressional committees to refuse to answer questions. In June and December of that year, his statements made the first page of the *New York Times*. Senator McCarthy's response: "Einstein is a danger to America."
- In 1955, just a few days before Einstein died, he signed the Einstein-Russell anti-war declaration that was the basis for organizing the international Pugwash Conference. (The organization would win the Nobel Peace Prize thirty years later.)

Not a bad decade for an aging scientist whose main energies were devoted to research in math and physics!

Were he alive today, Einstein would surely put his knee to the ground with Colin Kaepernick, he would be front and center in opposing the warmongers and the neo-McCarthyites, be they Democrats or Republicans, he would speak out against those who give themselves the right to recolonize Asia and Africa, he would probably be part of the BDS movement, and would surely call out the Confederate-flag-waving marchers in Charlottesville (and elsewhere).

"If this be Treason...." *

EINSTEIN IS SUBJECT OF AN FBI "TREASON" FILE

In a letter to my attorney, retired U.S. Justice Department official Richard L. Huff first let it slip: "Mr. Einstein is the subject of one Headquarters Office main file, entitled Treason."

"Treason? Einstein? That's amazing!" is the reaction of most people when they hear this news. First they are amazed to hear that the FBI even has a Treason File—"Never heard about that before!" And then, that Einstein should be included in such a category is…well, you tell me!

"Why Einstein?" "When did they put him in the Treason category?" are but a few of the questions I get when I tell people.

"Must have been a mistake!" is another frequent reaction. One wag responded: "You must have mis-read him—the guy from the Justice Department—or maybe he wrote it wrong. He must have meant to say 'Reason.' That sounds more likely: The FBI has set up a 'Reason' category, and Einstein's FBI file is one of the Bureau's main 'Reason' files. That must be it."

But no. Reasonable as that might sound, it is not the FBI. The FBI now acknowledges that its "Central Records System Classification" includes category #61: "Treason"—a category they have maintained and expanded for nearly 100 years (since 1921)." The Bureau also acknowledges that this "Treason" category contains their reports on more than 22,000 organizations and individuals, including Einstein.

"Well, 22,000 is not really such a large number," claims one FBI official. "After all," he argues, "the FBI has hundreds of thousands of people

---

* "If this be treason, make the most of it," said Patrick Henry, 30 May 1775, speaking of the coming American Revolution.

** See Gerald K. Haines and David A. Langbart, *Unlocking the Files of the FBI, A Guide to Its Records and Classification System*, Scholarly Resources Inc., Wilmington, DE, 1993.

THE EINSTEIN FILE

and groups in its 'Subversive' files." Maybe so, but Treason is arguably the most serious crime in the country—the only crime defined in the U.S. Constitution, since many of the "founding fathers" had been accused of Treason against the King of England. While—so far—none of the 22,000 has been charged with Treason, let alone tried or convicted, presumably they have all been (or still are) at least suspected of Treason. After all, they are not in File #32, Bank Robbery or File #272, Money Laundering. All 22,000 are included in File #61.

As Gore Vidal put it, "the only question really worth asking: Why?" Why did the FBI begin a "Treason" file in 1921? Why 22,000 names? And, our question: Why Einstein?

It might be simply a coincidence that 1921 was only four years after the Russian Revolution of 1917—history's first successful socialist (communist) revolution inspiring millions of radicals and rebels around the world. In any case, be it coincidence or cause and effect, just four years after the Bolsheviks took power in Russia, the U.S. Justice Department decided it needed a stronger more centralized Bureau of Investigation, including a new file on what the government considered «Treason.»

Now consider this comment in a note I received from the FBI's Historian John Fox, Ph. D:

> The 61 file classification [Treason] began in the early 1920s as domestic subversion investigations, and so its earliest files concern the activities of anarchists, communists, and others considered political radicals or revolutionaries in their day.

This is confirmed by the names of the individuals and organizations listed in the Treason file. At least two extremely detailed research projects have gone through most or those listed by the FBI under "Treason."* I urge readers to comb through these studies. They are very revealing.

And, yes, the people and groups listed in the FBI's Treason File are mostly left-wing or left-leaning, radicals, socialists, and Communists—also many who might not be, but whom the FBI would nonetheless have considered as troublemakers, dangerous and quite possibly treasonous. And in the 1920s— as the researchers have so thoroughly revealed—the FBI was extra-interested in accusing African Americans as troublemakers and dangerous.

How did Einstein get on the FBI's Treason list in 1933? He was not yet a U.S. citizen, but was universally hailed as the world's greatest scientist and

---

* Regin Schmidt, *Red Scare: The FBI and the Origins of Anticommunisim*, Tusculanum Press, Stockholm, Sweden (2000); *Federal Surveillance of Afro-Americans (1917-1925)*; *The First World War, The Red Scare and the Garvey Movement*, project of University Publications of America, Frederick, Md. (1986) with a detailed introduction by Theodore Kornweibel, Jr.

had not the slightest trouble becoming a citizen in 1940. No one but Hitler and the Nazis in Germany (who put a price on his head), had accused him of Treason—well, almost no one. How and why did the FBI do it?

Dr. Fox, the FBI Historian:

> In 1933, the FBI was still focusing its #61 [Treason] investigations on subversion—anarchists, communists and others considered radicals or revolutionaries. At that point, the Woman Patriot Corporation, an anti-radical (as they defined it) group, accused Einstein, who was considering emigrating to the US, of being a political radical.
>
> Future materials obtained by the FBI on Einstein were included in his original file as it was already open. In the mid-1930's, the 100 case classification ["Domestic Security"] became the standard for domestic intelligence/domestic subversion investigations; this was what the Bureau's interest in Einstein consisted in and it is the class that would have been assigned to his main file had it been opened several years later, rather than in 1932.

But the accusation from the Woman Patriot group was enough for the Bureau to assign the 61 label to Einstein.

Readers will recall—see Chapter 1—that the Woman Patriot group was led by a Mrs. Randolph Frothingham. They will also recall that most of these women were married to Senators or other political muckety-mucks, the Alt-right of their day.

But just so no one will forget how far right these Alt-right ladies were, it's worth repeating here that after U.S. women won the right to vote in 1919, despite the Woman Patriot Corporation's efforts, the group quickly turned to working to defeat the proposed Constitutional amendment outlawing child labor—an amendment they denounced as "a communist plot." Every issue of the group's newspaper, *The Woman Patriot*, proclaimed across the top of its front page: "FOR THE HOME AND NATIONAL DEFENSE, AGAINST WOMAN SUFFRAGE, FEMINISM AND SOCIALISM." When they attacked Einstein, they also said: "Not even Stalin himself is affiliated with so many anarcho-communist international groups to promote this 'preliminary condition' of world revolution."

These days, the FBI Historian and other FBI personnel today have all wanted to make it absolutely clear that the Bureau does *not* consider Einstein in any way involved with Treason. Yet the letter from Mr. Huff to my attorney said simply: "Mr. Einstein **is the subject** of one Headquarters Office main file, entitled Treason" (emphasis added). And as long as the FBI says that "the accusation from the Woman Patriot group was enough for the Bureau to assign the 61 label [Treason] to Einstein," it leaves little room for a defense.

What if the next FBI Historian changes his mind? Or doesn't want to discuss the question? Or is appointed by someone from today's Alt-right?

(Not so hard to imagine.) Is there no way to amend the FBI's file... perhaps a sticker that says, simply "Alt right." Or, are we simply to say to Mrs. Frothingham and her superpatriotic folk, "You win." And hope that does not encourage the new superpatriots to new charges of Treason.

* * *

Many questions remain: Are people and groups still being added to the FBI's Treason file? Who decides about what category to assign each file? How much accountability or review exists for these decisions within the Justice Department? Is there any way of correcting or amending a file? Most important, why?

Why does the FBI *still* maintain a Treason File? The Bureau acknowledges that practically none of the file's 22,000 people and groups has been charged with anything, let alone arrested, tried or convicted. By now, many (like Einstein) are no longer alive. Many others (like Einstein) have never done anything remotely resembling treason, have never had a treasonous thought—so why keep the Treason file?

Could this be anything like the FBI's old "Det-com" list collected during the 1950's? These were (reportedly many thousands of) people to be put in "detention camps" in case of war with Russia? Or war with China? Or Korea? Or other national "emergency"? The FBI would probably deny this, of course, but in the event of a war or national emergency, they might decide that rounding up "Treason suspects" would seem to make sense. Seem to. Until you think of Einstein being put in a U.S. "detention center." Or until you think of who today's targets of the FBI would be (or targets of the NSA or the Homeland-First-ers). They have already begun "warnings" against "radicals" and "identity groups"—a term that would surely be applied to Black Lives Matter, among other groups critical of the government. The "suspect" list would surely grow, considering the slippery slide to the right of U.S. politics. Once again, as James Baldwin said, "History wouldn't matter, if history were past. But history is present. We live our history. We are our history."

The Treason File may well be the focus of future studies, books, perhaps even a TV series. But for now it is worth imagining what Einstein would say if he knew he was on the list. My guess is that he would most likely give us one of his winks and nod towards the statue of Patrick Henry, and then say simply, "Let us make the most of it."

It is fitting that the Albert Einstein Memorial in Washington, D.C. is a favorite place for children since Einstein always talked to children as if they were real people. (Photo: Fred Jerome)

Notes

PREFACE

1. Several conversations with Grunwald, 1990-1992.
2. In the past twenty years, Einstein biographies by Sayen and Brian have included some discussion of chapters on Einstein's politics, including references to the FBI file. Pais's *Einstein Lived Here* and Calaprice's *Expanded Quotable Einstein,* although not biographies, contain useful political references.
3. "… hundreds of pro-Communist groups.": FBI's Einstein file, Section 10.
4. "If a man has such esteem…": Bucky, p. 32.
5. Interview with Dyson, Institute for Advanced Study, April 10, 2000.
6. On "objectivity": Describing the renowned historian W. E. B. Du Bois—whom we will meet again in the Einstein file—Aptheker argued it was his "intense partisanship, on the side of the exploited and therefore on the side of justice, that makes possible the grasping of truth. That partisanship is, at least, the highway leading to that accumulation of knowledge that brings one closer and closer to the real but not reachable final truth": Aptheker, *Afro-American History, The Modern Era,* New York, 1971, p. 52, cited by Robin D. G. Kelley, *Journal of American History,* June 2000, p. 155.
7. "… fought for social justice": letter to *The Nation* from Lester Rodney, January 22, 2001. Well before Jackie Robinson was hired by the Dodgers, Rodney, as sports editor of the *Daily Worker,* called for ending the color line in Major League baseball.
8. Einstein's 1949 comment on the flag, in the original, hand-written German:
   Die Fahn' ist ein Symbol dafür
   Dass noch der Mensch ein Herdentier
   The original couplet, signed by Einstein and dated 1949, is reproduced here courtesy of The James and Elizabeth May Collection. It was included (exhibit 87) in the 1979 Einstein exhibition at the Smithsonian National Museum of American History commemorating the one-hundredth anniversary of the scientist's birth.

INTRODUCTION

1. Federal agencies cooperating with the FBI on the Einstein investigation: Intelligence departments of the U.S. Army (G-2), Navy (ONI), and Air Force (Special Investigations), the Immigration and Naturalization Service (INS), the State Department, the Atomic Energy Commission, and the CIA.

…more than one thousand eight hundred pages! Includes three hundred-plus previously withheld pages and blacked-out sections released when in the spring of 2000, the Public Citizen Litigation Group, on my behalf, obtained the relatively unredacted file (see Preface).

2. For a full discussion of these "personal" files, see Theoharis, *From the Secret Files of J. Edgar Hoover.*

3. ...because of "Einstein's prominence throughout the world...": January 9, 1955 memo from Agent Branigan to A. W. Belmont at FBI headquarters, Einstein file, Section 10. Also G-2 memo to Hoover, March 31, 1951 (Section 1): "The prominence of Einstein requires extreme discretion."

4. *Time's* "absentminded professor" paragraph is excerpted from the magazines' politically sterilized "overview" piece by Managing Editor Walter Isaacson (December 31, 1999). As mentioned earlier, Fred Golden's article, "Relativity's Rebel," paints a more political portrait.

5. A list of 135 political articles and 150 *New York Times* citations just through 1950, prepared by Margaret C. Shields, appears (pp. 691-695) in *Albert Einstein Philosopher-Scientist,* edited by Paul Arthur Schilpp. (This collection also includes an autobiographical article by Einstein, twenty-five critical essays, and "Einstein's Reply to His Critics.") The *Bibliographical Checklist and Index to the Collected Writings of Albert Einstein* lists additional Einstein articles published after 1950. The total number of Einstein's non-science ("general") essays and articles listed in the *Checklist* as published between 1920 and 1955 is actually 307.

1. "WHAT'S THIS, AN INQUISITION?"

1. "You will never see it again.": Friedrich, p. 374, and Frank, p. 226.

2. Germany's "three million unemployed of 1930 became six and a half million by the end of 1932.": Delmer, p. 103.

3. *100 Authors Against Einstein:* Clark, pp. 508-509: "...his life is not safe here anyrnore": General Hans von Seeckt, commander in chief of the German Army, cited by Valentin (full account, pp. 202-209).

4. Those who fled the Nazis in 1932, those who stayed: Friedrich, pp. 371-2 and 383.

5. "Einstein ... was anxious.": Bentwich quoted by Clark, p. 508. Einstein told friends and colleagues he would be back in Berlin by April: letter to M. Solovene, 11/20/32, cited by Fölsing, p. 654.

6. Call from the consulate general in Berlin ("much to his surprise"): *New York Times,* December 6, 1932, p. 1.

7. Mrs. Frothingham's previous service to the DAR: *New York Times,* December 11, 1932: "Forbidding Lady-Fingers."

8. The Alien Exclusion Act passed in 1920 barred "Aliens who believed in, advise, advocate, or teach, or...write, publish, or cause to be written or published, or knowingly circulate, distribute, print or display, or knowingly...have in their possession for the purpose of circulation ... any written or printed matter advising, advocating or teaching opposition to all organized government or...(1) the overthrow by force or violence of the Government of the United States or of all forms of law, or (2) the duty, necessity or propriety of the unlawful assaulting or killing of any officer...of the Government of the United States, or (3) the unlawful damage, injury, or destruction of property, or (4) sabotage..."

9. "... promote treason...": From "Charges Filed against Admission of Albert Einstein to the United States"—Memo from the Woman Patriot Corporation to the U.S. Department of State, November 22, 1932. (Einstein file, Section 1, pp. 1-16.)

10. Under its letterhead, THE WOMAN PATRIOT CORPORATION, 710 Jackson Place, NW, Washington, D.C., the memo simply lists the group's officers (headed by Mrs. Frothingham) and its Board of Directors. Dated November 19, 1932, it is addressed to the Honorable A. Dana Hodgdon, chief [of] Visa Division, Department of State, Washington, D.C. Stamps on the FBI's copy indicate that State promptly sent the Bureau a copy, which arrived on December 1, 1932.

...Far-right groups. Sources cited by Jeansomme in *Women of the Far Right* include Minott. *Peerless Patriots,* Pencak. For *God and Country,* and Dilling: *The Red Network.* Dilling (see "Banned from the Bomb") was not a member of the Woman Patriot Corporation, but shared their views and even quoted them in her own book's extensive entry on Einstein. Also see Schrecker, *Many Are the Crimes* and Powers, *Not Without Honor,* pp. 91-94. "The most important person of this [far-right set] was Dilling...."

11. Two of the group's most prominent founding mothers:

Mrs. James Wolcott Wadsworth, Jr., the organization's first president, was also president of the National Association Opposed to Women's Suffrage. Her husband, a Republican senator from New York and former Speaker of the N.Y. State Assembly, was also a director of the Genesee Valley National Bank and Livingston County Trust Co. He was the son of a congressman and grandson of a U.S. Army general.

Mrs. Robert Garrett, the new group's secretary, was married to a leading Baltimore banker, head of the banking firm Robert Garrett & Sons, a director of four major Maryland banks, the Baltimore & Ohio Railroad, and the Davison Chemical Company, among other corporations.

12. In its entry for Louis A. Frothingham, Appleton's *Cyclopedia of Biographies* (1918-19) strays from its usually detached historical tone with uncharacteristic enthusiasm:

> Not to every man has it been given to have no less than four Mayflower Pilgrims on the boughs of his family tree, but upon this one are the names of William Bradford, second governor of Plymouth...Eider William Brewster, Richard Warren and John Holland. This is besides a New Hampshire branch bearing the names of Judge Nathaniel Weare, famous jurist of Hampton and the Reverend Stephen Bachelor.

Following the family tradition, Louis attended Adams Academy, Boston Latin School, and Harvard, where he played both football and baseball, before going on to Harvard Law School. From there, after a stint in the Officers Corps, he followed the family roadmap into business and politics. Besides serving as president of Blackstone Savings Bank, director of the Federal Trust Company, and an Overseer of Harvard University for eighteen years, Louis A. Frothingham, brother to the Reverend Paul Revere Frothingham, was a proud member of the Society of Mayflower Descendants.

13. *The Woman Patriot,* December 1932: "The full text of the charges... was released to the press, November 30."

14. Einstein's "reply" to the Woman Patriot: Besides the December 4, 1932 *Times* article (an AP dispatch), see *Ideas and Opinions,* p. 8. Einstein's attitude toward women may well be reflected in some of the essay's sexist terminology (e.g., "cackling of its faithful geese").

15. *The Woman Patriot,* op. cit., p. 1.

16. Sayen, pp. 6-7.

17. Embassy grilling: Numerous press reports have described the interview and reactions (cables of concern sent to the Einsteins, and the protest from Mrs. Swope's group). See especially *New York Times* during the first week of December, 1932. A blow-by-blow account of the interview was given by Elsa to the *Times* Berlin correspondent and appeared in a page-one story datelined December 5, 1932, the same day as the consulate confrontation. The AP

dispatch also had a December 5 Berlin dateline. It is virtually certain that the media could not have latched onto the story so quickly without a call from the Einsteins. (U.S. consular officials would never have released such embarrassing details.)

For footnote fanatics (and for the record): A new version of the embassy events has "emerged" recently. It is a case study in how fiction can become history with just the slightest little nudge. In his recent Einstein biography, hailed as "definitive" by many critics, Fölsing first gives the older version, as reported in the *New York Times,* where Einstein demands and gets a visa within twenty-four hours. Fölsing then adds: "According to recently released U.S. government papers however, Einstein did something different. He signed the declaration demanded of him, confirming that he was not a member of any radical organization" (p. 654). As his source for this new information, Fölsing cites (fn. 98, p. 811) "Brief biography of Einstein in the files of the U.S. Army relating to the security clearance of physicists for the atomic bomb project in 1940. See R. A. Schwartz, *Einstein and the War Department* in *Isis,* vol. 80, 1989."

The truth is that the "brief biography of Einstein in the files of the U.S. Army" is a page-and-a-half sketch prepared by the FBI, undocumented and loaded with misinformation and a bias that seems to echo pro-Nazi media reports. (See Chapter 4, "Banned from the Bomb.") Schwartz cites that FBI sketch only in the course of thoroughly debunking and discrediting it.

That FBI memo is hardly a credible source. Also, to call it "recently released U.S. government papers," or even a "brief biography of Einstein in the files of the U.S. Army," is quite different from identifying it as an undocumented FBI sketch. Finally, when Fölsing writes, "See R. A. Schwartz [article] in *Isis,*" it implies that Schwartz cites the FBI piece as documentation, and gives no hint that Schwartz debunks it.

The embassy confrontation as described here was reported in numerous press accounts, including the Woman Patriot Corporation's own newspaper (See *WP,* December 3, 1932) and never challenged or denied. The only source for the claim that Einstein signed a loyalty oath comes from the discredited FBI "sketch". There is not a shred of evidence that Einstein signed anything at all in the Berlin Embassy, let alone such a loyalty-oath type of document that he found so repugnant.

In fact, Einstein "was told a visa had been granted him" according to the *New York Times* (December 7, 1932), "despite his refusal yesterday to submit to an examination by consular officials as to his political creed."

18. Mrs. Gray quoted in the *New York Times* of January 9, 1933: the Einstein issue of *The Woman Patriot,* December 1932.

2. FLASHBACK

1. Learning to play the violin: 1940 letter to Philipp Frank, cited by Fölsing, p. 26.

2. It was widely known as a politically liberal, forward-looking school and had been recently enlarged to include modern languages. It also had a new physics laboratory.

3. "...purest, most fervent...": Reiser, p. 50: "I 'played hookey' a lot...": Einstein in *Autobiographische Skizze,* p. 10, cited by Folsing, p. 50. Einstein, in *Autobiographical Notes* (translated in Schilpp, p. 17): "This [skipping classes] gave one freedom in the choice of pursuits...a freedom which I enjoyed to a great extent and have gladly taken into the bargain the bad conscience connected with it as by far the lesser evil. It is, in fact, nothing short of a miracle that the modern methods of instruction have not yet entirely strangled the holy curiosity of inquiry...."

Swiss Ethical Culture Society: Fölsing, p. 51.

4. On the cause-and-effect link "at least on a pre-conscious level...": Gumbrecht, p. 339. *New York Times* headlines on Russian uprising: January 23, 1905, p. 1.

5. "...prize hen": *Nova's* two-hour TV Special on Einstein.

6. He remained a political outsider in Germany: Goenner and Castagnetti, p. 325.

7. Einstein's interaction with pacifist circles: *Ibid.,* p. 327. The Goenner-Castagnetti article presents a thorough and careful description of Einstein's cautious first steps into politics.

8. Einstein's lecture disrupted by "excesses of an anti-Semitic mob": *Vorwarts,* February 13, 1920, cited by Pais *(Einstein Lived Here),* p. 153. According to Einstein expert Robert Schulmann, the disruption was actually "a protest against what some students viewed as unfair practices of the university in admitting unregistered students." But Schulmann adds: "That there was an anti-Semitic component is undeniable." (Note to author, November 1, 2001)

9. F. Sthamer, September 2, 1920, cited by Fölsing, p. 464.

10. Secret KKK-like force inside German Army: *Paris Herald Tribune,* December 28, 1921.

11. Transforming international education: Clark, pp. 440-442. "... marched with the crowd, rather than against it": p. 428.

12. Einstein's "2 percent solution" to war: Nathan pp. 116-117. His Upton Sinclair interview: Nathan, p. 120.

13. Speeches at Caltech: the *New York Times,* January 26 and February 28, 1932.

14. *City Lights* premiere "went down in legend": standing ovation for Einsteins: Robinson, p. 414.

15. Einstein's speech in Chicago, calling for antimilitary civil disobedience: *New York Times,* March 4, 1931. The same article states: "Among those who visited with the scientist were Frank Lloyd Wright, architect." The Chicago speech and meeting with Wright are also reported in Einstein's FBI dossier: memo May 11, 1954 from the LA SAC to Hoover.

16. "... He hated the hubbub": Frank, pp. 330, 468-469.

17. Einstein's mixed reviews of America: letters to Belgium's Queen Elizabeth, February 2, 1931, and Paul Ehrenfest, April 3, 1932. Princeton Archives.

3. REFUGEE

1. Fifty-thousand-dollar price on Einstein's head: Bucky, p. 59-60. Brian (p. 249) says the rumored amount was $5,000, but he confirms Einstein's wry response.

2. "...a wound that refused to heal": Vallentin, p. 172: also Highfield and Carter, p. 215. In the summer of 1934, Elsa sailed to Paris, where she found Ilsa near death, under the care of her sister Margot. After Ilsa's death, Elsa returned to Princeton in August, accompanied by Margot and carrying Ilsa's ashes.

3. Breckenridge Long and anti-Semitism in the State Department: See footnote, p. 13.

4, "... alleged mistreatment of Jews...": Hull also told the delegation from AJC and B'nai Brith: "I am of the opinion that outside intercession has rarely produced the results desired and has frequently aggravated the situation." (Morse, pp. 112-114 and 122.)

—"... undesirable classes including Communists...": A. Dana Hodgdon, chief of the State Department's Visa Division, quoted by Morse, p. 141.

5. Requirements for admission: Morse, pp. 140-141.

6. "...stopped wearing socks": Halsman, cited in French *(Centenary Volume),* pp. 27-28. Halsman's famous portrait of Einstein was the cover photo for *Time* magazine's "Person

of the Century" issue, December 31, 1999. (A previously unpublished Halsman photo of Einstein with Otto Nathan appears in the photo insert.)

7. The newly released pages in Section 9 include a list of names of the refugees Einstein sponsored.

8. Einstein's letter to Eleanor Roosevelt, July 26, 1941: Einstein Archives, Princeton. Einstein met with the First Lady in July 1941. Morse, p. 316.

9. Texaco's oil to Franco. Loftus and Aarons, p. 63.

10. For a more complete but still concise summary of the Lincoln Brigade, see entry by Sam Sills in *Encyclopedia of the American Left*, pp. 2-4.

11. In recent years, historians on both left and right have tended toward cynicism in evaluating Roosevelt's motives. Zinn (p. 112) argues that Roosevelt's shift to an anti-Nazi policy occurred only when "Japan and Germany threatened U.S. world interests.... Roosevelt was as much concerned to end the oppression of Jews as Lincoln was to end slavery during the Civil War." Einstein, Szilard, and the majority of Americans did not share this view.

12, "He was very quick...and willing to assume responsibility...": Weart and (Gertrud) Szilard, p. 83, cited by Rhodes *(Atomic Bomb)*, p. 305. Initially, Szilard and Wigner had asked Einstein to write to his longtime friend Queen Elizabeth of Belgium urging her to stop uranium shipments from the Belgian Congo to Germany. After considerable discussion, and with input from Alexander Sachs, an economist and unofficial adviser to Roosevelt, Szilard and Einstein agreed that writing to the President would be more effective.

13. "Imagine Belgium occupied by present-day Germany!": Einstein's letter to Alfred Nahon, July 20, 1933, in *New York Times*, September 10, 1933, cited by Nathan, p. 229.

14. "... a deep antipathy...": Einstein to Paul Hutchinson, editor of *The Christian Century*, reprinted in Einstein's booklet *The Fight Against War*, cited by Nathan, p. 98.

15. "Peace was not above...": Paul Doty, *Einstein and International Security*, Holton and Elkana, p. 353.

16. *Kristallnacht* report: *New York Times*, November 11, 1938, p. 1.

17. "But with the rise of Fascism...": Einstein to a student at Missouri University, July 14, 1941, Nathan, p. 319. The letter begins, "My abhorrence of militarism and war is as great as yours. But..."

   a town where thieves and murderers are organized....": Paragraphs omitted from a letter to Phi Beta Kappa, February 1, 1939: Nathan, p. 283.

18. Among those in on the Einstein-Szilard letter to FDR project were Wigner, Edward Teller (also a Hungarian-born physicist refugee), and Alexander Sachs, Russian-born economist and businessman working for Lehman Brothers, a friend of the President. The decision to write to Roosevelt actually took two meetings with Einstein and several interim discussions with Sachs. It was Sachs who actually delivered the famous letter to Roosevelt.

19. The letter was actually prepared by Szilard, based on a shorter draft Einstein had written in German. See Nathan for both the letter sent to Roosevelt (p. 294-296) and a translation of Einstein's draft (p. 293).

20. Einstein's criticism of U.S. half measures to support England: August 16, 1940 letter to Harold Urey. Nathan pp. 315-317. Urey, then at Columbia, had won the Nobel Prize for Chemistry six years earlier for his discovery of heavy hydrogen.

21. For most of the text of Einstein's "I Am An American" speech: Nathan, pp. 312-314.

4. BANNED FROM THE BOMB

1. Vannevar Bush not convinced an A-bomb was possible: Rhodes *(Atomic Bomb)*, p. 338. Bush was "initially more interested in proving the impossibility of such a weapon than in rushing to build one: the Germans could not do what could not be done."

2. For a list of all thirty-one names nominated for the NDRC advisory committee, as well as most G-2's loyalty-clearance evaluations and relevant correspondence between G-2 and the War Department, see National Archives, G-2/8930-B-254. Also, for more on G-2's correspondence on Einstein, see Schwartz, "Einstein and the War Department."

3. General Miles' letter to Hoover requesting the Einstein file, June 26, 1940 (National Archives, War Department files).

4. The Woman Patriot anti-Einstein memo was copied to the FBI almost as soon as the State Department received it. Stamp on Page of the memo shows it arrived at the Bureau on December 1, 1932.

5. Einstein turned down participation in the 1932 Amsterdam Conference: Nathan, pp. 181-182: Einstein's letter of August 24 1932, addressed to Henri Barbusse: "When Japan attacked Manchuria, the conscience of the civilized world was not strong enough to prevent this crime. Business interests of industries profiting from war proved to be stronger than the peoples' urge for justice. It now becomes clear to everyone that the intention to weaken Russia with a military assault and hinder its economic development was behind this attack....May this congress, by the power of public opinion, contribute to steps taken by the governments of the superpowers to prevent further harm." (Nathan, p. 181.) Besides Barbusse, those who took part in the conference included: Madame Sun Yat Sen, John Dos Passos, Maxim Gorki, George Bernard Shaw, Augusto Sandino, H. G. Wells, Heinrich Mann, Martin Alexander Nexo, Romain Rolland, Micheal Karolyi, and Bertrand Russell.

6. Hoover's letter, dated August 15, 1940 to General Miles and the "Biographical Sketch." See FBI Einstein file, Part 1, and Army Intelligence files, National Archives (G-2/8930-B-254). General Miles' handwritten warning appears only on the National Archives copy. In re the "Biographical Sketch," Schwartz *(op. cit.)* is convinced it was prepared by the FBI and he is probably correct. There is some evidence that the undated, unsigned document may have been prepared by G-2. It is identical in format and typeface to biographical sketches in at least two other G-2 security files (Irvin Stewart and Alexander Sachs). These other sketches, however, may also have been prepared for G-2 by the FBI. Whichever agency prepared the sketch, of course, does not alter its inaccuracies or proNazi bias.

7. General Strong's letter has apparently disappeared from Army Intelligence files. But Vannevar Bush was shown a copy. See note 14.

8. The FBI reported that Einstein said Szilard was "honest, reliable and trustworthy... an outspoken democrat...[who could be trusted] without any fear whatever that Szilard might disclose confidential information to a foreign government." Source: The Einstein file, Section 2, Correlation Summary, pp. 129-132. A less detailed account of the interview, but including Einstein's endorsement of Szilard's loyalty, is in Szilard's FBI file. See Leo Szilard home page, copyright 1995 by Gene Dannen.

Strangely, in an account of the same FBI interview, Ernst Straus leaves out Szilard's name, using "Mr. X" instead—perhaps out of a commitment not to name names, even in 1980, although it's unlikely that Szilard could have been hurt by the story of Einstein's endorsement. ("Reminiscences" by Straus, in Hotton & Elkana, p. 417.)

9. "Virtually all nuclear physicists...had vanished...": Fölsing, p. 718. "Einstein was probably able to form a picture of the state of affairs."

10. Szilard visited Einstein "about the uranium project": Interview with FBI (above). Einstein file, p. 131.

11. "... utterly impossible..." to take Einstein into his confidence: Bush to Frank Aydelotte, director of the Institute for Advanced Study in Princeton, December 30, 1941: National Archives OSRD files.

ONI approves Einstein for war work: The FBI's Einstein file, Part 2, Correlation Report, p. 116.

Einstein "felt very bad about being neglected...": Lieutenant Brunnauer, "Einstein and the U.S. Navy," cited by Fölsing, p. 715. Brunnauer adds that Navy explosives experts regularly "brought him problems such as the optimal detonation of torpedoes. His solutions...were accurate."

"...I don't want to do any other work.": Brian, p. 334.

In the Navy without having to get a haircut: Pais, Subtle is the Lord, p. 12. Einstein's letters to Lieutenant Brunnauer were declassified by the Navy in 1979. Copies available from the National Archives.

12. Bush asks Einstein to serve as OSRD consultant: Nathan, p. 303.

Bush told Nathan (p. 665, fn.9): "I did not know of any relationship of [Einstein's] with the Navy..." He also claimed that when he had earlier excluded Einstein from discussions about the bomb project, he hadn't known about Einstein's 1939 letter to Roosevelt (Sayen, p. 148).

13. Einstein turns down Bush's offer: Nathan p. 303. Einstein also refers to Bush's offer in his letter to Commander Brunnauer of August 13, 1943: National Archives, U.S. Navy records. "...supported the national effort...": Balibar, p. 87.

14. "... the Army could not clear.": Letter from Vannevar Bush, director of the Office of Scientific Research and Development, to Major General R. C. Moore. Source: National Archives, OSRD files, OCS/16253-46.

15. "unable to locate the letter...": Elaine C. Everly, assistant chief for the Navy and Old Army Branch of the General Services Administration to Richard A. Schwartz, October 26, 1983, courtesy of Professor Schwartz. See also "Einstein and the War Department," p. 1.

16. Gentry, p. 313: "Hoover's frequent ally, General George V. Strong..."

17. Political screening of individual scientists for the Manhattan Project by FBI and Army Intelligence, beginning in 1940: Military Intelligence files, National Archives.

General Miles on Urey's political activity: letter to the Army's War Plans Division, July 31, 1940. Military Intelligence files, National Archives: G-2/8930-B-254).

—Urey's FBI file (116-18315) lists his "front" organizations on p. 2 of its summary "Re: Harold Urey," June 17, 1953.

18. "I had lots of Communist friends": Oppenheimer in Time's cover story, November 8 1948, p. 76. Whether or not Oppenheimer himself was a CP member, he, Kitty, Frank, and Frank's wife Jacquinette were "all sympathetic to the left and made financial contributions to the Party," according to Steve Nelson, the Communist Party's organizer in Berkeley during the early 1940s (Nelson, p. 269).

19. Levine's comments are recorded in the raw footage of an interview by Chris Koch and Richard Elman, October 10, 1962. Pacifica Radio Archives tapes BB1397a, b, and c.

20. "We needed experts....": Letter from Bethe to author, November 11, 1996.

21. Einstein's expertise in demand: The problem involved how best to use a process called gaseous diffusion in the separation of uranium isotopes-a necessary step in

developing the atom bomb. Bush tried to approach Einstein through Frank Aydelotte, then director of the Institute for Advanced Study. Einstein's response to the Bush-via-Aydelotte request stated that he would need additional information in order to deal more thoroughly with the problem. Bush called in Harold Urey, then head of the U.S. gaseous-diffusion project, who agreed that Einstein would need more information and urged Bush to have more confidence in Einstein. See Bush-Aydelotte and Bush-Urey letters: G-2 files in the National Archives.

22. "... favorite outdoor sport...": Hoover rarely missed a Saturday at the track. "His favorite sport is horse racing." *(Nation's Business,* January 1972.)

23. Isolationists' promise of AG job to Hoover: Loftus and Aarons cite a confidential source formerly in NSA and another confidential informant they don't identify. On Nazi contributions to congressmen, they cite the top-secret private files of the U.S. attorney general, kept in a vault on the sixth floor of the main Justice Department building in Washington, which they have read: p. 577, fn. 66 and 67. Higham *(American Swastika,* p. 38) also indicates a Nazi connection to several members of Congress, citing, besides Wheeler, Minnesota Senator Ernest Lundeen. But Higham does not support the thesis that Hoover had a connection to this group.

24. "... most successful covert operation...": Volkman, p. 185.

25. Exposing Wheeler's Nazi ties: Gentry, p. 269.

26. "...anti-Semitic, lunatic right...": Dilling described by Powers *(Not Without Honor),* p. 129: "crackpot" (p. 132): Powers says her book "twisted the history of the left and the American reform movement into a bizarre and breathless melodrama...."(p. 129).

27. On the Dilling factor: "Most historians contend that Hoover did not pay much attention to *The Red Network*...but its findings are, in fact, liberally sprinkled throughout the writers' files": Robbins, p. 76. "Hoover's agents used Dilling's *Red Network*...as often as they used *Current Biography*": p. 103.

28. Hoover's invitation to Himmler to attend the international police conference: FBI file 65-3598: his reception of Himmler's aide and correspondence with German officials: Summers, p. 134: his letter to KRIPO chief counsel W. Fleischer: Donner, p. 86.

29. Einstein on Hitler's hit list: the Einstein file, Section 3, p. 242.

30. "The Bureau's fervent anti-Communist ideology...": Schwartz, *Isis,* p. 284.

31. "During the McCarthy era, the Federal Bureau of Investigation accepted statements picked up from extreme right-wing newspapers and the testimonies of obscure propagandists as serious sources....": Hentschel, Letter to ISIS, v. 81, No. 2, 1990, pp. 279-280.

32. "... primdonnas...": Rhodes *(Atomic Bomb),* p. 449.

33. "... a number of Manhattan Project scientists considered quitting....": My interview with Rotblat, London, October 2, 1996. Rotblat reported that Army officials at the Manhattan Project told him in 1944 that the bomb would most likely be used against Russia or Japan. He was harassed by FBI officials, who were convinced that his decision to leave must have meant he was a Russian spy.

34. Einstein's 1918 letter to his mother: Nathan, p. 24.

35. "War is won...peace is not": *New York Times,* December 11, 1945. Full text of speech: Nathan, pp. 355-356.

5. EMERGENCY COMMITTEE

1. Hiroshima casualties: Estimates don't vary by much. Former Defense Secretary Robert McNamara, interviewed on the *Robin McNeil Newshour,* February 22, 2001, said the U.S. bombing of Hiroshima "killed 180,000 people."

2. Truman's diary: Rhodes *(Atomic Bomb)*, p. 690--91, and Robert Ferrell ("Truman at Potsdam," *American Heritage,* June-July, 1980) "...treat him as a beast": Truman to Samuel McCrea Cavert, general secretary of the Federal Council of Churches, who had cabled him, "Many Christians deeply concerned..." The council's statement was signed by Bishop G. Bromley Oxnam and, surprisingly, by future conservative secretary of state, John Foster Dulles. *(New York Times,* August 10, 1945, p. 6—"Oxnam, Dulles Ask Halt in Bomb Use.")

3. "Who is barbarian?": *The Crisis,* September 1945, p. 249, cited by Boyer, p. 199.

4. Einstein described Roosevelt as "above the petty bickering of the day...without any selfish interest": *New York Times,* March 30, 1948.

5. Einstein's *Sunday Express* interview, August 18, 1946, cited in his FBI file, Section SUB A: Memo from Agent Fletcher to Deputy Director Ladd, recorded August 30, 1946. A United Press dispatch reporting the interview appeared in the Washington *Times Herald,* August 19, 1945.

6. Byrnes told historian Herbert Freis he had felt "it would be regrettable if the Soviet Union entered the [Pacific] war....": Byrnes to Freis in 1958, cited in Rhodes *(Atomic Bomb),* p. 690: "...before the Red Army entered Manchuria": Alperovitz, pp. 665-066. After a detailed case (pp. 664-668) demonstrating that an anti-Soviet motive was at least partly behind the atom bombing, Alperovitz concludes: "However, we simply do not have enough information to make a final judgment as to emphasis."

"...tantalizing hints that Roosevelt was troubled...": McGeorge Bundy, quoted by Alperovitz who concludes, "At best, Roosevelt's position was ambiguous and, if anything, suggests he had considerable doubts about attacking a city ... however ... whatever thoughts Roosevelt may have had about the use of the weapon, the real-world situation changed radically in the final months [after his death] before Hiroshima" (pp. 661-662).

7. Einstein to FDR: "I have much confidence...": Weart and Szilard, p. 205. Einstein's meetings with Otto Stern and Bohr: Sherwin, p. 110, and Clark, pp. 697-701.

8. Szilard's petition was signed by sixty-nine Manhattan Project scientists at the Chicago Metallurgical Laboratory and eighty-eight at Oak Ridge (before General Groves' staff stopped its circulation). At Los Alamos, Edward Teller decided not to circulate it "after consulting with Oppenheimer" (Alperovitz, p. 190).

9. "...dumping our gear overboard": Stephen McKie recalling his Navy days in an interview in his home in San Jose, California, February 19, 2001.

10. "The greatest thing in history": Rhodes *A-Bomb,* p. 734 (quoting Truman in *Year of Decision,* p. 421).

11. Public opinion polls on the atom bomb: Boyer, pp. 22-24. Media opinions: Alperovitz, pp. 427-428, and Boyer, pp. 12-19.

12. "...survival is not assured": Edward R. Murrow on CBS radio, August 12, 1945: *New York Herald Tribune,* August 7, 1945: *Life,* August 20, 1945 (p. 25).

13. *Catholic World:* September 1945): another leading Catholic magazine, *America,* declared (September 1945), that the Japanese surrender had been under preparation for some time before the bombing...": Alperovitz, p. 438.

"... sinned grievously...": Commission on the Relation of the Church to the War in the Light of the Christian Faith, Federal Council of the Churches of Christ in America, March 1946.

Other Protestant spokesmen joined the critics. The *Christian Century* said the bombing "placed our nation in an indefensible moral position" (August 29, 1945).

14. Richard Strout's piece was published in *The Progressive,* August 10, 1945.

15. *Washington Afro-American,* August 18, 1945. *Chicago Defender* articles by Hughes, White, and Du Bois, August 18, September 8, and September 15, 1945, respectively.

16. Newspapers in several cities...: Boyer p. 197.

17. "... sacrifice was urgent and necessary...": *New York Times,* March 15, 1958, p. 1. Truman's response, thirteen years after the fact, to protest from the City Council of Hiroshima-which cited more than 200,000 lives lost in that city.

18. "Military necessity will by our cry....": Lawrence in *United States News* (soon to become *U.S. News & World Report),* August 17, 1945, cited in Alperovitz, p. 438. Also see reference (p. 439) to Felix Morley, editor of the conservative *Human Events.*

   U.S. Strategic Bomb Survey, *Japan's Struggle to End the War,* Washington, D.C., 1946: Boyer, p. 186, and "Hiroshima and Nagasaki... concentrations of population": Zinn, p. 126.

19. "Instantaneous death...": description of the U.S. Air Force photo of the atom bomb explosion over Hiroshima: John Faber, *Great News Photos and the Stories behind Them,* Dover Publications, Inc., New York, 1947, p. 94.

20. "...will curse the name...": Morrison in 1945, Goodchild, p. 169. Also includes Oppenheimer's quote from the Bhagavad Gita.

21. "...no hope of clearing my conscience...": Teller, July 1945, quoted by Rhodes, *Atomic Bomb,* p. 697.

22. The first issue of the *Bulletin* appeared in December 1945. The following May, "Einstein, one of the *Bulletin's* godfathers, wrote in a...fund-raising letter: 'The unleashed power of the atom has changed everything save our modes of thinking, and thus we drift toward unparalleled catastrophe.'" ("A Brief History of the Bulletin," published on-line by the Educational Foundation for Nuclear Science, Chicago, 1999.)

23. The Association for Atomic Education was formed by FAS later in 1946 as a non-profit group to at least partly facilitate receiving funds from the ECAS. For a detailed history of ECAS: Clark, pp. 716-719, and Smith, *A Peril and a Hope,* especially pp. 495-497 and 509-511.

24. "...a chain reaction of awareness and communication": *NY Times Magazine,* June 23, 1946. "The Real Problem is in the Hearts of Men," by Albert Einstein in an interview with Michael Amrine.

25. Science has become "a nightmare that causes everyone to tremble.": Einstein letter to Belgium's Queen Elizabeth in 1954, quoted by Eugeniusz Olszewski (Whitrow, p. 89).

26. On *Hiroshima,* "Millions ... over ABC radio...": Jennings and Brewster, *The Century,* p. 291-2: "The power of Hersey's reporting (delivered devoid of melodrama, in an unaffected style) was to bring human content to an unimaginable tragedy and the response, in turn, was overwhelming...it was impossible to ever again see the bomb as just another weapon."

27. Cold War as cause of drop-off in FAS membership: Boyer, p. 342. FAS members vote for "production of atom bombs": Boyer, p. 96. Einstein on public indifference: quoted by David Lilienthal, "Democracy and the Atom," *NEA Journal,* February 1948, p. 80.

28. Golden's memo to Secretary of State Marshall, June 9, 1947, *Foreign Relations of the U.S. 1945-1950* (v. I, pp. 487-489).

29. "Nowhere (does Golden's report contain] any analysis of Einstein's ideas...": Sayen, p. 196.

30. "Atomic War or Peace": FBI's Einstein file, Section 1. First printed in *The Atlantic Monthly,* then reprinted by ECAS in January 1948, this is the only Einstein article to be found in the FBI's file, which actually includes two copies, sent in by two different paid informants.

31. "...militarization...will undermine the democratic spirit...": April 28, 1948, speech in Carnegie Hall. *(New York Times,* April 29, 1948): "Disagreements among Committee members over total disarmament": Sayen, p. 194: over Einstein's criticism of the UNAEC: Smith, p. 508, and working with the State Department: p. 327. "The UN had been "ineffectual": Golden's memo to Marshall on his interview with Einstein. (See fn. 28, above.) The ECAS remained dormant until formally dissolved in September 1951. In 1948, its members voted to turn over all remaining funds to the *Bulletin of Atomic Scientists:* Nathan, p. 558.

32. The Einstein file: Ladd-to-Hoover memo, February 15, 1950, p. 3.

33. Einstein file, Correlation Report, p. 503 (March 12, 1946 memo from Washington field office) and p. 628 (December 1946 memo from G-2). A similar memo in June (p. 564) reports the Newark office is probing whether the committee is "communistically infiltrated and dominated" and whether Einstein "was the actual force behind the organization or...being used as a respectable front for others."

34. "...$100,000...": August 5, 1953 Summary Report, p. 107. The FBI actually refers to the newspaper as the *"New York Times Herald."* It is one of the less significant errors in the Einstein file.

Foreign correspondence: Ladd-to-Hoover memo February 15, 1950, p. 3.

35. FBI's erroneous belief about Einstein's nuclear knowledge: Correlation Report, pp. 395, 427, 503.

36. EPA to FBI: "He was not a consultant." Einstein's FBI file (Section 4): Correlation Report, p. 657.

37. The Bureau's final assessment of ECAS: Einstein's FBI file (Section 5): Correlation Report, p. 730.

38. Einstein's vision of nationwide public discussion: *NY Times Magazine,* June 23, 1946 (see fn. 9).

39. Among the groups committed to bridging the science-media-public gaps, perhaps the most successful (until its funding ran out in 1995) was the Scientists' Institute for Public Information, founded by Margaret Mead in 1963.

40. Einstein on guilt: Olszewski, *op. cit.*

41. *"I made one mistake...":* (Linus Pauling's diary): Clark, p. 672: Einstein's exchange with Katusu Hara and other Japanese journalists and scientists: Nathan, pp. 583-591: "My part consisted of. .. " (letter to *Kaizo* magazine): *Ideas and Opinions,* Modern Library ed., p. 181.

6. AMERICAN CRUSADE TO END LYNCHING

1. "Ostentatious": Reiser, p. 187. Einstein actually called the honorary degrees "rolls of ostentatious."

2. "We held the ceremony...in the Grove": Phone interview with Mrs. Bond, June 17, 2000: "first institution in the world...": Horace Mann Bond, *Education for Freedom,* Chapter 1, cited on Lincoln University's home page Website.

3. "...a very simple man came to Lincoln...": *The Lincolnian, v.* 17, No. 4, June 4, 1946.

4. Note from Julian Bond, June 2000.

5. One brief item inside the next day's *New York Times* reported: "Dr. Einstein said he believed there was 'a great future' for the Negro," and he "asked the students 'to work long and hard and with lasting patience.'" Assuming the *Times* received a copy of Einstein's entire speech, it is interesting to note the difference between what they

singled out to publish and the nonprofessional report by a Lincoln student: "Then this man...spoke of the disease that humanity had [and] that he could not be silent."

6. Address at Lincoln University: It is not certain that these were the exact words of Einstein's speech. He seems to have used the same text as appeared in his *Pageant* magazine article, five months earlier. However, aside from other considerations, it is unlikely he would have used exactly the same words as at least some of that article is directed to a white readership: "Your ancestors dragged these black people from their homes by force: and in the white man's quest for wealth and an easy life, they have been ruthlessly suppressed and exploited...." Nonetheless, based on the student article (fn. 3, above), it would seem that these words were at least the gist of what Einstein said. The *Pageant* article was reprinted (as "On the Negro Question") in a collection of essays Einstein himself selected, called *Out of My Later Years.*

7. David Williams, *Hit Hard,* Bantam War Book Series, Toronto, 1983. See also Emily Wax, "Blacks' Other WW II Battle," *Newsday,* November 8, 1998.

8. "...four or five men in the white mob were killed...": Raymond Lockridge, a black carpenter who was in Mink Slide during the attack, quoted by Juan Williams, p. 134.

9. "...closer to German storm troopers.": Thurgood Marshall, quoted in *New York Times,* March 2, 1946, p. 26.

10. Star-studded Committee for Justice in Columbia, Tennessee: O'Brien, p. 263, fn. 86.

11. Details on the near lynching of Marshall: Juan Williams, pp. 131-142.

12. Hoover sent nine white agents...black witnesses reported...in 197-page report supporting the Tennessee State Police: O'Brien, pp. 194-200. (Top-secret "race riots" memo from Agent Tamm to DM Ladd, March 2, 1946: fn. 53, p. 197: "...very ignorant type of Negro": Hoover to President's Committee on Civil Rights, p. 196.)

13. The killing of J. C. Farmer occurred on August 3: Macio Snipes was shot on July 20. Sources of lynching reports, taken from press accounts, include: NAACP, *30 Years of Lynching:* Ginzburg *100 Years of Lynchings:* David Montgomery's introduction to *The Cold War and the University,* and the Civil Rights Congress *We Charge Genocide.*

14. Monroe, Georgia, lynching reports: excerpted from the *New York Times,* July 27 and 29, 1946. The source of the AP report on the Louisiana lynching of John C. Jones is *We Charge Genocide.* (See note 13.) The *New York Times* did carry the story on Aug. 16—on its last page—but omitted many of the most gruesome details.

15. Dr. Joseph L. Johnson, Dean of Howard Medical School: Metz T. P. Lorchard, editor in chief of the *Chicago Defender:* Rabbi Irving Miller of the American Jewish Congress: and several church leaders, including Mrs. Harper Sibley, president of the United Council of Church Women. *(New York Times,* September 2, 1946, p. 16: also cited by Duberman, p. 674). Actress Mercedes McKendrick also was a sponsor of the Crusade.

16. "...banishment to paradise": quoted in Sayen, p. 64: "...almost ashamed of living in such peace...": Letter to Belgium's Queen Mother Elizabeth, March 20, 1936 (Princeton Archives).

17. *Crisis,* February 1932, "the determined effort of the American Negroes...deserves every recognition and support."

18. "Explaining" why Princeton should remain a white-only school: *Princeton Herald,* September 25, 1942.

19. Description of Princeton: Wright, p. 33: "... townspeople "talking against Negroes,": Bucky, p. 46: Princeton as WASP-dom: *Ibid,* p. 44.

20. Marian Anderson: She felt "honored": Anderson, p. 267: "...stayed there whenever she came to Princeton: Margot Einstein, quoted by Sayen, p. 222: "...artistic master...": *Princetonian,* April 17, 1937.

21. World's Fair speech: Calaprice, p. 194: interview with Mrs. Floyd at home in Princeton, October 17, 2001.

22. The Tuskegee Institute reported four lynchings in 1941 (when the U.S. didn't enter the war until December), three in 1938 and five in 1937: *New York Times*, January 1, 1942, p. 31.

23. Hoover's early file on "Radicalism and Sedition among Negroes" and his citing of Randolph's *Messenger* and Du Bois's *Crisis*: Lewis, pp. 6-7: "Negro Activities" file and attack on Garvey: Theoharis, *The Boss*, p. 57. Theoharis cites Lowenthal (p. 90), as well as Robert Hill, "'The Foremost Radical Among his Race': Marcus Garvey and the Black Scare, 1918-1921," *Prologue*, Winter 1984 and a 1984 paper by Theodore Kornweibel, Jr., "The FBI and Black America 1917-1922."

24. The ACEL-related entries were compiled into two FBI reports within the Einstein file—the Correlation Report released in 1952 and the Summary Report of August, 1953. Some of the items were written after the September 23, 1946 protest in Washington, while others were written earlier, which explains why the tense shifts from past to present and back again.

25. "...ironclad practice...never to evaluate...": J. Edgar Hoover, *New York Times*, March 29, 1953.

26. ACEL description in the Einstein file, fills ten pages from Section 4, the 1952 Correlation Report, beginning on p. 572. The excerpt with the revealing tagline is from p. 582. The item describing Robeson's "long record of Communist affiliations" was written seven years after the Washington event, appearing in Section 8, pp. 29-30 of the FBI's August 5, 1953 Summary Report.

27. Confrontation with Truman: Press reports include: *New York Times*, September 24, 1946, *Chicago Defender*, September 28, 1946, and ("Robeson told newspapermen he assured the President it was not a threat, merely a statement of fact about the temper of the Negro people....") *Philadelphia Tribune*, September 24, 1946.

28. Besides the papers cited in note 27 above, *The Washington Post*. September 24, 1946, and numerous black papers, notably the *Baltimore Afro-American*, October 5, 1946, gave the White House confrontation extensive coverage. The *Times* piece citing Einstein's letter appeared September 23, 1946.

29. "After analyzing the electoral defeat...": Goldfield, p. 253.

30. FBI attacks on Truman's Civil Rights Committee: Internal memos between Hoover, Ladd, Tolson, and others, cited by O'Reilly, p. 26, note 43.

31. "...what the world thinks...": Report from Truman's Committee on Civil Rights, cited by Zinn, p. 151.

7. THE EINSTEIN WATCH

1. Wollenberger break-in described in FBI Correlation Report, pp. 251 (Section 3) and 111 (Section 2). The entry on page 111 spells his name as Wallenberger and the name of his "maternal aunt" as Helen Ducas. It states that he was "Chairman of 'Friends of Free Germany' in Cambridge."

2. FBI agrees to release withheld pages: "Einstein Subject of FBI Probe, Files Show," by Erica Craven, *Public Citizen News*, November-December 2000.

3. FBI memo on Hemingway from Mickey Ladd to Hoover: Mitgang, pp. 44-45: memo on Hughes, also from Mickey Ladd to Hoover, *Ibid.*, p. 179: description of Writers War Board: Folsom, pp. 227, 229, 231. Two years later, the same Mickey Ladd managed the FBI's "investigation" into the Mink Slide case in Tennessee, and four years after that, Hoover put him in charge of the Einstein case.

4. Endorser of Committee to Aid Spanish Democracy: *The Tablet,* February 25, 1950, and letter to Mayor of Stalingrad, both cited in INS file on Einstein. (See Chapter 16.)

5. Fund-raising appeal for the NAACP: FBI's Einstein file, p. 298 (Section 3).

6. FBI memo on Einstein's phone number and "Correlator's note": Einstein file, p. 476 (Section 3).

7. Tapping "not advisable," p. 490 (Section 4).

8. FBI monitoring in the Einstein file: mail cover on Weisskopf, Section 2, p. 137: on Godel, Section 6, p. 1040: Hogness-Condon phone tap, Section 5, p. 731: Einstein's phone calls, Section 4, pp. 491 and 597: birthday telegram, Section 6, p. 975.

9. ...even J. Edgar Hoover thought he was irresponsible: Mathews wrote that the American Communist Party's largest group of supporters were Protestant ministers— Theoharis *(The Boss),* p. 295.

—The official name of Washington's HUAC was the Washington State Joint Legislative Fact-Finding Committee on Un-American Activities. It was established in 1947.

10. Matthews testimony: Einstein File, Section 5, pp. 885-890 and Section 8, pp. 15-16. Also see: Center for the Study of the Pacific Northwest, *UWIRED Outreach* on-line: "Joint Legislative Fact-Finding Committee on Un-American Activities."

11. "This room is wired...my house is closely watched.": Einstein file, Section 8, p. 75. The FBI reports that the dinner party took place at the residence of Dr. Nissin Mayorah, Bulgarian Minister to the U.S., and Einstein directed his remarks to Polish Ambassador Winiewicz.

12. Pais believed Einstein had no knowledge of specific FBI probe: Pais interview in his office, October 29, 1999; it was "common knowledge" among physicists that they were "under surveillance": Sayen, p. 256.

8. RIGHT TIME

1. This foreign-born agitator...: Rankin, *Congressional Record,* October, 25, 1945.

2. ...rally for American-Soviet friendship: Einstein file, Section 3, p. 461.

3. Handwritten memo: If it's not derogatory...: Einstein file, Correlation Report, p. 1153.

4. Wallace speech, March 19, 1946: University of Iowa archives, cited in Culver, p. 414.

5. "Your courageous intervention...": Einstein letter to Wallace, September 18, 1946 (two days before he was fired) and other messages of support: Wallace Archives, University of Iowa, Culver, p. 418.

6. Truman's diary entry on Wallace and Reds, September 19, 1946: Donovan, p. 227.

7. Truman's personal dislike for Hoover has been widely cited. He reportedly also feared that the FBI would become another Gestapo. At first, he asked Congress to give the Civil Service Commission primary jurisdiction for loyalty investigations, but Congress balked, voting to give most power to the FBI. In November, Truman agreed to give Hoover's Bureau *all* authority for investigating government employees.

8. "In answer to insinuations that FBI files were being 'leaked' to favored members of Congress, Hoover said: 'I can say unequivocally that is an absolute lie'": Whitehead, p. 354: "...we gave McCarthy all we had": Sullivan, pp. 45 and 267: "...undermining constitutional guarantees...": Theoharis *(The Boss),* p. 17.

9. Custodial Detention Index: Holmes, pp. 88-89, fn 18: Hoover's switch to Security Index: Theoharis *(Spying on Americans),* pp. 41-44: "Hoover [saw] Communists coming up out of the sewers": William Hundley, formerly with the Justice Department's Internal Security Section, quoted by Demaris, *Esquire,* Nov. 1974, p. 147.

10. "... importance...cannot be overemphasized.": order to FBI field offices, July 7, 1945, FBI Smith Act files, X, quoted by Schrecker (*Many Are the Crimes*, p. 191).

11. "...the one case Hoover really wanted...": Hundley, in Demaris, op. cit., p. 147: the FBI's 2000-page "brief" and Hoover's pressure: The indictments were actually drawn up in mid June, but Clark, worried about negative public reaction, held off issuing them until after the Democratic Convention in July: Steinberg, pp. 95-110.

12. "... powerful national figures...": Theoharis ("*JEH, Sex and Crime*," p. 164).

13. Hoover-Dewey deal: Sullivan, p. 44.

14. Hoover to George E. Allen denouncing National Science Foundation and Shapley: Steinberg, p. 36.

15. "...before we corrode our hearts.": Condon, cited by Caute, p. 470.

16. The Condon case: Boyer, pp. 104-105, and Kevles, p. 379.

17. The AEC memorandum clearing Condon in July 1948, stated there was "no question whatever" about his loyalty and that "his continued clearance is in the best interests of the atomic energy program." (*Chicago Tribune*—in a four-paragraph story-July 16, 1948, p. 2.)

18. "... honest warning": Einstein statement, May 12, 1947, Nathan, p. 407.

19. "...while there is still time": Einstein to Shapley, Nathan, pp. 483, 486.

20. Einstein continued to support the conference: The Einstein file, Section 8, p. 133. Wang questions how much Einstein was actually involved in the conference (p. 126, fn. 19), citing a 1992 article by Robbie Lieberman, who claimed that although Einstein "was a sponsor," his name was missing from "a partial list of sponsors" on the conference call. But neither Wang nor Lieberman mentions the fact that Einstein's exploratory surgery in December 1948 had left him quite debilitated. Now the newly released pages of Einstein's FBI file show that he was, in fact, listed as a sponsor at the time of the conference.

21. "...none was more wrong than 1949": Belfrage, p. 99: additional details on the Einstein-Mann initiative and the "Cultural and Scientific Conference for World Peace," pp. 92-99.

22. Letter to Max Brod, February 22, 1949, Einstein Archives, quoted by Calaprice, p. 11: Father Coughlin's radio attack: Higham (*swastika*), p. 71.

23. "...coming to terms with the Arabs...": Albert Einstein letter to Chaim Weizmann, November 28, 1929 (*Albert Through the Looking Glass*, p. 91): power-sharing proposal: *New York Times*, March 5, 1931.

24. "... remained highly critical of its political leadership": *Looking Glass*, p. 84.

25. "If he accepts...": Yitzhak Navon, in Holton and Elkana, p. 295, and *Looking Glass*, p. 94: "... they would not like to hear": Sayen, p. 247.

26. "... complete equality for the Arab citizens": Einstein letter to Zvi Lurie, January 5, 1955, cited by Calaprice (*Expanded*), p. 142.
Thesis that Einstein was essentially pro-Israel: Isaiah Berlin in Holton and Elkana, pp. 281-292.

27. "should have been deported..." Rankin, on Einstein's call for a World Government: *Dallas Times Herald*, February 14, 1950.

28. Soviet scientists' criticism, *Moscow New Times*, November 26, 1947: Einstein's response, *Bulletin of Atomic Scientists*, February 1948: reprinted in *Ideas and Opinions*, Modern Library, pp. 146-165.

29. On Zionism, Einstein file Correlation Report, pp. 972, 1032: on World Federalism, Einstein file, Correlation Report, pp. 892-99, 949 and Section 1, February 15, 1950 memo, pp. 4, 8.

30. FBI and California HUAC citations re the Wallace campaign: Einstein file, Section 8, pp. 83-85.

31. "… to permit a nonsegregated audience.": *New York Times*, April 23, 1948: Wallace campaign speech on labor, *Times*, April 24.

32. FBI dossier report on Einstein's "Why Socialism": Section 6, p. 1002.

33. Nehru's visit to Einstein took place on November 5, 1949. The visiting party included Nehru's sister, who was also India's ambassador to the United States, his daughter Indira Gandhi, who would later become India's prime minister, and Amiya Chakravarty, Nehru's colleague. Four days later, Chakravarty wrote to Einstein that Nehru felt that meeting Einstein had "fulfilled…the great expectation of his life." The same letter reported that the conversation with Einstein had strengthened Nehru's conviction "that India must stand outside the two big blocs…": Einstein Archives, Princeton.

34. Einstein opposing "the complete militarization of this country…": Nathan, pp. 513-14: NATO "a horror": letter to Wallace, note 35.

35. "…half-fascistic": letter to Wallace, Einstein Archives, January 26, 1949.

9. THE LIST

1. "…gone fishing.": Pais, *Einstein Lived Here*, p. 43.

2. "…fame at the service of his moral indignation": Stern, *Dreams and Delusions*, p. 27.

3. FBI Einstein file, Correlation Report, p. 720.

4. "…planted press story…" and mixing informer reports with news stories: Donner, p. 129.

5. …authorities enlarged their lists: In 1947, the attorney general's subversive list included seventy-eight organizations: by the end of 1950, it had grown to 197. In addition, HUAC issued its own list, designating 624 organizations as "subversive.": Caute, p. 581, fn. 18. Mini-HUAC's in several states also issued subversive lists.

6. Seventy groups: The Einstein file later (in its 1955 retrospective summary) claims he was "affiliated or his name extensively associated with literally hundreds of pro-Communist groups," but no specifics are listed to back up that figure. The more accurate number is probably seventy.

7. Besides the Basque children's group and the Exiled Writers Committee, this category includes: Spanish Refugee Relief, American Relief Ship for Spain, Loyalty Committee of Victims of Nazi and Fascist Oppression, National Committee to Aid Victims of German Fascism, International Relief Association, Russian War Relief, Non-Sectarian Committee for Political Refugees, and the Jewish Black Book.

8. Other anti-fascist groups on the FBI's subversive list: American Council for Anti-Nazi Propaganda, Committee to Aid Spanish Democracy, Free Germany Institute, German American League for Culture, the National Conference on the German Problem, and Japanese-American Committee for Political Democracy.

9. Besides ECAS, WRI, and NCAC, Einstein's "Red front" anti-war groups included Committee for Peace through World Cooperation, Conference for Peaceful Alternatives to the Atlantic Pact (NATO), Scientific and Cultural Conference for World Peace, American Soviet Friendship Council, World Congress Against War, Scientists for Atomic Education, and Committee for Conscientious Objectors.

10. Interview with John Swomley, April 8, 2000, New York City.

11. Other anti-McCarthy-Hooverism groups: Committee to Defeat the Mundt Bill (actually, the Mundt-Nixon bill: it would have required members of the Communist

Party and "Communist fronts" to register with the government), Defense Committee for the Hollywood 10, American Committee for the Protection of the Foreign Born, and National Political Action Committee.

12. Other arts-sciences-professions groups included National Council of the Arts, Sciences, and Professions: Society for Social Responsibility in Science: Motion Picture Artists Committee: World Congress of Intellectuals: Korean-American Cultural Association: American Pushkin Committee: American Committee of Jewish Writers, Artists, and Scientists: and Scientific and Cultural Conference for World Peace.

13. Roosevelt was honorary member of the League of American Writers from 1938-1940: Folsom, pp. 95, 121, 264. A sampling of League members includes Agee, Auden, Dos Passos, Dreiser, Hemingway, MacLeish, Millay, Steinbeck, and Thurber, as well as Sherwood Anderson, Conrad Aiken, Van Wyck Brooks, Pearl Buck, Frank Marshall Davis, Walter Duranty, Ralph Ellison, Malcolm Cowley, Lillian Hellman, Langston Hughes, Dorothy Parker, Irwin Shaw, Rex Stout, William Carlos Williams, Richard Wright, and Frank Yerby.

10. DU BOIS AND ROBESON

1. "...no one really wants to talk about...": Anna Quindlen, "The Problem of the Color Line," *Newsweek*, March 13, 2000.

2. "Race prejudice...an American tradition...": Einstein interview with *Cheyney Record*, Nathan p. 502: "Every right-minded person...": Message to the Southwide Conference on Discrimination in Higher Education, Atlanta University, 1950, sponsored by the Southern Conference Educational Fund.

3. Two civil-rights affiliations not included in the FBI's list of Einstein "Red fronts": the NAACP Legal Defense Fund and the Committee to Free the Negro Victims in Columbia, Tennessee (1946), also organized by the NAACP.

4. Willie McGee's last letter to his wife: "Defending Willie McGee": Jessica Mitford in Fried, pp. 377-378.

5. Gerald Horne in *The Encyclopedia of the American Left*, pp. 134-5. For more extensive treatment, see Horne's 1987 book on the CRC, *Communist Front?*

6. Horne, *Ibid.*, calls CAA "the premiere organization pushing decolonization and antiapartheid." p. 135.

7. "Hens have more teeth..." No references to Robeson: After this book was written, two small but welcome hens' teeth arrived: The UPI photo of Einstein with Robeson, Henry Wallace, and Frank Kingdon that appears in this book was included in *Albert Through the Looking Glass,* published by the Einstein Archives, Hebrew University, Jerusalem (describing Robeson as "the baritone and civilrights campaigner."), and in her expanded edition of *The Quotable Einstein*, Alice Calaprice added references to Robeson and the American Crusade to End Lynching.

8. Einstein scheduled as Du Bois' first defense witness: my interview with Herbert Aptheker, February 19, 2001. Also see: *Paul Robeson Speaks* p. 565, and Lewis, p. 553.

9. Report on W. E. B. Du Bois from FBI Atlanta office, November 12, 1942.

10. "...thundering heaven...": Eduardo Galeano, *Century of the Wind*, p. 147.

11. FBI tapped Robeson's phone, opened his mail, fed HUAC and SISS: O'Reilly, p. 31 The Bureau also fed "items" on Robeson to gossip columnist Hedda Hopper.

12. Robeson's FBI file includes Hooveresque "reviews" of many of his stage and screen roles. One example:

[Informant's name deleted] has submitted information in regard to the motion picture, *Native Land*. From this source it was learned that this motion picture is receiving copious reviews in the New York press...*Native Land* is obviously a communist project. It is produced by the Frontier Films, which is a communist instrumentality: it is directed by Paul Strand (communist) and Leo Hurwitz who has many communist connections. The commentary is written by David Wolff, is spoken by Paul Robeson, an avowed communist, and the music is by Marc Blitzstein, a communist songwriter. It is noted that this picture... purportedly includes scenes that portray violations of civil liberties in the United States.

—FBI note on *Native Land* from Robeson file
(memo from NY office to Hoover, December 8, 1942).

13. "Why can't they stop the lynchers?": Duberman, p. 305.

14. His 1949 statement that black people would not fight the Russians undoubtedly cost Robeson some support in the black community, given the anti-communist fear then gripping the country. But among millions of African-Americans, Robeson's name remained respected—if spoken at times in whispers. The *NY Times* (April 21, 1949) reported that Robeson said, "It is unthinkable that American Negroes would go to war on behalf of those who have oppressed us for generations against a country [the Soviet Union] which in one generation has raised our people to full human dignity." A number of black leaders, including A. Philip Randolph and Bayard Rustin, denounced Robeson's statement. Jackie Robinson (among several others) went before HUAC and called Robeson's statement "silly." In response, Robeson denounced HUAC, but refused to attack Robinson. ("That's exactly what the other group wants us to do") and said he and Robinson were "brother victims of [HUAC's] terror." (Duberman, p. 362.)

15. FBI item on JAFRC from the Einstein file, Section 8, p. 43: item on photo with Robeson and Wallace, Section 8, p. 84.

16. Robeson was barred from appearing at a Chicago high school and Ohio State and Michigan State Universities (Duberman, pp. 318-319), and even the once-liberal CCNY student government voted to bar him in 1954 (*The Campus*, October 14, 1954).

17. Telephone interviews with Lloyd Brown, October-November 1998.

18. Robeson's monthly column, "Here's My Story," in *Freedom*, November 1952.

11. HOW RED?

1. "grossly unequal punishment...": Urey's letter to *NY Times*, January 5, 1953.

—"perjured testimony.": The trial was so flawed that even Radosh and Milton, who have long held that the Rosenbergs were guilty, called it "a grave miscarriage of justice" (p. 451). Schrecker states that Greenglass "appears to have doctored his story a bit in order to make a case against his sister." (*Many Are the Crimes*, p. 177.) "Would Ethel have been convicted if her brother had told the truth?" Roberts asks (p. 487). His answer: "No."

2. Einstein's letter to Truman, January 11, 1953: Reported but not reprinted, *NY Times*, January 13, 1953.

3. Einstein's letter to Judge Kaufman: Einstein file (Section 8), Summary Report, p. 80.

4. "...does not change our opinion.": Telephone interviews with Walter Schneir, April 2000, and *The Nation*, August. 14 and 21 and October 16, 1995: "tragic irony": Volklman, p. 162, fn.: Haynes and Klehr: pp. 15-16: Feklisov's different story: "Red Files," PBS, September 27, 1999.

5. "...used as an instrument...": Letter to Roger Bird, September 12, 1953 (Princeton Archives, 41-571): comment heard by Earl Ubell: conversation with Ubell, April 2000:

"bordering on treachery...": letter to Attorney Irwin Edelman, September 8, 1954, in Princeton Archives. Another report, although second hand if not thirdhand, of Einstein's split with the Rosenberg Committee comes from former FBI Agent Robert J. Lamphere, who writes that in the spring of 1953, "when the Committee to Secure Justice pressured him for an affidavit that would say that Greenglass's sketch of the bomb had been nonsense, Einstein refused, saying he thought that the cause had become 'Communist-inspired.'" (*The FBI-KGB War*, p. 264.)

6. ..."suspected" CP member, Einstein file Correlation Report (memo from Chicago FBI office) p. 149: "Communist adherent," p. 646: duplicate, p. 628: deluded, p. 642: criticism of U.S. policies, Ladd report to Hoover, February 15, 1950.

7. To anyone who would listen, the CRC argued "the defense of the Communist Party is the first line in the defense of civil liberties for everyone": Gerald Horne in *"The Encyclopedia of the American Left,"* p. 134.

8. "... obligation to do good for his fellow men.": Bucky, p. 32.

    ... some have claimed: Sidney Hook, for one, would not believe Einstein could arrive at some of his left-wing views by himself, and blamed his assistant Leopold Infeld and his friend Otto Nathan for exerting undue leftward pressure on Einstein (Brian, p. 300-301). But Einstein's letter to Nathan on his sixtieth birthday (copy in the Einstein Archives at Princeton, translated from German by Claes Smith-Solbakken), states, "We always agree fundamentally." Other letters from Einstein to Nathan contain similar comments—e.g., "You are my closest confidant."

9. "...he seemed naïve in the field of international politics and mass human relations." Golden's memo to Secretary of State Marshall, June 9, 1947, *Foreign Relations of the U.S. 1945-1950,* (v. I, p. 487.)

10. "...wasn't in the least naïve": C. P. Snow in *Centenary Volume,* p. 79: "...he seemed naïve in the field of international politics and mass human relations." Golden's memo to Secretary of State Marshall, June 9, 1947, *Foreign Relations of the U.S. 1945-1950,* v. I, pp. 487-489. (Chapter 4, fn. 28.) Brecht, in his journal on October 28, 1945, wrote that Einstein "a brilliant brain in his own subject, housed in a bad violinist and an eternal schoolboy with a penchant for generalizing about politics": cited by Balibar, p. 87.

11. ...the Committee for Spanish Freedom: Full text of letter in Einstein Archives, Princeton.

    "... not...by blindly sticking pins...": A few additional examples:

    Exhibit A: In 1932, he sent a message criticizing Japan's invasion of Manchuria to be read at the First World Congress Against War and Fascism (held in Amsterdam), but he refused to sponsor or even attend the event because he felt it "was entirely under Russian Communist domination." Einstein also refused to sign the statement announcing the conference, because of "its glorification of Soviet Russia." See Nathan, pp. 178-181.

    Exhibit B: When Einstein and Otto Nathan were invited to take part in the Soviet-sponsored World Conference of Intellectuals in 1948 in Wroclaw (Breslau), Poland, they prepared a statement for Nathan to present. (Einstein was unable to attend.) The statement included a call for World Government. Moscow (like Washington) sharply disagreed with this proposal, and the conference sponsors agreed to allow the speech only if that reference were deleted. Nathan refused. The conference leaders substituted a brief letter of greeting that Einstein had sent them two months earlier. Einstein angrily sent his excluded statement to the *New York Times,* which published it August 29, 1948. Einstein also wrote a sharp protest to Conference Chairman Julian Huxley, citing among other things the fact that his letters to Nathan in Wroclaw had been delayed for up to two weeks, and when Nathan did receive them, they appeared to have been opened. Huxley's excuse-filled "letter of apology" to Einstein: Einstein Archives, Princeton. For excerpts from Einstein's disallowed statement, see, besides the *Times,* Clark, p. 723.

Exhibit C: Although he had publicly advocated clemency for Ethel and Julius Rosenberg after their espionage conviction and expressed public dismay at their death penalty, as we've reported, Einstein refused to support the Rosenbergs' defense (Committee to Secure Justice for the Rosenbergs), arguing that it was "used as an instrument by the Communists."

"...carefully studied the information...": Nathan provides five pages (364-368) of examples of the scientist's rejections of requests just in 1945. In addition, Sayen's research confirms (p. 203) that, "The myth that Einstein lent his name indiscriminately to any liberal-sounding movement is refuted by a careful study of the Einstein Archives, which provide numerous instances of Einstein's refusal to accede to requests for his support."

12. "...within his rights.": Einstein, quoted in Bucky, p. 32.

13. Holton, *History & Other Passions,* p. 14. Other leading Einstein scholars agree. The director of the Einstein Papers Project at Boston University, Robert Schulmann, and John Stachel, director of the Center for Einstein Studies, also at BU, have both stated they don't believe Einstein was naïve. Stachel *"Exploring the Man Beyond the Myth"*: Einstein "chose his issues carefully. He was well aware that his fame gave him a vast audience for his views: but he also realized that he had to use this instrument sparingly if it was to remain effective." Schulmann's comments during a conversation in his office, July 22, 1997.

14. Equality in Russia "was not an empty phrase.": Memo from Ladd to Hoover, February 15, 1950.

The most pro-Soviet pubic statement Einstein would make: Einstein's remarks over the phone (because of poor health), October 25, 1942: Nathan, pp. 232-234.

15. Soviet scientists denounced World Government: "It would benefit only the capitalist democracies...further the unbridled expansion of American imperialism...," For the full statement and Einstein's response, see *Bulletin of Atomic Scientists,* February 1948. Einstein's differences with Soviet positions also appear frequently in his letters in the Princeton Archives. (Also see Chapter 8, n. 28.)

16. The *Times* of London article: September 16, 1933, p. 12 It seems likely the "press statement" was legitimate, even though it does not appear in the Einstein Archives, and he was not in the habit of issuing press statements, and even less so while traveling. (The *Times* of London piece appeared just a week after Einstein's arrival in London, where he stayed briefly before returning to the U.S.) But he was in London when the statement appeared: he certainly could have renounced the *Times* piece if it were untrue.

17. Under the headline, EINSTEIN JOINS CONDEMNATION OF RED PURGES, The *Star Ledger* article (January 22, 1953) reads, in part: "The *New Leader,* a weekly anti-Communist magazine, published the text of a telegram it sent to Einstein and other persons who have sought clemency for Ethel and Julius Rosenberg, sentenced to death for atomic spying...In reply, Einstein said: "It goes without saying that the perversion of justice which manifests itself in all the official trials staged by the Russian government, not only that in Prague, but also the earlier ones since the second half of the 30's, deserves unconditional condemnation..." The Newark FBI office, which never missed reading the *Star Ledger,* totally ignored the article.

18. Einstein's letter to Stalin: The original memo from the U.S. Embassy in Moscow is dated July 19, 1946. It was withheld from release by the FBI, but is available in the

G-2 files in the National Archives. If the story is true, the memo continues, Soviet Foreign Minister Molotov received the letter and "Molotov directed the Ministry of Internal Affairs to immediately investigate the cases mentioned by Einstein…[and] as a result…certain high Soviet officials were discharged for anti-Semitism. The professors named by Einstein were then elected to the Academy." Nonetheless, Einstein stayed in Princeton.

19. Kapitsa wrote to Bohr in London in April 1944: Clark, p. 698. Bohr and his son escaped from Denmark to Sweden in a small boat in October 1943. They spent several months in London before coming to the U.S.—and Los Alamos—in the summer of 1944.

20. "…atheistic communist dictatorship…": Hoover's comments from a 1961 speech, cited by Welch, p. 97.

21. "…investigations have already undermined…": Letter to Felix Arnold, March 19, 1954, and "…no citizen is obligated…": Letter to Corliss Lamont, January 2, 1954, both in the Einstein Archives, cited by Calaprice, pp. 140-41.

22. Besides in the May 1949 issue of *Monthly Review* magazine, this essay is included in Einstein's *Ideas and Opinions,* and available on at least one of the many Einstein Web sites on the Internet.

23. Einstein on communism: Bucky, p. 64.

24. "The fear of communism…": Address to Chicago Decalogue Society, February 20, 1954, *Ideas and Opinions,* pp. 38-9. "Nothing astonishes me so much as…": Letter to Queen Elizabeth, January 2, 1955, in Nathan, p. 616.

25. "…distemper of the times.": Sayen, p. 203.

26. Letter to Norman Thomas, March 10, 1954: Princeton Archives, quoted by Sayen, p. 278.

12. "ELEANOR COULD HAVE TRIGGERED IT…"

1. Interview with Welch in his home in Sarasota, Florida, June 16, 1998. An FBI agent for thirty years, Welch worked at most levels within the Bureau. In 1977, he was on President Carter's "short list" of candidates to succeed Hoover as FBI Director.

2. "…because God made a woman like Eleanor Roosevelt.": Welch, p. 15: "old hoot owl," et al., Summers, pp. 161-2: "…if she wasn't encouraging them.": Sullivan, p. 37.

3. On Mrs. Roosevelt as "his deadly enemy": Powers *(Secrecy and Power)* p. 265: and fn. 110: "…developing a Gestapo…": ER to FDR, March 12, 1943.
On FDR's virtually 100 percent support for Hoover: Among numerous JEH biographies, see Theoharis, pp. 179-181: Gentry, pp. 223-4: Summers, pp. 117-19: and John T. Flynn, *The New Republic,* 1940: "Hoover could not continue these activities for ten minutes in the administration of a man who did not approve them."

4. Hoover's hatred for Mrs. Roosevelt, and especially for her anti-racism: Numerous Hoover biographies: See especially Gentry, Chapter 21.
   "in love with a Negro.": Sullivan, p. 37.
   Hoover and Tolson called her "n … -lover": Summers, p. 162.

5. The Eleanor Roosevelt file: Ladd memos to Hoover, September 11, 1942, and Tamm, October 21, 1942. The FBI also had secret files on ER's activities with the American Youth Congress and the International Students Service (ISS), both acquired through illegal FBI break-ins into the offices of those groups in January 1942 and December 1942, respectively. They described ER as arguing that working with the Russians was essential for the bigger picture (to win the war). Memo: Ladd to JEH December 1, 1942

says that ISS gives in to "practically every demand of the Russian delegation." Hoover's comment: "This is nauseating." Theoharis, *The Boss*, p. 191.

On "Eleanor Clubs," see O'Reilly, *Racial Matters*, pp. 19-20, for more details.

6. Spy headlines during week of February 4-11, 1950: *Chicago Tribune*, February 4: *NY Daily News*, February 5: *Chicago Tribune*, February 5 and 8: *New York Times*, February 11, and *New York Journal American*, February 12.

7. McCarthy's speech: Full text, Schrecker, pp. 211-215. When McCarthy entered the speech into the *Congressional Record* (February 20), he reduced the number of subversives from 205 to 57.

8. Hoover's articles in *U.S. News*, August 11: *Educational Forum*, May: and *Coronet*, December. Other political pieces with Hoover's byline in 1950 appeared in *Education*, the *New York Times Magazine* (see Bibliography), *Elks Magazine*, *Scholastic*, and *American City*.

9. Hoover's warning of Red uprisings in France: Richard Gid Powers, *Not Without Honor*, p. 194. He also bombarded the White House with reports of undercover Communists in government, frequently targeting Treasury Department official Harry Dexter White. Called before HUAC while recovering from a heart attack in the summer of 1948, White died three days later.

10. "... might hit upon a 'super-duper' atom bomb and be off to Russia.": Senator Knowland, quoted in Dupre and Lakoff, p. 128: HUAC's attack on scientists: R. Williams *(Klaus Fuchs)*, p. 161.

11. Twenty thousand to fifty thousand out of work: Caute, p. 461.

12. NIH blacklist: Holmes, pp. 244-245, and Bryce Nelson. *Science*, July 18, 1969, p. 269, and January 9, 1970, pp. 154-56.

13. Interviews with Lederman, May 1998, and Seifter, January 26, 1998.

14. Einstein's ten-dollar contribution to Struik's Defense: The Einstein file, Section 8, p. 89.

15. Interview with Struik, May 1999, in his home in Belmont, Massachusetts. Under the Massachusetts Anti-Anarchy Law, first passed in 1919, Sruik faced up to five and a half years in jail if convicted. Dr. George Sarton, Harvard professor emeritus of the History of Science, headed a committee "of more than sixty professors, clergymen, and other citizens...to raise funds for the defense of Professor Struik" *(New York, Times*, December 5, 1951).

Struik made no secret of his socialist sympathies, writing and speaking publicly in support of Marxism, the Soviet Union, and indicted Communist Party officials, several of whom were his friends. But as for attempting to overthrow Massachusetts: "Absolute nonsense" was the way Struik described the charges, according to the *Times*. "The Netherlands-born Professor of Mathematics...declared that he was a 'Marxist scholar'...[and] was in sympathy with the communist fight for civil rights but disliked party discipline."

13. SPY HUNT 1: FUCHS

1. The FBI tailed Oppenheimer when he traveled from Los Alamos: FBI's Oppenheimer file, memo from Mickey Ladd, Document 65. "Army security officers hounded [Oppenheimer] mercilessly [and) interrogated him frequently...": Rhodes *(Atomic Bomb)*, p. 571.

2. Interview with Rotblat, October 2, 1996 (London).

3. "...the greatest single contribution to Moscow's ability...": Wolf, p. 253: quoting Soviet nuclear scientist Igor Kurchatov: Fuchs "saved him several years of research": p. 256.

4. Fuchs didn't work in the area of plutonium chemistry: Herken, p. 322. The debate on how much Fuchs gave the Russians is somewhat out of date today, but included:

"There is little doubt the Russians would have made the atom bomb without Fuchs": Princeton physicist Henry DeWolf Smyth, author of the landmark 1945 Report "Atomic Energy for Military Purposes" *(Bulletin of Atomic Scientists,* 1950).

Shortly after Fuchs' arrest, Robert Oppenheimer told a meeting of the State Department Policy Review Group: "If the Russians were able to make any advances... on the basis of the information they received from Fuchs, they were marvelous indeed." *(Foreign Relations of the U.S., 1945-50,* published by U.S. State Dept., 1950, vol. I, p. 173).

Military analyst Herbert York cited a number of factors in the Soviets' atom bomb program, which "argue that espionage did not play an essential role." But York (p. 37), writing in 1976, added, "Unfortunately, there is as yet not enough information to form a certain judgment."

The Joint Congressional Committee on Atomic Energy declared in 1951 that Fuchs did more damage "than any other spy, not only in the history of the United States, but in the history of nations." Such shrill congressional charges were common during the McCarthy period and often had little relationship to facts. But in this case, the Committee, while still shrill and exaggerating, was not too far off.

5. Fuchs on the postwar tripartite review committee: Reported by Rotblat during my interview with him (fn. 10, above), and his subsequent letter, July 24, 1998.

6. General Groves' anti-British buck-passing, *New York World Telegram,* February 4, 1950: "...anti-American sentiment among the British...": Moss, pp. 174-76.

7. "Ali hell broke loose...": Lamphere and Shachtman, p. 137.

8. "FBI teams were mobilized across the country...": more than five hundred suspects: Albright, pp. 214-215.

9. Bethe: "A scientist...works for the world": The FBI's Fuchs "Foocase" files File 4, 1975 Series-show that Hoover ordered that Hans Bethe be placed under surveillance (Herken, p. 322). "Perhaps the greatest impediment...": Bethe, cited by Caute, p. 462.

10. The Tellers' close friendship with Fuchs: my interview with Priscilla MacMillan at Harvard's Center for Russian Studies, June 5, 1998: Hoover's pursuit of Teller partly because of Hall, who was already, in 1950, high on the FBI's list of suspects: Albright, pp. 215-216. Before Teller's turn to the right, he supported "world government" in 1948 as "our only hope for survival.": Rhodes *(Atomic Bomb),* p. 766.

11. On Hoover's morning routine: Crawford picked him up at 8:30, etc., and quotes from Allen: Demaris in *Esquire* ("The Private Life of JEH,") September 1974. Sullivan and Wick quotes: Demaris *(The Director),* pp. 30-31.

12. Rushmore not only worked for McCarthy, he gave the senator access to his information from FBI files: Theoharis and Cox, p. 283. Rushmore apparently also had access to files of the Immigration and Naturalization Service. One of his columns included a before-the-fact report on the INS attempt to deport Sophie Gerson, the wife of a Communist Party official: Caute, p. 227.

13. "This astonishingly dense person...": *New York Times,* December 14, 1967.

14. Ladd's rise through the ranks due to "loyalty": Gentry, p. 369. "...Ladd was in charge of *all* investigations...": My interview with Moore, in his house, November 6, 1997.

15. FBI Einstein file 100-32986, memo from McKee to Hoover, may 17, 1949

16. LA dismissed Kimbrough's story: Memos from LA SAC, May 5 and May 17, 1949: Ladd's confirming memo to Hoover, March 10, 1950 (Einstein file, Section 1).

17. J. Edgar Hoover in the *New York Times Magazine,* April 18, 1950. Favorable information as much as negative: *New York Times,* March 29, 1953, Section IV.

18. Emma Rabbeis letter, written February 25, 1950 and translated by the FBI, as well as a two-paragraph "Translator's Summary" ("Dr. Einstein is not altogether politically untainted") are both strangely missing from the newly released version (March 2000) of the Einstein file. They are contained in Section 1 of the file that the Bureau released in 1983. It's possible that the FBI reviewers found some previously unrecognized threat to national security in the two documents and without giving any explanation, withheld them. It seems more likely that in the confusion that apparently has affected many aspects of the FBI recently, someone accidentally spilled coffee on the pages or they were simply lost in the paper shuffle.

19. FBI's Heineman file memos dated May 2, 1947, and Sept. 22, 1949.

20. See note 27.

21. "...all information in her possession...": Hoover as quoted in Moss, p. 174.

22. *Ibid.,* p. 173: Since Einstein was not involved in the Manhattan Project or work on the bomb, Kristel Heineman's "report" reflected an "obviously distorted mind."

23. All specific references to these interviews, conducted February 2, 5, 10, and 14, are drawn, unless otherwise indicated, from the FBI's Heineman file, including memos from Agent Gordon to Boston SAC, Boston office to Hoover, and Hoover to Boston office, February 5, 7, 13, 16, 17, September 28, and (final report from Agent Gordon, listing Dr. Hadley as T-1) December 2, 1950 FBI file No. *65-3304. Espionage-R.*

24. The FBI also showed Ms. Heineman photos of: Arthur Weber, Abraham Rothman, Martin Deutsch, Gerhard Wolland, and Alexander Bogrow. (Memos: Agent Gordon to Boston SAC, February 13, 1950 and February 16, 1950.

25. Robert Heineman first told FBI agents his wife had told him Einstein "was instrumental in gaining the release of Fuchs from internment," but then told them that he (Robert) knew of "no direct relationship between Fuchs and Einstein" (Einstein file, Section 3, p. 240, Section 6, p. 1072).

26. Einstein file (Section 1): G-2 (MID) Report on Rabbeis interview: VIII-12915/D-137899, June 22, 1950.

27. Fuchs "knew of no activity" by Einstein "on his behalf.": FBI Einstein file, Correlation Report, January 1953, p. 1081.

28. G-2 promise to send more meaty report: Cover letter with Rabbeis interview, stamped July 31, 1950.

14. FAR OUT

1. Mrs. Apostolina's tale: Einstein file, Section 2, Correlation Report, p. 32.

2. Death-ray tale: *Ibid.,* Correlation Report, pp. 76, 852.

3. Sheafe's tale: *Ibid.,* Section 1, February 10, 1950.

4. Lloyd's tale: *Ibid.,* Section 7, letter to Hoover, April 21, 1953.

5. FBI's investigation of Lloyd's tale: *Ibid,* Section 9. Confidential FBI Report, LA 105-1636: Internal Security-R (for Russia).

15. SPY HUNT 2: OPERATION CABLE-DROP

1. Unless otherwise indicated, documents relating to Einstein's alleged Berlin cable-drop connection are from the FBI's Einstein file, Part I, and G-2 files in the National Archives.

2. Grosskopf was arrested by the Nazis in 1933 but survived the war, and at the time of this G-2 report in 1950, he was chief of police in Soviet-controlled East Berlin. Besides Grosskopf, the others listed as having known about the Einstein cable-drop are: Paul Ruegg, Wilhelm Bahnik, Friedrich (Fritz) Burde, Herrmann Duennow, Albert Gromulat, Alfred Kattner, Karl Hans Kippenberger, Dr. Gruenther Kromrey, Johannes Liebers, Leo Roth, Adolf Sauter, Elena Welker, Wilhelm (Willi) Wloch, Karl Wloch, and Wilhelm Zaisser. Of these, Burde, Liebers, and Zaisser were reportedly members of the Ruegg/Noulens group in Shanghai. The subsequent espionage activities of each of these men is described in detail in the report. (Kattner, for example, was "turned" by the Nazis and became a double agent before he "was eventually liquidated by the Communist underground in about 1934.")

The five "couriers" who allegedly picked up cables at Einstein's house included Burde, Kattner, Willi Wloch, and Grosskopf, who, *Source* said, was the liaison man for only about three months in 1929. The fifth courier was a man *Source* identified only as "Fritz."

3. Einstein "...must have become aware...": For the sake of brevity, the cited paragraph combines excerpts from both G-2 reports and the FBI's later Summary Report (p. 8) of August 5, 1953.

4. "...which of us to lock up...": Wise, *The American Police State*, p. 313.

5. Hoover's statements and escalating numbers of Reds: Capehart in *Chicago Tribune*, February 8, 1950 (p. 3): Mundt in *NY JA* (p. 1), February 12, 1950: 12,000 Communists, *Washington Post*, September 8, 1950 (p. 19): 14,000 Reds, *NY Times*, April 28, 1951 (p. 1).

6. Welch interview, June 16, 1998.

7. "...identity of informants...": Hoover's request for information, dated October 23, 1950, went first to G-2 Assistant Chief of Staff John Weckerling in Washington, who relayed it to Major Hudson, director of intelligence for the U.S. Army in Europe, along with an explanation of the whole Einstein-espionage situation to date.

8. G-2's recommendation "that RSHA personnel be interviewed" and that "...no further exploitation of *Source* be made..." as well as their estimate that *Source* "...is probably accurate...": G-2 report of January 25, 1951, in both the FBI's Einstein file and National Archives' G-2 files.

9. G-2's door-to-door investigators in Germany were Gustav Bard and Joseph Hotter, both from CIC Region VIII. Excerpts cited are from their memos of February 14 and March 29, 1951.

10. "...the possibility of compromise...": November 26, 1952 memo from Eucom to G-2 headquarters in Washington.

"...requires extreme discretion.": Cover letter to Hoover, sent with the January 25, 1951 report, by G-2 Assistant Chief of Staff Paul G. Guthrie. From FBI's Einstein file and CIC files in National Archives.

11. "Paean from Pravda," *Newsweek*, May 22, 1947, pp. 29-30.

12. Einstein's letters to Sharp dated April 2, 19 and 16, and June 17, 1953: Nathan, pp. 543-545: Sharp's last letter to Einstein, November 6, 1953, mailed from the federal penitentiary in Danbury, CT: Nathan, p. 677.

13. ...forty such anti-communist films... : Zinn, p. 139: production peaked in 1952: Whitfield, pp. 134-136.

14. State sedition acts: Caute, p. 71, citing, among other sources, *Political and Civil Rights in the United States* (p. 429), by Thomas I. Emerson and David Haber.

15. Walk-in witness: FBI Einstein file (Section 9). The memo from SAC Miami (100-12677) to SAC Newark (100-32986), September 4, 1953, was sent by registered mail, a means of communication rarely used by the FBI in that pre-computer, pre-fax era.

16. Hentschel, a Teaching Fellow at the Technical University of Berlin, identified Weyland as the Miami informant in his 1990 letter to *ISIS*, 81: 2: 307. It was corroborated in incontrovertible detail in 1992 by Kleinert (University of Halle). Professor Kleinert's lecture, "Paul Weyland, the Einstein-Killer from Berlin," to a Sigma Xi luncheon at Smith College, December 8, 1992, was printed in an expanded version in *HOST*, v. 3, No. 1, January 1995. ISSN No. 1192-084 X. The combined evidence of these two pieces leaves not the slightest doubt that the September 4, 1953 "walk-in witness" was Weyland.

17. A translation of Einstein's entire article in the August 27, 1920 *Berliner Tageblatt*—"*My* Answer re: Theory of Anti-relativity, Inc."—is reprinted (4 pages, single-spaced) in the FBI's Einstein file. The translation by Olivia B. McMahon is dated December 2, 1953. It also appears *in* an anthology, edited by Gerald Tauber, on Einstein's General Theory of Relativity.

18. "...science is racial...": Lenard in *Deutsche Physik*, v. IV., cited by Clark, p. 639.

19. "The German Foreign Office believed that Ford was a financial supporter of Weyland": Brian, p. 110.

20. Most of the biographical material on Weyland (e.g., Weyland's postwar job as interpreter, p. 7: his U.S. citizenship, p. 9) comes from Kleinert's detailed research summarized in *HOST*, *op.* cit. Additional sources include Hentschel, Folsing, and Frank.

21. References to Ruegg and Sorge: Einstein file (Section 8), Summary Report, pp. 11-12. Cameo appearances: Ruegg's name (alias Hilaire Noulens) did appear in the original G-2 charges against Einstein, but the specific allegation about his use of the scientist's address is totally new. Sorge's name was not mentioned at all in G-2's original charges. His name does appear once in the Einstein file, on page 1150 of the Correlation Report, which refers to a G-2 report of August 2, 1951 on "The Richard Sorge Case," which includes "Miscellaneous Records," one of which mentions Einstein's name.

22. "...soup kitchens...": Gibarti's Comintern activities described in letter (March 27, 2000) from former FBI employee Susan Rosenfeld citing Gibarti's letter of March 22, 1930 to the secretariat of the USCP. (Emory University, Theodre Draper Papers, Box 1, Polder 23.)

23. Gibarti left the Party in 1938: my interview with Andy Rabinbach, June 7, 2001.

24. Gibarti's friend and closest colleague was Willi Muenzenberg, one of the Comintern's top organizers. In 1938, Muenzenberg criticized Stalin's xenophobia, and was expelled in early 1939. The Stalin-Hitler pact led Muenzenberg to launch an anti-Stalinist journal, based in Paris. When the Nazis arrived, he headed south but was murdered shortly after he left Paris. Some say he was done in by Stalin's agents, but at least as much evidence points to the Nazis as his killers.

25. Gibarti was paid 20,000 francs: FBI's Einstein file, Section 6, p. 1071: Gibarti's Senate Internal Security Subcommittee testimony: FBI's Gibarti file (61-6629). Gibarti's FBI testimony about Einstein in January 1951: FBI's Einstein dossier, Section 2, p. 25 (pages released in 2000), and Section 8, p. 97.

26. "...both sides of the political aisle": Telephone interview with Gruber in Paris, June 3, 2001.

27. "Oh, that's the little physicist...": Thomas Kuczynski's e-mail message about his grandfather Robert, August 5, 2001. The same message reports: "My grandfather admired all the time Einstein's 'wise unpretentiousness.'" Also: *Freunde und Gute Bekannte. Gesprache mit Thomas Grimm,* by Juergen Kuczynski, Berlin, 1997, pp. 36-38.

28. The KPD "utilized" Robert Kuczynski: Louis Gibarti, quoted in the FBI's Einstein file, Section 6, p. 1121.

29. "...most brilliant Soviet agent.": Volkman, p. 122.

30. Ruth Werner/Ursula Kuczynski, also known by her code-name Tonya, died at the age of ninety-three on July 7, 2000, in Berlin. The *New York Times* obituary (July 23) called her "a colorful and successful Soviet spy whose exploits included radioing invaluable atomic bomb data to Moscow."

Juergen introduced Fuchs to Soviet agents: and Ruth's transmissions of Fuchs "squiggles" from the U.K. saved the Soviets years: Wolf, pp. 255-256: Polmar and Allen, p. 320.

31. "It will be appreciated...": Hoover letter to G-2, October 14, 1953 (Einstein file, Section 9).

16. "UNDESIRABLE ALIEN"

1. INS newsletter: Not to be confused with the left-wing magazine, *Monthly Review,* which published Einstein's *Why Socialism* essay in 1949.
2. "A number were badly beaten...": *New York Times,* November 8, 1919, reporting on the first of the two raids.
3. "Lawless acts of a mob.": Lowenthal, p. 137.
4. Rankin, from Mississippi: *Detroit Times,* October 28, 1945.
5. Morality articles: *The Tablet,* February 11, 18 and 25, 1950.
6. HOOVER CITES...: *The Tablet,* February 27, 1954.
7. Pais calls it "strikingly anti-Semitic.": *Einstein Lived Here,* p. 210.
8. "...always right.": See references to *Brooklyn Tablet* in Crosby *(God Church and Flag).*
9. 8,226 "subversives" investigated: Schrecker *(Science & Society),* p. 416: "The Justice Department's aim...": Caute, p. 227, Harriman quote, p. 230, statistics on deportations, etc., pp. 226-229.
10. "...aliens as wicked people...": Texas Congressman Maury Maverick, quoted by Caute p. 231: same page: "...bigoted, destructive and arrogant." Caute cites INS District Directors Ed Shaughnessy in New York and Ed Barber in San Francisco as prime examples.
11. The Legion's Contact Program: described in FBI files, quoted by Theoharis, *"The Boss,"* pp. 193-198.
12. Wiggins approval: Zimmerman memo in FBI's Einstein file, Adj. 2185-P-4009: Kelly follow-up memo to Hoover: Einstein file, C-5013865 Irv.
13. "Once he resolved...": Initially, a turf battle between the FBI and INS had stalled the Einstein denaturalization effort. By maneuvering memos among FBI offices in Washington, Newark, and Philadelphia, asking, requesting, and advising in the unmistakable language of delay—"who has authority to issue clearance to proceed within the designated jurisdiction," etc.—Hoover effectively blocked the project for nearly *two years.* It was only after the FBI and INS had gotten past that inter-agency jockeying—Commissioner Mackey's arrival seemed to help—that Hoover finally resolved to work in partnership with the INS on the Einstein case.
14. FBI memo from Newark office to Hoover with copy to INS, Philadelphia, February 23, 1952: SECRET and CONFIDENTIAL. Title: Albert Einstein. Tagged INTERNAL SECURITY-R [for Russia]).
15. Most of the pages that "originated with the INS" were actually records the INS obtained from HUAC, other congressional committees, and the Office of Naval Intelligence. One committee that sent a report on Einstein (again, listing the same "subversive" affiliations) to the INS in late 1953 was something called the "Senate Subcommittee Overlooking Subversion in Government Departments"—a

name that defies logic, whichever meaning of the word "overlooking" one chooses to use.
16. HUAC and Tarantino: From the INS Einstein file.

17. TURNING TIDES

1. "...roughly ten thousand" jobs lost according to Yale's Ralph S. Brown: Schrecker, *Age of McCarthyism*, p. 76. The Committee gave data on 60,000 people to employers: Caute, pp. 102-103.
2. ...fifty-one separate investigations: Gelhorn, p. 117: "over a hundred hearings...": Rabinowitz, p. 115.
3. In 1952 and again in 1955, House Speaker Sam Rayburn ordered TV cameras barred from hearing rooms, and HUAC's own rules gave a witness the right to refuse to be televised (see Caute, p. 94). Nonetheless, TV cameras were a fixture at most congressional hearings.
4. Einstein's "depression" letters: Indiana letter, cited by Nathan, p. 538-39: "...the dear Americans have assumed the Germans' place..." and "...one stands by, powerless." (to Queen Mother Elizabeth, January 6, 1951): Nathan, p. 554: "...hardly ever felt as alienated..." (to Gertrude Warschauer, July 15, 1950): Calaprice, p. 24: "Saddest of all..." (to Elizabeth, January 3, 1952): Nathan, p. 562.
5. ...book-banning: "The purge, especially distressing Mann and Einstein was that of books and of teachers....": Belfrage, p. 92.
6. Robin Hood a "Red": Diverse media coverage, including *NY Times,* November 14, 15, 17, 1953.
7. *New York Times* Shaftsbury story, October 29, 1953. UPI dispatch on loyalty oaths, datelined Chicago, January 18.
8. Nazi book-burning: Friedrich, p. 385, and Frank, p. 237.
9. January 31, 1951 to the editor of *The New Republic*. Cited by Nathan, p. 554.
10. "...rallying educators and the public to resist...": letter from William Frauenglass, May 1953 (source: Richard Frauenglass).

"...incorrigible nonconformist": Einstein's recorded remarks were broadcast on the radio May 4, 1953, as he accepted an award from Lord & Taylor for nonconformity in science. Although the award recognized only his *scientific* nonconformity, Einstein consciously made the link to politics. He donated the award money, $1,000, to the American Committee for Emigré Scholars (a group that Hoover somehow neglected to include on his list of "Communist fronts": Nathan, p. 591. Text of the taped address in *Ideas and Opinions,* pp. 35-36.

"...ingrate immigrant...": Pegler's syndicated column, June 14, 1955.

"...freeloader ...above the laws...": in the official publication of the California Republican State Committee, March 1954: Gerald L. K. Smith: *New York Times,* April 23, 1955, p. 8.

"...should not be permitted to impede...": AP dispatch on O'Conner's speech to the Pennsylvania Railroad Holy Name Society in Philadelphia, June 14, 1953. (Pais, *Einstein Lived Here,* p. 240.)
12. The *Times'* dismissal of journalists, and even print-shop employees, with suspected communist sympathies, described in Aronson, pp. 145-146. For a more detailed account of loyalty purges inside major media, see Caute, Chapter 24, pp. 446-455.
13. Source of Wuchinich notes and quotes, unless otherwise indicated: interview with Sarah and David Wuchinich in Sarah's home in Mt. Kisco, NY, November 11, 1998, and correspondence with David.

14. Details of Wuchinich's parachute drop behind Nazi lines to join the Yugoslav guerrillas come from David Wuchinich and from *Secret Warriors,* documentary aired on The History Channel, January 1999. RAF Special Duty Squadron No. 143, assigned to drop agents and supplies behind Nazi lines in the Balkans, used British Halifax and Hudson bombers and a few American B-24 Liberators.

15. "...their political background didn't fit our German operation": Persico, p. 82.

16. *"Captain* Wuchinich...": Nelson, p. 306; also OSS sent Wuchinich to China...: his weekly radio program aired on WLOA in Braddock, PA: although he never joined the Party...: unable to find steady work.

17. The Wuchinich and Frauenglass news coverage also ran in adjacent columns in *Time* magazine, June 22, 1953.

Excerpts from Einstein's letter to Wuchinich, courtesy Sarah and David Wuchinich.

"Restrict myself to having publicly and clearly stated my position.": Letter to Shadowitz January 14, 1954 in Einstein Archives. The letter explains: "You must...consider that many people in a similar position are approaching me."

18. Quotes, unless otherwise indicated, are from conversations with Shadowitz at his home in Tarpon Springs, Florida, June 15, 1998.

19. "...the well-known subterfuge...of the Fifth Amendment...": From Einstein's original letter to Frauenglass, later deleted, by mutual agreement, from the version published in the *New York Times* on June 12, 1953. Source: Richard Frauenglass.

20. "...taking the Fifth...an 'admission of guilt' ": Einstein told the *Newark News* (December 17, 1953) that he had "advised" Shadowitz to use the First Amendment as the basis for refusing to answer the committee. Einstein clearly had second thoughts about having gone along with Frauenglass' use of the Fifth Amendment. He said so directly when the Frauenglass family visited him. (Source: Tillie Frauenglass notes provided by Richard Frauenglass.) Regrets are also found in Einstein's letter to Corliss Lamont, January 2, 1954 (Einstein Archives, Princeton University).

21. The eventual ruling by the U.S. Court of Appeals that "the subject of 'subversive activity' was outside the committee's jurisdiction" came in July 1955, nearly a year after McCarthy's demise.

22. FBI's Einstein file on Frauenglass and Shadowitz: Section 9, June 24, 1954 and November 23, 1953.

23. Wuchinich blackout in FBI file: The classification code listings on the blacked-out paragraphs indicate that the information was:

(b)(l)(A) "specifically authorized...to be kept secret in the interest of national defense or foreign policy... " and

(b)(2) "related solely to the internal personnel rules and practices of an agency:" and

(b)(7)(D) "could reasonably be expected to disclose the identity of a confidential source..."

—From "Explanation of Exemptions" Subsections of Title 5, U.S. Code, Section 552 (Freedom of Information Act).

24. Nathan thought Einstein seemed frightened, and the two discussed withdrawing the Frauenglass letter: Sayen (interview with Nathan), p. 272.

25. Nathan filed a successful suit, forcing the State Department to return his passport in 1955 after he declared he was not a member of the Communist Party: he was acquitted of the Contempt of Congress charges in 1957.

26. "...only by speaking out": "On the Negro Question," *Out of My Later Years,* p. 133.

27. Statistics on NYC teachers fired: Iversen, p. 267: *New York Times,* Sept. 15, 1953, *NY Herald Tribune,* January 7, 1954 (cited by Caute, p. 610).

NOTES   367

28. Eisenhower's landslide victory in November 1952 was widely attributed in large part to his pledge to end the war ("I'll go to Korea").

29. Senator Lehman's "creeping McCarthyism" speech to the Democratic State Committee, April 29, 1953, reported in the next day's *New York Times*. Media coverage of these examples includes *New York Times* May 17 and 21 and CLER ICS VEHEMENT ON 'M'CARTHYISM': July 6, 1953, p. I ("...the threat of McCarthyism to intellectual freedom").

30. McCarthy a nut case: President Eisenhower publicly criticized McCarthy for "book burning," in a speech at Dartmouth, June 14, 1953, and again on June 26 ("a zealot"), echoed a few days later by Vice-President Nixon, and on July 3 by Attorney General Brownell and Michigan's Republican Senator Potter. Even North Dakota's Senator Mundt, known for his right-wing views, chimed in. *(New York Times* page-one articles, June 15, 27 and July 4, 1953: for Senator Mundt, July 6, p. 10.)

31. Not a political activist: "It would not be in the best interests of the cause were I to engage in political action, such as speaking before assemblies or sending messages to them. If I should do so, I would be regarded more as a political partisan than simply as an individual with a social conscience and certain convictions on public issues."— Einstein letter to War Resisters League, January 29, 1954: Nathan, p. 599.

32. Novikoff's letter to Einstein and his response, courtesy of Phyllis Novikoff. (For more on Novikoff, see David Holmes' book on his case: also Schrecker, *No Ivory Tower*, and Caute.) Background on Einstein Medical College: interview with Prof. Sam Seifter and Phyllis Novikoff at the college, January 26, 1998.

33. "...good for our morale": letter to author from Irving Adler, September 28, 2000: two more teachers refuse to answer: *New York Times*, December 19 and 22, 1953; 100 pacifists pledge: Nathan p. 598.

34. Source of Frauenglass notes and quotes, including Tillie Frauenglass's record of the family's June 30, 1953 visit with Einstein: Richard Frauenglass, interviewed January 4, 1999 at his home on New York's Long Island. William Frauenglass died in 1998. Tillie was in a nursing home. "My father's legacy to me was to ingrain in me a sense of honesty, even as a child," Richard explained. "It was only later that I realized the social importance of what he had done."

35. At the time, Helen Dukas asked the Frauenglass family not to publicize their visit. Honoring that request, the family kept their notes a guarded secret. In releasing this information forty-five years later, Richard Frauenglass writes, "It is felt that the spirit and intent of Ms. Dukas' request has not been compromised."

36. "...never seen him so cheerful...": Kahler quoted by Sayen, p. 272.

37. "Enfant terrible...": Letter from Einstein to Queen Mother, Elizabeth, March 28, 1954. Nathan, p. 604.

38. Despite the fact that the plumbers union conferred Einstein with an honorary membership (a reflection of his celebrity), this statement reveals an interesting information gap in Einstein's knowledge. If Einstein had actually been a plumber, he would have been required to sign a non-communist loyalty oath or lose his job. The leadership of the plumbers union, like that of most unions, went along completely with the McCarthy/Hoover campaign and required their members, even their apprentices, to sign loyalty oaths. The construction trades included the most loyalty-oathed jobs in the country.

18. THE UNRAVELING

1. The translated article reached Hoover on December 4, 1953: The Einstein file (Section 9).

2. Gibarti's testimony against Juergen Kuczynski: In a not-unusual FBI snafu, their interview with Gibarti, blacked out in the version of Einstein's file released in 1983, is cleared in their recently released pages in Section 2 (p. 25), but Gibarti's name remains blacked out in Section 8 (p. 97).

3. "...of which Einstein was in charge": Einstein's dossier (Section 8), Summary Report, p. 12. Phone calls from Stein: p. 12 and p. 119 (Section 8).

4. Kuczynski's memoirs: Describing his visit to Einstein in May 1938, the memoirs report that the previous time Juergen had seen Einstein was "six years earlier," in 1932, before Einstein had moved to the U.S. After the visit, the next contact recorded in JK's memoirs was a letter from Einstein that he received in London a year later, in 1939. *(Memoiren,* Berlin, 1972, pp. 309-311.) Far from having "frequently visited" Einstein: Gibarti could have made up the part about frequent visits or, as seems more likely, the FBI could have garbled the story. In the FBI's first report on their interview with Gibarti in 1951, it was Robert Kuczynski, not his son Juergen, who "frequently visited" his old friend in Princeton: "Gibarti stated that Robert Kuczynski went frequently to Princeton to see Einstein..." (Einstein file, Section 6, p. 1121, New York memo, February 9, 1951.) In his Summary Report, Murphy could have miscopied the earlier memo, accidentally or otherwise, since frequent visits from Juergen would appear to be more incriminating than visits by his father.

5. Kuczynski's spy career: Polmar and Allen, pp. 319-320.

6. FBI censors have blacked out or withheld 80 percent: FBI Gibarti file (61-6629), memos of October 8 and 17, 1951.

7. ...distributed to INS and G-2: Hoover letter, October 14, 1953 (Section 9).

8. "...humanitarian...": Memos to Hoover March 26 and May 17, 1954 (Section 9).

9. couldn't—or wouldn't—come up with anything: Memo from G-2 in Heidelberg to Hoover, December 15, 1953: "G-2...has received no instructions to conduct further investigation...": Einstein's FBI dossier (Section 9): "It will be appreciated...": Hoover's memo to G-2, October 14, 1953. Hoover sent G-2 similar requests on December 5, 1951, September 1, 1952, and in 1954 on January 15, June 17, and September 21: Einstein's dossier and G-2 files, National Archives. W. A. Perry's "Investigation is pending" response: June 24, 1954.

10. ...fan the flames of discontent: The United States "had waged an active propaganda campaign that encouraged dissatisfaction with the Communist regime [but] had not worked directly to foster open rebellion." (CIA "Documents on Intelligence War in Berlin, 1946-1961," released, June, 1999.)

11. von Laue interview: Memo from G-2 Agents Sylvester and Tangney (66th CIC), dated September 1, 1954, from both FBI and G-2 files.

12. "Helen Dukas, according to informants, has corresponded with one Otto Katz...": Einstein file, Section 3, p. 317 (1944 letter) and p. 394.

13. Pravdin contact: Einstein file, Section 6, p. 1159.

14. Katz, "according to the files of the NY office, was a reported Soviet agent and was presently writing for the *Freies Deutschland* . . . in Mexico City...": Einstein file, Section 3, p. 317. Katz, who often used the pseudonym Andre Simone, was the chief editor of *The Brown Book of Hitler Terror and the Burning of the Reichstag,* published in London in 1933, just months after the Nazi regime came to power. *The Brown Book* was sponsored by the World Committee of the Victims of German Fascism, whose honorary chairman was Albert Einstein. Another possible nonespionage reason for calls from Katz could

have been to discuss articles in left-leaning publications such as the German-Jewish periodical *Aufbau*. Einstein had three articles in *Aufbau* in 1940, three in 1944, three in 1945, and one in 1946. *(Bibliographical Checklist and Index to the Collected Writings.)*

15. Hoover's letter to Brownell, July 27, 1953, exposing the McCarthy-Spellman-Kennedy plot: Gentry, p. 436: Hoover's split with McCarthy: Nash, p. 107.: "McCarthy, pushed by...Senator William Benton (D., Conn.) and a few others to identify [his sources], blurted out that he possessed a chart prepared by the FBI...Hoover...swiftly denied [its] existence."

16. "...new phase of the Cold War...": Theoharis *(The Boss)*, p. 302.

17. "...because of her close connection to Albert Einstein...": January 9, 1955 memo from Agent Branigan to A. W. Belmont at FBI headquarters.

18. Dukas interview February 23, 1955, in both FBI's Einstein file and G-2 files in National Archives.

19. Since Newark was the FBI office coordinating the Einstein investigation, it had sent out Murphy's Summary Report. New York was apparently the FBI office Gibarti reported to. The New York SAC reported to Hoover on May 23, May 26, and May 27 that letters of November 23, 1953 and January 15, 1954, as well as the 1953 Summary had been "changed to properly attribute the information to Gibarti by name and character-ization [T-136]." On June 8, the Newark SAC sent memos to thirteen FBI offices around the country that had previously received Vince Murphy's Summary. Newark advised all these offices to make appropriate changes and deletions in that report.

19. EINSTEIN THE SPY?

1. "...Einstein was aware that his Berlin office was used...": Liaison Report (G-2 to INS), December 30, 1952 (Ernest J. Hover, acting investigator, Investigations Division, ID No.'s: C-5013865, C-5013867, p. 8. The newly declassified (after my appeal) report was released to me on April 21, 1999 with a cover letter from Russell A. Nichols, chief, FOI and Privacy Office, U.S. Army Intelligence.

Even after being redeclassified, nearly eight pages of the ten-page report remain blacked out. The section quoted is from one of its few unredacted paragraphs.

Revealingly, the same report (p. 9) describes the unsupported 1932 anti-Einstein accusations from the Woman Patriot Corporation simply as "an interesting document."

2. Einstein's "other office": Litten: "Einstein and the Noulens Affair," *British Journal for the History of Science* (1991, 24, 465-7).

3. The sixteen who knew about the alleged Einstein cable-drop: See Endnote 2, Chapter 15, above.

4. "...no connection with any organization or institution.": January 25, 1951 memo from G-2 to Hoover, Einstein file, Section 1.

5. Einstein "...must have become aware...":

6. "...so fond of his rural existence.": Folsing, p. 615.

7. Seventy-five arrested at Berlin protest: *New York Times* September 8, 1930, p. 3.

8. *International Cable Register of the World,* compiled: and published [in English, Spanish, French and German] by the International Cable Directory Company, New York and London. None of the directory's editions, from 1915 through 1931, contain any listing for Einstein.

9. Einstein's alleged listing in the Cable Directory: Einstein file, Section 1, G-2 memo to Hoover, January 25, 1951. The same memo includes the statement that Einstein received a flood of international cables "from around the world."

10. Einstein's fiftieth birthday greetings from around the world, and absence of international cables over the years: Einstein Archives, Princeton. Two Western Union telegrams were delivered to Einstein's house, but they were addressed to his home on Haberlandstrasse, not to an international cable address.

11. Einstein's "trip" to Russia: Frank, pp. 203-204.

12. The National Conference on the German Problem met at the Waldorf Astoria. Besides Einstein and Mrs. Roosevelt, others attending included Henry Morgenthau, Jr., Sumner Welles, Helen Gehagan Douglas, and former Ambassador to France, William Bullitt: Higham *(American Swastika)*, p. 205.

13. "German specialists and scientists in the U.S. under the protective custody of the Joint Intelligence Objectives Agency," cited in a memo from Ladd to Hoover, January 6, 1947 (p. 632 of Correlation Report in the Einstein file).
"...Einstein was among those who did protest." In the same memo, Ladd also reports reading about the protesting group in a *New York Times* article, December 30, 1946.

14. "...Nazis...accepted by the West...: Polmar and Allen, p. 233.

15. "...the FBI also had its share of Nazis...": Postwar recruitment of Nazis to FBI and CIA, Loftus/Aarons, pp. 223-4:
Valerian Trifa: "...my good friend J. Edgar Hoover...": p. 224. "... instead of arresting them," p. 508.

16. G-2's "network...of former Nazis": Simpson in *Blowback*, p. 69.
—More records of "ex-Nazis working as inside sources for the CIA and FBI" can be found in the British Foreign Office microfilm files, and also the Berlin Document Center: Simpson, p. 210. Also, FBI File No. 105-40098 reportedly lists many of these former Nazis: Aarons/Loftus, p. 509.

17. The Einstein file, section 1, G-2 report, January 25, 1951.

18. "...from former well-placed KPD members.": Letter to Hoover, July 31, 1950, from G-2's Chief of Intelligence, Brigadier General John Weckerling (Einstein file, Section 1).

19. Markus Wolf interviewed in the Berlin Jewish Community Center, July 2000.

20. Extensive research in Germany has tentatively identified three men, from the list of sixteen, who, separately or in combination, could be *Source-former* Communists who switched to the Nazis and then to the U.S. Occupation forces after the war. But the research has not yet been published or peer-reviewed and until then, it would be irresponsible to mention their names.

21. Hentschel: Letter to ISIS, v. 81, No. 2, 1990, pp. 279-280.

CONCLUSION

1. Loftus and Aarons, p. 6: the wrong-man file, Folsom, pp. 128-144.

2. Vacuum-cleaner approach: Kessler, *The FBI*, p. 81.

3. Clark quoted by DeMaris ("Office Politics of JEH"), *Esquire*, November 1974, p. 144.

4. "Hoover Answers Ten Questions on the FBI," the *New York Times Magazine*, April 18, 1950.

5. Innocent victims: Schrecker *(Many Are the Crimes)*, pp. 275-277. Among the examples she cites:
Kendrick Cole, a fifty-year-old FDA inspector who liked camping, lost his job because, while hiking in the mountains, he had met some members of the Nature Friends of America (a group on the Subversive List) and paid them $1.50 for firewood.
Actor Everett Sloan was blacklisted in the early 1950s because the FBI confused his name with that of a former communist named Allan Sloane.

6. Caltech speech, February 16, 1931: Nathan, p. 122.

7. ...DOCTORED TESTS: *New York Times,* March 7, 2000: M.I.T. PHYSICIST SAYS PENTAGON 15 TRYING TO SILENCE HIM: *New York Times,* July 27, 2001.

8. "...the ugly underside of the McCarthy era.": Navasky in *The Nation,* July 16, 2001, p. 46.

9. "...to tire in that struggle...": tape-recorded address to the Decalogue Society of Chicago, February 20, 1954. *Ideas and Opinions,* pp. 37-39, and Nathan, pp. 600-601.

POSTSCRIPT

1. The report of an amorous relationship between Einstein and Konenkova and its unsubstantiated hints at an espionage connection are discussed in my *New York Times* op-ed article, "Looking at a Genius, Seeing a Spy," June 8, 1998. For more debunking of the spy story, see letter to the *Times* from Walter Schneir, June 5, 1998.

2. "...a complete fabrication.": Sagdeyev telephone interview, May 1998.

3. Romerstein and Breindel quote the FBI's Einstein file on p. 279.

Sources on Einstein

Aichelburg, Peter C., and Sexl, Roman U., ed., *Albert Einstein: His Influence on Physics, Philosophy and Politics,* Friedr. Vieweg & Sohn, Braunschweig/Weisbaden, 1979. Published under the auspices of the International Society on General Relativity and Gravitation.

Balibar, Francoise, *Einstein: Decoding the Universe,* Harry N. Abrams, Inc., Publishers, NY, 1993 (English translation, 2001).

Berlin, Isaiah and five others, *Einstein and Humanism,* papers from the Einstein Centennial Symposium, Jerusalem, 1979.

Bibliographical Checklist and Index to the Collected Writings of Albert Einstein, prepared by Nell Boni, Monique Russ, and Dan H. Lawrence, Pageant Books, Inc., Paterson, NJ, 1960.

Brunnauer, Lt. Stephen, "Einstein and the US Navy," *Heterogeneous Catalysis,* Washington, DC, 1983.

Brian, Denis, *Einstein, A Life,* John Wiley & Sons, Inc., NY, 1996.

Bucky, Peter A., *The Private Albert Einstein,* Andrews and McMeel, Kansas City, MO, 1992.

Calaprice, Alice, *The Ultimate Quotable Einstein,* Princeton Univ. Press, 2011.

Calder, Nigel, *Einstein's Universe,* Viking Press, NY, 1979.

Castagnetti, Giuseppe and Goenner, Hubert, "Albert Einstein as Pacifist and Democrat during World War I," *Science in Context,* 1996, 9, 4, pp. 325-386.

Clark, Ronald, W., *Einstein, The Life and Times,* Avon Books, 1972.

Cline, Barbara Lovett, *The Questioners,* Thomas Y. Crowell Co., NY, 1965.

Cohen, I. Bernard, "An Interview with Einstein," *Scientific American,* v. 193 (1955), pp. 68-73.

Dukas, Helen and Hoffman Banesh, eds., *Albert Einstein: The Human Side,* Princeton Univ. Press, 1979.

Eddington, Allen Boyce, ed., *Essential Einstein,* Pomegranate Artbooks, San Francisco, 1995.

Einstein, Albert, *The Evolution of Physics,* (with L. Infeld), Cambridge Univ. Press, 1947.

—, *Ideas and Opinions,* based on *Mein Weltbild,* introduction, Alan Lichtman, Modern Library, NY, 1994.

—, *Out of My Later Years,* The Philosophical Library, NY, 1950.

—, *The World As I See It (Mein Weltbild),* Amsterdam, 1934, revised edition edited by Carl Seelig, Zurich, 1953.

—, "Education & World Peace," *New York Times,* Nov. 24, 1934, p. 17.

—, "Message to the Southwide Conference on Discrimination in Higher Education," Atlanta Univ., 1950, *Discrimination in Higher Education,* SCEF, New Orleans, 1951.

—, "Most Fateful Decision in Recorded History," *Southern Patriot,* May 1949.

—, "The Arabs and Palestine," *Princeton Herald,* April 14 and 28, 1944.

—, "To American Negroes," *The Crisis* (NAACP magazine), 1932, Vol. 39, p. 45.

—, "Victim of Misunderstanding," London *Times* (letter), Sept. 16, 1933, p. 12.

—, "Why Socialism?" *Monthly Review,* Vol. I, No. 1, May, 1949.

Feier, Lewis S., *Einstein and the Generations of Science,* New Brunswick & London, 1982.

Fölsing, Albrecht, *Albert Einstein: A Biography,* Viking, 1997.

Frank, Philipp, *Einstein: His Life and Times,* 1947, Alfred A. Knopf, NY.

French, A. P., ed., *Einstein, A Centenary Volume,* Harvard Univ. Press, Cambridge, MA., 1979.

Golden, Fred, "Relativity's Rebel," *Time,* Dec. 31, 1999. Grundmann, Siegfried, *Einsteins Akte,* Springer, Berlin, 1998.

Grüning, Michael, *Ein Haus für Albert Einstein,* Verlag der Nation, Berlin, 1990. Herneck, Frederick, *Einstein Privat,* Buchverlag Der Morgen, Berlin, 1980.

Highfield, Roger, and Carter, Paul, *The Private Lives of Albert Einstein,* St. Martin's Press, NY, 1993.

Hoffmann, Banesh (with Helen Dukas), *Albert Einstein, Creator and Rebel,* Hart-Davis, MacGibbon, London, 1973.

Holton, Gerald, *Einstein, History and Other Passions,* Addison Wesley, NY, 1996. Holton, Gerald, and Elkana, Yehuda, ed., *Albert Einstein: Historical and Cultural Perspective,* Princeton Univ. Press, 1982 (from the Einstein Centennial Symposium in Jerusalem).

Einstein and Humanism, the Aspen Institute for Humanistic Studies, NY, 1986. Infeld, Leopold, *Albert Einstein,* Charles Scribner's Sons, NY, 1950.

Jerome, Fred, "Einstein and Martin Luther King Share Common Enemy, Racism," *Our World News* on-line, Jan. 20, 1998.

—, "Looking at a Genius, Seeing a Spy," op-ed, *NY Times,* June 8, 1998. Kantha, Sachi Sri, *The Einstein Dictionary,* Greenwood Press, 1996.

—, with Rodger Taylor, Einstein on Race and Racism, Rutgers Univ. Press, 2006

—, Einstein on Israel and Zionism, His Provocative Ideas about the Middle East, St. Martin's Press, NY, 2009.

Marianoff, Dimitri, and Wayne, Palma, *Einstein: an Intimate Study of a Great Man,* Doubleday, Doran & Co, 1944.

Nathan, Otto, and Norden Heinz, eds., *Einstein on Peace,* Simon & Schuster, NY, 1960.

Pais, Abraham, *Einstein Lived Here,* Oxford Univ. Press, NY, 1994.

—, *Subtle Is the Lord,* Oxford Univ. Press, 1982.

Reiser, Anton, *Albert Einstein, A Biographical Portrait,* A. & C. Boni, NY, 1930.

Richards, Alan Windsor, *Einstein As I Knew Him,* Harvest House Press, Princeton, NJ, 1979.

Rosenkranz, Ze'ev, ed., *Albert Through the Looking Glass,* Hebrew Univ. Press, Jerusalem, 1999.

Rowe, David E., and Schulman, Robert, Einstein on Politics, Princeton Univ. Press, 2007.

Ryan, Dennis, ed., *Einstein and the Humanities,* reports from a seminar at Hofstra Univ., Greenwood Press, 1987.

Sayen, Jamie, *Einstein in America,* Crown Publishing, Inc., New York, 1985.

Schilpp, Paul Arthur, ed., *Albert Einstein Philosopher-Scientist,* Open Court Publishing Co., La Salle, IL, 1949, Library of Living Philosophers, Inc., 1970.

Schwartz, Joseph, and McGuinness Michael, *Einstein for Beginners,* Pantheon Books, NY, 1979.

Schwartz, Richard Alan, "Einstein and the War Department," *ISIS,* June, 1989.

—,"The FBI and Dr. Einstein," *The Nation,* Sept. 3-10, 1983.

Simmons, John, *The Scientific 100,* Carol Publishing Group, Secaucus, NJ, 1996.

Stachel, John, "Exploring the Man Beyond the Myth, Albert Einstein," *Bostonia,* February, 1982.

—, "Einstein and Infeld, Seen Through Their Correspondence," Acta Physica Polonica B. v. 30, No. 10, 1990 (presented at "Infeld Centennial Meeting," Warsaw, Poland, June 22-23, 1998).

Stern, Fritz, *Einstein's German World,* Princeton Univ. Press, 1999.

Vallentin, Antonina, *Einstein: a Biography,* London, 1954.

White, Michael, and Gribbin, John, *Einstein A Life in Science,* A Dutton Book, Penguin Books, NY, 1993.

Whitrow, G. J., ed., *Einstein the Man and His Achievement,* Dover Publications, NY, 1975, original BBC publication 1967 (based on three BBC radio broadcasts in 1966).

Builders of the Universe; U.S. Library Assoc. Inc., Westwood Village, Los Angeles, CA, 1932.

VIDEOTAPES

"A Day with Einstein, Recollections by Lucien Aigner," 1940 photo session in Princeton, Herbert Wolff, K2 Productions, Lenox, MA, 1994.

"Einstein: Light to the Power of E(2)" by David Devine and Richard Mozer, Devine Productions, Ltd., Toronto, 1997.

"Einstein Revealed," Nova, WGBH, Boston, 1996.

"Einstein's Universe," BBC and WGBH, narrated by Peter Ustinov, 1997.

SOURCES ON HOOVER AND FBI

Chams, Alexander, *Cloak and Gave/ PB/ Wiretaps, Bugs, Informers, and the Supreme Court,* Univ. of Illinois Press, Urbana, 1992.

Cook, Fred J., *The PB/ Nobody Knows,* Macmillan, NY, 1964.

Corson, William R., *The Armies of Ignorance,* The Dial Press, NY, 1977. DeLoach, Cartha, *Hoover's FBI,* Regency Publishers, 1995.

Demaris, Ovid, *The Director: An Oral History of JEH,* Harper's Magazine Press, NY, 1975.

De Toledano, Ralph,/. *Edgar Hoover,* Arlington House, New Rochelle, NY, 1973. Donner, Frank J., *The Age of Surveillance,* Vintage Books, NY, 1981.

Elliff, John T., *Reform of FBI Intelligence Activities,* Princeton Univ. Press, 1979. Gentry, Curt,/. *Edgar Hoover, the Man and the Secrets,* Penguin Books, NY, 1991. Hoover, J. Edgar, *Masters of Deceit,* Henry Holt, NY, 1958. Pocket Cardinal Edition,

Pocket Books, NY: first printing Aug., 1959, 27th printing, March, 1968.

Jeffreys, Diarmuid, *The Bureau,* Houghton Mifflin, NY, 1995 (companion to BBC documentary).

Keller, William W., *The Liberals and J. Edgar Hoover,* Princeton Univ. Press, 1989.

Kessler, Ronald, *The FBI,* Pocket Books (Simon & Schuster), NY, 1993. Kuntz, Tom and Phil, eds., *The Sinatra Files,* Three Rivers Press, NY, 2000.

Lamphere, Robert J., and Shachtman, Tom, *The FBI-KGB War, A Special Agent's Story,* Random House, NY, 1986.

Lowenthal, Max, *The FBI,* William Sloane, NY, 1950.

Mitgang, Herbert, *Dangerous Dossiers,* Ballantine Books, NY, 1988. Nash, Jay R., *Citizen Hoover,* Nelson-Hall, Chicago, 1972.

O'Reilly, Kenneth, *Black Americans: The FBI File,* Carroll & Graf Publishers, NY, 1994.

—,'Racial Matters': *The FBI's Secret File on Black America, 1960-1972,* The Free Press, NY, 1989.

Powers, Richard Gid, *Secrecy and Power: The Life of J. Edgar Hoover,* The Free Press, NY, 1987.

—, *G-Men: Hoover's FBI in American Popular Culture,* Southern Illinois Univ.

Press, Carbondale, 1983.

Robbins, Natalie, *Alien Ink,* William Morrow and Co., NY, 1992. Schott, Joseph, *No Left Turns,* Praeger, NY, 1972.

Sullivan, William C., with Bill Brown, *The Bureau: My 30 Years in Hoover's FBI,* W. W. Norton, NY, 1979.

Summers, Anthony, *Official and Confidential: The Secret Life of J. Edgar Hoover,* G. P. Putnam's Sons, NY, 1993.

Swearingen, M. Wesley, *FBI Secrets,* South End Press, Boston, 1995.

Theoharis, Athan, and Cox John Stuart, *The Boss,* Temple Univ. Press, Philadelphia, PA, 1988.

Theoharis, Athan, *From the Secret Files of J. Edgar Hoover,* Ivan R. Dee, Chicago, 1991.

—, *J.Edgar Hoover, Sex, and Crime,* Ivan R. Dee, 1995.

—, *Spying on Americans,* Temple University Press, 1981.

—, *The FBI: An Annotated Bibliography and Guide,* Garland Publishers, Inc., New York, 1994.

Turner, William W., *Hoover's FBI, the Men and the Myth,* Sherbourne Press, Los Angeles, 1971.

—, *Rearview Mirror: Looking Back at the FBI, the CIA and Other Tails,* Penmarin Books, Granite Bay, CA, 2001.

Ungar, Sanford, *The FBI,* 1975, Little Brown, Boston.

Welch, Neil, and Marston, David W., *Inside Hoover's FBI,* Doubleday & Co., Garden City, NY, 1984.

Whitehead, Don, *The FBI Story,* Random House, NY, 1956.

Wise, David, *The American Police State,* Random House, NY, 1976.

—, "The FBI's Greatest Hits," *Washington Post Magazine,* Oct. 27, 1996.

Wise, David and Ross, Thomas B., *The Invisible Government,* Random House, 1964.

Articles

"The Private Life of J. Edgar Hoover," Ovid Demaris, *Esquire,* Sept., 1974. "The Office Politics of J. Edgar Hoover," Demaris, *Esquire,* Nov., 1974.

"A Postscript on Einstein and the FBI," Klaus Hentschel, *ISIS,* 81:2:307 (1990). "Hoover Answers Ten Questions on the FBI," *New York Times Magazine,* April 18, 1950.

"J. Edgar Hoover Speaks Out," interview in *Nation's Business,* Jan., 1972. "How Communists Operate," *US News & World Report,* Aug. 11, 1950.

"How Hoover Sold Out 'An Authentic American Hero,' " Seth Kantor, *Atlanta Constitution,* July 4-6, 1980.

"The Truth About J. Edgar Hoover," William S. McBirnie, Community Churches of America, Glendale, CA, 1975.

"The Last Days of J. Edgar Hoover," Drew Pearson and Jack Anderson, *True,* Jan., 1969.

"Reform of the FBI," H. H. Wilson, *The Nation,* February, 1971.

"Hoover: Monument of Power for 48 Years" (obit), *Washington Post,* May 3, 1972.

"J. Edgar Hoover Made the FBI Formidable..." (obit) *New York Times,* May 3, 1972.

Videotapes

"Hoover's FBI." Videotape by Burbank Video, 1991. "The Bureau," BBC Documentary, see Jeffreys, above.

"J. Edgar Hoover, Personal and Confidential," TV documentary, A & E channel *(Behind the Badge* series), May, 1999.

SOURCES ON ESPIONAGE

Albright, Joseph, and Kunstel, Marcia, *Bombshell,* Times Books, NY, 1997. Banford, James, *The Puzzle Palace,* Penguin Books, NY, 1983.

Cave Brown, Anthony, *Bodyguard of Lies,* Harper & Row, NY, 1975. Corson, *Armies of Ignorance* (listed above).

Dallin, David J., *Soviet Espionage,* Yale Univ. Press, New Haven, CT, 1955. David Dallin Papers, NY Public Library, special collection.

Dasch, George, *Eight Spies Against America,* Robert M. McBride Co., NY, 1959. Deakin, F. W., and Storry, G. R., *The Case of Richard Sorge,* Harper & Row, Publishers, NY, 1966.

Haynes, John Earl, and Klehr, Harvey, *Venona: Decoding Soviet Espionage in America,* Yale Univ. Press, 1999.

Koch, Stephen, *Double Lives: Spies and Writers in the Secret Soviet War of Ideas Against the West,* The Free Press, NY, 1994.

Lazitch, Branko and Drachkovitch, Milorad M., *Biographies of the Comintern,* Hoover Institute, Stanford Univ., 1986.

Moss, Norman, *Klaus Fuchs,* Grafton Books, London, 1987.

Persico, Joseph, *Casey: From the* OSS *to the CIA,* Viking Penguin, NY, 1990. Polmar, Norman, and Allen, Thomas B. *Spy Book: The Encyclopedia of Espionage,* Random House, NY, 1997.

Popov, Dusko (Tricycle), *Spy/Counterspy,* Grosset & Dunlap, NY, 1974. Rabinowitch, Eugene, "Atomic Spy Trials: Heretical Afterthoughts," *Bulletin of Atomic Scientists,* May 1951.

Reinhardt, Guenther, *Crimes without Punishment,* Hermitage House, Inc., NY, 1952. Romerstein, Herbert and Eric Breindel, *The Venona Secrets,* Regnery, NY, 2000.

Stevenson, William, *A Man Called Intrepid,* Ballantine Books, NY, 1976.

—, *Intrepid's Last Case,* Villard Books, NY, 1983. Volkman, Ernest, *Spies,* John Wiley & Sons, Inc., NY, 1994. Whymant, Robert, *Stalin's Spy,* St. Martin's Press, NY, 1998.

Williams, Robert Chadwell, *Klaus Fuchs, Atom Spy,* Harvard Univ. Press, Cambridge, 1987.

Wolf, Markus, with Anne McElvoy, *Man without a Face: The Autobiography of Communism's Greatest Spymaster,* Jonathan Cape, London, 1997.

The Sorge Spy Ring: A Case Study in International Espionage in the Far East, Supreme Commander Allied Powers, Central Intelligence Section (CIS), #7, Garland Publishers, NY, 1989.

ADDITIONAL SOURCES

Adler, Irving, and Zelman, Benjamin M., "Aftermath of a Witch Hunt: New York's 'Subversive Teachers,'" *The Nation,* April 9, 1977.

Alexander, Stephan, *"Communazis"* Yale Univ. Press, New Haven, 2000.

Alison, David, *Searchlight: An Exposé of New York City Schools,* Teachers Center Press, NY, 1951.

Allen, George E., *Presidents Who Have Known Me,* Simon & Schuster, NY, 1960. Alperovitz, Gar, *The Decision to Use the Atomic Bomb,* Random House, Inc., NY, 1995.

Anderson, Marian, *Lord What A Morning,* Univ. of Wisconsin Press, Madison, 1956. Aptheker, Herbert, *A Documentary History of the Negro People,* v. 5, Carol Publishing Group, NY, 1993.

Belfrage, Cedric, *The American Inquisition, 1945-1960,* Bobbs-Merrill, Indianapolis, 1973.

Bernstein, Barton J., ed., *Politics and Policies of the Truman Administration,* Quadrangle Books, Chicago, 1970.

Beyerchen, Alan D., *Scientists Under Hitler,* Yale Univ. Press, New Haven, 1977. Bialer, Sewerin, *Stalin and His Generals,* Pegasus, NY, 1969.

Bonanno, Bill, *Round by Honor,* St. Martin's Paperbacks, NY, 1999.

Bower, Robert T., *Television and the Public,* Holt, Rheinhart and Winston, NY, 1973.

Boyer, Paul, *By the Bomb's Early Light: American Thought and Culture at the Dawn of the Atomic Age,* Univ. of North Carolina Press, 1994.

Brecher, Jeremy, *Strike!,* Straight Arrow Press (Book Div. of *Rolling Stone),* San Francisco, 1972.

Brown, Lloyd, *The Young Paul Robeson,* Westview Press, Boulder, CO, 1997.

Buhle, Jo; Buhle, Paul, and Georgakas, Dan, ed., *Encyclopedia of the American Left,* Univ. of Illinois Press, Urbana, 1992.

Carr, E. H., *The Twilight of the Comintern,* The Macmillan Press, Ltd., London, 1982. Carroll, Peter N., *The Odyssey of the Abraham Lincoln Brigade: Americans in theSpanish Civil War,* Stanford Univ. Press, 1994.

Caute, David, *The Great Fear, the Anti-Communist Purge Under Truman and Eisenhower,* Simon & Schuster, NY, 1978.

—, *The Fellow-Travelers: Intellectual Friends of Communism,* Yale Univ. Press, New Haven, 1988.

Chaplin, Charles, *My Autobiography,* Simon & Schuster, NY, 1964. Craig, Gordon A., *Germany,* Oxford Univ. Press, NY, 1978.

Crosby, Donald F., *God, Church and Flag,* Univ. of North Carolina Press, Chapel Hill, 1978.

Culver, John C., and Hyde, John, *American Dreamer: A Life of Henry A. Wallace,* W. W. Norton & Company, NY, 2000.

Davis, Nuel Pharr, *Lawrence and Oppenheimer,* Simon & Schuster, NY, 1968. Delmer, Sefton, *Weimar Germany: Democracy on Trial,* Macdonald Library of the 20th Century, London, 1972.

Dilling, Elizabeth, *The Red Network,* C. N. Caspar Co., Milwaukee, 1934.

—, *The Plot Against Christianity,* published by Elizabeth Dilling, Chicago, undated.

Donovan, Robert J., *Conflict and Crisis, the Presidency of Harry S. Truman, 1945- 1948,* Norton, NY, 1977.

Duberman, Martin Baum, *Paul Robeson,* Alfred A. Knopf, NY, 1988.

Dupre, J. Stefan, and Lakoff, Sanford B., *Science and the Nation, Policy and Politics,* Prentice-Hall, Englewood, NJ, 1962.

Fainsod, Merle, *International Socialism and the World War,* Harvard Univ. Press, 1935.

Fariello, Griffin, *Red Scare: Memories of the American Inquisition, An Oral History,* W. W. Norton & Company, NY, 1995.

Fast, Howard, *Peekskill,* published by the Civil Rights Congress, NY, 1951. Fermi, Laura, *Atoms in the Family,* Univ. of Chicago Press, Chicago, 1954. Frank, Reuven, *Out of Thin Air,* Simon & Schuster, NY, 1991.

Fried, Albert, *Communism in America: A History in Documents,* Columbia Univ. Press, NY, 1997.

Friedlander, Saul, *Nazi Germany and the Jews,* v. I: 1933-1939, Harper Collins Publishers, NY, 1997.

Friedrich, Otto, *Before the Deluge: A Portrait of Berlin in the 1920's,* Harper & Row, NY, 1972; Fromm International Publishing, 1986.

Garber, Marjorie, and Walkowitz, Rebecca L., eds., *Secret Agents: The Rosenberg Case, McCarthyism, and Fifties America,* Routledge, NY, 1995.

Gellately, Robert, *The Gestapo and German Society,* Clarendon Press, Oxford, 1990.

—, *Backing Hitler: Consent and Coercion in Nazi Germany,* Oxford Univ. Press, Oxford, 2001.

Gellhorn, Walter, "Security, Secrecy, and the Advancement of Science," in *Civil Liberties Under Attack,* Univ. of Pennsylvania Press, Philadelphia, 1951.

Ginzburg, Ralph, *100 Years of Lynchings,* Black Classic Press, Baltimore, 1962. Goldfield, Michael, *The Co/or of Politics,* The New Press, NY, 1997.

Goodchild, Peter, *J. Robert Oppenheimer, Shatterer of Worlds,* Houghton Mifflin Co., Boston, 1981.

Gruber, Helmut, *International Communism in the Bra of Lenin,* Cornell Univ. Press, Ithaca, NY, I965.

—, *Soviet Russia Masters the Comintern: International Communism in the Era of Stalin's Ascendancy,* Anchor Press Doubleday, Garden City, NY, 1974.

Gumbrecht, Hans U., In *1926,* Harvard Univ. Press, Cambridge, MA, 1997.

Harper, Alan D., *The Politics of Loyalty,* Greenwood Publishing Corp., Westport, CT, 1969.

Herken, Gregg, *The Winning Weapon,* Alfred A. Knopf, NY, 1980. Higham, Charles, *American Swastika,* Doubleday, Garden City, NY, 1985.

—, *Trading with the Enemy,* Delacorte Press, NY, 1983.

Hobsbawm, Eric, *The Age of Extremes: The Short Twentieth Century, 1914-1991,* Michael Joseph, 1994.

Hoffman, Peter, *The History of German Resistance, 1933-1945,* MIT Press, Cambridge, 1977.

Holmes, David R., *Stalking the Academic Communist,* Univ. Press of New England, Hanover, NH, and London, 1989.

Horne, Gerald, *Communist Front? The Civil Rights Congress, 1946-1956,* Farleigh Dickinson Univ. Press, 1987.

—, "The Civil Rights Congress," essay in *The Encyclopedia of the American Left.* Hunt, Linda, "San Antonio's Nazi Connection," *San Antonio Current,* June 22, 1995. Iversen, Robert, *The Communists and the Schools,* Harcourt Brace, NY, 1959.

Infeld, Leopold, *Quest: The Evolution of a Scientist,* Doubleday, Doran & Co., 1941.

—, *WI Left Canada,* McGill-Queens Univ. Press, Montreal, 1978. Jeansomme, Glen, *Women of the Far Right,* Univ. of Chicago Press, 1996.

Jenkins, Philip, *Bringing the Cold War: The Struggle for Pennsylvania's Ethnie Communities,* Univ. of North Carolina Press, Chape) Hill, 1999.

Jennings, Peter, and Brewster, Todd, *The Century,* Doubleday, NY, 1998.

Jungk, Robert, *Brighter than A Thousand Suns,* Harcourt Brace & Co., NY, 1956. Kamen, Martin, *Radiant Science, Dark Politics: A Memoir of the Nuclear Age,* Univ. of California Press, Berkeley, 1985.

Kanfer, Stefan, *A Journal of the Plague Years,* Atheneum, NY, 1973. Kempton, Murray, *Part of Our Time,* Dell Publishing Co., NY, 1955. Kershaw, Ian, *Hitler,* W. W. Norton, NY, 1998.

Kevles, Daniel J., *The Physicists,* Alfred E. Knopf, NY, 1978.

Kleinert, Andreas, "Paul Weyland, the Einstein Killer from Berlin," *HOST,* v. 3, No. 1, Jan., 1995.

Kuznick, Peter J., *Beyond the Laboratory: Scientists as Political Activists in the 1930's,* Univ. of Chicago Press, 1987.

Lawson, John Howard, *Film in the Battle of Ideas,* Masses & Mainstream, NY, 1953. Leslie, Stuart, *The Cold War and American Science,* Columbia Univ. Press, NY, 1993. Lewis, David Levering, *W. E. B. Du Bois,* Henry Holt & Company, NY, 2000.

Loftus, John and Aarons, Mark, *The Secret War Against the Jews,* St. Martin's Griffin ed. NY, 1997.

Mayer, Henry, "How the Loyalty-Security Program Affects Employment," *Lawyers Guild Review,* v. 15, 1955-56.

McDermott, Kevin, and Agnew, Jeremy, *The Comintern,* The Macmillan Press, Ltd., London, 1996.

McWilliams, Carey, *Witch Hunt: The Revival of Heresy,* Little Brown, Boston, 1950. Morse, Arthur D., *While Six Million Died: A Chronicle of American Apathy,* Random House, New York, 1968.

National Association for the Advancement of Colored People (NAACP), *30 Years of Lynching in the US,* published by NAACP, NY, 1946.

Nelson, Steve, *Steve Nelson, American Radical,* Univ. of Pittsburgh Press, 1981. O'Brien, Gail Williams, *The Color of the Law: Race, Violence and Justice in the Post-World War II South,* Univ. of North Carolina Press, 1999.

Peat, F. David, *Infinite Potential, The Life and Times of David Bohm,* Helix Books, Addison Wesley Publishing Co. NY, 1997.

Powers, Richard Gid, *Not Without Honor: The History of American Anti-Communism,* The Free Press, NY, 1995.

Radosh, Ron and Milton, Alice, *The Rosenberg File,* Henry Holt & Co., NY, 1983. Ranney, Austin, *Channels of Power,* Basic Books, Inc., Publishers, NY, 1983.

Rees, Tim, and Thorpe Andrew, eds., *International Communism and the Communist International, 1919-1943,* Manchester Univ. Press, UK, 1998.

Rhodes, Richard, *Dark Sun: The Making of the Hydrogen Bomb,* Simon & Schuster, NY, 1995.

—, *The Making of the Atomic Bomb,* Simon & Schuster, NY, 1986. Roberts, Sam, *The Brother,* Random House, NY, 2001.

Robeson, Paul, *Paul Robeson Speaks,* ed. Philip Foner, Citadel Press, NY, 1978.

—, *Here I Stand,* Beacon Press, Boston, 1998 ed.

"Paul Robeson: Here I Stand," videotape, co-production of Thirteen/WNET and Menair Media International, directed by St. Clair Bourne, 1999.

Robinson, David, *Chaplin, His Life and Art*, McGraw-Hill Book Co., NY, 1985. Rose, Paul Lawrence, *Heisenberg and the Nazi Atomic Bomb Project*, Univ. of California Press, Berkeley, 1998.

Sayre, Nora, *Running Time, Films of the Cold War*, The Dial Press, NY, 1982. Scales, Junius, *Cause at Heart*, Univ. of Georgia Press, Athens, GA, 1987.

Schrecker, Ellen W., *The Age of McCarthyism*, Bedford Books of St. Martin's Press, NY, 1994.

—, *Many Are the Crimes, McCarthyism in America*, Little, Brown & Company, NY, 1998.

—, *No Ivory Tower*, Oxford Univ. Press, NY, 1986.

—, "Immigration and Internal Security: Deportations During the McCarthy Era," *Science and Society*, v. 60, No. 4, Winter 1996-1997.

Schultz, Bud and Ruth, *It Did Happen Here, Recollections of Political Repression in America*, Univ. of California Press, Berkeley, 1989.

Schwartz, Richard Alan, *The Cold War Reference Guide*, McFarland & Co. Inc, Publishers, Jefferson, NC, 1997.

—, *Cold War Culture*, Facts on File, NY, 1997.

Sherwin, Martin J., *A World Destroyed: The Atomic Bomb and the Grand Alliance*, Alfred A. Knopf, NY, 1975.

Sime, Ruth Lewin, *Lise Meitner, A Life in Physics*, Univ. of California Press, Berkeley, 1996.

Simpson, Christopher, *Blowback. America's Recruitment of Nazis and Its Effects on the Gold War*, Weidenfeld & Nicolsen, NY, 1988.

Smith. Alice K., *A Peri/ and A Hope: The Scientists Movement in America, 1945-47*, Univ. of Chicago Press, 1965.

Smith, John Chabot, *Alger Hiss, The True Story*, Holt, Rhinehart & Winston, NY, 1976.

Steinberg, Peter L., *The Great "Red Menace," US Prosecution of American Communists, 1947-1952*, Greenwood Press, Westport, CT, 1984.

Stern, Fritz, *Dream and Delusions: The Drama of German History*, Alfred A. Knopf, NY, 1987.

Stewart, Jeffrey C., *Paul Robeson, Artist and Citizen*, Rutgers Univ. Press, New Brunswick, NJ, 1998.

Swomley, John M., *Confronting Systems of Violence: Memoirs of a Peace Activist*, Fellowship Publications, Nyack, NY, 1998.

Szasz, Ferenc, *The Day the Sun Rose Twice*, Univ. of New Mexico Press, Albuquerque, 1984.

Szilard, Leo, "The AEC Fellowships: Shall We Yield or Fight?," *Bulletin of Atomic Scientists*, June, 1949.

Theoharis, Athan G., *The Truman Presidency* [documents], Earl M. Coleman Enterprises, Inc, Publishers, Stanfordville, NY, 1979.

Wang, Jessica, *American Science in an Age of Anxiety*, Univ. of North Carolina Press, 1999.

Wallace, Irving, *The Writing of One Novel*, E. P. Dutton, NY, 1968. Wax, Emily, "Blacks' Other WW II Battle," *Newsday*, Nov. 8, 1998.

Weart, Spencer R., and Szilard, Gertrud Weiss, eds., *Leo Szilard: His Version of the Facts*, MIT Press, Cambridge, 1978.

Williams, David J., *Hit Hard*, Bantam War Book Series, Toronto, 1983.

Williams, Juan, *Thurgood Marshall, American Revolutionary*, Times Books, NY, 1998. Wistrich, Robert S., *Antisemitism: The Longest Hatred*, Schocken Books, NY, 1991. Wright, Bruce, *Black Robes, White Justice*, Lyle Stuart, Secaucus, NJ, 1987.

York, Herbert, *The Advisors: Oppenheimer, Teller & the SuperBomb*, Stanford Univ. Press, Stanford, CA, 1976.

Zangrando, Robert L., *The NAACP Crusade Against Lynching, 1909-1950*, Temple Univ. Press, Philadelphia, 1980.

Zinn, Howard, *The Twentieth Century, A People's History*, Harper & Row Publishers, NY, 1980.

ESSAY COLLECTIONS

The *Atomic Age, Scientists in National and World Affairs,* selected articles from the "Bulletin of Atomic Scientists," eds: Morton Grodzins and Eugene Rabinowitch, Basic Books, Inc., Publishers, NY, 1962.

The Gold War, 1945-1991, Benjamin Frankel, ed., Gale Research, Detroit, 1992.

The Gold War & the University, Andre Schiffrin, ed., The New Press, NY, 1997.

INTERVIEWS

Irving Adler
Julia Bond
Lloyd Brown
Manuela Dobos
Freeman Dyson
Fanny Floyd
Richard Frauenglass
Robert Gellately
David Gelmarn
Gillett Griffin
Helmut Gruber
Martin Klein
Peter Lax
Henry Meyers
Philip Morrison
Doris Nathan
Phyllis Novakoff
Abraham Pais
Melba Phillips
Joseph Rotblat
Jamie Sayen
Walter Schneir

Robert Schulmann
Sam Seifter
Al Shadowitz
Chris Simpson
Callie Caraway
Sinkler Marian Smith
John Stachel
Dirk Struik
John Swomley
Sanford Unger
Emery Wimbish
David Wise
Markus Wolf
Sarah and David Wuchinich

FBI FILES, OTHER THAN THE EINSTEIN FILE

Charlie Chaplin
W. E. B. Du Bois
Louis Gibarti
Robert and Kristel Heineman
Otto Nathan
J. Robert Oppenheimer
Paul Robeson
Eleanor Roosevelt
Harold Urey

NON-FBI FILES ON EINSTEIN

G-2, INS, CIA, ONI, HUAC

CORRESPONDENCE FILES

Army Intelligence (G-2, CIC) War Department
Office of Scientific Research and Development
U.S. Navy
U.S. Army War Plans Division (1940)

Acknowledgments

A hundred times every day I remind myself that my inner and outer lives are based on the labors of other people, living and dead, and that I must exert myself in order to give in the same measure as I have received and am still receiving.

—*Einstein, "The World As I See It"*

The success of my FOIA effort to obtain the previously withheld («redacted») 25 percent of the FBI's Einstein file was due primarily to the Public Citizen Litigation Group (David Vladeck and the diligent and persistent efforts of Erica Craven), and to Carl Stern. Thanks also to Duncan Levin and Kate Martin at the Center for National Security Studies.

For sharing their memories and allowing me to barge into their lives, I am indebted to Irving Adler, Julia and Julian Bond, Lloyd Brown, Manuela Dobos, Freeman Dyson, Fanny Floyd, Richard Frauenglass, Gillet Griffin, Thomas Kuczynski, Peter Lax, Leon Lederman, Henry Meyers, Philip Morrison, Doris Nathan, Phyllis Novikoff, Abraham Pais, Melba Phillips, Joseph Rotblat, Jamie Sayen, Sam Seifter, Al Shadowitz, Callie Carraway Sinkler, Dirk Struik, John Swomley, and David and Sarah Wuchinich.

Several current and former FBI agents and employees, some of whom disagreed with many of the points in this book, also were quite forthcoming with suggestions, views, and recollections. Some spoke only on a promise of anonymity. Others include Herb Clough, Hank Flynn, Donald E. Moore, Sam Papich, Susan Rosenfeld, Rex Tomb, William Turner, Neil J. Welch, and Fred Whitehurst. I am grateful to all of them. Two former Newark-based agents, Vincent Murphy and Thomas Kelly, who worked on the Einstein case were, perhaps understandably, unwilling to make any comment, even off the record.

Many people provided valuable help in contacting sources, obtaining documents, and contributing generously with advice and criticism, including: Peggy Adler, Steve Adler, Janet Basu, Wolf Beigelbock, Marian and Fred Bonem, Bill Broad, David Burnham, Alice Calaprice, Tonya Foster, David Garrow, Robert Gellately, David Gelman, Helmut Gruber, Abe Habenstreit, Tony Hiss, Doug Hostetter, Harvey Klehr, Martin J. Klein, Stephen Koch, John Loftus, Bruce Lewenstein, Mary Maher, Priscilla McMillan, Herb Mitgang, Klaus Peters, Andy Rabinbach, Kenneth O'Reilly, Yoshi Rosen, Tom Ross, Irene Runge, Walter Schneir, Jack Schwartz, Chris Simpson, Janet Stern, Athan Theoharis, Earl Ubell, Sanford Unger, David Wise, and William Worthy.

I am grateful, too, for advice and encouragement from: Herbert Aptheker, Laurel Bauer, Peter Benjaminson, Deborah Blum, James Boyd, Howard Boyer, Richard Brush, Debbie Burrell, Ira Flatow, Reuven Frank, Marvin Gettleman, Erica Goode, Ernie Herman, Margaret Herring, Roald Hoffmann, Debbie Jones, Helene Karman, John Levin, Frank McCulloch, Jack Monet, Maureen Nappi, Steve Quigley, Ben Patrusky, Bill Reuben, Barbara Rich, Carol Rogers, Roald Sagdeev, Bill Schaap, Gwen Simmons, and Michael Spielman.

A number of librarians and curators also provided valuable support, including Wayne Furman and his staff at the New York Public Library who opened the door to the Wertheim Study, Marjorie Charlante, Marvin Russell and numerous others at the National Archives, INS Historian Marian Smith, Wendy Chmielewski, curator of the Swarthmore Peace Collection, Harold Augenbaum at the Mercantile Library Writer's Studio, Victor Berch, archivist for the Veterans of the Abraham Lincoln Brigade, Marcia Tucker at the Institute for Advanced Study, Peggy Sherry, who guided me through the Einstein Collection at Princeton, and Paul Forman, curator of the Modern Physics Collection at the Smithsonian National Museum of American History. Also thanks to Ze'ev Rosenkranz, curator of the Albert Einstein Archives at the Hebrew University in Jerusalem, and his super-competent assistants Dina Carter and Barbara Wolff, for help with information and reprint permissions for letters and photos.

Invaluable assistance in clearing the way for the publication of photos and excerpts from Einstein's writings also came from the Princeton University Press, publisher of The Collected Papers of Albert Einstein © Hebrew University and Princeton University Press; Charles Blockson of the Charles L. Blockson Afro-American Collection at Temple University; Laure Lion at Corbis Images; Mike Silverman and Yvette Reyes at the Associated Press/ Wide World Photos; Thomas McCarter of the Landshoff estate; Jane Halsman at the Philippe Halsman Studio; Doris Nathan; and Emery Wimbish, Dean of Libraries at Lincoln University, with help from

Ed Gibson and Brenda Snyder, who generously made available valuable historical records at the university's Langston Hughes Memorial Library.

Special thanks to Richard Alan Schwartz for his time and dedication in first obtaining Einstein's FBI file and his generosity in sharing it.

Thanks also to Charles Blackburn, Wendy Bouser, and John Sullivan, whose gracious hospitality enhanced my all-too-brief stay at the Weymouth Writers Residence in Southern Pines, North Carolina; and to Martha Heinz, Liz Cox, Hugh Miller, Gay Bowman, Glen Rounds, Rusty Jobe, and all my other good friends in the Sandhills area for their encouragement and criticism; to Susan and her mother, Rita Richardson, for their warm generosity in opening their cottage and introducing me to the good people of Hopewell Manor; to Joanna Korman for her photographie skills; to Jackie Boyd for her ace research; to Bob and Raphael Apter for sharing their apartment and advice; and, above and beyond the call, thanks to Nils and Gunilla Smith-Solbakken for their generosity in providing a warm and welcoming writing place.

Absolutely invaluable research, translation, and other assistance in Germany was provided by Stephan Ahlf, who also enlisted the help of several German scholars and historians, including Siegfried Grundmann, Klaus Hentschel, Heinz Hohne, Andreas Kleinert, and Horst Muhleisen.

Thanks cannot express my feelings of gratitude to my editor extraordinaire at St. Martin's Press, Michael Denneny, and to my marvelous agent Frances Goldin and her associates Sydelle Kramer and Sam Stoloff, all of whom generously contributed critical insights; to Meyer Kukle and Ingrid Risop for sharing their valuable time and suggestions; to John Stachel and Robert Schulmann for their Einstein expertise, their careful, meticulous, and constructive editorial help, and their support; to Linda Regan for initially taking on this project at the erstwhile Plenum Press; to the my longtime friends and colleagues Alan McGowan and John Harnett for their unflagging encouragement; and to my oldest (longest-time) friend Dorothy Zellner for irreplaceable and selfless editorial assistance, and for believing.

Finally, this book would never have been possible without the forbearance (that means putting up with me) and loving support of my wife, Jocelyn—as well as the consistent cooperation from our children and their partners: Rebecka and Claes, Mark and Melanie, and Daniel and Angela, who produced a total of five grandchildren-Annika, Dakota, Savannah, Ty, and Xiomara—while this book was in gestation, and still found time to provide valuable suggestions and assistance.

Index

ALSO AVAILABLE FROM BARAKA BOOKS

Washington's Long War on Syria
Stephen Gowans

Patriots, Traitors and Empires
The Story of Korea's Struggle for Freedom
Stephen Gowans

Slouching Towards Sirte
NATO's War on Libya and Africa
Maximilian C. Forte

Rwanda and the New Scramble for Africa
From Tragedy to Useful Imperial Fiction
Robin Philpot

The Question of Separatism
Quebec and the Struggle over Sovereignty
Jane Jacobs

The Complete Muhammad Ali
Ishmael Reed

Justice Belied
The Unbalanced Scales of International Criminal Justice
John Philpot & Sébastien Chartrand, Editors

Songs Upon the Rivers
The Buried History of the French-speaking Canadiens and Métis
From the Great Lakes and the Mississippi across to the Pacific
Robert Foxcurran, Michel Bouchard, and Sébastien Malette

Rebel Priest in the Time of Tyrants
Mission to Haiti, Ecuador and Chile
Claude Lacaille

Scandinavian Common Sense
Policies to Tackle Social Inequalities in Health
Marie-France Raynault & Dominique Côté

Printed by Imprimerie Gauvin
Gatineau, Québec